# Kindertransport: A Lifelong Journey of Survival and Redemption

# Kindertransport: A Lifelong Journey of Survival and Redemption

The Story of Ralph W. Mollerick, A Kind

David H. Herschler

Library of Congress Cataloging-in-Publication Data
Library of Congress Control Number: 2017910291
CreateSpace Independent Publishing Platform
North Charleston, South Carolina


ISBN: 9781548067458
ISBN: 1548067458

Dedicated to
Ralph W. Mollerick
and
all the *Kinder* who had the courage to tell their stories
and to
Evey Herschler

*"Now, as then, the face of an innocent child is my
guiding light of hope for the world . . . the reason to
survive, to achieve and to work for the future."*
Nathan Shapell, Holocaust survivor

*"Education and remembrance are the only
cures for hatred and bigotry."*
Miriam Oster, Holocaust survivor

*"Believe in the power of the individual to
make a difference in this world."*
Vera Federman, Holocaust survivor

# Contents

# *Preface*

THIS BOOK HAD its origins in late February 2013. My wife, Evey, and I were visiting our good friends Ralph and Phyllis Mollerick in their Lake Worth, Florida, home for a few days in advance of taking a Caribbean cruise. Ralph knew of my interest in his personal history and was eager to share an article that he had written and that was soon to appear in *Prism*, the journal of Yeshiva University. The article had been selected from among dozens submitted for a special issue relating to the Kindertransport and, in particular, the personal recollections of the experiences of *kinder*, as survivors of the Kindertransport program are known. These children were sent by their parents out of Germany, Austria, and German-occupied Czechoslovakia to the relative safety of England between December 1938 and September 1939. Ralph and his older sister, Edith, had been among the nearly 10,000 children rescued and probably saved from almost certain death at the hands of the Nazis as a result of the Kindertransport program. He had been speaking extensively to both senior groups and school-age youth for more than a decade about his personal experience and about the Kindertransport within the context of the Holocaust. Ralph had also been actively engaged in the work of the Kindertransport Association of North America (KTA) in a number of leadership roles for 15 years. He had been the subject of local newspaper and newsletter articles both in the United States and in his childhood town of Wolfhagen, Germany, but until 2012 he had never considered writing a substantive account of his Kindertransport experience for publication. Because of my background as a professional historian, Ralph wanted me to read the article and showed me the proofs as we sat around the breakfast table, which I read with great interest, and which I found impressive for its contents but also intriguing for what was absent from the article. There was, I believed at the time and still do, an important and fascinating story to be told based on what I knew about Ralph's past—in fact, right up to the present, as I knew that he had been uniquely honored by his childhood town of Wolfhagen two weeks earlier. The *Prism* article was something in which he took great pride, but he acknowledged that it had been a struggle for him because he did not consider himself much of a writer. "I would really like to tell my life's story, but I'm not equipped to write a book-length account," he said to me. It took but a nanosecond for me to respond, "Hello—I'm available."

The timing was almost perfect. In February 2013, I was less than a year away from retirement from a 37-year career as a historian and archivist with the United States government. Having been a manager most of my career and preoccupied with two volunteer organizations outside of my profession for much of that time, I had not had the opportunity to take on a book project of my own ever since completing my doctoral dissertation, and had been contemplating writing a book such as a personal biography soon after retirement. The opportunity to tell Ralph's story was fortuitous in that it very much fit the type of book project I wanted to undertake. Evey and I purchased a retirement home in Delaware and moved from Maryland halfway through 2014, spending much of the ensuing few months settling in. As it turned out, Ralph's term of service on his home owner's association board—an extraordinarily time-consuming responsibility—was due to expire at the end of 2014, and so the timing was right immediately thereafter for both of us to embark on what would be a multiyear project to produce a personal account of Ralph's life. After several days of discussions and looking through materials at Ralph's Florida home in February 2015, I developed a detailed chapter outline and we began a long process of planning and undertaking the research necessary for the project.

I first met Ralph Mollerick in the spring of 1977 when Evey and I affiliated with Mishkan Torah Congregation in Greenbelt, Maryland, shortly after arriving from the Midwest where I had just completed my doctorate in United States history at Indiana University, Bloomington. Ralph was quite active at the synagogue and it was not long before I joined the executive board as a committee chair and Ralph and I attended board meetings together. Although I knew that Ralph was employed at The National Aeronautical and Space Administration's (NASA) Goddard Space Flight Center, I did not know much about his personal life or his past other than having seen his wife and three children on the High Holidays and a few other occasions over several years. I also recognized that Ralph was a hard worker on the board who had served as synagogue president and was relatively soft-spoken compared with some of the other board members. Because he was almost 17 years my senior with teenage children, whereas Evey and I had just started a family, we did not socialize with Ralph and his family at that time and I really only got to know him well outside of the synagogue more than a decade later, around the time that I was synagogue president. By that time Ralph was divorced from his first wife and dating a congregant at Mishkan Torah who had also recently been divorced, and who was closer to our age and someone with whom Evey and I had been friendly. We became good friends with Ralph and Phyllis even before they were married and remain close friends today even though we now live in Delaware and they live in Florida. That friendship has paralleled a remarkable time in Ralph's life, really a second life story that developed from a turning point more than midway through his life that is directly tied to the earlier time. In the aggregate, the two life components amount to a lifelong journey of survival and redemption, and that is, at the core, what I believe makes Ralph's story so compelling.

Taking a step back from the excitement of telling a good friend's life story, the historian in me considered at some length first, whether doing so in a book would contribute materially to existing literature on the Kindertransport within the larger context of the history of the Holocaust, particularly from an individual participant's personal perspective. There are, indeed, now an impressive number of published personal accounts about kinder, mostly autobiographical, although until fairly recently the vast majority of these have been article-length or shorter and tended to appear in a variety of published compilations of such accounts. Some stories have been incorporated into documentary films such as the award-winning *Into the Arms of Strangers,* or *My Knees Were Jumping*, among others. Many of the kinder have recorded video interviews as part of Steven Spielberg's sponsored *Shoah* Foundation project, which is available from the United States Holocaust Memorial Museum and elsewhere. Most of these personal accounts, even those that are book-length and autobiographical, tell fascinating personal stories but fall short on providing historical context, which is critical to fully comprehending the very nature of the personal story. For a variety of reasons, many kinder have been reluctant, even unable, to tell their stories, finding their past too painful to relive; others have moved on with their lives and did not want to look back; still others may well have been willing to share their stories and have done so in group settings such as at meetings of the KTA, but did not want to spend the time or felt ill-equipped to write and publish their accounts. Time is growing short for these individuals to contribute to the literature. Less than 30 percent of the nearly 10,000 kinder are still living, and the vast majority of those individuals are now in their mid-80s or older; within the next decade or so, virtually the entire universe of this historic group is likely to be gone.

A second consideration for the historian in me concerned whether Ralph's life story was in some way unique enough from the many other published accounts so that the reader could come away with more than just a good read, thereby justifying publication. Herein is where the earlier mention of Ralph having experienced a life in two distinct, but closely connected phases that inspired the title of this book comes into play. Although the story of Ralph's survival of the Holocaust is intrinsically interesting, in the broader historical context it is probably not unlike those of thousands of other survivors—certainly with respect to the stories of other kinder. It is, really, how Ralph's life has transpired ever since the early 1990s—the story of what he has accomplished for himself, for the town and country of his birth, and most of all for public knowledge and history, and how he did so—that sets his life story apart from those of most other kinder survivors. To be more specific without completely giving away the details, Ralph experienced something of an epiphany in 1993 that, coming closely on the heels of two other life-altering events, turned his life trajectory around. Thereafter he was able to experience a personal redemption, which enabled him to serve as a catalyst for, and to immerse himself in, the redemption of his childhood town of Wolfhagen. This epiphany also enabled him to become actively engaged in working with other surviving kinder and their succeeding generations through leadership in the KTA and related organizations, and to dedicate much of his time during his senior years telling his story within the context of the broader history of the Holocaust, particularly to students both in the United States and in Germany—thus contributing directly to public knowledge about the Holocaust. It is the extraordinary story of Ralph's redemption more so than his survival that makes his life truly unique. But that component of his life cannot possibly be fully meaningful to the reader without also understanding the story of Ralph's survival.

Given, therefore, what I believe is a legitimate justification for undertaking this book-length project, a third consideration for the historian in me relates to the availability and nature of sources for a book such as this, along with a related fourth consideration of how Ralph's life story should best be written. With regard to the latter question, there are a number of reasons why I chose to write the book as a narrative in the third person rather than in Ralph's voice. First and foremost, it was important to me to infuse the narrative with historical context, which sets it somewhat apart from most of the autobiographical published accounts by kinder; from a technical standpoint this consideration is facilitated by writing in the third person. Secondly, writing the story in the third person allows me to distinguish between Ralph's personal reflections and my own analysis; differentiating between the two became increasingly important during the writing of the manuscript. Finally, it is important that the reader understands that while Ralph collaborated closely throughout the project, I take full responsibility for both its content and format; telling the story in the first person would only confuse the reader on that account. The second, and from a historian's perspective, more fundamental decision that had to be made about the writing of the book was whether it should—or even could—be presented as a scholarly study. After weighing a number of considerations, not the least of which included the most likely audience, the nature of the sources used, the advantage to the reader in proceeding through the material unencumbered by annotation, and my personal preference in presenting the information, I decided to write the story as a nonfiction personal narrative rather than as a scholarly biography.

With regard to sources, there are several points to be made. Identifying primary sources for a personal narrative ranging over 80 years is, under any circumstance a daunting challenge. Covering a life where some of the most critical components date from the Nazi period in Germany is all the more difficult. Documentary trails are, by the very nature of projects such as this one, often minimal and strewn with gaps. This was certainly the case for this book project but to a considerably lesser extent than I had initially anticipated. Ralph had saved an impressive but disorganized collection of correspondence over the course of his childhood, early adulthood, and to a far greater extent over the past 20-plus years. In tracking down information about his family, including cousins with whom he reconnected after nearly a half-century, he had managed to collect a few highly important letters written by his parents dating back to the Nazi period. He also viewed and obtained—with the assistance of a local researcher—information from records relating to his parents from an archive in Hamburg, as well as his own and his sister's official files from the Refugee Children's Movement obtained from an archive in England, again with the assistance of a local researcher. After considerable search, Ralph found among materials saved throughout his life three separate personal daily journals covering key aspects of his past between 1945 and 1950, as well as a treasure trove of photographs dating back to his childhood in Germany, a selection of which appears in this book and some of which proved invaluable in confirming historical facts. For the portion of his life beginning in 1993, besides fairly extensive correspondence, Ralph provided copies of speeches, other oral presentations, newspaper and newsletter articles and clippings mostly in English or already translated into English from German (but a few that the author had translated into English from the original German), and a handful of miscellaneous organizational documents relating to the KTA. From Günter Glitsch in Wolfhagen I obtained copies of correspondence, speeches, newspaper clippings (again, most of which were already translated from German to English but a few that the author had translated) and miscellaneous documentation relevant to Ralph's connection with the town. From Ernst Klein in Volkmarsen I received materials and references to websites relating to organizations involved today in the preservation of Jewish history in Germany. Along with this collection of mostly contemporaneous primary sources, I also consulted information from published official Department of State documentation in the Foreign Relations of the United States series, the *Hansard Digitized Official Debates of Parliament*, and secondary sources in print and online—the latter including the comprehensive websites of the United States Holocaust Memorial Museum, the World Holocaust Remembrance Center at Yad Vashem, the National Archives of the United Kingdom, the Kindertransport Association of North America, the Association of Jewish Refugees, and even Google Maps—as well as in video format, mostly for the purpose of providing historical context to the narrative.

By far the single greatest research-related undertaking and most important collection of information for this project was the nearly 600 pages of transcriptions of oral history interviews I conducted with Ralph, members of his family, friends, and officials in Wolfhagen and Hamburg, and several other individuals important in his life. It would, of course, have been fortuitous to have the opportunity to interview

Ralph's sister, Edith, and his oldest son, Jeffrey, but Edith was long gone, and Jeffrey died tragically in 2003 at age 45. The oral history interviews were conducted over a four-month period that included an extended visit to Ralph's Florida home, a visit by Ralph and Phyllis to my Delaware home, as well as a 10-day visit Evey and I made with Ralph and Phyllis to Germany and also a few telephone interviews. Although essential to a book project such as this, oral history interviews of course can be risky with respect to accuracy and sometimes even to credibility, especially in this case because they rely mostly on the memory of a person in their 80s and delve as far back in time as early childhood. I found Ralph's memory to be quite extraordinary, considering his age and the number of years we covered. It was particularly interesting for me to distinguish what he actually remembered from his childhood and youth from what he remembered from things he learned about that time much later in life. During the course of transcribing and reviewing the oral history interviews, nonetheless, there were several small gaps, inconsistencies, and discrepancies, as one would expect. Fortunately most of the gaps were able to be closed, the inconsistencies resolved, and most of the discrepancies were able to be clarified, corrected, and confirmed as either absolutely accurate or identified as the most logical conclusion based on follow-up communication with the interviewees and cross-referencing the transcripts with other available contemporaneous sources or reliable secondary materials. This greatly mitigates—but of course does not completely eliminate—the risk of minor inaccuracies in the personal account presented herein.

The reader also should be aware of the way in which primary source material has been directly incorporated into the narrative text. There were a number of options available in this regard, but because of a curiosity in portions of the oral history transcriptions wherein the inter-viewee recalled actual verbatim exchanges with other individuals, which more likely should be considered to be re-creations of any recollected actual exchanges that occurred, such portions of the personal account have been presented as dialogue or commentary set within quotations.

Other portions taken directly from oral history transcripts are generally identified as a recollection. Unless a quoted source has otherwise been identified, the reader should assume the source is from a transcribed oral history interview. The advantage in presenting the transcribed material in this fashion is that it makes for a livelier presentation and better draws the reader into the story. The disadvantage, of course, is that the reader is being asked to at least partially suspend reality in a personal account that in virtually every other respect is a more traditional nonfiction work. For the same reasons, and especially because this book is a personal account rather than a scholarly monograph, it was decided to eschew the use of footnotes in the text as well as the inclusion of a formal bibliography, other than the note on sources included herein as part of these prefatory comments.

It would be presumptuous and unfair to omit a note of acknowledgement to those whose assistance has been essential to producing this historical personal account. First and foremost, I am indebted to Ralph Mollerick for his constant devotion to this project, for the dozens of hours of recorded interviews and follow-up discussion, for his indefatigable energy and persistence over the course of more than two years in searching for and locating invaluable source materials hidden away and long forgotten in his home and elsewhere, and for introducing me to—and helping to arrange oral history interviews with—friends, family, officials, and colleagues in Germany and in the United States. Ours has truly been a collaboration of love, even through the few but inevitable moments of frustration in resolving inconsistencies in the recorded interviews. I hope this book does justice to his life story. I am likewise indebted to Phyllis Mollerick for her support and collaboration in the course of this project, and for her influence on Ralph's life that, in my judgment, contributed immeasurably to his personal redemption and all the benefits to the world that derived as a result.

I could not be more grateful to the several wonderful people in Wolfhagen for the gift of their time and knowledge in sitting for interviews, and especially for their friendship and hospitality, inviting us into their homes and offices—all of which reflects their love and admiration for Ralph and Phyllis. Included in this group are Bürgermeister (Mayor) Reinhard Schaake; Dekan of the Lutheran Church Dr. Gernot Gerlach; Ralph's childhood friends Heinz Abel and Heinrich Schwarz and his wife, Gertrud; former school headmaster Arne Pillardy; former Bürgermeister Giselher Dietrich; and especially Günter Glitsch, for providing so many essential documents as well as his invaluable translating assistance during interviews I conducted while in Wolfhagen and in nearby Volkmarsen, for his special insight into Ralph's importance to Wolfhagen, for showing us around the Wolfhagen area, and for providing key follow-up information by telephone. I am also indebted to Ernst Klein, chairman and director of *Rückblende Gegen das Vergessen* ("Flashback Against Oblivion"), an extraordinarily impressive exhibit and organization dedicated to the restoration and preservation of the history of German Jewry in the north Hessen region. Besides contributing to the oral history for this book, Herr Klein provided a fascinating tour of Jewish sites in Volkmarsen and of his exhibit. In Hamburg, Christine Zinn and Thorsten Lührig provided their expertise on the archival records relating to Ralph's parents and other family members who lived in that city, as well as a fascinating tour and explanation of the Jewish neighborhood in which Ralph's family lived, and especially of the Stolpersteine dedicated to his parents.

There are several others to whom I am indebted for their contributions to this book project. Ralph's sole surviving son, Glen Mollerick, and Harry Rosenthal, one of Ralph's few remaining cousins, provided invaluable information through oral history interviews; the same is true for Melissa Hacker, president of the Kindertransport Association of North America. In England, Jeanette Rosenberg undertook research on Ralph's past and provided a copy of Ralph and Edith's invaluable files maintained by the Refugee Children's Movement that are housed in the World Jewish Relief Archive. Evey Herschler, Kristin Ahlberg, and Sharon Walder have read all or parts of the manuscript, providing essential advice on content, style, and grammar; Rebecca Grilliot provided a technical copy edit of the manuscript with great skill. Their editorial expertise has improved this personal account immeasurably. I am especially indebted to Evey, most of all, but also to friends, family, and our Delaware community for their patience and support during the course of this project.

# Introduction

THE MORNING OF February 13, 2013, should have begun like most others for Ralph Mollerick, but the profound knot in his stomach told him that this day something was different. As the fog of sleep faded from his brain in the predawn hours, the sound of a rooster crowing entered his gradually awakening consciousness. Trying to identify the source of his angst, he looked around his first floor room, number 17 of the Hotel Zum Schiffchen, still shrouded in semidarkness. His wife of 22 years, Phyllis, lay beside him still asleep. Occasional gusts of wind buffeted the two elongated windows overlooking the rear of the hotel. Without wak-

ing Phyllis, Ralph quietly stepped to one of the windows, pulled the curtain aside, and gazed out into the brightening, clear sky at a familiar scene below. Fields of various muted colors interlaced with brilliant yellow rapeseed stretched from the southern edge of town just beyond the street below his window to the horizon a few kilometers to the south. More than a dozen turbine windmills—each giant blade the size of the wing of a wide-bodied jet aircraft—dotted a single, visible hill abutting the fields just

outside the town center. Ralph realized that the familiarity of this scene was due to the fact that this was his 10th visit to Wolfhagen over the past 20 years, his town of birth located in central Germany in the northern part of the state of Hessen. Thinking about those visits filled him briefly with a sense of warmth and satisfaction.

His presence in Wolfhagen this winter morning, however, suddenly reminded Ralph why he felt a knot in his stomach. A few months earlier he had received a phone call at his Lake Worth, Florida, home from his friend, Günter Glitsch, in Wolfhagen. That Günter would be calling him was not unusual; for nearly 20 years they had spoken to each other long-distance on a regular basis. Only on rare occasions had Günter called for a special reason, and this had turned out to be one of those occasions. Günter, who had served on the town council for many years but had since stepped down, had called with an official invitation for Ralph from the town of Wolfhagen to travel there during the second week of February. In their previous nine visits to Wolfhagen, Ralph and Phyllis had never come in the dead of winter. Ralph's recollection of Wolfhagen as a child reminded him how harsh the winter weather could be, so Günter's invitation—an official one at that—was puzzling. Günter explained that the people of Wolfhagen had a special surprise for Ralph, that he was going to be honored by the town, and that he should prepare some very brief remarks that he would deliver publicly in German. Although Ralph was well-accustomed to speaking before large audiences, the thought of having to speak publicly in German filled him with dread. Having left Germany as a child and willfully abandoned his native tongue, he felt ill-equipped to deliver even the briefest of comments in German. A knot in the pit of his stomach began to form as Günter made his request. A second matter of concern was the nature of the honor he was to receive. All Günter had told him about the honor was that, in preparing his speech, he should think about what it would be like for him to be welcomed to Wolfhagen in an "unusual way." Despite an ongoing curiosity about the upcoming event, Ralph had dutifully prepared brief remarks—quite brief for him, filling less than one page of large print—and faxed the document to Günter so that he could translate the speech into German.

Now, staring out of his hotel window, realizing that today was the big day but still unclear about how he was to be honored, Ralph's uneasiness grew. He later recalled that the prospect of delivering his remarks in German "froze me, because I'm not very good at German." When Ralph and Phyllis arrived in Wolfhagen on February 10, Günter had provided the translated remarks to Ralph, as well as a transliterated version so that he could present the speech without the relatively few errors in pronunciation that he typically made. He had spent much of the previous day, February 12, rehearsing the speech, with Günter constantly reminding him to slow down the pace of his delivery. But upon awakening on the morning of the ceremony, Ralph's concern about doing the speech was pervasive. Trying to distract his nerves, he took a shower; the hot water offered some relief as he directed the handheld flexible shower head over his body. The bathroom window was open a crack; stepping out of the shower, Ralph inhaled deeply the outside air, which felt expectedly brisk and laden with the fragrance of manure and farm animals, an aroma that was highly evocative of his childhood in the town. Quickly drying and dressing, he returned to the larger window in the bedroom and could see glimpses of people in the yard below the rear of the hotel and heard the sounds of chickens filtering up to his room. It had come as a bit of a surprise that there was absolutely no evidence of snow on the ground and that the sun was now shining brightly on the horizon, something that had been a rarity in recalling his childhood winters in Wolfhagen. Only the occasional sound of the wind blowing against the building reminded him of the season and that once outside he was likely to feel the chill of winter, as had been the case each day since arriving in Germany. While Phyllis awakened and readied herself for the day ahead, Ralph could feel himself alternating between excitement and anxiety.

The breakfast room of the Hotel Zum Schiffchen was located on the ground floor to the left of the staircase looking down from the stairwell.

The aroma of coffee was present as Ralph and Phyllis descended the staircase carrying their outer garments with them, and entered the breakfast room. Several guests were engaged in rather loud conversation throughout the room during the eight o'clock hour. Gazing around the room from the entranceway, Ralph noticed a group of men who appeared to him to be possibly a construction crew finishing their breakfast and getting ready to head out for work. There was an American family seated in the room, people whom Ralph and Phyllis had not formally met but who were also there because of an official invitation from the town of Wolfhagen. Also present in the breakfast room was Lutz Kann, the only other surviving former Jewish resident of the town whom Ralph and Phyllis had first met 20 years earlier on their initial visit to Wolfhagen. Lutz was there to be honored along with Ralph; accompanying him from Berlin for the occasion were his children and grandchildren, although his wife could not be present due to illness. They greeted each other curtly; there was a strained history between Ralph and Lutz dating back to their first encounter that prevented an extended or warm conversation that morning. Ralph and Phyllis then found their usual table along the front wall, set down their coats, and helped themselves to the buffet breakfast and coffee. Ralph sat down and ate his usual breakfast at this hotel: cereal, accompanied by juice and bread with marmalade on it. He ate in silence— something quite different from previous breakfasts in Wolfhagen. As he later recalled, "I was totally preoccupied with how I was going to conduct myself for the event that evening."

Following breakfast, Ralph and Phyllis crossed to the opposite side of the hotel to return their room key. The Schiffchen had been modernized to include most amenities, with the exception of an elevator and air conditioning. The room key, however, was something quite different; rather than using electronic cards, the Schiffchen had large, fairly heavy metal keys with the room number engraved on them. It would have been inconvenient, if not impossible, to carry such a key around all day, so the hotel required patrons to drop off their keys at the reception desk when leaving the hotel and retrieve them when returning. The reception desk itself was located in the restaurant, which was divided into a pub room where the reception desk was situated and a more private dining room adjacent to the pub. The hotel's restaurant was one of the primary gathering places in the town each evening. Ralph and Phyllis had discovered the Schiffchen quite by accident on their first visit to Wolfhagen, and it became their hotel of choice shortly thereafter.

Having returned their room key, Ralph and Phyllis turned toward the hotel's front door when they were intercepted by Günter, who entered the hotel wearing a heavy jacket and gloves. On most occasions, Günter joined them in the breakfast room, but on this particular morning he had been running a bit late. Günter spent a few minutes discussing the plan for the day. They would walk to the home of Heinz Abel where Ralph would rehearse his presentation again. Heinz had been Ralph's closest childhood friend and still lived in the same house adjacent to the house Ralph had lived in as a child. Like Günter, Heinz and his wife, Gisela had become very close friends with Ralph and Phyllis almost immediately during Ralph's first return visit to Wolfhagen. Günter expected the Abel's daughter, Britta, to be there, since that day was Ash Wednesday and many people were not at work. Britta wanted to work with Ralph on his pronunciation in German. It was also likely that another childhood companion, Heinrich Schwarz and his wife, Gertrud, would join everyone for lunch. This was no surprise to Phyllis; in referring to their visits to Wolfhagen, she recalled that she and Ralph, Heinz and Gisela Abel, Heinrich and Gertrud Schwarz, and Günter Glitsch "were always a group—we were together almost constantly." Günter invited Ralph and Phyllis to spend some time with him at his home during the afternoon before returning them to the Schiffchen to change clothes and prepare for the early evening ceremony.

The historic center of Wolfhagen was not large and could easily be traversed by foot despite the central square in the town, with the large Lutheran church immediately adjacent to it, being situated at the top of a fairly steep hill. The geography of the historic center thus allowed for a truly dramatic view of the town from a short distance away, especially on the north side, where the highest point dropped off precipitously into a ravine. Three streets bisected the historic town center in roughly an east–west direction: Schützebergerstraße is the longest and northernmost street; Burgstraße runs parallel along the southern part of the center, passing the central square and the Lutheran church as well as the City Hall; Mittelstraße branches off from Schützebergerstraße just west of the central square, passing the square and running roughly parallel to Schützebergerstraße and Burgstraße. All of these main streets are fairly narrow, with shorter crossing streets not much wider than alleyways. The Schiffchen was located at the southwestern corner and just outside of the historic town center along a busy thoroughfare that served as the southern bypass of the historic center.

Ralph, Phyllis and Günter braced for the cold and stepped outside the hotel entrance. The brisk air enhanced by gusting winds hit them almost immediately. Ralph determined that he was "definitely underdressed for the weather," despite Günter having given him a warmer coat to wear than the one he brought from Florida. He wore Günter's coat given to him the previous day when they had attended a carnival in a neighboring town that included a parade replete with floats depicting the Grimm fairytales for which the area is known. But the frigid weather this morning was particularly bitter, with the wind pounding them in the face as they walked toward Schützebergerstraße. Turning onto this cobblestoned street, they walked toward the center of the town, passing one house after another displaying the half-timber architecture for which Wolfhagen, as well as much of Germany, is known. They passed the Alte Rathaus (Old City Hall) Hotel and Restaurant, where they had stayed on their very first visit to Wolfhagen, noting the point just prior to reaching this structure where Mittelstraße branches off and climbs past the northern edge of the central square, where sits a statue of a wolf on a stone base marking the year 1216 when the town was established. The bone-chilling cold prevented much conversation, and Ralph was not inclined to say much, feeling all the more introspective the closer they came to the home of Heinz Abel.

As the group approached their destination, Ralph gazed up and once again saw his childhood home, part of which was still known as the Steinkammer at Schüzteberg-erstraße 37. The house itself was typical half-timber in design but the adjoining family business part of the complex was unique both in its size, being considerably larger than any of the other structures on this street, and in its architecture. Instead of the more common half-timber look, the building was made completely of stone (hence the name Steinkammer) that rose to four levels in height with a Dutch-type architecture featuring a step-like roofline façade that narrowed to a flat peak at the top. The family store on the ground floor of the Steinkammer had long ago been replaced and now housed an Italian restaurant and a wine tasting shop. The first level above had been converted to a movie theater, and the large clock that had been cantilevered from the second level of the Steinkammer over the street was long gone. Ralph thought about how special it was each time he had returned and looked at the structure from this same angle. His thoughts then turned to his parents. He wondered how they would have felt knowing that the town was honoring him later that day. He imagined that his father would have been proud of his having had the courage to return to his town of birth after his personal traumatic survival and all the horrors that had occurred to his parents and so many others at the hands of the Nazis; and how proud his father would have been of all his many achievements in his life, not least of which included the way in which he had conducted himself every time he returned to Wolfhagen—what he had accomplished for his own redemption and for the redemption of the town.

Thoughts of the town reminded him of why he was there—to be honored—and about how different he felt being in Wolfhagen this time compared with prior visits. He felt his angst returning as he wondered again how he was going to handle himself at the ceremony, and whether he could successfully pull off his speech in German before hundreds of residents, town and regional officials, and the press. Staring at the Steinkammer, Ralph suddenly felt a deep, inner chill far more intense than the bitter cold air on his skin. He began to shiver convulsively as the pleasant aroma of food being prepared drifted from the Steinkammer onto the street. In his mind's eye he envisioned his mother standing in the kitchen, cooking; he envisioned himself as a child watching from his window as Hitler Youth marched by below; he envisioned his father sternly standing over him. Ralph closed his eyes and became immersed in his past.

# PART I

## Survival

# CHAPTER 1

───── ⚭ ─────

# Wolfhagen (1934–1937)

ROLF WOLFGANG MÖLLERICH shuddered with the sharp sting he felt across his backside. Tears began to run down his face with a second smack of the stick at the same location. He looked up at his father peering down at him before allowing himself to stand and face him. Without a word, Josef Möllerich returned the very thin, child-sized cane walking stick to its place behind the door to his son's room and walked out. Although only four years old, Wolfgang (as he was called by virtually everyone) had become accustomed to his father's style of discipline. Josef was strict with his son and there could be any number of offenses for which young Wolfgang would receive the stick. These included, in his pre-school years, staying late outside riding his tricycle with friends, principally with his next door neighbor and best friend, Heinz; or failing to identify the correct color of crayons other than yellow, blue, or black, because he was colorblind (but of course as a young child he would have had no way of knowing that—and neither, apparently, did his father). Once in school, Wolfgang experienced multiple episodes with that stick because he would lie about how he was doing. He would say that everything was fine at school; but his father knew it was not fine because he had a report saying that he was not doing his homework, or that he was annoying other students, or that he would deliberately do the opposite of what the teacher told him to do. He recalled that on such occasions his father would say to him: "Wolfgang, get me that cane!" "I trembled," he said, "because I knew what was going to happen."

Discipline aside, Wolfgang's childhood life in Wolfhagen was very much centered on his family—in sometimes challenging but usually less painful ways. He was born on May 27, 1930, in nearby and much larger Kassel and this had been, so he later surmised, because there were complications surrounding his birth due to his mother, Selma, having been 35 years old at the time of his birth. His arrival came nine years after his sister, Edith who, in 1934 at the age of 13, attended school in Frankfurt-am-Main and so was not around very much. The nine-year gap between the siblings was unusual in those times, and Wolfgang later suspected that his mother may have experienced one or more miscarriages, which also would explain the need for his birth to occur in a city hospital with more extensive medical facilities than there had been in his hometown. The age gap between Wolfgang and his sister also had something to do with a dark and complex component to their relationship that would emerge very early in Wolfgang's life and continue pretty much unabated long into his adulthood; it would also be a central preoccupation for Wolfgang throughout his life.

Wolfgang enjoyed considerable material comfort as a result of his father's successful business and elevated standing in the town. His paternal grandfather, Wolf Möllerich, was considered the family patriarch. Born in Wolfhagen in 1849, Wolf married Frederike (Richschen) Speyer Weissenbach and the couple raised five children (and lost three others at or shortly after childbirth). Wolf established what turned out to be the highly lucrative Wolf Möllerich Firm that included sales of large appliances, hardware, grains and lumber. He also owned considerable property in and near the town that included approximately one acre on which the business—and his residence—was located, as well as about two acres of land near the southern edge of town that was rented to farmers and others for the purpose of growing fruits and vegetables. The business and property were inherited by his two sons, Moritz and Josef, upon Wolf's death in 1912. Josef was nine years junior to his brother, having been born in 1885. The brothers shared equally in the family business, but divided up the responsibilities so that Josef ran the appliance, grain, and lumber sales components while his older brother ran the hardware store and mostly kept the books. Later estimates suggest that the firm did the equivalent of a half million dollars of business annually (in early 1930s US dollars) and was probably worth more than the equivalent of a million US dollars. Young Wolfgang could not have realized it, but his father was most likely a millionaire at the time Hitler came to power.

Besides his business success, Josef Möllerich was a pillar of the community. He had served on the town Parliament during the days of the Weimar Republic and was well respected throughout the area as a philanthropist. During his tenure on the town Parliament he arranged and personally paid for the development of a small rock garden as part of the main square with the design of the Star of David embedded within (which, of course, was removed once the National Socialists came to power). Josef also contributed heavily both to the local synagogue and the separate *Jüdische Schule* (Talmud Torah school) over the course of many years. He was a firm believer in education and supported the local schools both financially and with his time, speaking to students at the public school on multiple occasions prior to 1933 about the value of education. Josef provided both credit on the sale of his products and outright loans to people he knew in the town who were in need, and the company kept fastidious records of all transactions in the attic of Moritz's home, from which Moritz ran the hardware store on the ground floor and which was adjacent to the Steinkammer and separated from the stone building by an alley. The ground floor of the Steinkammer served as an appliance store with a large display in the front showing such items as washing machines, vacuum cleaners, and ovens. The latter were cast iron and among the best available in Germany at the time and had the family name, Möllerich, emblazoned on them.

The residence part of the complex that included the Steinkammer at Schützebergerstraße 37 had nearly 4,000 square feet of living space, mostly on the three levels above the ground floor. Many of the buildings in central Wolfhagen characteristically had shops on the ground level with living quarters above the shops, such as the one housing the hardware store and Moritz's family living quarters. Wolfgang's home was a bit different in two respects: the ground level combined an entrance on the right side of the half-timber building that comprised the residence with a stairway going up to the living quarters and a passageway into the Möllerich's appliance store on the ground level of the Steinkammer. There was also a gate to the street on the left side of the ground level of the residence that allowed trucks and other vehicles to pass under the residence through a driveway and enter a massive courtyard behind the house where the lumber was stored. The first floor, one level up, had a large living room with four windows facing the street. It was elegantly furnished, as was the formal dining room immediately behind this room, which had no windows at all but had a door leading to the central corridor and another leading to the large kitchen at the rear of the house. The kitchen overlooked the courtyard and because there was a steep hill behind the courtyard, it was possible to see the buildings down the hill, including the *Jüdische Schule*. Beyond the homes and streets one could see the fields that surrounded Wolfhagen, except for one large hill on the east side of the town. Most of the rooms in the Möllerich home had timber pillars measuring nearly a foot in diameter, some of which went all the way down to the foundation.

The next level of the house had mostly bedrooms along a corridor similar to the first level. The large master bedroom occupied the front of the house with windows overlooking Schützebergerstraße. There was a full bathroom immediately behind the master bedroom but not adjoining it, with an oversized closet adjacent. There were two somewhat smaller bedrooms at the rear of the corridor, one occupied by

Wolfgang and the other belonging to his sister; both of these bed-rooms had windows facing the courtyard. Up the stairs from the second level, the layout became a bit unusual. There was a landing halfway up to the top living level, with a half-bathroom—a toilet and a sink and a small window overlooking the alley—located off the landing. Wolfgang and Edith generally used this bathroom. The stairway then continued to the landing at the top level, which was somewhat smaller than the lower levels of the house because of the roof being gabled from the front to the rear. Here there was a suite—a large bedroom with adjoining sitting room and a separate full bathroom—that was reserved for Wolfgang's maternal grandparents when they were not staying in their own house in town.

Given the exigencies of the business, in which Selma Möllerich also assisted, and the strict environment in which he was raised, Wolfgang had a loving but not necessarily close relationship with his parents, al-though he got along much better with his mother than his father be-cause he was afraid of the cane. What Wolfgang remembered most about his mother was how she insisted on keeping everything tidy in the business space, so much so that it annoyed his father, who would often flick cigarette ashes on the floor just to tease his wife (so he later learned). Wolfgang loved spending time with his mother in the kitchen. "She was a really good cook," he recalled; "I loved her food and when she baked I was always there to help her, stirring and pouring a little of this and a little of that." But his mother was "really more involved with the office work and therefore not very attentive to me," he remembered.

Josef and Selma were not only busy during the day but often hosted gatherings in their home in the evenings. Wolfgang found these social occasions particularly uncomfortable during his pre-school years. He recalled feigning sleep in order to avoid being cuddled by, and having to kiss, everyone in the room, family and guests alike. He was expected to greet the friends and relatives and would be handed from one to the other like a football. "The relatives were the worst," he recalled, "because they wanted to pick me up, wanted to swing me and I just didn't like to have that done to me;" nor did he enjoy being bounced on a variety of knees for minutes at a time. There was heavy smoking in the room during these occasions—an acrid combination of cigarette and cigar fumes—from which Wolfgang recoiled. He had a keen sensitivity to odors from early childhood and so it was understandable that Wolfgang sought refuge in his room as quickly as he could manage whenever his parents hosted parties.

During the daytime Wolfgang received most of his attention and affection from his maternal grandparents, Jonas and Bertha Meyer, whose actual names he didn't learn until much later in life; as a child he called them simply Opa and Oma. It was German custom to address people, even those known well, by their titles, such as *Herr* and *Frau,* and this custom carried over for Wolfgang until he was well into adulthood. His grandparents had a house a short distance away on Mittelstraße, but on occasion occupied the top level of Wolfgang's house on Schützebergerstraße (Jonas and Bertha Meyer were in their 70s at this time but Wolfgang considered them to be "still very active; they could climb stairs"). Wolfgang enjoyed taking walks with his grandfather. Jonas loved to smoke cigars but his wife didn't allow the smoke in their house so he would often ask young Wolfgang to join him for a walk while he smoked his cigar, and Wolfgang described these walks as "the best." They would always begin with Jonas telling his grandson to "go to the bathroom" first. "But Opa," Wolfgang would say, "I've already been; why do I have to go again?" Jonas would then respond, "You go because I said so; if you want to come with me you have to listen to me." Once outside, Jonas would light his cigar and begin puffing on it and flicking the ashes. He then would hold out his thumb and tell Wolfgang to grab his thumb and not let go of it. They would walk to the edge of town and in the fields where there was a stream, and they would just "hang out" by the stream while Jonas smoked his cigar and told his grandson stories about his service in the army. On one of these walks, Wolfgang asked his grandfather if he could try the cigar. "Yes, of course you can," Jonas replied as he bent down and put his thumb in his grandson's mouth. "That was hysterically funny for me," Wolfgang later explained, "because I didn't realize at the time and thought his thumb was the cigar and I thought that was how he smoked." Upon returning to his grandparent's house, Wolfgang excitedly told his Oma that Opa had let him smoke the cigar. "She looked at me," he recalled, "and then looked at him and he showed her his thumb and they both just laughed."

When Wolfgang was together with both his parents during his childhood while living in Wolfhagen he spent considerable time on family outings, which he very much enjoyed. His father had one of the better cars made at the time; it probably predated 1933, but it was large enough to hold six people easily. As he grew a bit older, Wolfgang took great interest in the car; in fact he took great interest at a very early age in almost anything that had mechanical parts, including his tricycle and a fairly sophisticated erector set with motors, which was called a "mechano set," that he had been given by his parents; this, along with his oversized comic books and his tricycle proved to be his most prized possessions during his time in Wolfhagen. The outings with his parents—and sometimes with his sister and maternal grandparents—were almost always special times for Wolfgang. They would drive into the countryside and take long walks in parks or travel to neighboring towns, passing other cars and also horse-drawn wagons along the way. They went on rides in amusement parks and ate at cafes. He later recalled that "we always had a good time."

Many of the family outings involved visits to relatives in nearby towns, especially Volkmarsen. With the exception of his grandparents, most of Wolfgang's relatives that he knew as a child were on his father's side. His Uncle Moritz and Aunt Jette, of course, lived next door to him in Wolfhagen. They had one daughter, Gretl (whom everyone later called Margaret) who, like all of Wolfgang's first cousins, was considerably older than he, having been born in 1914. Josef also had three sisters, Sophie, Bertha, and Alma. Sophie married Hermann Schwarz and moved to Volkmarsen, where they raised four sons (Max; Ludwig; Otto;

and Eugen) who were all older than Wolfgang's cousin Gretl. Bertha married Jacob Mansbach and moved to Gudensburg where they raised a son, Julius, and a daughter, Brunhilde (later called Hilde) who were both older than Wolfgang's cousin Gretl. Alma, who was the youngest of Wolfgang's aunts, married Julius Schloss and they also moved to Volkmarsen where they raised a son, Werner, and a daughter, Ruth; both were a bit younger than Wolfgang's other first cousins but older than Edith and much older than Wolfgang. It was Aunt Sophie who left the greatest impression on Wolfgang from the outset. She and her family lived in a big red house just off the main square in Volkmarsen that had been named a historic site, not because Wolfgang's relatives lived there but because of an earlier owner who had been a dignitary who controlled much of that part of Hessen. Wolfgang enjoyed the visits to this house because, unlike his own home where each room was set apart from another, the main level of this home had an open design that allowed him to run around the whole perimeter, much to the annoy-

ance of his older cousins who lived there or who visited this home on the occasions when Wolfgang was there. Wolfgang nevertheless recalled many joyful meals at his Aunt Sophie's house and talking to his cousin Otto who, at 25 years his senior was old enough to be his uncle; but after a while at these gatherings Wolfgang would be left to play pretty much on his own while the others played cards and smoked.

Being left largely to his own devices during the day was a fairly common occurrence for young Wolfgang. With his parents generally preoccupied, his cousins in a different age bracket, his sister attending school in Frankfurt-am-Main, and with almost no other Jewish boys in the town—of any age—Wolfgang relied on the friendship of non-Jewish boys for day-time companionship. His neighbor next door, Heinz, was six months younger than he and was, according to Wolfgang, "like a brother." Kurt Giese lived around the corner down the alley and was the same age as Wolfgang, as were Rolf Franke and Heinrich Bergmann, whose cousin, Heinrich Schwarz was friendly with Wolfgang even though he was two years younger and thus too young to play with the others much at the time. Wolfgang recalled that "on most days we all got together on our tricycles and that's how we passed the time." They rode along the cob-blestone sidewalks of Schützebergerstraße, stopping at the nearby cor-ners to walk across. Wolfgang and Heinz also rode in the large upstairs storage area of Heinz's house, and the group sometimes rode in the enormous courtyard of the Steinkammer where the lumber was stored, provided the area wasn't congested with workers and trucks. They also used the latter space to play tag, but did not engage much in sports, partly because the boys were a bit young and partly because there was really not much space in the center of town to kick a ball around.

For the most part—at least until sometime in 1936—there was no indication of the influence of National Socialism within the small circle of Wolfgang's playmates. Their families also seemed to get along well. In particular, Heinz later recalled that his father and Josef would sit out-side their houses on a bench having a beer together, talking, smoking, and watching people go by. Heinrich Schwarz recalled Wolfgang's par-ents visiting his home on social occasions. Among several of the neigh-boring families, a purchase would be concluded with a handshake, written down in the business ledger and paid for at a later time with no questions asked. But Wolfgang found, especially after he began public school, that some of the boys in the town would gang up on him, and so he learned to take care of himself. Although slight of stature and small enough for his age that some of the younger boys were physically larg-er, Wolfgang learned to be "a tough kid" and was capable of wrestling one or two of them—even those who were physically larger—to the ground. He later recalled: "I did that only when I had to; if someone pulled me off the tricycle, they were in trouble." He was also agile and fleet afoot, even at a young age. This tough veneer, as well as his speed and agility, served him quite well throughout his childhood.

The lumber yard behind the Möllerich house served as a favorite hiding place for Wolfgang. It was often a busy place during the work day, as trucks would enter through the gate on Schützebergerstraße, pass under the house, enter the large courtyard and make a partial circle, coming to a stop where the lumber was stored. Wolfgang recalled that he found the lumber yard "the most fascinating place to be." Hundreds of pieces of varieties of wood, each about 20 feet in length, all organized by grade and type, were stored under a lean-to-like structure standing on end along the wall of the Steinkammer. Once he finished playing with friends, or had to run away from kids in the town when things turned "viral" and there were too many to take on, Wolfgang found little reason to go into the house, from which there would be no escape for the remainder of the day, so he would seek refuge in the lumberyard behind the rows of wood. He loved listening to and observing the activities, peering through spaces between the wood while he was wedged between the wood and the Steinkammer wall. There was a lumberjack who would cut the wood, bundle it and, using a mechanical lift, load each bundle into the trucks. Sometimes as many as three trucks would be in the lumber yard at one time. Wolfgang took great interest in watching the work there and sometimes spent up to two hours at a time, hoping he would not be discovered. The family had a German shepherd, and Wolfgang loved that dog because "he was absolutely silent about where I would be." But there was considerable risk of being exposed, as he recalled: "People would be requesting different types of lumber and I was concerned that they would pull out the stack near me and there I would be hiding," he later recalled. "How embarrassing that would have been for me because my father would have been very angry," and Wolfgang knew full well what would have been in store for him had he angered his father.

Of greater concern to Wolfgang as a child in Wolfhagen was Edith. Because of the nine-year gap in their ages, and because Wolfgang was the only Jewish boy born in Wolfhagen over the same nine-year time-frame, he received considerable attention, especially from the family, which did not sit well with his sister who enjoyed the limelight, being bright, lively, and exceptionally attractive. Like several of the Jewish girls in town, Edith had attended the *Jüdische Schule*, which had virtually all girls attending and was considered a better learning place than the public school (where Edith had earlier been in the same class as Lutz Kann). But after Hitler came to power in 1933, the *Judische Schule* was closed and Edith, who was 12 years old at the time and ready for the equivalent of middle school, was sent to a boarding school for Jewish girls in Frankfurt-am-Main. Her absence made young Wolfgang's life relatively peaceful, but Edith would return home from time to time on weekends and for holidays, and Wolfgang mostly dreaded these occasions. "As soon as she came home," he recalled, "she would push me aside and say, 'Get out of my way!' and go into her room." Wolfgang wanted to speak to her, to hear about her school experiences, where she had been and what she had been doing. Edith would have none of it, largely ignoring her younger brother except to verbally and physically abuse him. Wolfgang later recalled: "It was a constant battle with Edith; there was no love when she was around. I was beaten up by her often just because she was no longer the lone child in the family."

As a result of his immediate family's absence or preoccupation with business matters, Wolfgang spent considerable time in the house left alone to amuse himself. He enjoyed books, even before he could read, because he had an inquisitive mind and because he liked the illustrations. His favorite was in the style of a comic book, but with a hard cover with enough pages to be perhaps an inch-and-a-half thick. Once he was in public school and began reading, his parents gave him more serious books, stories about people's lives, about inventors or important German historical figures. But most of all he loved his "mechano set," which allowed him to create things, and this would lead eventually to his greatest lifetime professional interest. "I was at total peace with myself; I would be entertained for hours playing with this set and building structures bigger and bigger. And then my sister would come in and say, 'That's silly—take it apart!' And she would start undoing it." These encounters with his sister set the stage for the relationship between Edith and Wolfgang that would in many ways dominate much of his thinking throughout childhood.

One aspect of Wolfgang's early childhood in Wolfhagen that remained consistently positive was his association with the synagogue. The building was located in the center of town on a corner along Mittelstraße not far from the main square and just past the point where Triangelstraße branches off from Mittelstraße and runs parallel to Schützebergerstraße heading to the east end of the center of town. Constructed in 1859, the synagogue was reasonably large, running the length of the short block between Mittelstraße and Triangelstraße. Like most Jewish congregations in Germany, the synagogue was orthodox, but what by today's standards would probably be characterized as "modern orthodox," as compared with the more traditional orthodox congregations located throughout the rest of Europe. When full, the building could seat close to 200 people, with men and women separated for services; but by 1934 only 29 Jewish families remained in Wolfhagen, and so the building was never truly full as far back as Wolfgang could remember. Rows of benches stretched from the *bima* and ark at the front all the way to the rear of the building, brightly lit by chandeliers suspended from a high ceiling on either side of the center aisle. Wolfgang later described the décor as "ornate with gold pillars and crowns on the Torahs." The front row, directly behind the reader's table, located centrally at the front of the *bima*, was reserved for the largest donors, and this was where Josef and Wolfgang sat for Shabbat and holiday services. Wolfgang attended nursery school at the synagogue, but what he remembered most about Jewish life in this building was the service on the Jewish festival of *Simchat Torah*. The bench seats all had lids that would lift up; they stored such items as *siddurim* (prayer books) and *talleisim* (prayer shawls). But on *Simchat Torah* they were filled with a variety of candy, especially chocolates which, at a designated time, the children were allowed to take. Wolfgang felt safe inside the synagogue, even once Hitler and the National Socialists came to power.

Early in 1935, Wolfgang's father took him out of the synagogue's nursery school and placed him in the public school kindergarten class. The school was located on Burgstraße, directly across the street from the large Lutheran church that abutted the main square; it was an easy walk, even for a child of four or five years old, of perhaps 200 yards to the bottom of the main square and beyond to Schützebergerstraße and on to his home at No. 37. Wolfgang was the only Jewish boy in the school—at least in the elementary level; there were perhaps eight or nine Jewish girls in the school, but none in his kindergarten class. Nevertheless, he recalled that for the most part all the children were treated the same at that time. The entire school population sometimes had outings that included attending programs in another building, and while young Wolfgang noted that the Jewish children were all seated in the last row, he thought nothing of it. "Kindergarten was fine," he later recalled. The same would not be true for first grade.

September 1935 marked a turning point in Wolfgang's life. On the first day of school, a man who was markedly stooped over and was known by most of the students in the school as "the hunchback," walked into Wolfgang's first grade classroom and said in a booming voice, "*Heil Hitler!*" He explained to his five- and six-year-old students that they were all to observe the precepts of Adolf Hitler and National Socialism, that it was the best and safest way of life and if they were not part of it, they were out. This was possibly the first time, at age five, that Wolfgang had been exposed to blatant Nazism and when later asked how he felt about what the teacher said, he recalled: "I didn't have any feelings; I didn't know, so I accepted that."

Wolfgang's ambivalence did not last long. According to later recollections, within minutes the hunchback, whose name was Herr Ickler, called out to him: "Möllerich—come to the front, turn around and face the students!" Wolfgang did as he was told. "Students," the teacher said, "here is an example of what the Third Reich does not want; here is a dirty Jew. Take a look at him, see what you think, and let's talk about it." Nobody said a word. The hunchback pointed at Wolfgang and spoke on: "He is below us; he is not part of our society." He then told Wolfgang that henceforth in this class he would stand in the corner facing the wall; he would be responsible for completing homework assignments but he was not given any books. The predictable result was that Wolfgang was unable to do his homework and thus received poor grades that were reported to his parents. His father got "very angry" over the failing grades, for which Wolfgang received the usual punishment, despite protesting that he had been singled out by Herr Ickler and was unable to do his work or learn in the class. This pattern continued until early 1936 when Josef removed his son from public school and arranged to have him tutored by his cousin, Ruth Schloss, who had moved from Volkmarsen to Wolfhagen in order to take a job working in Moritz's hardware store, and who lived in Moritz's home during that time.

Josef Möllerich's decision to remove Wolfgang from public school was based in part on his gradually accepting his son's protests about the teacher's treatment, and in part on Wolfgang soon becoming exposed to incidents of anti-Semitism and harassment on the way home from school. A member of the town later recalled that Wolfgang was "humiliated and reviled at school. The way home from school was a thorny road for him, day by day." He would be accosted by gangs of boys usually numbering between six and eight at a time—some from his class and others from older classes—while crossing the main square where he would be taunted and humiliated with shouts of "dirty Jew," pushed to the ground and pummeled. Sometimes Wolfgang would argue with them and pushing and shoving would ensue. On occasions when his tormentors were fewer in number and closer to his age he would fight back, usually taking one or two to the ground before being pulled away by the others. As these incidents grew in frequency, Wolfgang became more wary and when he sighted any group of boys approaching he would make a dash for his grandparents' house, and most of the time he would outrun the group and arrive safely.

Sometimes Wolfgang wasn't so fortunate. During 1936, even after his parents took him out of public school, he and others who knew him at the time recalled incidents where some of the older boys in the town—but not those with whom he was friends—harassed and mistreated him because he was Jewish. On one occasion, a couple of neighbors of the Möllerich family were walking to Engelhardt's Bakery across the street from Wolfgang's house and came upon Wolfgang near the truck entrance to the bakery strung up by his wrists to the railing where the trucks would back into the driveway. Wolfgang later recalled that he had not been tied up for very long, maybe 10 minutes, before his neighbors walked by. At first they thought he was playing with friends, but when they realized he had been tied up, they released him and he ran into his house without a word and without later telling his parents. On another occasion, during the summer of 1936, he had been at the town pool when a thunderstorm struck quite suddenly with bolts of lightning clearly visible close by. Everyone quickly climbed out of the pool and ran to escape the storm. Wolfgang, who at age six was not a swimmer so he could only go in shallow water, was terrified of thunder and lightning; he was in such a rush to get dressed and run for cover that he put his pants on backwards. Some of the older boys noticed him leaving the pool, ridiculed him and forced him into an empty water barrel just as a bolt of lightning struck very close by simultaneously with a crash of thunder. The boys laughed and taunted him, calling him a dirty Jew, and then ran off; Wolfgang dragged himself out of the barrel and ran as fast as he could to his grandparents' house on the next street, screaming "Oma, Oma!" as the tears streaming down his face blended with the rain falling on him.

As traumatic as these incidents were for young Wolfgang, it was, somewhat curiously, a very different kind of situation that brought home to him a true understanding of why he was being harassed by other kids. From time to time, soldiers from nearby who knew many of the families in Wolfhagen would ride into the town on horses wearing long coats and carrying bags that hung from both sides of the saddles that were filled with small coins. They would gather in the main square, which slopes from Burgstraße to Mittelstraße. The soldiers would reach into their bags and throw the coins all over the square, encouraging the children to pick them up. When Wolfgang tried to pick up some coins, a soldier rode up to him and said: "You're a dirty Jew; you don't get to pick up any coins!" Wolfgang later recalled: "This was so fundamental because it set me apart from everybody else. I was not allowed to pick up the coins because I was a Jew, and that was my first real

understanding that I was different, and the difference was that I was Jewish." He also later recalled watching from the window of his house as Hitler Youth marched through the streets of Wolfhagen and later reflected ironically how at the time he had resented that most of the boys he knew in the town eventually participated in the Hitler Youth program and he could not.

It was also during 1936 that some of Wolfgang's small group of non-Jewish playmates, really all of them except for Heinz, began to become "unavailable" to ride their tricycles and play tag. He recalled them telling him things such as, simply, "I cannot come out and play with you—sorry." Wolfgang also recalled that as time went by during the year 1936 his parents inexplicably put restrictions on his playing with friends, causing him to withdraw from them just as they had withdrawn from him, again probably with the exception of Heinz, who later noted: "I think ours was a very perfect neighborhood because I never noticed anything that happened between our families." Wolfgang was troubled by this situation, nonetheless, and asked his grandmother what he had done to cause the kids to stop playing with him, because while he had begun to understand what the epithet, "dirty Jew" meant, his friends really never used that phrase or led him in any way to believe that his being Jewish was cause for their standoffishness. His family was not particularly helpful, however; Oma merely said to him: "Forget about those boys, you're a good boy—you're okay. There's something wrong with their families and you have to understand that because of those problems which they have, they are not permitted to play with you anymore." He also recalled asking his sister, who was equally vague: "My sister knew and she didn't want to talk about it. For the longest time I asked her why the kids in town were against me, and she said to me, 'Someday you'll understand but right now you don't need to know.'" His father repeatedly told him, "Don't worry about it." Wolfgang thought it was "awful" that his family would not be open with him about what was happening, especially because his heart told him something was very wrong with life in Wolfhagen. He had experienced harassment and had been bullied, and he had observed outward displays of force, having seen the Hitler Youth marching through the streets and observed an increasing presence of soldiers in the town.

Wolfgang also noticed changes in the way his parents and family interacted with other people in the town. In particular, the frequent parties held in the family room of his house began to taper off and, when they were held, fewer of the non-Jewish people attended, even those who had almost always come to these gatherings in the past. Wolfgang recalled that many of the people who came to his house for social events did business with his father's firm on a regular basis. He also recalled that of the 29 Jewish families in the town, perhaps half of them would attend the socials hosted by his parents. That "mix" of business and social friends and acquaintances became increasingly unbalanced during 1936. These evenings, however, could also result in some fun at the guests' expense. He recalled that when his sister was present for these parties his parents gave the two of them the assignment to gather the cigarettes and place them in a serving tray. The instructions also included placing a microscopic firecracker in the center of perhaps a half dozen of the cigarettes. "There would be a BANG!" he recalled, "and everybody jumped; then there was another BANG as people puffed away on their cigarettes, and everyone thought it was hilarious." If there was any tension among the small group of guests, this practical joke tended to break the ice. Everyone gathered around to see whose cigarette would go off next. Not surprisingly, when Edith was not in town for one of these parties, Wolfgang would have nothing to do with this game because he was loath to encourage more smoking in the house.

As the months passed, Wolfgang spent more of his time at home and with members of the family. He was especially fond of his cousin Ruth who made learning fun for him as his tutor. She would work with him in his house each day, teaching him arithmetic, German grammar, and Hebrew. She also taught him songs and sang with him, which helped him enjoy the learning experience. Although he was increasingly insulated by his immediate family from the extent of the worsening conditions for Jews in and around Wolfhagen and really couldn't imagine what the changes that he had experienced would mean for him, he had learned that his cousin Otto had been forced to leave the university and his cousin Eugen, who wanted to become a doctor, was forced to leave medical school. By the end of 1935, his Aunt Sophie and Uncle Hermann had moved with their four sons from Volkmarsen to Hanover, a medium-sized city to the north about halfway between Kassel and Hamburg. At home, starting in late 1936 and continuing in 1937, he overheard whispered conversations among his parents and his Uncle Moritz, sometimes involving Edith—conversations from which he was barred and most of which took place at night after he was supposed to have gone to bed. He did not understand much of what was being said, but plans were being discussed, and the word "America" was mentioned multiple times.

Wolfgang, of course, would have had no way of knowing on that first day of school in September 1935 that a systematic campaign had begun almost immediately after Adolf Hitler became Germany's Chancellor in January 1933 to strip the nation's Jews of their rights, freedom, wealth, and eventually their existence. Anti-Semitism had occurred in Europe throughout most of the second millennium, fueled mainly by religious differences, in particular the Jews' rejection of Christianity. The Jews of Europe had been subjected to exile, segregation, and humiliation. According to the website of The World Holocaust Remembrance Center of Yad Vashem, however, in the second half of the 19th century anti-Semitism, influenced by social Darwinism, took on heavy racial overtones, emphasizing economic, social, and political factors rather than matters of faith that highlighted the differences between Jews and Christians. This singular development had an immediate impact on Adolf Hitler and the National Socialists in Germany as they ruthlessly implemented anti-Semitism as a political tool. Within weeks of assuming leadership of Germany, even before the process of consolidating power as *Führer* (absolute dictator) had been completed, Hitler and his closest supporters instituted a program of anti-Semitic edicts and policies against Germany's Jews that would ultimately lead to the most profound example of global genocide that the world had ever known.

The program began in early March 1933 with a series of organized but widely scattered attacks on Jews across Germany. On April 1, members of the Nazi Party and its affiliated organizations (the SA—*Sturmabteilung* or Storm Detachment, better known as the Brownshirts or Stormtroopers; the SS—*Schutzstaffel* or Protection Squads; and Hitler Youth, all of which developed in the decade preceding Hitler's accession to national control in Germany) organized and implemented a nationwide boycott of Jewish-owned stores and businesses by standing at the doors in order to block patrons from entering and by holding anti-Jewish signs. According to the United States Holocaust Memorial Museum website, they often smeared the word *"Jude"* or painted a yellow Star of David on store windows and marched through the streets chanting anti-Jewish slogans. On April 7, the German government issued the Law for the Restoration of the Civil Service, the purpose of which was largely to exclude Jews from all civil service positions. The same day the government issued a law mandating the disbarment of non-Aryan lawyers by September 30, 1933. Initially, these measures exempted Jews who were veterans of World War I, but these exemptions soon were overturned.

By the end of 1933, through a series of laws and official decrees, Jews were ousted or banned from virtually all aspects of professional, economic or cultural pursuits within Germany, including attending universities, practicing medicine, serving in the armed forces, working in the fields of journalism, literature, theater, film, broadcasting and fine arts, or inheriting farms. German public schools were to limit enrollment of Jewish children to 1.5 percent of the student body, except in areas where Jews constituted more than 5 percent of the population, in which Jewish enrollment in public school could extend to a maximum of 5 percent. In May, German student organizations supported by Nazi Party members and its affiliated groups organized public demonstrations across Germany where books written largely by Jews were burned in the streets for the purpose of purging German libraries of non-Aryan literature. On January 24, 1934, the government banned Jews from membership in the German Labor Front, effectively preventing them from obtaining employment in wage and salaried private sector jobs, and excluding those already employed from the benefits available to non-Jews.

On August 2, 1934, German President Paul von Hindenburg died. Supported by German military forces as well as Nazi Party affiliated organizations, Hitler assumed the office of president of Germany. Barely two weeks later, Hitler abolished the office of president and declared himself *Führer* of the German Reich and People, while retaining himself as Chancellor of Germany. In this capacity, Hitler's decisions were not subject to the laws of Germany, effectively eliminating the last vestiges of legal or constitutional limits to his authority. The German nation became known as The Third Reich.

The initial progression of anti-Jewish legislation and edicts reached a peak on September 15, 1935. At its annual party rally in Nuremburg, the National Socialist government announced The Reich Citizenship Law and the Law for the Protection of the German Blood and Honor. These "Nuremburg Laws" effectively made Jews second-class citizens, setting their personal status in society apart from the "Aryan race." The laws extended the definition of a Jew to someone who had three or four Jewish grandparents, prevented Jews from marrying Aryans, and essentially disenfranchised Jews and stripped them of their rights as German citizens so that they became more like subjects as a result of their segregated status in German society. The laws classified as Jewish those who had converted out of Judaism or had not practiced Judaism for three generations. They also institutionalized many of the anti-Semitic racial theories underpinning Nazi ideology. The viral effect of the Nuremburg Laws, compounded by two and a half years of anti-Semitic policies, spread at varying rates and levels of intensity around the country depending to a considerable extent on the level of local affiliation with the Nazi Party.

The Jews of Germany—only a little more than 500,000 people comprising less than 1 percent of the total population in 1933—according to the United States Holocaust Memorial Museum website—initially largely assumed a posture of denial. Most considered themselves loyal

Germans, many having served their nation with distinction in the First World War. They had excelled in business, literature, science, and the arts to a far greater extent than their numbers indicated; and many had immersed themselves in German culture and society even to the point of engaging in intermarriage and conversion to Christianity. There was a widespread belief among German Jews, at least at the outset of the Third Reich, that the role they played in German society was so essential to the nation that they would be immune from long-term consequences of the radical policies that were beginning to be implemented. But after what had transpired since early 1933 and especially after the enactment and enforcement of the Nuremburg Laws, increasing numbers of Germany's Jews came to realize that they could no longer sustain the kind of lives that they had built for themselves in Germany and determined that the time had come to leave—a decision that was, until October 1941, encouraged by the National Socialist regime provided departing Jews were willing to leave an increasingly large portion of their accumulated wealth behind and could find a country to which they could emigrate.

The hushed discussions in the Möllerich household became more intense during the winter of 1936–1937. The number of Edith's periodic returns to Wolfhagen increased to at least monthly and the family used these occasions to discuss their plans, mostly without Wolfgang present in the room. He continued, however, to overhear the conversations which often became heated and sometimes occurred with him in the room pretending not to pay attention. The elevated tone of these discussions was due mainly to a clear split in opinion between Josef on the one hand and his wife and brother on the other. Selma increasingly argued that conditions in Germany had worsened for Jews and there was no relief in sight. Wolfgang recalled hearing his mother say: "Josef, don't you see what's going on around you? When are you going to wake up and understand that we have to leave?" Wolfgang later recalled his uncle telling his father: "Josef, we've got to get out of here;

this is getting bad. People are leaving—people are getting arrested." For a period of time lasting several months, Josef stood firm and argued that he was "immune to Nazism" because he was a decorated veteran of the war and a pillar of the community. "They're not going to trouble me," he said. "This situation is madness; it can't last long. We'll just wait it out."

The arguments in favor of leaving, however, had merit. Although conditions for the small Jewish community in Wolfhagen were initially not as bad as in many other parts of Germany—there were few, if any *"Jude Verboten"* (no Jews allowed) signs on stores and Jews were not yet required to wear the yellow Star of David—Jewish families were politely turned away from, or discouraged from patronizing restaurants and shops. Herr Engelhardt, the baker, was an exception, however, and set aside and hid baked goods for the Jewish families in Wolfhagen. But Wolfgang's cousin Ruth Schloss later wrote that she was chased through the streets of the town and harassed when walking in Wolfhagen at night; and there had been the occasional act of vandalism, as in a stone being thrown through the shop window owned by the Kron family (but repaired quickly by the father of Heinrich Schwarz). By 1937 several of these Jewish families in the town had moved to nearby cities like Kassel seeking greater anonymity. News soon arrived that most members of the Möllerich family in the nearby towns had left their homes and many had departed—or would soon leave—the country. Eugen, Otto, and Max Schwarz had received visas to the United States, had met the American quota requirements, and had departed Hannover and moved to New York City, settling in Washington Heights where there was a growing community of German Jews. It was later learned that their brother, Ludwig, found his way to Palestine with his wife, Ellen, and they settled on a kibbutz with other German émigrés where their son, Jack, was born in 1939. Josef's sister Sophie and her husband, Hermann Schwarz remained in Hannover until their sons arranged to sponsor and send visas for them to join them in New York in the first half of 1941. Josef's sister Bertha and her children Julius and Brunhilde also were able to obtain visas and favorable quota numbers from the United States and moved from nearby Gudensberg to Chicago. Josef's nephew, Werner Schloss, also from Volkmarsen, had been arrested in early 1937 because of outspoken political views and for refusing to say, "Heil Hitler." Shortly after being released he was able to immigrate to England, where he began a new life, later assuming the name Bernard Rutherford (the surname of his English wife). His sister, Ruth, applied for and received a visa to the United States, cleared the quota, and settled in the same Washington Heights neighborhood of New York as her Aunt Sophie. Their parents, Alma and Julius Schloss, were unable to leave Germany due to poor health and perished in a concentration camp in 1943. As for Moritz's daughter, Gretl, she married Josef Rosenthal (whom the family sometimes referred to as Seppl) in 1937 and they settled in Wetzlar to be closer to his parents. They applied for and received visas to the United States that same year but could not meet the quota until 1939, after they had managed to reach England (Gretl actually departed Germany on September 1, 1939, the day Germany marched into Poland sparking the onset of World War II). They arrived in New York in August 1940, and settled in upper Manhattan—north of Washington Heights—where their son, Harry, was born the same month.

These circumstances, and the increasing pressure from Selma and Moritz, convinced Josef in early 1937 that the time had come to leave Wolfhagen. Moritz pushed his brother; Wolfgang remembered him telling his father: "'It's better to leave now than tomorrow—or the day after.'" But Josef was, by nature, meticulous and disciplined to the point of being methodical. He was consumed by the need for order, especially when making significant decisions. He was willing to have his wife and brother's strong desire to leave prevail, but if they were going to leave, it would be done his way. A three-part plan emerged: the two families and Selma's parents would apply for visas to the United States and then sail by ship to New York City once their US immigration quota numbers became available. Everyone would determine what to take with them and the business would have to be sold and items shipped to the United States that would allow Josef and Moritz to start a new business in America. Josef began formulating a notion that both personal items, including furniture, and the products and other items necessary to start a new business could be shipped to New York in massive crates (referred to by the family as "lifts") that could be stored by relatives already in New York until he and his family arrived there. Wolfgang suddenly found himself brought into the discussion. He was told to identify the items that he wanted to take away with him, as was his sister. He later recalled: "The discussion in the house centered on what we wanted to take. I indicated what I wanted most was my "mechano set" and my comic books; those were a must." Edith then indicated what she wanted to take, particularly her bicycle, and Selma of course listed a variety of items ranging from household linens, blankets, and silverware to personal items such as jewelry. She then spoke to her parents about what they wanted to pack. As the planning meetings progressed, Selma became overwhelmed: "How are we going to do all of this?" she worried. Josef felt the pressure: "You're rushing me," he would say. "Let's do one step at a time. Let's just list everything that you can identify." When Moritz was asked what he and Jette wanted to pack, he responded, "We're not going to do that; when we leave, we're just going with whatever we can get into suitcases and what we can carry in our pockets."

Josef's tripartite plan to move the family to New York encountered a crushing challenge almost immediately over the extent of his personal assets and those of the Wolf Möllerich Firm. In order to have exit visa applications approved by German authorities, it was necessary for all hopeful émigrés to determine their wealth so that the appropriate exit tax (sometimes referred to by those German Jews trying to emigrate as the "Jude Tax") could be assessed, a process that had to pass through several bureaucratic entities, including the tax office. The exit tax had not originated with the Nazis, having been enacted in 1931 by the Reichstag during the heart of the Great Depression to discourage wealthy Germans from emigrating. A 25 percent tax was to be levied on assets over 200,000 RM (over $700,000 in 2016 US dollars), but the Nazis lowered that amount in 1934 to 50,000 RM to further benefit from the assets of émigrés. Beyond that, any cash prospective emigrants received from the liquidation of assets such as homes, autos, land, or businesses were assessed a fee of 20 percent in 1933, but in September 1936 that amount more than quadrupled to 81 percent, and increased again in the summer of 1939 to 96 percent. Setting aside for the moment the initial problem of obtaining an approved determination of actual assets, in 1937 the effective impact of the combined exit taxes and fees that Wolfgang's family would have had to pay would have cost more than 75 percent of their total accumulated wealth, a price that all but perhaps Josef would have gladly been willing to pay at the time, but a staggering loss nonetheless.

The exorbitant exit fees notwithstanding, because of the business, it became necessary for Josef and Moritz to have the books of the Wolf Möllerich Firm audited by an independent, non-Jewish accountant. This was done in the late winter of 1937, and shortly thereafter Josef and Moritz were summoned to the tax office in Kassel for what turned out to be a very difficult day. The building was crowded with Jewish businessmen from all over northern Hessen. When it was their turn, Josef and Moritz had to explain what turned out to be a number of discrepancies in the books that showed *zoll und haben* (debt and credit). Upon returning home, Josef explained to his family, as Wolfgang later recalled, that he had tried to "shield other people by not including them as having a debt owed to him." In fact, records indicate that in 1937 there was more than 65,000 RM in outstanding debt owed to the firm by several individuals and businesses in and around Wolfhagen. One of these people, it was later learned, was Otto Abel, Heinz's father. There were many others in Wolfhagen to whom Josef had loaned money that he shielded in his application in the same way. The rationale probably was, in fact, to keep these non-Jewish neighbors out of the books of a Jewish firm for their own protection, but it also lowered the total assets of the firm for the purpose of paying government fees. The consequence of having these discrepancies in the financial report, however, was catastrophic: Josef and Moritz were ordered to have the accountant revise the report so that the numbers were accurate. The process became bogged down in the bureaucracy largely, one would surmise, because of the high level of the assets involved (the report actually was sent to Berlin, causing further delay), but also because of the ever increasing volume of paperwork the tax office had to process. The result was that while other members of the family who had significantly fewer assets had their paperwork pass seamlessly through the process and approved, thus allowing them to obtain exit visas without delay, Josef and Moritz were caught in an ever tightening web of financial scrutiny that held up their planned emigration in ways that they could not have imagined at the time they initially filed for emigration in early 1937.

With the plan to emigrate directly to the United States stalled and with likely no hope of a quick resolution, Josef and Moritz began planning for an interim move to Hamburg. Because many of the families that constituted the small Jewish population of Wolfhagen had moved away, there was concern that the Möllerich family—no matter how much they were respected by their neighbors in Wolfhagen—would become so conspicuous in the small town that they could be subjected to harassment by the German authorities at best or arrested and imprisoned by the Gestapo at worst. Besides, ownership of property and businesses by Jews had become very difficult by 1937 and there was undoubtedly pressure for them to sell the business and property and leave Wolfhagen. Hamburg was not only one of the largest cities in Germany, offering the hope of greater anonymity, but a major port from which overseas transport might facilitate their ultimate emigration once the financial paperwork could be resolved and the business sold. In the spring of 1937, Moritz proposed a move to Hamburg and made several trips there by train, where he found a neighborhood that was largely Jewish, with two synagogues and a Talmud Torah school and shops within easy walking distance of each other, and found two sizable apartments not far from each other to house himself and Jette in one and Josef and his family, including Selma's parents, in the other. Within weeks, the two brothers rented and furnished their respective apartments and made plans to move, which Moritz and Jette did in late May.

About a month later, Wolfgang was told to pack for a trip that would be coming up in a few days. Until that time he had been told virtually nothing about a move to Hamburg and had assumed that the family was awaiting approval to immigrate to the United States. His life had become somewhat consumed by his sister's return from Frankfurt, where she had completed her school year. Her presence at home on a full-time basis, he later recalled, "was bad because we fought—we were not friends. I could not ever feel comfortable in the presence of my sister because she didn't like me and so she beat me up." With his mother's help, Wolfgang went through his cabinet and drawers, packing clothing and a few personal items. He desperately wanted to take his "mechano set," which had become his most treasured possession, but his father told him: "If you take that then you can't take a single book because the weight will be too much and everything has to fit in the trunk of the car." Much to her chagrin, Edith was told that she could not take her bike with her. It had been decided that the family would load the car after dark and depart in the dead of night, virtually disappearing from the town without telling anyone their destination. This was done for their own safety as well as the safety of their neighbors who could then honestly say, when asked by the authorities where family Möllerich had gone, that they knew nothing. Wolfgang recalled that the back of the car had been cleaned out to maximize storage space. Very late one night early in July, Josef and his family, along with Selma's parents—six people in all—piled into the car loaded with limited belongings, and departed Wolfhagen. At first excited about the trip, Wolfgang wondered if he would ever see his home again. The lateness of the hour and the motion of the car made him drowsy and he soon fell asleep on his mother's lap.

# CHAPTER 2

## Hamburg (1937–1938)

THE CAR PULLED up in front of a light grey four-story apartment building at Beneckestraße 26. The drive from Wolfhagen to Hamburg had taken much of the shortened summer night so that the Möllerich family arrival in Hamburg coincided with the break of dawn. Despite the long drive, Wolfgang slept most of the way and had to be stirred when the car stopped at its destination. Wiping sleep from his eyes as he stepped onto the sidewalk, Wolfgang looked around in the quickly increasing early light. Buildings lined one side of the street; the building next to the one where he was standing was located on a corner and was darker in color than the one in front of him and more ornate with several small spires on its roof. There was a park directly across the street that contin-

ued beyond the street corner closest to where he stood. Bewildered, Wolfgang turned to his father and asked him how long they were going to stay there. Josef said to him simply, "This is your new home." He allowed his father's words to sink in for a moment and then asked him why they had to leave so late at night, without his being able to say goodbye to anyone in Wolfhagen. "Don't ask; just accept," his father responded. "Be patient because we have a lot on our minds. I know you are young and that this is very confusing for you, but in time you will understand why we did this." As he later recalled, Wolfgang understood enough to realize that "it was like one chapter of my life was finished and a new chapter was about to begin."

The apartment at Beneckestraße 26 was one flight up from the street and turned out to be large enough to occupy half the building from front to back on that level and was separated from the equally large other apartment by a center stairs and outer hallway. Inside the apartment, a long corridor connected the rooms. There were three bedrooms facing the front with an excellent view of the park across the street. Wolfgang and Edith each had their own room here as did their parents. There were two more bedrooms (one of which was occupied by Wolfgang's grandparents) and a full bathroom at the rear of the apartment. In between, there was a very large living room where the door to the apartment from the outer hallway was located; a formal dining room sat behind the living room, with the kitchen situated behind this room. In all, the apartment was easily over 2,000 square feet of living space but felt considerably smaller than the home in Wolfhagen.

Although the block of Beneckestraße where Wolfgang's apartment was located was almost entirely a residential street, there were shops on the ground level of many of the buildings on the adjacent block where the house numbers decreased. It was at this end of the street where two synagogues stood almost directly opposite each other. The neighborhood, which had developed around the turn of the 20th century and was known as New City, had very quickly become heavily populated with Jewish residents. The more visibly striking of the two structures was the Bonnplatz Synagogue, a huge, freestanding building located at the foot of Beneckestrasse that was built in 1910 and had a large dome above the sanctuary. The second synagogue, known as the New Dammtor Synagogue, was actually the older of the two congregations. The building was smaller and located at the end of a row of houses situated on a pedestrian walkway between Beneckestraße and the next street running parallel to it, and thus was somewhat hidden from view, unlike the larger Bonnplatz Synagogue. The New Dammtor was more traditional orthodox than was the Bonnplatz Synagogue, which was more liberal in observance, so much so that it was sometimes referred to as a "temple." The Möllerich family joined this congregation and attended services there on a regular basis. There was a Talmud Torah school located just a few steps down the street from the Bonnplatz Synagogue and around the corner from Beneckestraße; Wolfgang attended classes at this school. The street behind the New Dammtor Synagogue was a major thoroughfare with many shops and had a streetcar running along it, from which it was possible to travel virtually anywhere

else in the city via the existing network of streetcar lines. It was also possible to use the streetcar to get to Moritz Möllerich's apartment, which was located at Isistraße 15, a distance of about one to two kilometers from Wolfgang's apartment; but most of the time the two families walked to each other's homes.

It took a bit of time for Wolfgang to adjust to life in one of the largest cities in Germany, having lived prior to this in a small, mostly rural environment. He would walk around the immediate neighborhood, having no bicycle during the time he was in Hamburg. He walked to and from the Talmud Torah, and around the corner to the street where most of the shops were located. Often he would accompany his grandfather on walks so that his Opa could smoke a cigar. His father would sometimes send him to purchase beer at a shop near the Bonnplatz Synagogue, especially when his parents hosted gatherings at their apartment. These social occasions involved far fewer people than the ones his parents held in Wolfhagen; visitors in this instance were almost entirely Jewish and consisted of a mix of neighbors or fellow congregants at the synagogue, along with a few distant relatives who had mostly been living in and around Hamburg long before the Möllerich family had moved there.

Wolfgang found life in Hamburg, even in the largely Jewish neighborhood in which he lived, to be characterized by an interesting contradiction with regard to the way in which he observed the influence of Nazism on his life. On the one hand, the presence of Hitler Youth and German soldiers was far greater in Hamburg than in Wolfhagen. From his apartment bedroom window, he would watch Hitler Youth marching along the street or in the park directly across the street. This park was also the site of a number of political and military rallies in which Nazi officials would speak from a temporary platform that had been set up. Wolfgang recalled that on one occasion, it appeared that the guest speaker was a very high ranking official—in fact he believed at the time it might have been Hitler, but later in life realized that this relatively small park, located in the center of a highly Jewish community, would not have been a likely location for Hitler to speak. Wolfgang recalled on this occasion hearing from his open apartment window a fiery speech clearly anti-Semitic in tone. He also recalled that many of the Jewish shopkeepers in the neighborhood complained about lack of sales because of the national boycott against Jewish businesses. He noticed that it became increasingly difficult for people in the neighborhood to purchase many of the items they needed, such as hardware, and so they were forced to travel to other parts of the city to purchase these items, so long as the non-Jewish store owners did not identify their customers as Jewish.

On the other hand, Wolfgang observed that he and his family, and many of his Jewish neighbors were able to go about their lives relatively unabated, at least for the first year or so in which he lived in Hamburg. Jews were not required to wear the yellow Star of David, nor did Wolfgang notice any *Jude verboten* signs on store fronts, and so it was largely possible to travel to other parts of the city where the population was not Jewish and blend in with relative anonymity. Wolfgang recalled that he loved to take walks to parks around the city with his family, sometimes stopping for a snack such as ice cream, and the family usually would be served with no questions asked. But there were times when such outings made him nervous because he remembered experiences from his time living in Wolfhagen. On one such occasion, his parents and sister went with him to a park in a non-Jewish section of the city and found a table located under a tree at a café and sat down. While they waited to place their order, a group of Hitler Youth came along, and Wolfgang said to his family, "Let's go," because he knew what was going to happen. "They would recognize me and want to know why I was not in uniform," he later recalled. His sister told him to "calm down" and everything would be fine. Just at that moment, a bird flying by relieved itself and the result of that landed on his father's forehead and ran down his nose, causing everyone to laugh hysterically—except for Wolfgang. "I was absolutely petrified about the Hitler Youth," he remembered, "because I saw what happened in Wolfhagen," where his Oma had told him to be wary of the Hitler Youth, because they "could identify Jews and get them in trouble." This warning stuck with Wolfgang; the sight of the Hitler Youth at the Hamburg café caused him to panic and he was ready to run off on his own, but Edith grabbed him and said, "You're not going without us," at which point Josef calmly said, "Wolfgang's probably right; let's get out of here," and they left the café without any confrontation and without having placed their order.

Despite the relatively peaceful living conditions for the Möllerich family, especially through the early fall of 1938, Wolfgang found himself to be unhappy most of the time. He missed his friends from Wolfhagen, most of all Heinz; he missed the relative freedom he had enjoyed being out of the house and spending time in the lumber yard in his hometown; he missed his tutor, his cousin Ruth; and he missed the family German shepherd, who Wolfgang had tormented by playing the harmonica in his presence, and whom he learned had been slaughtered for meat shortly before he had left Wolfhagen. Although he attended the Talmud Torah School in his Hamburg neighborhood, there were few children his age, certainly very few boys, and so he was largely bereft of peer companionship. Nor did the Talmud Torah provide enough learning in arithmetic and German for him to develop foundational intellectual skills, even though he craved such learning. His teacher, Herr Steinhof, reported that Wolfgang was well-behaved but not particularly diligent in any of his subjects, and the boy received mostly average grades largely because he was unhappy and bored. Occasionally his father would spend time with him on arithmetic and language, but that proved to be a poor substitute for the regular daily drilling required to retain what he was being taught. Unlike his sister, who at age 16 was permitted to spend significant time outside the apartment and find a few friends with whom to socialize, Wolfgang at age 7 had no such privileges. He recalled that he was "bored, because I had nothing to do" except play with the few toys he had, sometimes for hours at a time. His father had replaced his "mechano set" left in Wolfhagen, and Wolfgang's only real pleasure was in building "fantastic things that had drives and a motor," such as Ferris wheels that were as high as three or four feet. As in Wolfhagen, he confided in his Oma, whom he recalled saying to him, "Don't worry—this isn't going to last this way forever; we're going to see better times." She taught him Hebrew and sat with him when he recited the *Sh'ma* (a principal daily prayer) each night.

As time passed in Hamburg, Wolfgang was distracted by two things: his aunt Jette had passed away suddenly on August 10, 1937; and he wondered what had become of the plan to go to America. He knew that his father had been absent for a day or longer on a few occasions since the move to Hamburg, but there was not much in the way of family conversations about moving to America, and he presumed his father's absences were related in some way to the business. In fact, both Josef and Selma had traveled back to Wolfhagen overnight in September 1937 to transport much of the furniture they had stored in their home to Hamburg. Josef had leased the Wolfhagen house and adjacent Steinkammer to Otto Matthias, a civil servant in the land registry office in Wolfhagen. He and his wife moved into the Möllerich house at the beginning of July after receiving special permission from the National Socialist Party to rent from a Jewish landlord. Matthias later recorded in a letter to Wilhelm G. Winter that he found Josef and Selma Möllerich "obliging and helpful," referring to Selma as "a beautiful woman," and that he and his wife "were regarded more as sort of trustees rather than tenants." In that letter Matthias described what happened the day in September 1937 when Josef and Selma came to transport their remaining furniture to Hamburg: "The unskilled laborer Krowkowski drove up in front of the house with a platform truck in order to load all their property," he wrote. "The couple climbed up into the truck and Mrs. Möllerich wept bitterly." It is likely that the Abel family who lived next door may have seen the Möllerich couple at this time as well, because Wolfgang's friend Heinz later recalled, "I was just seven years old, but I noticed that they (the Möllerich family) had gone," and that his parents heard that they were in Hamburg, so it is possible Josef mentioned it to Otto Abel the day they were in Wolfhagen to move the furniture. Matthias also noted a time early in 1938 when Josef returned to Wolfhagen "to settle business matters." While Matthias was undertaking military service at the end of 1938, he learned from his wife that the Steinkammer and the adjacent building they were renting had been sold to Eugen Schiffmann and his family, and so Matthias and his wife rented and moved into another place further down Schützebergerstraße at the end of May 1939. These events remained unknown to Wolfgang in Hamburg, who became increasingly curious about moving to America. Whenever he asked his sister about that, her typical response was, "When we have to go, we'll go, and that's all there is to it." And so Wolfgang's ennui in Hamburg continued well into the autumn of 1938, when he found himself suddenly shaken to the core by an event of monumental consequence.

Herschel Grynszpan was born in Hannover to Polish Jewish parents who immigrated to Germany in 1911. Never allowed to become German citizens, the family was among roughly 12,000 Polish Jewish refugees who had settled in Germany and, in the case of the Grynszpan family, made a modest living, although they never assimilated into German culture and spoke mostly Yiddish. Herschel attended public school until 1935 when, after passage of the Nuremburg Laws, Jewish children were no longer able to attend most public schools in Germany. He went to a Yeshiva in Frankfurt and studied Hebrew and the Torah. While there, he determined to go to Palestine but was told he was too young, so he decided to make his way to Paris to live with his aunt and uncle and entered France illegally in September 1936 at the age of 15. There he worked odd jobs and lived a bohemian lifestyle, unable to take on a real job because he was constantly under pressure of being deported by the authorities. He was described as a shy, intelligent young man who often became emotional about the plight of world Jewry. He also spoke openly with great love for his family in Germany.

On October 26, 1938, an order was issued for the Gestapo to arrest and deport all Polish Jews residing in Germany, including Herschel's family. Forced to walk about two kilometers across the border, the refugees were prevented from entering Poland and were placed in a detention camp under deplorable conditions in which they were fed by the Polish Red Cross. Herschel received the news on November 3 in a postcard from his sister. He pleaded with his uncle to send assistance to his family, but his uncle said he did not have the means to provide help and the two argued, with Herschel storming out of the house, taking with him all the money he had—300 francs, a small portion of which he used to stay the night of November 6 in a cheap hotel. The next day Herschel purchased a revolver, wrote a farewell note to his parents, and went to the German Embassy where he asked to see the Ambassador on the pretext that he had a highly valuable document. He was directed to the office of Ernst Vom Rath, a junior clerk on the embassy staff. When Vom Rath asked to see the highly valuable document, Grynszpan pulled out the revolver and shot the German five times in revenge for the treatment of his family and the 12,000 Polish Jews evicted from Germany. Grynszpan made no attempt to escape and was immediately arrested while Vom Rath was rushed to a hospital in critical condition. He died from the gunshot wounds on November 9.

The day Vom Rath died coincided with the 15th anniversary of the 1923 Beer Hall *Putsch* in 1938, still an auspicious date for the National Socialists, whose leadership had gathered in Munich—the site of the *Putsch*—to commemorate the occasion. After private discussions with Hitler and others, Propaganda Minister Joseph Goebbels delivered an inflammatory speech to the crowd of assembled "Old Guard" party leaders, in which it was made clear that "World Jewry" was responsible for the assassination in Paris and that while there would be no "official" acts of retaliation ordered, should "unofficial" demonstrations occur, they would not be disrupted. Within hours, word spread among party officials throughout Germany and its annexed territories: Austria, which had become part of the Third Reich in March 1938 as a result of the *"Anschluss,"* and the portion of western Czechoslovakia known as the Sudetenland, which had been annexed by Germany as a result of the "Munich Agreement" between Germany, England, and France signed in September 1938. By nightfall, a massive *pogrom* erupted against Jewish communities throughout Germany and the annexed territories, led by Hitler Youth and Nazi Stormtroopers. Jewish homes and businesses were vandalized, looted, and sometimes completely destroyed; Jewish cemeteries were desecrated; more than 250 synagogues were burned. According to the United States Holocaust Memorial Museum website, although the record shows that only 91 Jews were killed during the demonstrations, units of the SS and Gestapo arrested nearly 30,000 Jewish men, especially younger adults, who were thrown into local jails or sent to concentration camps. The demonstrations were the most intense in Berlin and Vienna, the two largest centers of Jewry in the Third Reich, but erupted all over throughout the night of November 9 and into the next day. Known as *Kristallnacht* (Night of Broken Glass), the pogrom of November 9–10, 1938, was the first instance of mass violence and incarceration of Jews under the Third Reich simply because of their ethnicity. It also marked a turning point for Jews in the manner in which they were treated by the Nazi government thereafter and in renewed efforts by Jews to leave Germany and the annexed territories before it was too late.

The events of November 9–10, 1938, had a direct, significant impact on the residents of the Hamburg neighborhood of New City, including the Möllerich family. News of the assassination of the German diplomat in Paris had been reported on the radio the day after the shooting, November 8. The family again took pains to keep the news from Wolfgang, speaking in hushed tones when he was in a different room. But Wolfgang realized that something was going on. He noticed a buildup of activity in the neighborhood streets that included the presence of more Gestapo and other officials wearing armbands with a Swastika emblazoned on them, as well as increased numbers of Hitler Youth marching, especially on the afternoon of November 9. He asked Edith what was happening. "Something bad has happened that will probably have consequences that will affect us," she told him. That night, Wolfgang went to his bedroom window and saw many Nazi officials and uniformed men (most likely Stormtroopers) going through the street in front of his building, going into buildings on his street, even into his own building. "They were knocking on doors, looking for Jews," he later recalled. He was scared, partly because of what he had seen outside and partly because everyone around him seemed concerned about what was taking place. But there was no knock on his door on that night—possibly because there were no young adult males living there. Wolfgang was told to stay away from the windows and so he went to bed, not able to hear or see much of what was going on outside the apartment. He later recalled the faint smell of something burning in the distance, but eventually he went to sleep.

The next morning, there was considerable talk among the family around the breakfast table, but Wolfgang was more interested in observing what was going on outside. He silently slipped out of the apartment and stood in front of his building. The smell of something burning was much stronger in the air out there, but he could not see anything actually burning from his vantage point. There was some activity on the next street where it appeared stones had been thrown through store windows, leaving considerable broken glass on the sidewalk. Before long, Selma came down and Wolfgang asked his mother what had happened. She merely said to him: "Get in the house," and took him by the arm and led him upstairs. He could tell from her voice that she was very upset and "jittery" and when he went upstairs he heard the others saying that there were reports that both the Bonnplatz Synagogue and the New Dammtor Synagogue had been burned. He was ordered not to go out in the street by himself, however, and that ended any opportunity he had to see what had taken place. He later recalled that his life in Hamburg, which had not been a happy one from the outset, became even more intolerable in the aftermath of Kristallnacht. He was "haunted" by the "fear of isolation and restriction from going outside." If he had a bike, he would be riding up and down the street and in the park across the street, he later lamented. "But I didn't have a bicycle in Hamburg so there was nothing for me to do but to be a good boy and listen to my parents and grandparents." At the time Wolfgang—who had turned eight years old the past May—believed he was "traumatized" by "being closed in and not being trusted" by his parents. Later in life he realized this had been done to "shield him" from the worst of what was happening to the family under Nazism.

What Wolfgang did not know until many years later, but his family undoubtedly learned almost immediately, was that his cousin Gretl's husband, Josef Rosenthal, living in Wetzlar with his wife and his parents, had been one of the young Jewish men arrested on Kristallnacht and had been sent to the concentration camp at Buchenwald. He and Gretl had taken their honeymoon in Italy earlier in 1938, and he had been accused of smuggling funds out of the country. The charge, like many of the charges that landed young German Jewish males in jail on November 9 and 10, 1938, had no legitimate basis. Josef and Gretl had already received visas to immigrate to the United States prior to

Kristallnacht but were awaiting the availability of their United States quota number. A few weeks after Josef was sent to Buchenwald, Gretl paid a hefty fee to have him released, and not long after that Josef was able to go to England until he was later joined by Gretl and they waited for their quota number in the safety of England. Not everyone arrested on Kristallnacht was so fortunate. Hundreds died in the camps as the result of the harsh treatment to which they were subjected, although the majority ended up being released.

The burning and looting subsided in the New City section of Hamburg after November 10, but the knocking on doors by Gestapo officers and Stormtroopers continued—in fact increased. Like most of their neighbors, the Möllerich family hunkered down each night dreading the sound of the butt of a rifle or a revolver knocking loudly on apartment doors. Shortly after Kristallnacht, the family heard the sound of several loud footsteps coming up the stairway of the building and then stopping. There was a sharp knock on the door across the hallway from their apartment; the man of the house was taken away in a truck. Josef was well aware that the records of his business were still under scrutiny by the government. He had traveled to Wolfhagen at least twice in the past 16 months in an effort to sell his home and tie up some of the loose ends regarding the business so that he and Moritz could sell it as soon as the extended audit on the business was resolved. Realizing that the Gestapo could be coming for him, he devised a plan that he hoped would work. Earlier in his life he had suffered a severe case of pneumonia that had actually required surgery on one of his lungs. Ever since that time he had been on an extensive regime of medication. After Kristallnacht, each night Josef would prepare for bed early, line up his medicine bottles by his bedside, leaving some bottles open so the aroma of medication would be present in the room, and wait for the sound of knocking on the door. The night the Gestapo came for his neighbor, Josef had crawled into bed at the sound of the knocking. Two days later, it happened; there was a loud knock on the apartment door caused by the butt of a rifle carried by a Stormtrooper, who entered the apartment along with a Gestapo officer wearing a Swastika on an armband. Selma and Edith stood near the doorway while Wolfgang was held and partially shielded by his grandparents. "Where is the man of the house,' the Gestapo agent demanded. He was shown to the master bedroom where Josef lay under the covers, hacking and moaning. "What is wrong with this man," the agent again demanded to know." Selma answered, "He has pneumonia; he is very sick." The intruders took a moment to look around and then the Gestapo agent turned to the Stormtrooper and said, "Let's go," and they abruptly left the apartment.

The family exhaled a collective sigh of relief after that incident, but the level of fear from that moment on was pervasive. Efforts to prepare to move to America accelerated immediately. Wolfgang later recalled: "After Kristallnacht there was a dramatic change in my parents' behavior. They were scared; they were rushing around." Selma stepped up her pleas to Josef to do whatever it would take to get the family out. A bit of good news arrived from New York that visas for Josef and his family—except for Selma's parents but including Moritz—were on their way. Moritz was ready to go; Josef was determined to carry through with his plan to ship as much as possible to New York so the family would have what it needed and so that he could start a business once they arrived in the United States. But he understood the urgency and moved forward with the packing of the "lifts," which he had stored in the basement of the building and began to fill them with china, linens, and furniture from the apartment which were added to the furniture that had been transported from Wolfhagen the previous year. Wolfgang at first remained mostly a silent observer to this flurry of activity engaged in by his family. Then his father took him aside and said to him: "I need your help. We have to pack up immediately, and I want you to organize my coin and stamp collections." Josef had a massive stamp collection with thousands of stamps, most of which were "first day of issue." Besides their value, the stamp collection was one of his most prized personal possessions that he and Moritz had accumulated over the years and that Josef had held onto for himself and his older brother. Wolfgang did the best he could to pack up the coins in a box, which was easy, and tried to organize page after page of the stamp collection, which was much harder to do. He later recalled, "I assembled these stamps day after day by removing the stamps page by page and placing them into sealable envelopes; that was my entire job and I did it, and that was fine because it gave me something to do."

While Kristallnacht galvanized Josef Möllerich and his family into action in anticipation of the arrival of visas and with hope of their quota numbers becoming available quickly to allow a move to the United States, the events of Kristallnacht also led almost immediately to new anti-Semitic measures in the Third Reich that would severely cripple those efforts. On November 12, the German government issued the Decree on the Elimination of the Jews from Economic Life, preventing Jews from operating retail stores, sales agencies or from conducting trade of any kind. Jews had already been made ineligible for employment in the public sector and engaging in professions in the private sector; this measure prevented them from working in businesses in the private sector. On December 3, the government issued the Decree on the Utilization of Jewish Property, requiring the sale of all Jewish businesses to Aryan owners; it became the law of the land for Jews to sell land, homes, stocks and businesses to non-Jews, usually at prices far below their actual value. Also in December, the government froze all Jewish assets. Henceforth it would be required for Jews to submit written, itemized requests for the use of any of their funds not in their personal possession, even for the basic monthly necessities of life, as well as for one-time expenses for such routine items as eyeglasses. Every written request for funds was reviewed by a government official and stamped "approved" or "denied" (often the denied requests would be annotated with a question of why a particular item would be needed by a Jew), and signed "in the name of Adolf Hitler" with the officer's signature. The latter two government edicts, in particular, caused further delay in the Möllerich family's efforts to pack and ship to New York the "lifts" that Josef was preparing and, combined with the ongoing audit of the business records, made it far more difficult for the brothers to sell their business even though they were legally required to do so. It would take several months and complex paperwork before the lifts could be shipped to New York. Kristallnacht, however, would have another immediate and historic result—one that would change the course of Wolfgang's life, and Edith's, forever.

While public pressure mounted on governments in the United States and much of the rest of the world to take action in order to relieve the heightened suffering of Jews and other non-Aryans within the Third Reich and its annexed territories, several factors had prevented these countries from significantly increasing immigration quotas beyond the existing limitations. The United Kingdom, however, among all the nations of the world, developed as an exception to its immigration policy a program known as the Kindertransport to allow children 17 years old or younger to travel to England from Germany, Austria, and the Czech Sudetenland, thus rescuing them from the ever-tightening grip of Nazi persecution. Organized and largely implemented by charitable and religious organizations within England with the blessing and support of the British government, aided and abetted by individuals and groups within the Third Reich and its annexed territories as well as in The Netherlands and Belgium, the Kindertransport brought nearly 10,000 children (about 75 percent of them Jewish) out of harm's way between December 1938 and September 1939. As if this accomplishment was not sufficiently impressive, the Kindertransport program was conceived, approved, organized, and implemented in scarcely more than a fortnight, and stands as one of the largest and most unique and successful rescue missions in history.

The Kindertransport had its antecedents in an initiative by United States President Franklin D. Roosevelt in March 1938 to convene an international conference devoted to finding solutions to the growing crisis of refugees seeking to emigrate from Germany and Austria. Roosevelt had called for the conference very shortly after Hitler's *Anschluss* in

Austria increased the number of Jews under the control of the Nazi regime by approximately 185,000. Delegates from 32 nations and several
refugee organizations gathered at Evian, France, on the shores of Lake
Geneva in early July. The nine-day conference turned out to be largely
a showcase to enable each delegation to speak out against German
treatment of the Jews and other non-Aryans, but among the nations in
attendance the only one to increase its immigration quota as a result of
the meeting was the Dominican Republic. As for the remaining participants, particularly the United States and the United Kingdom, excuses
for inaction included the difficulty of modifying existing legislated immigration quotas and concern that a massive influx of immigrants stripped
of their assets would create both an impossible burden on the state and
competition for jobs at a time when each nation's economy was still re-
covering from the Great Depression. It has also been argued and largely
accepted after the fact that anti-Semitism in the United States, especially among some senior Department of State officials, contributed to
the failure of the United States to further open its doors to German and
Austrian Jewish refugees. The Evian Conference delegates established
an Intergovernmental Committee on Refugees for the purpose of seeking countries willing to provide "permanent settlement" for refugees
emigrating from Germany and Austria (and after September 1938, the
Czech Sudetenland), and to seek cooperation from Germany both in establishing a process for orderly emigration and in encouraging Germany
to allow émigrés to take with them some significant portion of their assets. The committee established an office in London under the directorship of George Rublee, a veteran American diplomat, who attempted in
vain to make significant headway with both the potential nations of final settlement and the German government, including German Foreign
Minister Joachim von Ribbentrop, during the fall of 1938. The refugee
question became entwined with larger foreign policy issues among
the major international powers, further inhibiting progress. It took
Kristallnacht to elevate the plight of Jews in the Third Reich among the
American and British public. Rublee reported to the US Department of

State from London that "the public reaction in Great Britain to the recent attack on the Jews in Germany is deep and widespread." Ironically, the horrors of November 9–10 succeeded where the Evian Conference and the ensuing efforts of the Intergovernmental Committee on Refugees failed, at least when it came to England and a relatively small but significant component of those seeking emigration from the Third Reich.

In the immediate aftermath of Kristallnacht, newspapers in London and throughout the United Kingdom published editorials and letters to the editor that reflected a public outcry against inhumane treatment of Jews within the Third Reich and its annexed territories. Driven by moral responsibility for humanitarian principles as well as political objections to the British government ceding the Sudetenland in Czechoslovakia to Nazi control at Munich and obstructing expanded Jewish emigration to Palestine, religious groups representing Jews and Christians—most notably Quakers—launched a direct appeal to the British government. Because it was unsafe for British Jews to travel to Germany to assess the problem, the Friends Service Council, which had been working with Jewish refugee organizations both in England and in Germany, sent a delegation to Berlin to meet with Jewish leaders there. The Quaker group was able to determine that parents were, according to a British government source, as appearing in the spring 1994 issue of *The Kinder Link*, the quarterly newsletter of the KTA, "almost unanimously" willing to allow their children to travel alone to the safety of England rather than risk "the unknown dangers with which they are faced in Germany." On November 15, a small group of influential Jewish Britons representing the Council for German Jewry met with British Prime Minister Neville Chamberlain and proposed a plan that called for the admission into England of children age 17 and under from Germany and Nazi-controlled Austria and Czechoslovakia. Chamberlain was unconvinced during the meeting, but the next day the British Cabinet took up the proposal and decided that the government must take immediate action to alleviate the humanitarian refugee crisis. It prepared a resolution for Parliament in which the British government would waive or alter certain immigration requirements to allow entry into England of an un-specified number of children. On the morning of November 21, Home Secretary Samuel Hoare met with a large group representing various Jewish, Quaker, and other non-Jewish activist groups who had formed themselves into an organization initially called the Movement for the Care of Children from Germany and which later became known as the Refugee Children's Movement. As home secretary, Hoare—who was from a Quaker family—would be crucial to government support of the motion. The representatives promised to find homes for the children and fund the program, as well as provide a 50-pound sterling guar-antee to cover eventual re-emigration costs. These assurances proved sufficient to gain the home secretary's backing.

A historic debate occurred in Parliament's House of Commons on a resolution presented by Philip John Noel-Baker, on the evening of November 21, 1938. According to the *Hansard Digitized Official Debates of Parliament*, Noel-Baker, a Member of Parliament repre-senting the Labor Party and future winner of the Nobel Peace Prize, launched into a compelling, 5,000 word condemnation of Kristallnacht and subsequent measures taken by the German government and an impassioned justification for assistance to prospective refugees victim-ized by the Third Reich policies in the wake of November 9–10, whom he referred to as a "pitiful human wreckage." Several other members of Parliament rose to speak in favor of the resolution over the course of nearly four hours, including David G. Logan who said, in referring to Kristallnacht and its immediate aftermath: "I feel that some of the incidents of the past three weeks have brought about a different point of view in the whole English-speaking race, and that we people will be able to recognise and bring about in this House a common unity which we could never achieve under any conditions of political parti-sanship." When it became the turn of the home secretary to speak, Samuel Hoare relayed the substance of that morning's meeting with the leaders of the Refugee Children's Movement, and stated that his government "shall put no obstacle in the way of children coming here and living" in the manner described by the group that morning. He concluded his remarks by referring to the leadership of that group: "Let me assure them as Home Secretary that I will do my utmost to facilitate their work, to extend its scope and to show that we will be in the forefront among the nations of the world in giving relief to these suffering people." The resolution passed resoundingly at the end of the evening.

With the action of Parliament, the home secretary made good on his commitment to provide entry to all child refugees from within the Third Reich and its annexed territories whose maintenance could be guaranteed, dropping the requirement for individual visas in lieu of details about the child in the form of an identity card. The Refugee Children's Movement immediately launched a massive effort that had essentially three simultaneous components. One aspect of the initiative involved finding foster homes, hostels, and other places to house the children upon their arrival in England. Refugee Children's Movement co-chairs Sir Wyndham Deeds, a Christian former military general and social service worker, and Lord Herbert Samuel, a Jewish-born diplomat and politician, broadcast an appeal over the BBC Home Service Radio on November 25 that resulted in more than 500 positive responses almost overnight. Raising money to cover the cost of the care of the emigrant children became another priority for the Refugee Children's Movement. On December 8, former British Prime Minister Stanley Baldwin made a broadcast appeal for donations to the Lord Baldwin Fund, which raised about 500,000 pounds sterling, about 200,000 of which went to the Refugee Children's Movement for the Kindertransport program. The Society of Friends undertook separate fund-raising efforts that resulted, according to later estimates, in contributions of some kind toward the refugee relief programs, including the Kindertransport, from nearly every one of the almost 20,000 Quaker households in England. The most complex aspect of the Kindertransport initiative, however, involved the identification of children to be rescued, organizing of the transports—which involved volunteers in England, Germany, Austria,

Czechoslovakia, Poland, The Netherlands, and Belgium—and developing the process by which Kindertransport children arriving in England would be managed, from their initial encampment to their assigned homes or hostels or farms, to monitoring their welfare (i.e., schooling and other progress) over time until they were old enough to be on their own or were reunited with their families. With regard to the selection of children to be rescued, priority lists were established in an attempt to identify children most imperiled, those who were orphaned or left homeless or who were in danger of arrest or whose parents were too impoverished to keep them. This system of prioritization worked in part; but the selection and scheduling of children for the Kindertransport also came about as a result of the initiative on the part of parents to make the necessary connections and obtain passage for their children. The Refugee Children's Movement coordinated multiple networks of organizers, who worked feverishly to accomplish each of these essential aspects of the Kindertransport rescue program.

The results of this most complex coordination effort were astounding. The first transport of about 200 children, who were mostly victims of a destroyed orphanage, departed Berlin on December 1, 1938—just three weeks after Kristallnacht—and arrived in Harwich, England, the next morning. Special sealed trains carried the children from Berlin, Vienna, and other major cities within the Third Reich and its annexed territories mostly to the Hook of Holland, or a port in Belgium, and from there the children were transported by ferry to Harwich, England, and taken to holiday camps nearby, such as Dovercourt, for initial training in English language and customs and assignment to a foster home or youth hostel, farm, or some other place of boarding. Some of the children came directly by ship, such as from Hamburg, or Gdansk, Poland, or by plane; but the vast majority was transported by train and ferry. The first transport from Vienna departed on December 10, largely due to the efforts of Geertruida Wijsmuller-Meijer, a Dutch woman activist who went directly to Adolf Eichmann's headquarters in Vienna and demanded that he allow her to transport over 600 children; after an initial refusal, and somewhat to Wijsmuller-Meijer's surprise and amazement, Eichmann then readily agreed. Germany, in fact, largely cooperated with the Kindertransport rescue effort, providing old trains and officials at train stations and other points of departure to check in children prior to their journey and monitor their journey until they left German-controlled territory. Later, on May 14, 1940, on the day Germany invaded The Netherlands, Wijsmuller-Meijer rounded up as many Jewish children as she could find in the Netherlands (74 children), put them on a freighter in the port of Ijmuiden near Amsterdam, and they departed for England as the final transport in the program. After Germany marched into the remainder of independent Czechoslovakia in March 1939, transports from Prague were quickly organized largely through the efforts of Nicholas Winton (much later knighted for his role in the operation), who in December 1938 was a young stockbroker of German-Jewish heritage who had traveled to Prague to begin organizing efforts that resulted in the rescue of 669 children. In most cases, Winton prearranged foster homes by convincing British families to take the children in. The Kindertransport rescue effort continued through much of the summer of 1939 but, with the exception of the one Dutch transport in May 1940, had to be halted with the start of the Second World War on September 1, 1939. Nearly 10,000 children in all were rescued as a result of the Kindertransport program. For their efforts, many of the leaders of the Refugee Children's Movement as well as Wijsmuller-Meijer, Winton, and the Society of Friends, among others, were later recognized and honored in a variety of ways, including their being recorded among the righteous at *Yad Vashem* in Jerusalem.

Snow was falling and it was bitter cold one morning early in December 1938 when Josef Möllerich went out of his Hamburg apartment without saying a word. He took the streetcar into the city center and made two stops, first at the British consulate and then at the Hamburg office of the German Transportation Ministry, which was located adjacent to the central railroad station. By the time he returned to the apartment much later in the day, the snow had subsided, but Josef had begun coughing violently due to the frigid air and his weakened lungs. He took his medication and went to bed, again without saying anything. Two days later, still coughing badly, Josef put on his coat and left the apartment in silence and this time returned even later in the day. Upon arriving home, Josef summoned Selma and his two children and said to them, "Let's sit down; I need to speak to you about something very important."

Wolfgang, of course, knew absolutely nothing about what had taken place in the days leading up to his father's summons, other than his father's disappearance in the snow and cold, but he was soon to find out what the outings were about. Josef had listened to the BBC on the radio and had learned of the British Parliament's action in late November regarding accepting children from Germany unaccompanied by their parents without the requirement of visas. He and Selma had carried on private discussions late at night, weighing the painful choice of sending their children out of Germany with the possibility that something would happen either to the children or to them that would prevent their ever seeing Wolfgang or Edith again. After a few nights of anguished discussion, they made their decision, finally swayed by the knowledge their children would likely be safe and the hope that with their United States visas soon to be in hand that Josef could sell the business and resolve any remaining financial issues with the government so that they could join their children in England within perhaps a few months and await availability of their United States immigration quota clearance from there. On the day it had snowed, Josef had visited the British consulate, learned more about the Kindertransport program, completed the required forms that provided information about his two children, and then went through a similar process at the office of the German Ministry of Transportation. He had come home with two passes for transport dates for Wolfgang and Edith designated for several months into 1939, the later dates assigned, no doubt, because Wolfgang and Edith would not have met any of the top priorities set by the Refugee Children's Movement for selecting children.

This fact undoubtedly troubled Josef because he had no idea how long the Kindertransport program would actually continue. The next day Josef learned from a fellow congregant at the synagogue that a family nearby had obtained two Kindertransport passes for December 14. Josef knew the family slightly and realized their financial situation was very poor and thus their children would have satisfied one of the Kindertransport selection priorities. As it turned out, both children had become too sick to travel so soon, and so Josef had offered to exchange the tickets he had obtained for Wolfgang and Edith for the earlier transport dates, which could not be used by the family whose children were ill. He had gladly sweetened the offer with a hefty sum of money, which the father of the two sick children accepted. The next day the two men visited the British consulate and German Ministry of Transportation and had the papers for their children's transports duly adjusted to reflect the exchange.

Now, sitting around the dining room table, Josef told his children that they would need to pack a single bag of their belongings because they were going on a journey to England. Wolfgang later recalled that Edith immediately spoke up and said, "To England—why not to the United States?" Josef responded, "That would be ideal but we don't have that choice. So here's what we're going to do: we're going to send you on a train called the Kindertransport by way of Holland, then by ferry overnight to England." He explained to his children that they would be leaving in two days and that they could take only one suitcase each that had to be small enough that they could each carry. There would be room only for clothing and a few essentials like a toothbrush. Because of space limitations Wolfgang was unable to take his favorite book with all the comic illustrations inside, and of course it would be impossible for him to take his "mechano set." Josef also told his children that he and their mother would come for them in England hopefully in three months. Wolfgang later recalled that "The urgency of getting us going started to mount; the pressures and anxieties were very obvious to me that something big was going to unfold in my life—a journey to a country that I'd never been to, where they speak a language that I do not know, and had different customs that I would have to learn."

The ensuing 36 hours went by with Wolfgang in a semi-fog. His Uncle Moritz came for dinner on the evening of December 13 to say goodbye. His Oma and Opa were very subdued and said little; Bertha looked particularly sad and seemed to be holding back tears. On his last night in Hamburg, Wolfgang's mind was in turmoil. On the one hand he found himself to be excited to be taking a journey to England; on the other hand, three months was a long time and he would miss his parents—not to mention having to travel with Edith filled him with considerable anxiety. He finally fell asleep wondering how the next day would unfold.

# C H A P T E R   3

⸙

# Kindertransport Journey (December 1938)

ON THE MORNING of Wednesday, December 14, 1938, Wolfgang was awakened early by his mother and told to get dressed for travel. He glanced outside his window at the park, its trees barren of leaves; looking up he noticed a leaden late autumn sky. His one small suitcase was already packed full of clothing, a few bare essentials and two or three small comic-style periodicals. Wolfgang, Edith, and their parents quickly ate breakfast, checked everything to make certain nothing had been forgotten and that nothing more was taken than was required by the rules of the Kindertransport program, as had been explained in the materials Josef had brought home from the British consulate and the German Ministry of Transportation days earlier. There was little time for conversation; just one lingering hug and kiss for Oma and Opa, a quick photograph taken of Wolfgang and Edith (see front cover), and the two parents and their children were out the door. As Wolfgang later recalled, "On the day that we left it was hurry, hurry, hurry, with very few words spoken from the time we left the house until we arrived at the Hamburg railway station."

Like most large city railroad terminals in Europe, the Hamburg Central Railroad Station was a massive brown stone structure a full square block in size, including the entry plaza on one end and on the side, with a semi-curved roof displaying translucent glass on it as well as at the far end of the building where the trains exited the terminal. At the near end, a long open space extended across the width of the

63

terminal, allowing considerable space for people waiting for their train to be called, with ticket windows on one side and stairways leading down to platforms and the tracks on the other. There were occasional announcements of train departures being made that at most times could be heard above the din in the waiting area. But on this morning, most regular announcements of train departures were inaudible. As Wolfgang, Edith, and their parents walked into the terminal carrying their individual bags and dressed for winter weather, they were struck immediately by "a cacophony of sounds," the likes of which Wolfgang had not heard before. At one end of the waiting area there were hundreds of people gathered into small family units engaged in rushed, excited, stressed conversation or, in many cases, weeping or screaming or audibly praying. Wolfgang recalled passing families where parents issued loud, last-minute instructions to their children.

Finding a small open space, the Möllerich family huddled together. Selma instructed Edith to take good care of her 8-year-old brother and handed her a small *siddur* (prayer book) so that she could say prayers for them and hopefully the prayers would be answered favorably and they would meet again in three months. The book was inscribed in Selma's handwriting; her hand trembled as she reached out and handed it to Edith. Josef turned to his son, kneeling down and placing his hands on Wolfgang's shoulders, and said, "The most important thing I can tell you is to get an education because that is one thing that nobody can take away from you." Thinking back on this moment later in life, Wolfgang understood that his father used those specific words because so much of what Germany's Jews had was being systematically taken from them, and so Josef dwelled on the importance of education for perhaps a minute, which seemed like a long time to Wolfgang. Tears welling in his eyes, Josef told his son to "be a good boy and listen to your sister." The last sentence was nearly drowned out by the blast of a whistle that silenced much of the conversation in the terminal. Instructions were issued for the Kindertransport children to form a line of twos and go toward gate 14 at the top of the stairway leading to the platform. Hurriedly, Josef and Selma hugged their children amidst sobs. Wolfgang wanted to linger in his mother's embrace but they were being instructed to hurry to the gate so as not to delay the train. He later recalled that his parents' arms "were outstretched as they slipped off our arms and down to our hands; they just held our hands for a second or two until we separated from them. I could see their tears; I could hear the quiver in their voices as we slowly disappeared in the crowd."

There were a series of checking stations on the path to the stairway. At the first checkpoint they were stopped and Wolfgang and Edith were asked their names and dates of birth and were each handed a card with three digits on it that was connected by a looped string and were told to place it around their necks and not to take it off at all—at any time during the trip—and the officer also identified them as Jews. Other than to answer questions of officers, the children were instructed to be silent as they went through the check-in process and boarded the train. Gripping each other's hands, Edith and Wolfgang followed the line a few steps to another checkpoint where a uniformed officer asked for their names and dates of birth and checked them against the numbers around their necks. The process repeated a third time near the top of the stairway leading down to the platform where another uniformed officer checked them off his list. Now descending the stairway, Wolfgang noticed a Track 14A and Track 14B on either side of the platform, which was located at the far end of the terminal from the side which they entered. At each track sat trains that were visibly older than the trains being used for general public transportation on the other tracks. These older trains were made available especially for the Kindertransport, but on this day, only the train on Track 14A was being used. The children walked two at a time along the platform until they were told to board the train. Each car had small steps making it possible for them to climb up and into the doorway of the train. Wolfgang and Edith were instructed to enter one of the cars and were assigned seats next to each other on a wooden bench with Wolfgang at a window and his sister adjacent to the aisle.

The significance of the numbers on the identification cards fascinated Wolfgang almost from the outset. Although he was somewhat preoccupied by the very unique circumstance to ponder the question at the time, the subject proved to be one to which he gave considerable thought and study over the years, finding it difficult to reach a firm conclusion. He remembered that he and Edith had consecutive numbers on their cards but could not recall the specific number except that the first digit was "3." Later in life he actually did some research and spoke with other participants of the Kindertransport to get their views, receiving a variety of responses ranging from the question never occurred to them to a couple of different theories. At one time he had been convinced that the first digit on the card designated the transport sequence, but he later rejected that notion and eventually concluded that the first digit identified the car number of his particular train and the next two digits represented the assigned seat number within that car.

Upon being seated on the train, Wolfgang examined his surroundings. The train was old and in relatively poor condition, with the bench seats "pretty worn and without any pads." The window had a shade which, for the moment was up and it was possible to open the windows. There was a uniformed guard—not a soldier but most likely a railroad official—at either end of their car. Almost immediately upon being seated, the guards told everyone to lower the shades and that there would be no talking at all during the trip. Besides the guards, Wolfgang noticed that two children were sitting with adult women whom he later learned were chaperones for children with special needs, although he saw no wheelchairs or any other visible evidence that either child required special assistance. It was also unclear to him, as he later recalled, whether the chaperones were provided by the railroad or by some organization associated with the Kindertransport program. Looking around, Wolfgang saw one of the children in his car pull out a hard cover comic book that appeared to be exactly like his own favorite book that he had so much wanted to take along with him but could not because it would not fit into his small suitcase. When he saw that book, as he later recalled, "I freaked out" and said to his sister, "That's my book," to which Edith responded, "It's not your book; it belongs to another child." He would not accept that and demanded that she ask the guard if someone could find his parents and have them return home and bring him his book. "That can't be done," she told him, but he persisted so Edith got up to speak to a guard—possibly to inquire if she could get Wolfgang a comic book in the waiting area of the station— but she was abruptly stopped. "Sit down in your seat and keep your mouth shut," the guard told her. Wolfgang continued to complain until the guard came over to him and said, "If you don't shut up, I'll make you shut up." He later recalled that the guards on the train "scared the heck out of me."

Still upset about the comic book and unable to speak to Edith or any other child, Wolfgang grew increasingly anxious waiting for the train to depart. The train, it seemed to him, was waiting at the station for "a very long time" after everyone had boarded. He reached over to the window and lifted the shade enough so that he could look outside because he was curious about what was going on and wanted to know why the train hadn't yet moved. He observed officials in military uniforms all along the platform peering at the train, he presumed, to ensure that nobody got on or off and that nobody opened the windows. Immediately one of the guards on the train hit him on the head with the back of a hand and ordered him to put the shade down. Wondering about why the shades had to be down, he thought it might have been so that other people in the station would not know there were essentially only children on the train. He then tried to figure out how many children were actually on the train by counting the 25 or so in his car (not including the adults) and figuring there were probably about 8 cars on the train. Although his arithmetic skills were not yet very good, he was able to conclude that there were perhaps 200 children on the train. He also wondered why there was a second train across the platform from his, and whether it would be used for another transport that day or the next day. Such were the idle thoughts of young Wolfgang that were abruptly interrupted by a long shrill whistle as the train began to move. He could feel the click clack of the train wheels as it gradually gained speed. "As the train was going faster," he later recalled, "I could feel my heart beating faster, because I was experiencing an anxiety spell," a combination, no doubt, of fear of the unknown journey ahead and excitement over what he again thought would be an adventure for him. He looked at Edith and she was emotional, trying to hold back tears. Suddenly Wolfgang's nerves got the best of him and he trembled. Edith looked at him and then put her arm around his shoulders and said to him: "Calm down; everything will be all right." The train gained speed and Wolfgang fell asleep in the grip of his sister's arm.

A loud voice suddenly boomed through the car, waking anyone who had dozed off. "Lift the shades—we are in Holland," the voice announced, as Wolfgang snapped awake. The train had stopped. He quickly looked around and noticed that the German guards were gone. He glanced out the window where yellow-shaded meadows were visible in the faded December sunshine. Looking down, he saw tables set up along the track and many people were serving something in small paper cups. He opened the window, breathing in relatively mild December air, reached down, and was handed a cup filled with orange juice, something which he had never tasted before in his life, although he had eaten fresh oranges many times. He drank the juice straight down; the strong taste of orange momentarily filled him with joy. He reached out for a second cup to give to Edith just as the train began to move as the servers backed away from the train, and so Edith did not get the opportunity to have any juice.

Now wide awake, Wolfgang and everyone else in his car peered out the windows at the countryside as the train accelerated. The scenery was far different from anything Wolfgang had seen in Germany; windmills were visible in the distance. His excitement grew as he watched the Dutch countryside. "This was all new to me," he later recalled, "and even the air was different; it had fragrant odors associated with it." As the afternoon progressed, he watched animals grazing in the meadows as the train moved along at what seemed like a very fast pace. With the ban on speaking now lifted, many of the children engaged in excited conversation, sometimes related to what they were observing outside the train, sometimes discussing their curiosity and expectations about England. Wolfgang was one of the younger children in this car of the train, and so he said little, but listened with great interest to the talk about England. Some of the boys spoke about hearing that there were many caves to explore; others talked about the prospects of living in a city or on a farm. To some extent the talk was a result of the excitement of the moment and imaginations were running a bit wild. But some of the older children knew where they were going, that they would be met by a relative already in England or, more likely, by a foster parent to whom they had been pre-assigned. Soon the scenery changed and the train passed smokestacks and then docks with large ships, such as cargo vessels, with railroad tracks running adjacent to the docks in a manner similar to what Wolfgang had seen in Hamburg. After a few minutes more the train slowed and finally came to a halt at the Hook of Holland seaport.

Within moments, everyone on the train was told to disembark the train with their belongings, and so Wolfgang and Edith took their bags, buttoned their coats, and followed the others off the train. There were buses waiting not far from the train and picnic tables set up directly in front of where the buses were parked. The children were shown to these tables and handed a box meal consisting of a sandwich, a biscuit, an apple, and a small container of milk. They were told to "take this because you won't get anything on the boat." Wolfgang and Edith ate quickly because they were hungry and because it was quite cold sitting outside; once everyone had eaten, the children were directed to the buses. Holding Edith's hand, Wolfgang walked with the others in a line two by two straight onto a bus, which quickly loaded and drove the children a short distance to a pier where a ship—or what Wolfgang would later learn was an ocean going ferry—awaited.

The scene at the gangway of the ferry was far different from the orderly, detailed check-in process Wolfgang experienced at the Hamburg railroad station. Once departing the bus at the pier, something like 200 children gathered in one massive group and waited their turn to board the ship on a single narrow gangway. There was nobody with a list to cross check the numbers still being worn around the children's neck. The children were not required to board according to their number as they had been when boarding the train in Hamburg. There were only a few people directing and helping the children go up the gangway and onto the ferry, and one person checking off their number as they boarded. Once on board, the children were directed to a large inside space on the same deck on which they boarded, where cots had been set up in long rows and some children chose to sit, two on each side of a cot, while others chose to lie down. Some elected to watch the ship embark from the outside on that same deck, but the cold and wind on the outside deck that picked up as soon as the ship pulled away from the pier discouraged most of them from remaining outside for very long. Inside, Wolfgang sat down on a cot just with his sister, who encouraged him to lie down and sleep. After the excitement and stress of the day, having just eaten, Wolfgang suddenly felt drained of all energy; he later recalled that he was so tired "that it was as if I had been drugged." He quickly fell asleep before the ship left Holland. He also later recalled, "I was totally out and I don't remember the trip at all."

Edith allowed Wolfgang to sleep until the ship had arrived the next morning in Harwich, a port located on the southeast coast of England that served as the country's primary port on the North Sea, although it was little more than a large town with regard to both physical size and number of residents. Desperately trying to gain his bearing, Wolfgang realized the ship was not moving and that many adults were now circulating among them, inquiring as to the status of their health. It was explained that health inspectors had to ensure that there was nobody on board suffering from an infectious disease. Although the children had passed a very brief health screening before departure in Hamburg, and clearly nobody would have been allowed to travel if significantly ill, a handful of children indicated that they were a bit seasick or had a cough. The health inspection proceeded quite quickly, however, with the inspectors speaking to the children in German. When asked how he felt, Wolfgang said that he was "excited." He later recalled, "I was a little kid happy to go out and explore." He didn't realize that he was about to embark on a very new and different phase of his life, one in which he would virtually cease speaking German as a primary language forever and force himself to adapt to a new language, new customs, and a new lifestyle bereft of many of the comforts to which he had been accustomed in his hometown of Wolfhagen. Nor did he realize, at that moment, that he would not be addressed as Wolfgang again for a very long time, or that he might never see his parents again.

# CHAPTER 4

___ ❦ ___

# Prewar Life in England
# (December 1938–September 1939)

It DID NOT take long for excitement to fade and for reality to set in. On the morning of December 15, when the ferry carrying the Kindertransport that included the Möllerich children arrived at Harwich, the weather was sharply colder than it had been in Holland the day before. Rolf, as he was about to be addressed throughout his time in England and beyond that, later recalled that "the contrast between processing in Germany and processing in England was very obvious from the moment we arrived in Harwich." Once cleared by the health inspectors, the children disembarked the ferry and were herded onto buses in no particular order and with nobody checking their names off on a list or even recording their card numbers, which they were all still wearing around their necks. "When we got to Harwich they told us we were already processed," he recalled, so there was no need to check names against numbers. The children were told that they had entered the country legally, and "for me that was the most important part," Rolf later explained. They were escorted to waiting buses and it was a relatively short 25-minute ride to the Dovercourt Holiday Camp, a once popular summer resort facility that was completely available for use by the Kindertransport program during the month of December. The buses exited the port, driving south through the town of Harwich and along a narrow road that meandered through gentle turns that followed the water from Harwich harbor along the coast to Dovercourt Bay. The buses turned off the road onto the property of the Dovercourt Holiday

Camp and came to a stop in front of rows of low, barrack-like wooden buildings. Peering out the window at these barren structures as the bus came to a halt Rolf felt a growing knot in the pit of his stomach. He swallowed hard and followed Edith off the bus.

The motor transports had disgorged their passengers almost simultaneously, causing around 200 children to gather in a large group, without instructions, leading to a brief period of chaos. It took several minutes before the staff at the facility divided the new arrivals into groups of about 20 children, and each group was led into one of the barrack-style bunkhouses—boys and girls together. Rolf and Edith were in the group that entered the first of the bunkhouses; they followed several others inside through a swinging gate and wooden doors and were immediately confronted by multiple concerns. There was no heat in the building, as it had been constructed for the sole purpose of housing campers during the summer months. The temperature outside that morning hovered just above the freezing mark. Without the benefit of some form of heating, the temperature inside the wooden bunkhouse could not have been much higher than it was outside. The inside of the bunkhouse consisted of a large open room with two long rows of cot-style beds on either side, with a small shelf against the wall next to each bed. There was an enclosed room near the rear of the bunkhouse where the person who oversaw that group slept. Besides this person, there were two women chaperones that slept in a bunk at either end of the building. The shower, toilets, and sink were at the rear and opposite the bunk overseer's room, and were open except for a small wall in front of the toilets and showers. Rolf later recalled that "nobody was about to take a shower, even though we all stank of perspiration, because there was no privacy." But the absence of heating proved to be the most difficult issue for life in the bunkhouse, and everyone generally wore as many layers of clothing as they could find in order to stay relatively warm, both day and night.

The disagreeable physical conditions in which Rolf found himself at Dovercourt paled in comparison to a much greater concern, that

English was the language to be spoken from the outset. He knew virtually no English words and had no idea how to understand what was being said let alone speak the language. To that end, the very first thing after selecting a bunk, Edith sat Rolf down and told him that it was essential that he pay very close attention to the English words being spoken, and that he should start memorizing the words and what they mean. She had studied English for at least two years and had learned enough to comprehend fairly well and to speak the language, albeit with a strong German accent. Rolf later recalled Edith's instructions to him: "We have all day and you're going to listen to what I say and repeat after me; every sentence I say in German, I'll give you a translation in English and you will repeat it." She explained that the English he would hear from the people in charge of the camp and the chaperones would sound different than the English words she was speaking to him, but that was because she learned from a teacher in Germany and it was a second language for her. "And so my tutoring in English started immediately in that bunk on our first day in England," Rolf later recalled, "with Edith."

A second, and in some ways more formidable and certainly longer lasting problem returned for Rolf on that first day at Dovercourt—his ongoing resentment with the way in which his sister treated him. Edith was not an outwardly warm person to begin with, and she and Rolf had never gotten along, something which had troubled the boy as far back in his life as he could remember. The extraordinary circumstances of the previous day had drawn them together in ways that he had never previously experienced. Notwithstanding her initiative to assist Rolf in any way she could to learn the English language and dutifully taking overall responsibility as his guardian in the absence of their parents and grandparents, as instructed by her mother at the Hamburg Railroad Station, Edith had her own life and plans that she wanted to embark upon, and so Rolf sensed that much of her attention to him was done begrudgingly. He also began from that first day in England to realize that she would be calling the shots in his life, something that filled him with dread. He received a small introduction to this reality when, during the course of spending the day learning English, amid general clamoring for nourishment among the occupants of the bunkhouse, trays of food were brought in. Most of the children rushed to take what they wanted. Rolf held back because he wanted to find something light to eat. There were triangular sandwiches with a variety of meats and other items. Rolf took one with marmalade and one with peanut butter. Edith told him that this was insufficient and he needed to take some fruit, which he did not want to do. "You have to eat fruit," she told him, and so he did so, but it was a bitter pill for him to swallow that "she was totally in charge of my life." He recalled at that moment his adventure was "no longer exciting for me; now I was scared," because he felt insecure not only about learning English but about sharing living space with boys and girls comingled. It was notable, however, on that first night at Dovercourt, when it was bitter cold and with no substantial blankets available that Rolf recalled, "For me, the warmth came from my sister; she just embraced me and we both fell asleep."

The next day everyone was summoned outside and they were asked to line up, perhaps 200 or more children in total. The administrator of the camp, speaking in English so that Edith had to translate quietly for Rolf, impressed upon the children that in order to leave the camp and move on to a more permanent living situation they needed to learn the English language well enough to understand and speak a little, and they needed to learn something about British customs. Once they had met those basic requirements, they could leave either with the person who sponsored them—a prearranged foster parent or one without a child assigned to them who might select them at the camp—or go to a hostel or a farm or, in a few instances, perhaps to a monastery. It was explained that with respect to adapting to British customs, they would be expected to behave appropriately when food was placed on the table in the mess hall. The administrator then read from and had distributed to the children a set of guidelines entitled "Advice to Refugees," covering specific rules of behavior the children were to follow that included being polite at all times, especially in shops and waiting on queues, and taking care not to raise their voice or speak offensively or out of turn. "The English people," the printed guidance said, "have freely and liberally given you a place of refuge. Show them by your courtesy to others, your consideration for all people, your kindness, that they have been justified in their generosity." Rolf later recalled that the bunkhouse chaperones and, subsequently during his time in England supervisors of the Refugee Children's Movement and social workers, repeatedly advised him to "keep a stiff upper lip and act as an adult." During this general meeting, there were also questions about which children had any health concerns or dietary restrictions that they knew about. Rolf saw no reason to speak up since he was healthy, had no allergies to any foods that he knew of, and was disinclined to say anything about keeping a kosher diet. He had, in fact, other things more important than food on his mind.

With the exception of his intensive learning of the English language, which he took to almost immediately despite many roadblocks in his foundational education ever since the beginning of first grade more than three years earlier, Rolf was preoccupied with concern over his future. He would sit in little circles with several other children and listen to many of them speak about living with relatives in various parts of England. He listened to discussions among children from other bunkhouses who spoke excitedly about relatives meeting them in London once they left Dovercourt and then taking them to the United States; a few spoke of plans to travel to Australia. During these group discussions that began virtually as soon as the administrator had completed his talk and the meeting broke up that Friday morning, Rolf sat silently with a growing sense of dread. "I didn't know where I was going," he later recalled; "I was totally lost and uninformed about my future." What made matters worse for him was that he learned that his sister knew where she was going after leaving Dovercourt. She planned to go to London and attend nursing school. At age 17, Edith was among the oldest of the children in the Kindertransport program and would soon reach the age when she could be on her own. Before leaving Hamburg on the Kindertransport, she had communicated with her friend Lotte Rosenfeld, whom she knew from the school in Frankfurt and whose family was able to leave Germany and take up residence in London, and her father had made arrangements through the Refugee Children's Movement for her to stay with her girlfriend when she left the camp. It was obvious to Rolf that he could not go with his sister, since he was one of the younger children in the Kindertransport program and could not be on his own, and so his future was very much up in the air and weighing on him before bedtime that second night at Dovercourt. He missed having his mother tuck him in at night and his Oma hugging him and helping him say the Sh'ma, and he became distraught. Edith sat Rolf down and spoke to him in her firm voice words that would remain with him the rest of his life: "Listen to me: you must forget the past just as you must forget the German language. We are going to have a new life and you must concentrate on the present and then always look forward and never look back."

Two days later, December 18, was a Sunday, a very special day of the week at Dovercourt. Sunday was the day when prospective foster parents visited to select a foster child from among those children from the Kindertransport for which a specific foster parent had not been arranged. It was the day of the week that all the children wore their best clothes and tried to be on their best behavior in hope of impressing a prospective foster parent enough to select them. Later dubbed the "meat market" by many of the former Kindertransport survivors, these occasions were so important to a child's future that it caused extreme stress among them. Although the Refugee Children's Movement made every effort to identify as many foster parents as possible, there was never a sufficient number to accommodate the nearly 10,000 children of the Kindertransport. This was particularly the case during the first month or two of the program, because it had been put into place so quickly on an emergency basis that it was impossible to find foster parents for all—or even a significant majority—of the children who arrived in England in December 1938. Nevertheless, Edith made certain that

Rolf was dressed in his Shabbat clothing, which was the best of what he had brought with him. Most of the visitors that morning were there to pick up an already prearranged foster child. The remaining smaller group of prospective foster parents went through the bunkhouses and around the camp grounds looking over the children not spoken for, asking them questions about their health and observing their behavior and ability to converse in English.

Because Rolf was not one of the children who had a prearranged foster home, and because so many of the visitors that morning had come to pick up a specific child, he was not selected for a foster home. Unaware of these circumstances, the result only served to deepen Rolf's level of insecurity. He thought his appearance was not good enough and that his English, on which he continued to work diligently every day with his sister, was not good enough either, and he began to worry that he would be left to spend weeks in the cold and discomfort of the Dovercourt camp while his sister went off to London. Rolf's assumptions were incorrect on both counts. Within two days of the Sunday "meat market" he was deemed ready to leave Dovercourt and was told that he had been assigned to an orthodox hostel for boys located in the Clapton section of northeast London. In fact the logistics of the Kindertransport program, especially in the first month or two when there was a succession of transports out of Germany in very short order, required that the vast number of children from each transport be moved out of Dovercourt as quickly as possible, regardless of the pace at which they had learned the English language. With another transport scheduled for arrival, most of the remaining children from Rolf's transport were designated for assignment to a hostel or a farm during the week following his Sunday "meat market" experience. Six days after his arrival in England, Rolf departed Dovercourt the morning of December 21, 1938, on a special train from Harwich to Liverpool Street Station in London, along with Edith, who was, of course, much better prepared to leave and probably had waited until Rolf was scheduled to leave. The group of children were accompanied by a few escorts provided by a local committee of the Refugee Children's Movement. From Liverpool Street Station in London, where there is now a monument dedicated to the Kindertransport, Rolf was put on a bus for the short ride to his new home at the orthodox boys' hostel.

The bus carrying Rolf and the other boys from Liverpool Street Station came to a stop in front of a large corner building at 104 Nightingale Road. The two-story house looked more like a mansion to Rolf; it had a wrought iron fence about eight feet tall surrounding it along both Nightingale Road and Brooke Road. The stone façade displayed a faux half-timber Tudor design that reminded Rolf of his hometown of Wolfhagen. Peering at the house from behind the window of the bus as the other children gathered their belongings and began to exit, Rolf paused. The reminder of his home in Germany made him anxious about entering the house. As he stepped off the bus, Rolf was surprised and somewhat relieved to see Edith standing along the fence. He had no idea how she had gotten there, as they had said farewell when the train arrived at Liverpool Street Station. Thinking about that in later years, he presumed that she had been picked up in a car or taxi and driven to the hostel so she could meet him. There was no time for questions as the boys were led into the house. Rolf had been told this hostel was organized with a regimented Orthodox lifestyle, with studies both in Hebrew and English but heavy on the religious training, and with daily chores for all the boys. Given his insufficient basic education and spotty Hebrew education, he was apprehensive and hesitated, remaining with Edith who, in her direct tone said to him, "Just go." She told him she would contact him soon and walked off as Rolf slowly turned—thinking "what a cold goodbye"—and then hurried to catch up to the others entering the house.

Once inside, Rolf found that the house turned out to have a fairly typical layout, with a corridor running from the front entrance to the rear of the house that included a wide stairway to the upper level. There was a very large living room at the front of the house with windows facing both Nightingale Road and Brooke Road. The room had an upright piano that a few of the boys played from time to time. The large dining room was located directly behind the living room but the entrance to this room was off the main corridor, with no passageway directly from the living room. The oversize kitchen was located behind the dining room, but there was both a passageway directly from the dining room as well as a doorway from the kitchen to the main corridor. The hostel director's bedroom, which also served as his office, was located adjacent to the kitchen at the rear of the house. Upstairs there were two large bedrooms shared by the boys; the front bedroom resembled a dormitory because it ran the width of the house and about one-third the way from the front to the back and housed 28 boys, mostly in single beds, although there were a few bunk beds as well. The second bedroom housed 12 boys in single beds and occupied the middle of the second level. The two bedrooms thus accommodated a total of 40 boys. At the rear of this level were two smaller bedrooms for staff as well as a single, large bathroom shared by all the occupants of the house. Rolf wanted to have a bed near a window, but when he and the 11 other boys arrived they found that most of the beds were already occupied, and so he selected one of the single beds in the smaller of the two bedrooms.

Rolf quickly discovered that he was one of the youngest and also one of the physically smallest of the boys living in the hostel. He had been told before leaving Dovercourt that he would be among many boys his age at the hostel, but a vast majority of the boys were teenagers and the oldest were actually 20 years old. One of these 20-year-olds was a bit of a bully but was "very organized and neat," Rolf later recalled. Rolf was one of no more than a handful of children under 12 years old and there was only one boy younger—a year younger—than Rolf. Most of the boys had German names and spoke English with accents and so Rolf presumed that they had arrived very recently on the earliest Kindertransport departures, except for those boys who were older than 17. But a few of the boys spoke English with no German accent and Rolf later learned that they were from England and had been orphaned or came from a broken home where neither parents nor other relatives could support them. Two of the English boys turned out to be identical twins. In part because he was so much younger than the others, Rolf tended to gravitate toward the oldest boys; he enjoyed listening to their banter and found it both interesting and educational. One of these boys, a 17-year-old named Enoch, took a liking to Rolf from the outset. Enoch was very outgoing, self-confident, and a bit of a comedian. He loved to talk about his adventures outside of the hostel which, according to Rolf, often involved women, and he would sit Rolf down and give him advice about how to handle himself when with a female. "He said that someday I would meet a nice girl and go out with her, and I needed to know what to do and what not to do," Rolf later recalled. "I wasn't ready for that, of course, but even though I was only eight at the time I was all ears as he would ramble on about women in England."

The director of the hostel was a slender man in his mid-30s named Oscar Friedmann. Soft-spoken, youthful, and sporting a goatee, Friedmann was nevertheless a firm disciplinarian whom Rolf later characterized as "not a friendly person." He insisted that the boys address him as "Rabbi Friedmann" even though there was talk among many of the boys that he was not actually a rabbi, and Rolf later learned that he was, in fact, a psychologist. Friedmann insisted that English was to be the only language spoken in the house, except when chanting Hebrew prayers; studies were to be divided between learning English conversation and Hebrew. The boys were also expected not only to be familiar with the orthodox prayer services and songs, but to attend and even lead daily and Shabbat services. Rolf recalled that he memorized the prayers and recited them by rote but never led the services; nor was he ever interested in doing that despite the fact that the services were quite similar to those he had attended in Germany and some of the boys loved to lead services and became quite proficient at it. At mealtime an orthodox atmosphere was maintained. Over time Rolf became quite "observant" even though he would never develop much of a sense of faith. The dining room had long tables set up in a layout that resembled a "U." The walls were lined with sheets of paper with large Hebrew print containing the words to the blessings before and after the meal, which the boys were expected to learn and recite together. Eventually Rolf became more comfortable with the religious side of life in the hostel, but it was difficult for him. With respect to food, he found the dining options to be very acceptable and plentiful. "For meals we always had a big plate of food on the table and we were permitted to help ourselves but were told not to take more than we could eat," he later recalled.

Other than Friedmann, the staff included two teachers who came in daily or lived in one of the staff bedrooms in the hostel. Because of the small staff, the boys were not well supervised in the hostel, with some of them passing up services in order to get extra sleep. As for learning, most of the classes were held inside the hostel in the large living room, which impeded educational studies beyond training in English conversation and Hebrew in part because of the age ranges of the boys and in part because of limited space and staff. The older boys, once they had achieved an acceptable level of English comprehension, were able to attend a local public school to some extent, but many of them became apprentices in factories or found some other work instead in order to supplement the miniscule amount of spending money they received from the Refugee Children's Movement. The limited education provided at the hostel disappointed Rolf and caused him growing apprehension, especially later on during his time in England as he recognized that he had fallen behind other children his age in learning while he constantly was reminded of his father's final instructions to him before he left Hamburg that his top priority should be a good education.

Besides studies, the boys were expected to do chores around the hostel each day. Although staff cleaned the rooms, the boys were assigned specific duties when they were not in class. Being one of the younger boys, Rolf was assigned to collect all the prayer books and chumashim (books with the printed Torah) after the daily and Shabbat services. A gardener came regularly and Rolf was assigned to assist him. The gardener showed him how to grow asparagus and told him that everything he planted he probably would never see because it could take up to three years for the results of his work to be ready for harvesting; but he was able to harvest vegetables that had been planted in previous years. He found working in the garden to be one of the most enjoyable aspects of his time at the hostel—so much so that he would maintain an interest in gardening and horticulture much later in life. Another of Rolf's favorite pastimes at the London hostel, not surprisingly, was riding a bike. The hostel had received donations of several bicycles and it did not take Rolf long to learn how to ride one of the smaller two-wheelers around the neighborhood, even in the cold winter temperatures. He took great interest in the mechanics of the bikes located in the hostel's storage area and enjoyed cleaning the various moving components even though he was not required to do so.

Riding and working on the bikes led to one of Rolf's worst moments during his time at the hostel. He would ride the bike on dirt roads—sometimes wearing sandals because he became "tired of wearing boots"—and the dirt caked up on his feet. He would also pick up grime from cleaning the bikes in the hostel's storage area. Bathing was a concern for Rolf as he was not fond of the wooden bathtubs in the bathroom used by all the boys. For one thing the tubs "didn't look clean to me," he later recalled, and for another "I was kind of shy and standing naked in that bathroom didn't appeal to me." The result of the accumulated dirt and grime and not bathing was predictable; but discovery of the result was not. By chance, Edith decided to stop by to check up on Rolf one day after nursing classes just around the time Rolf's feet were at their dirtiest and when he was not wearing shoes. She immediately and correctly surmised that he had not washed for a long time and took him into the bathroom to check him over "from a nurse's point of view," she told him. She discovered a bit of ringworm under his chin and told him to get into the bathtub and started running the water. "I'm going to scrub you down," he recalled her telling him. "Oh, no you won't," he replied. Before he could protest further, she lifted him up, put him into the tub and bathed him "from head to toe." Afterwards she ordered ointment from the pharmacy at St. James Hospital where she studied nursing, and within a day or two the ringworm was gone. But the experience was humiliating for Rolf: "I remember vividly how she scrubbed me down with a brush in the wooden tub," he later recalled, "and how I was so embarrassed that she undressed me and I was standing there naked in the tub." Rolf learned an important lesson from this experience: "From that moment on," he remembered, "I developed very clean habits and learned to take better care of myself," to the extent that he would be almost obsessed with cleanliness and being neat about his personal belongings, especially during adulthood.

The bikes were not the only items donated to the hostel. Most of the boys came to the hostel with limited clothing and many of these items wore out quickly or needed to be replaced with larger sizes because so many of the boys experienced growth spurts. As a result, the older boys were sent around the neighborhood canvassing for donations of clothing. Rolf recalled being measured for clothing and receiving shoes, socks, and other items. Each of the boys had name labels placed in their clothing so that after they were laundered the clothes would be returned to the correct person. Later in life, when looking at photos taken during his time at the hostel, Rolf was not pleased with the way he had been dressed, recalling that "my parents would have never dressed me that way." Donations were donations, however, and the Refugee Children's Movement, especially in the early months of the Kindertransport program, was thrilled with any contributions each of the hostels could garner through their individual efforts. In this regard, one of the branch volunteer organizations, the North London Refugee Aid Society, sponsored a major fundraising event for the hostel on the evening of March 11, 1939. Invitations from the Mayor of Hackney, the district in which Clapton was located, were circulated throughout the area to what was officially deemed an "Opening Ceremony" for the hostel on Nightingale Road, even though the building had been functioning as a hostel primarily for Kindertransport children since the previous December. The event called for a prayer service to be co-officiated by the Bishop of Chelmsford and Rabbi M.L. Perlzweig, who was on the board of the Jewish Agency Executive and who would later serve on England's delegation to the World Jewish Congress. The printed invitation brochure included photographs of three of the younger children living at the hostel, with Rolf's photo in the center, and two extracts of testimonials printed below the photos written by family members who had heard from their children about the good work of the hostel. The message from Mayor Chas. G. Burton was simple and direct: "I issue this appeal, confident that you will take pleasure and pride in helping to make provision for the maintenance and training of forty boys at the Hostel. Help us to help the children." The invitation brochure concluded with a list of ways in which the community could help, including contributions of money, furniture, kitchen utensils, linens, books, games, tools, as well as volunteering their time. The ceremony drew an impressive turnout that included a number of prospective foster families, in part because of the strength of the existing society and in part because of the reputations of the guest officiates and that the mayor hosted the event.

Being one of the youngest and physically smallest of the boys at the hostel meant that Rolf was subjected to bullying from time to time by the older boys. The experience was not new for him, as he had been verbally and physically bullied by his sister as well as some of the older boys in Wolfhagen, and therefore being occasionally subjected to bullying was all the more "painful" for him. As had been the case with the boys in Germany, however, Rolf remained a tough kid and fought back. "They were older than me and I showed some of the older guys what I was made of," he later recalled. "If they came near me I would kick, and sometimes I took them to the ground and held them in a head lock." Occasionally he was "bullied" in ways that were more characteristic of a prank. He later recalled one time that the older boys told him to light the Shabbat candles, which he did. Friedmann came in and inquired who lit the candles, to which Rolf responded that he had done so. "What gives you the right to light the candles?" Friedmann demanded. "Someone asked me to do that," Rolf responded. Friedmann then confronted Rolf: "If someone asked you to cut your throat, would you cut your throat?" Rolf asked the director why his lighting the candles "was such a big deal." Friedman then said: "I have to give you a lesson in Shabbat. Here's the protocol: number one, you wait until everybody is here in this room; number two, you don't light the candles—the lady of the hostel is the one who lights the candles." The older chaps had to stifle their amusement during this exchange. Rolf also found himself often to be one of the last to get a seat at the table during meals, recalling that "they pushed me away so they could get to the table first, because at meals seating was everything; you wanted to be close to the food." There was one boy in the hostel who was younger than Rolf, and they became pretty good friends. But Rolf later recalled one occasion where he had the opportunity to bully this child. It happened during one of the regular Saturday night parties at the hostel, when Rolf's older friend, Enoch, offered to teach him how to dance. "We were doing some dancing and this one kid hid behind the drapes. We slowly danced over to the drapes and I deliberately lifted my hand up to go into the drapes, and I hit the kid on the chin. He fell to the floor and I thought I had knocked him out. To this day I regret what I did," he recalled, even though this younger boy was physically larger than Ralph.

Although Rolf was sometimes teased and bullied by some of the older boys, they also invited him to go on outings into central London from time to time. For Rolf, these opportunities to ride the double-decker bus, sitting on the top deck even in the dead of winter, visiting Buckingham Palace and Piccadilly Circus were special occasions and some of the best times he could recall while he was living at the hostel. For the cost of a few pence, they could ride the bus around the city; it gave Rolf a warm feeling of becoming part of living in England. "We were on our own and we explored," he later recalled. Most of the time Rolf had to rely on the older boys to treat him to the bus ride, since many of them had part-time jobs and Rolf received rarely more than a few pence spending money from the program and hardly any money at all from Edith. The one notable exception came just before Passover when he was asked to join another boy in placing "Kosher for Passover" labels on bottles of milk. They were driven to a farm where crates of milk bottles were stored in a refrigerated warehouse, with some crates set aside from the others. Rolf started at the near end of the row of these crates and the other boy at the far end and they labeled all the bottles, meeting up in the middle of the row. For this task Rolf was paid 7 shillings and 6 pence, which came out to a little more than one-third of a pound sterling. It was probably among the most spending money Rolf had at one time during the length of his stay at the London hostel.

Overall, Rolf adjusted surprisingly well to life in England considering his relatively young age and the circumstances under which he was separated from his parents. He did well in his English and Hebrew studies and was probably more proficient in English after no more than six months living in England than he had ever been in speaking or writing German. He also developed a reasonable comfort level with his day to day routines and interaction with the other boys in the hostel, even though most of the boys were considerably older than he. Despite this surface veneer of relative calm, however, Rolf remained troubled by an undercurrent of unhappiness that he only partly suppressed during his time at the hostel. Much of his concern involved the ever more complex relationship he had with Edith. On the one hand she had been there for him during the traumatic parting with his parents and journey to a new land and a new life, and had set him on a forward-looking course that enabled him to adjust to this new life. On the other hand, adjusting to that new course had been a struggle for him because it meant erasing much of his past—the positive and the negative—causing a lasting resentment of Edith that was in some ways compounded by her general absence from his life. From their first day in England and throughout his time in London, Rolf saw very little of his sister even though they were living in the same city. She was studying to become a nurse at St.

James Hospital in southwest London—some distance from the hostel. Rolf later recalled Edith taking him out only a few times. They attended a concert in Hyde Park, and one time she came to the hostel and when he came out to see her she said to him, "I don't like what you're wearing; let's get you a new shirt," and so she took him shopping. But Edith had very little money to share with Rolf, and he received not more than perhaps 10 shillings, the equivalent of two dollars from her every few months, as she was financially strapped due to her studies and having to pay half the rent on a flat she shared with her girlfriend. She could only work part time, mostly as a mother's helper. She had also taken an active interest in a social life very soon after arriving in London. For these reasons, Edith had little time to spend with Rolf, and because he was not permitted to use the phone in the hostel he rarely spoke to her by phone during his time there, so he really had minimal contact with her in London. Mostly that was fine with him because, as he recalled much later in life, "I didn't want to see my sister; I was afraid of being scrubbed again."

The other aspect of Rolf's angst during his time in London concerned his parents. His parents' promise that they would come for him in England in three months' time had been etched into his memory. But three months had come and gone without a single communication from them—not even a letter or postcard. Before the three months had passed, Rolf didn't think much about receiving a written communication; for a while he expected that his parents would just show up at the hostel. With the passing of winter 1939, however, still waiting for his parents and now hoping for a letter from them explaining the delay, Rolf became at first anxious and then resentful: "There were feelings that they deserted me," he later recalled, "and these feelings were hard to articulate at the time." Even if he had wanted to talk about his concern, there was really nobody for him to confide in. His sister was hardly available and it was difficult to speak to her about such things because of her unsympathetic manner. Rolf felt uncomfortable approaching the hostel director, "Rabbi" Friedmann, about his inner thoughts, and although the Refugee Children's Movement eventually assigned a social worker to each of the Kindertransport children, Rolf was not assigned a social worker until September 1940. The weeks and months during the spring and summer of 1939 passed for Rolf without word from his parents, and so his concern continued to mount. He had written a short postcard to them in early summer in a rare use of his inadequate German inquiring about their health and expressing the hope he would see them soon but without asking about the delay; it would be several months before he received a response. Meanwhile, at the beginning of September, an event with global consequences once again had a direct impact on Rolf that changed the direction of his life.

As dawn broke on September 1, 1939, forces of the Third Reich invaded Poland sparking the start of the Second World War. Using more than 1,300 aircraft, the Luftwaffe carried out massive bombing of Poland that caused the vastly undermanned Polish army and air force into retreat as 62 divisions of the Wehrmacht, including Panzer units and infantry, rolled across the plains and hills of western Poland toward Warsaw in a demonstration of power that became known as a *Blitzkrieg* (Lightning War). Two days later, England and France honored their guarantees of the integrity of Polish borders and declared war on Germany. So swiftly had the conquest of Poland been carried out, however, that England and France were unable to mobilize sufficiently to engage their considerable forces to assist the outgunned and outmanned Poles, and so within a week's time, German forces had reached the outskirts of Warsaw, where the Poles launched a valiant but futile resistance. On September 17, the Soviet Union invaded Poland from the east; 10 days later Warsaw surrendered and the Polish government fled into exile through Romania to London where it would remain for the duration of the war. In less than a month, Poland had been defeated and was divided between Germany and the Soviet Union.

To many observers at the time, and certainly in retrospect, Germany's invasion of Poland came as no surprise. Hitler had begun rearming Germany shortly after his ascent to power in 1933. He had signed a treaty of cooperation with Benito Mussolini on October 25, 1936, that led directly to creation of the Germany-Italy Axis alliance one week later. The German annexation of Austria (*Anschluss*), which occurred March 11–13, 1938, was accomplished with hardly any formal objection from England or France. Hitler then successfully negotiated the annexation of the substantially German-speaking Czech Sudetenland with the signing of the Munich Agreement with England, France, and Italy on September 29, 1938. British Prime Minister Neville Chamberlain returned from Munich and declared that he had achieved "Peace in our time." Six months later, however, Germany occupied most of the rest of Czechoslovakia even though these parts of the country had a much smaller German-speaking population. Then, on August 23, 1939, Germany and the Soviet Union shocked world capitals by signing a nonaggression pact. The agreement contained a secret codicil dividing Eastern Europe into German and Soviet spheres of influence, thus clearing the way for the invasion and occupation of Poland by the two powers.

The onset of the Second World War had two notable consequences that influenced Rolf Möllerich's life: war between England and Germany meant that the Kindertransport program came to an end, and transportation routes leaving Germany became more complicated, thus making it more difficult for Rolf's parents to get out of Germany. The second consequence of the onset of war took place in England, where a decision was made by the British government to evacuate children living in urban centers, especially London, to safer locations throughout the country. Known as Operation Pied Piper, the government relocated nearly one and a half million children along with some mothers of young children and pregnant women between September 1 and 4, 1939. Approximately another one and a half million children and young mothers were evacuated until September 1944, especially in the months between October 1939 and June 1940. Much like the Kindertransport program, British children were separated from their families and sent to live in foster homes or group accommodations; but the scale of the Kindertransport operation in terms of numbers of children paled in comparison to Operation Pied Piper. Despite the focus of this program on British children, the Refugee Children's Movement made similar relocation efforts, through its local committees, for as many of the younger children living in London as possible, including young Rolf Möllerich.

The radio at the London hostel on Nightingale Road was playing music on September 3, 1939, as it often did, and Rolf was among a group of boys listening and dancing, when a BBC news broadcast broke in and announced that war had been declared between England and Germany. For most of the boys, this interruption in the music was unwelcome and about as meaningful to them as listening to a commercial or to a public service announcement. Later, reflecting on the moment he learned that war had been declared, Rolf recalled: "There was no discussion about it among the boys; life went on as if nothing had happened." Nor did Rolf speak to his sister about the coming of war, recalling that "she was busy learning the profession of nursing." There was not even a phone conversation between them until two weeks later. Within a few days, however, Friedmann told the boys that it may be necessary to split up the group of 40 residents, that some of them might be sent out of London and that it would be up to the Refugee Children's Movement to decide who would be going and where some or all of the boys would be sent. Rolf then learned from Edith that she had received information from the Refugee Children's Movement that he would be moved shortly out of the hostel. "That was at her request," he later recalled. "When World War II was declared September 3, I was already nine years of age and Edith wanted me moved north where it would be safer and into a family setting where she thought I would have a more normal lifestyle." About a week before the end of September, Friedmann took Rolf aside and told him he would be moving out of the hostel at the beginning of October and that he was being relocated to a foster home in Peterborough. He was given no further details except that he would not be traveling with any of the other boys at the hostel and that he should prepare for this upcoming move. Rolf later recalled that "I was told it was getting dangerous for us to be there—that was it." He did what he was told, as usual, and began packing and preparing to move out of the London hostel, all the while wondering how yet another new chapter of his life would unfold.

# CHAPTER 5

———— ✿ ————

# Wartime and Postwar Life in England (1939–1946)

SHORTLY AFTER BREAKFAST on Sunday, October 1, 1939, Rolf was summoned from his bedroom at the London hostel and came downstairs carrying his packed suitcase. A couple who looked to be in their late 30s stood at the doorway with "Rabbi" Friedmann, who introduced them as Mr. and Mrs. Jeffrey. They had come to London by auto to transport Rolf to Peterborough. Rolf was prepared to go, and so he said his farewells to the boys at the hostel and quickly departed the building. Stepping into the rear seat of the black sedan, Rolf was introduced to the couple's 11-year-old son, Allen, who was lanky and very much resembled his father (except he had more hair than his dad). Mrs. Jeffrey explained that she and her husband had attended the ceremony and service at the hostel the previous March and had been very interested in serving as foster parents for one of the children but were only introduced to boys 14 years of age and older that evening and they preferred some-one closer to Allen's age. They had later learned that there were a few younger children at the hostel and had been thrilled when the Refugee Children's Movement contacted them recently about Rolf. During this explanation, Mr. Jeffrey had loaded Rolf's belongings into the boot and once that was done he got into the car and drove off without Rolf look-ing back at the hostel, but nonetheless experiencing a strong sense of apprehension about his future.

The town of Peterborough was located in the northern part of Cambridgeshire about 70 miles directly north of the London suburb of Clapton where the hostel was situated. Normally the drive would have taken perhaps two hours, but the Jeffrey family thought it would be interesting for Rolf to see a little more of the countryside, and so they took a detour to the northeast, passing through the historic college town of Cambridge and then on to a bay known as The Wash—a place roughly midway along the east coast of England where the North Sea cuts deeply into the English coastline at the juncture of the counties of Norfolk and Lincolnshire. This bay serves as the final destination for several rivers, including the Nene, which passes nearby Peterborough and through the city of Northampton to the west. Much of the coastline along The Wash consists of marshlands that today serve as one of England's largest and most important nature

preserves. The coastline is also dotted with lighthouses and at least one lightship, along with a few towns and it was in one of these towns, King's Lynn, that Rolf and the Jeffrey family stopped to have lunch and then took a leisurely walk along the coast. It was mid-afternoon by the time the car arrived at the Jeffrey home in Peterborough, with Rolf feeling far less apprehensive having spent the better part of a day in a family setting for the first time in nearly a year.

Peterborough is a typical English town whose center is dominated by a gothic style Cathedral that took over two centuries to build, and which was completed in 1375. The town became a major east–west stop on the railway line running from Edinburgh to the North Sea, and today is a city with a population of around 200,000; but much of this growth came after the Second World War, and so at the time Rolf arrived in Peterborough the town largely consisted of an agricultural economy.

From the center the town had grown mostly to the north, and it was there in the residential suburb of Walton—about three miles north of the town center that the Jeffrey family lived. Once inside the house, Mr. Jeffrey offered to show Rolf his ham radio station. Rolf found himself fascinated with the workings of the various pieces of equipment, which Mr. Jeffrey used to send messages to other ham operators around the world. Mr. Jeffrey asked Rolf if he wanted to say something to Hitler, but Rolf was afraid that he would get into trouble. "He assured me that nobody can trace the message and handed me the microphone," Rolf later recalled. "I told Hitler that he was bad and should burn in Hell." So much did Rolf enjoy this initial encounter with Mr. Jeffrey—in fact with the entire Jeffrey family—that his earlier apprehension about his future almost completely vanished and was replaced by a feeling that he could be content living with these people. He began eagerly looking forward to what would come next.

Rolf's sense of euphoria proved to be short-lived. Not more than an hour or two after his arrival at the Jeffrey home, Rolf was busy spending some time getting to know Allen and being shown around the house and so was oblivious to the sound of the telephone. A few minutes later, Mr. Jeffrey asked Rolf to join him and Mrs. Jeffrey downstairs and had him sit down with them at the kitchen table. The couple did not look happy. There had been a mix-up, they began to explain; they had indeed earlier been told that Rolf would be living with them but had just learned that he had been assigned to a different foster home located in a neighborhood not too far from their own. Mr. Jeffrey told Rolf to get his personal belongings and he would drive him to the home of Mr. and Mrs. Spain, to whom he had now been assigned. Rolf was stunned; in the course of less than a day he had developed a surprisingly strong attachment to the Jeffrey family. How could it be that he now had to be wrenched away from them? But he could not bring himself to articulate his feelings and so, as he had learned to do from the first week he arrived in England, he "kept a stiff upper lip" and did what he was told while internally he was in turmoil.

The drive to number 5 Abbey Road took only a few minutes. The street was a single block long with semi-attached, two-story brick homes lining both sides and with trees dotting the front yards of some of the residences, which were quite close to each other. There was a field located at the far end of the street that connected to a public school located around and behind the street adjacent to Abbey Road and so the street reached a dead end at this field. The home at 5 Abbey Road was the third from the beginning of the street and was occupied by Mr. and Mrs. Spain, along with their four-year-old son, Keith. From his initial impression of the Spain family Rolf had the sense that they were more reserved than the Jeffrey family, but not unfriendly. He rather liked the neighborhood, as the homes seemed comfortable enough and fairly new. He liked that the street backed on an open field which, while looking nothing like the hills around Wolfhagen, still had a country feel about it that reminded Rolf of his hometown. But at age four, Keith would not provide the kind of companionship that Rolf immediately experienced with Allen Jeffrey, and so he did not feel the level of comfort in the Spain home that he had with the Jeffrey family. Rolf could sense his anxiety returning during his first night with the Spain family.

The next day was a working day and so Mr. Spain was gone most of that day and for much of the rest of the week. In fact, Rolf recalled that later that week Mr. Spain was gone overnight. During this time, Mrs. Spain became ill and called for Rolf. "She was in bed throwing up," he later recalled, and asked Rolf to bring her a glass of water, which he did. He also grabbed a dish towel from the kitchen and used it to clean up the vomit on the floor next to the bed, and then rinsed the towel out in the kitchen sink. When Mrs. Spain learned about this she became angry, and blurted out to him: "You're the cause of my illness because you are not doing things in a way to observe cleanliness." The next evening when Mr. Spain returned, he listened to Mrs. Spain's complaint and then listened to Rolf's explanation of his actions. Mr. Spain said to him: "Okay, you cleaned up, but you didn't do it in a sanitary way; you contaminated everything because we are using the same dish cloth to wipe the plates we eat from that you used to clean up the vomit." He told Rolf in the future to use a rag and not one of the towels from the kitchen. A few days later—without any explanation, which caused him to believe the incident with the dish towel was involved—the local committee associated with the Refugee Children's Movement uprooted him again, this time moving him only three homes down the street to number 11 Abbey Road, the residence of the Jenkinson family. As it would turn out, he would remain with this family for more than four and a half years and would largely experience the kind of family setting that Edith was seeking for him and that Rolf desperately needed.

Rolf took a liking to Mr. and Mrs. Jenkinson almost immediately. As he later recalled, "the Jenkinsons were nice people." The couple was a bit older than Mr. and Mrs. Jeffrey had been—most likely in their early 40s—and had a son, Ronald, living with them who was seven years old when Rolf arrived, about 18 months his junior. The Jenkinsons also had a much older daughter who was about 20 years old. She had moved out several years earlier because her parents did not approve of the young man she was dating, and so the two young people had eloped. As far as Rolf could determine, Mr. and Mrs. Jenkinson did not see their daughter, nor speak to her, throughout his time living with the family; Ronald apparently hardly got to know his sister at all. Rolf found both Mr. Jenkinson and his wife to be soft spoken, even at times when the boys had to be disciplined, and this was in sharp contrast to Rolf's experience in the London hostel. Mr. Jenkinson, who was balding, had an office job that occupied much of his time during the work day. But he was quite skilled on the piano and loved to play every day. Rolf later recalled that Mr. Jenkinson "never got angry and spoke to him in a gentle voice." Mrs. Jenkinson was equally kind and a devout Christian. She insisted that the entire family go to church every Sunday, but also respected Rolf's Jewish background and made certain that he attended Shabbat services at the synagogue in town each week, as well. Although she was not outwardly affectionate toward Rolf, he "had the feeling that she was a loving woman" and was grateful that she provided a sheltering environment and ensured that he was well fed and clothed. For the most part, at least initially,

Rolf and Ronald got along well enough for Rolf to characterize him as "like a brother," which of course included the kind of sibling rivalries such as Ronald teasing Rolf and setting him up so that Rolf would get into trouble with Mr. and Mrs. Jenkinson. Understandably, this behavior would get under Rolf's skin to the extent that he sometimes wanted to "get tough" with the younger boy. But Edith during an early phone conversation advised him: "Don't fight; go along with it," probably because she did not want him to create friction with the Jenkinsons that might cause her brother to be moved again.

The Jenkinsons were among many families in the Walton section of Peterborough who had opened their homes to children who were evacuated from London and other large cities in the months following the start of the Second World War. Aside from humanitarian considerations, each foster family received 50 pounds sterling every month and a separate book of food ration tickets for such items as meat, butter, and eggs from the government. These supplemental payments and money to cover other costs of living for the foster children, such as for clothing and medical expenses, often better allowed families to make ends meet for themselves and their own children, as well as their foster children during wartime. Rolf's circumstance, of course, was different from the other evacuated children in the neighborhood because he was a refugee and not a British subject, whose status was under the administration of the Refugee Children's Movement. Once Operation Pied Piper was launched, nonetheless, it was possible for the Jenkinson family to receive the same support from the government for Rolf that other foster families received for housing British children. The Walton community was quite proud of its level of participation in providing foster homes for the evacuated children that included a group of at least

20 boys and about an equal number of girls. Rolf became quite friendly with one of the boys—a Jewish boy named Harold Cohen—who lived with an- other family on his street and was just nine months his junior. Rolf met Harold almost immediately after arriving in Peterborough while living at the Spain household and they spent time play- ing in both the Spain and Jenkinson backyards. Harold, in fact, later moved into the Jenkinson house with Rolf for a short time before his parents came to take him home.

It took very little time for Rolf to adjust to life in his foster home in Peterborough, as he quickly eased into daily and weekly family routines. He was given his own room, which was modest compared with his room in Wolfhagen, but he was none- theless thrilled to finally have some privacy after long months of sharing a bedroom with so many other children ever since arriving in England. It was the family's practice to not wear their outside shoes inside the house, and so the boys were responsible for storing the shoes in a loca- tion close to the front door. When Mr. Jenkinson came into the house, he would often ask Rolf to help remove his shoes and bring him his slip- pers; on Sundays the boys were responsible for cleaning all the shoes. Sunday was also a special day because the family would get dressed in their finest clothes and go to the local Church of England. In the begin- ning, Mrs. Jenkinson helped Rolf with his tie. He later recalled: "She would come over to me and say, 'I don't like the way your tie is done; let me show you.'" Eventually Rolf got the hang of it, but it felt good having an adult to assist him in that way. The family would then return home from church and Rolf and Ronald went to work in the kitchen preparing the Sunday meal. Although he had just turned eight years old, Ronald knew how to make a tasty roast and would test it, as he had been shown by his mother, to be certain it was tender. Rolf became an expert at making Yorkshire pudding. Rather than treating the Sunday cooking as a chore, Rolf loved making the meal; it brought back memories of assisting his mother with the baking in Wolfhagen, and he looked forward immensely to preparing the meal every Sunday. Above all, to his great delight, Rolf discovered that the family had a bicycle for him to use, and so he was able to explore the neighborhood and ride with some of the other boys. He also rode the bike the three miles to the synagogue, which at that time was the only one in town and was located just outside of the town center on Cobden Avenue. Although the Jenkinsons encouraged him to go to Shabbat services, they did not feel comfortable attending the services themselves and so except in extremely inclement weather, it was up to Rolf to get himself to and from services. The only aspect of family life that was missing for Rolf compared with his life in Wolfhagen, other than having his sister around, which had never been pleasant for him, was the absence of family outings. Unlike the many visits to relatives in and around Wolfhagen that Rolf had experienced as a young child, the Jenkinsons seemed not to have much of an extended family, nor were they inclined to take the boys outside of Peterborough on daily or overnight trips. Although it did not occur to Rolf at the time, it is possible that the war may have been partly responsible for the absence of family outings.

As soon as he arrived in Peterborough, Rolf began attending the public primary school located almost directly behind the block on which he lived. He approached this experience with great trepidation, in part because in his last encounter in a public school he had been ridiculed and bullied both by the teacher and his fellow students, and in part because his absence from a stable, formal educational environment for much of the previous four years had left him with feelings of insecurity because he was so far behind his classmates even in universal subjects such as math and science and history, but especially in English. Despite having been surprisingly adept at learning conversational English, he quite understandably found the technical aspects of English grammar difficult to grasp. "I was not a great student," he later recalled. "I copied on a piece of paper everything that was written on the blackboard so that when I went home I could understand what I had written." Fortunately, Rolf's teachers were patient with him regarding the language issue and encouraged him to ask questions if he didn't understand something, which he would do fairly often. "Once I asked about the difference between the words 'niece' and 'nice'—I didn't know which was which," he later recalled; "and the whole class laughed." Rolf remembered that the teacher silenced the class and said, "Students, this is not a funny question; how many of you know how to spell 'niece?'" Not a single hand went up. Rolf's teachers were "very good" with him. "They told me that I was a good student," he recalled, "that I was quick in learning, that my vocabulary was improving, and that even my speech sounded British." For the most part, Rolf very much "liked" and "was involved" with his primary school experience, and generally he got along pretty well with his classmates despite their teasing him about his language difficulties, especially during his first few years in the primary school when he and his classmates were still fairly young.

Rolf's attendance at services at the synagogue began almost immediately after his arrival in Peterborough. The single Jewish congregation in the town was Orthodox but tended to be more liberal than the congregations his family belonged to in Wolfhagen and Hamburg. Portions of the service included English readings, and some of the melodies he learned were used years later in the Conservative congregations to which he belonged. Rolf found himself comfortable with the Hebrew prayers, having learned them during his years in Germany and at the London hostel. The Peterborough synagogue, in fact, had a religious school, but Rolf attended classes there only sporadically, and so his primary connection with the congregation occurred on Shabbat and major Jewish holidays until he reached age 12. Rolf recalled that a typical Shabbat service drew perhaps 40–50 attendees, but he rarely saw more than one or two children at the services and found it difficult to develop friendships with them because they lived some distance from him on the opposite side of town. The spiritual leader of this congregation, Rabbi Greenberg, took some interest in Rolf, as did the congregation's president, Mr. Shaw, who Rolf recalled "had a magnificent singing voice that you might have thought he was a cantor, because he led the services most of the time." Rabbi Greenberg knew that Rolf had been born in Germany and had been part of the Kindertransport program, and Rolf had explained to him that his parents were still in Germany trying to get out and that he was worried because they hadn't come to England the previous winter as they had promised to do. To Rolf's great surprise, Rabbi Greenberg did not want to talk about the Nazis or his parents and—as Edith had already told him—said to him, "Don't think about that anymore." For the remainder of 1939 and well into the summer of 1940, concern about his parents continued to weigh on Rolf. By mid-August and especially in September, however, a new challenge had emerged.

Six months passed following the defeat of Poland in which a state of war existed between the Third Reich on the one hand and France and England on the other without any military land operations between the combatants taking place. With the exception of air attacks by both sides on seagoing warships and submarine (U-boat) attacks on shipping primarily in the Atlantic Ocean, the timeframe between October 1939 and March 1940 was typically marked by a continued mobilization and, in the case of England in particular, the purchase of wartime equipment from the United States at discount prices. England also engaged in significant air reconnaissance operations over Germany and dropped millions of propaganda leaflets instead of bombs. During this time, the French built up their massive complex of stationary defensive emplacements along the border with Germany in Alsace and Lorraine known as the Maginot Line. The absence of sustained military land engagement between the primary combatants was so pronounced during this period that it came to be known as the "Phony War."

Meanwhile, the Soviet Union attacked neutral and democratic Finland on November 30 and more than three months of "Winter War" ensued, ending with Finland ceding portions of territory in the north to the Soviets. Public opinion in France and England against Soviet aggression in Finland in part caused the resignation of French Prime Minister Édouard Deladier on March 20—just eight days after the "Winter War" ended—and led to a mobilization of British forces which could not be completed in time to come to the aid of the Finns. The Soviet defeat of Finland in the "Winter War" and the mobilization of British forces during that time led to a German attack on Denmark and Norway on April 9. Denmark surrendered that same day and was occupied by German troops; but Norway fought hard and British forces were sent into Norway on April 14. It took two months before Norway surrendered to Germany, but most of the fighting had ended in the southern, most heavily populated, portion of the country in fairly short order after the German attack despite the presence of the British forces, which were evacuated back to England just before Norway surrendered on June 9. Failure of British military operations in Norway led to a vote of no confidence against Prime Minister Chamberlain in Parliament in May. Although he survived the vote, Chamberlain resigned his position and King George V appointed Winston Churchill Prime Minister on May 10. The two architects of the highly unpopular "Munich Agreement" of September 1938—Chamberlain and Deladier—were thus removed from power by their respective governments just as the "Phony War" was about to end, plunging mainland Western Europe into all-out conflagration from which it would not emerge for five years.

On May 10, 1940, forces of the Third Reich launched a massive *Blitzkrieg* attack on the neutral countries of The Netherlands, Belgium, Luxembourg, and on France. Having been tested successfully in Poland eight months earlier, the coordinated and concentrated attack by the Luftwaffe, Panzer, and infantry units of Germany overran Luxembourg in a single day, The Netherlands in four days, and Belgium in 18 days. Much like the German initial attack during the First World War, the *blitz* through the Low Countries almost completely avoided the Maginot Line and within a week had pushed the defending French armies and a British Expeditionary Force that had been sent to mainland Europe toward the coast of the English Channel on the verge of potentially forcing a quick surrender by France and England and an end to the war. On May 20, however, the German advance abruptly halted, allowing the besieged French and British units to establish defenses around a beachhead at Dunkirk. Four days later the British launched a massive evacuation operation across the English Channel to the relative safety of England that over the course of nine days allowed more than 330,000 mostly British and French ground forces to live to fight another day. Following the Dunkirk operation, German forces turned south, occupying Paris on June 14 and causing the French government to flee. France signed an armistice agreement with Germany on June 22, thereafter setting up a "collaborationist" government in Vichy in southern France while German forces occupied the entire northern portion of France, including the coastline of the Atlantic Ocean and the English Channel. By the end of June 1940, forces of the Third Reich controlled all of Western Europe from France in the south to Denmark and Norway in the north to Poland in the east, leaving the island nation of Great Britain standing alone and separated from German forces only by the English Channel and the North Sea.

On June 18, 1940, just after Paris was occupied by forces of the Third Reich, newly appointed British Prime Minister Winston Churchill addressed the House of Commons: "The Battle of France is over," he stated; "I expect the Battle of Britain is about to begin." He went on: "Let us therefore brace ourselves to our duties, and so bear ourselves that if the British Empire and its Commonwealth last for a thousand years, men will say, 'This was their finest hour.'" Such inspirational rhetoric would rally Britons to withstand the bombardment by the Luftwaffe and anticipated invasion by the Wehrmacht in the ensuing months. But at the time of France's surrender, Hitler and his general staff had no plan for an invasion of Britain in place; such was their confidence that

England would follow France to the peace table. Nor was the German fighting machine prepared for a full-scale invasion of the British Isles, having sustained their successful *Blitzkrieg* across the Low Countries and France over the course of six weeks, thereby somewhat overextending their supply lines. By the beginning of July, Hitler's hope that England would sue for peace had faded and he directed his general staff to plan for an invasion of Britain as early as mid-August that would be preceded by extensive bombing operations by the Luftwaffe on British sea and air installations. The Germans, however, had poor intelligence regarding British defense systems, including the effectiveness of the Chain Home stations that employed the latest in radar technology available anywhere in the world at the time.

The first phase of the German invasion plan (Operation Sea Lion) called for the Luftwaffe, under the command of Air Marshal Hermann Göring, to destroy British shipping and port facilities and take out the Chain Home radar stations. Beginning on July 10, and continuing with increasing intensity over the ensuing month, these air attacks met with considerable success but failed to shut down the radar operation, thus allowing England early warning of targeted bombardment by the Luftwaffe. From the outset, moreover, the Luftwaffe met with fierce resistance from the Royal Air Force (RAF) Fighter Command, under the directorship of Air Marshal Hugh Dowding. The RAF possessed superior aircraft to the Luftwaffe and consistently shot down far more planes than it lost. Realizing the British superiority in the air, the Luftwaffe turned its bombing raids on RAF air bases throughout England beginning on August 13, resulting in heavy losses of pilots and aircraft for both sides and causing the German invasion plan to be pushed back until late September. By early September, however, the air battle of attrition over England resulted in the loss of more than 600 German aircraft while the RAF lost around 260 of its fighters. On August 30, Churchill spoke about the heroics of the RAF in the House of Commons in a presentation that included the now famous phrase: "Never in the field of human conflict was so much owed by so many to so few."

The ability of the RAF to destroy a high number of Luftwaffe bomb- ers and fighters, as well as a British bombing attack on Berlin in early September caused the Luftwaffe to make a major operational change. Göring ordered his bombers to target London and other industrial cit- ies such as Liverpool, Coventry, and Birmingham, and to switch to night raids in order to make it more difficult for the RAF interceptor fighters to shoot down his planes. The first night raid—a massive bombardment— hit London on September 7 and caused much of the city, particularly around the docks along the Thames to burn. The raid also forced most of the city's population into the Underground to escape the onslaught. A second massive night raid hit London on September 15, but this time the Luftwaffe sustained such heavy losses from the RAF that it served to demoralize Luftwaffe pilots. The bombing raids over England's major industrial cities that came to be known as "The Blitz" at the time would continue almost nightly until late October, and then more sporadically into the spring of 1941. The inability of the Luftwaffe to defeat the RAF over the skies of England or terrorize the British population to force their leaders to come to the peace table caused Hitler to postpone the invasion of Great Britain on October 12 until the spring of 1941. By that time, however, Hitler had focused his attention eastward, ordering a full-fledged attack on the Soviet Union (Operation Barbarossa) and spoke no further about invading England. The RAF victory in the Battle of Britain proved to be the first major turning point of the Second World War.

Two related events occurred on and around the street where Rolf lived in the Walton district of Peterborough during the middle of August 1940. Rolf observed that there was a noticeable increase in air traffic in the skies over his neighborhood; squadrons of fighter planes could be seen during the day and heard at night flying overhead. There were two large RAF installations south of Peterborough near Cambridge re- sponsible in part for the defense of Cambridgeshire. The bases came under attack by the Luftwaffe during August 1940 but they were too far away from Peterborough for Rolf to hear the sound of bombs or witness aerial dogfights in the sky at that time. Riding around the neighborhood on his bike, especially in the nearby fields, Rolf and his friends occasionally came across shell casings, which may have been from discharged aircraft rounds or from nearby anti-aircraft emplacements. The boys found these interesting but the adults in the community became concerned because these were indications that the war could be coming to their part of England. The second event more directly affected Rolf. Brick shelters were hastily erected along his street and throughout the neighboring streets. Four bomb shelters were constructed on Abbey road—roughly every third house apart—between the homes on one side of the street and the road itself. Each of the structures was about 24 feet wide by 12 feet deep with an open doorway on one end protected by a cement wall a foot or two in front of the doorway. Each shelter was designed to accommodate at least 16 persons, with eight double bunk beds placed inside each one. During drills, residents were told to go into the shelter and either turn to the left or the right to distribute themselves quickly. They were shown two bent metal handles at either end of the shelter and told that if the doorway ever became blocked, it was possible to escape the shelter by using the metal handles to force apart the bricks surrounding the handle, which were set in weak mortar. "We never had to do that," Rolf later recalled, "but people wanted to be close to that handle in case they had to escape from a collapsed shelter."

It wasn't long after the construction of the shelters that the residents were told to plan on spending their nights inside the shelter. "Around nine o'clock," Rolf recalled, "you got yourself into pajamas and went to the shelter." After a few nights of taking to the shelters with nothing happening, many of the people living on Abbey Road tired of doing that and reduced their nights in the shelter to about three times a week. Then, one night late in the first week of September, the air raid sirens went off and everyone quickly went into the shelters. Five minutes later the all clear sounded but many of the people spent the night inside the shelter anyway. About a week later the sirens went off again; this continued night after night for two or three weeks. On a few such occasions the sound of exploding bombs could be heard from somewhere close by the shelter, once exploding close enough that the residents in the shelter heard "a horrific explosion" and could feel the concussion causing the area around the shelter to shake. "It was scary," Rolf later recalled, "because you would never know how sturdy the shelter was going to be." When the all clear sounded and everyone came out of the shelter, it was morning. On the next street, almost the entire block of homes had been badly damaged and windows in some of the houses on Rolf's block had been blown out. That occasion was the worst of the bombing for Rolf, but he recalled that there were perhaps 15 nights when Peterborough experienced bombing and those times, in particular, were terrifying for many of the people in the shelter, especially for Rolf and the other children. Most of those occasions occurred during the height of the Battle of Britain in late September and October 1940. The bombings significantly subsided after that so that air raid warnings became much less frequent until they pretty much ceased by the spring of 1941. Rolf later contemplated these bombings of a residential community such as Peterborough which had few, if any, military targets. Because Peterborough was along the flight path from the North Sea to Birmingham, it is possible the Luftwaffe dropped their bombs in error or bombers were damaged by the RAF or anti-aircraft fire and had to drop their bombs prematurely. It is also possible, even likely, that as it became clearer that the Luftwaffe was losing the Battle of Britain, the night bombings were designed to terrorize Britons into coming to the peace table and so residential areas were more heavily targeted. In any event, for Rolf and many of his peers, the bombings over Peterborough began as an adventure but turned out to be a frightening experience.

Aside from the stretch of sustained bombings during September and October 1940 as part of the Battle of Britain, Rolf's daily life in Peterborough had settled into a relatively stable routine within the Jenkinson household that was reflected in the periodic reports entered into his permanent file by the social worker and staff of the Refugee Children's Movement. The first substantive welfare report entered on September 19, 1940, indicated that Rolf's health was fully "satisfactory," that he was attending primary school and religious services and was characterized by his teachers as a "well behaved, intelligent, and likeable little boy." Subsequent reports over the next 19 months were equally positive, especially the entry for April 14, 1942, which indicated that the Jenkinson home "appears to be a happy one and boy is well cared for," with the report from school indicating that "progress and conduct is good." The already positive home life had further improved for Rolf during the winter of 1941 when Harold Cohen moved into the Jenkinson home. Although Harold was a year behind Rolf in school, and therefore did not share the same classes, the two had been neighbors and good friends ever since Rolf's arrival in Peterborough. Harold joined Rolf and Ronald in the Sunday routine of going to church and then preparing the meal; Harold was responsible for preparing the vegetables. But unlike Rolf, Harold took no interest in attending synagogue, nor apparently did his parents ask the Jenkinsons to have him do so. By the summer of 1941, with the Battle of Britain concluded and the threat of German bombings mostly gone, some of the families who had evacuated their children out of London and other large cities began to retrieve them from their foster homes, and Harold was one of these children. Once Harold left Peterborough, Rolf never saw or heard from him again.

The departure of Harold Cohen had surprisingly little impact on Rolf in large measure because he had by then been in considerable inner turmoil regarding his family, as he continued to be preoccupied by the absence of his parents. He had received a postcard from them in 1940 and another in 1941, but neither mentioned anything about when they would be able to leave Germany and come for him. Shortly after the first postcard arrived, Rolf received a visit from his cousin Gretl Rosenthal toward the end of July 1940. She had joined her husband, Josef in England at the beginning of September 1939, on the eve of war, and they had been staying in London awaiting their quota number from the United States ever since. They had maintained contact with Edith because of their proximity to her, but Edith worked long hours in training to become a nurse and as a mother's helper, with subsequently even longer hours at St. James Hospital once the Battle of Britain began, and so the contacts had been few and far between. Edith had not once visited Rolf, which he very much resented, although she spoke to him on the telephone on average about once a month. The conversations generally were brief and focused on Rolf's needs and rarely included mention of their parents, with Edith deflecting questions and discouraging discussion of that topic whenever Rolf raised it. When Rolf's cousin Gretl appeared at the Jenkinson house in late July 1940, she was noticeably pregnant and explained that she and her husband had received their quota clearances and were sailing to New York in early August. When Rolf learned this, he became very excited, thinking Gretl had come to take him with her to New York. Taking her arm and refusing to let go as she prepared to leave, he pleaded: "Take me with you; please take me with you." But without an approved visa and affidavit, let alone a cleared US quota number, it was impossible for Rolf to accompany his cousins to America and so Gretl departed the Jenkinson home and Rolf remained in Peterborough.

The fact is that, unbeknownst to Rolf, Josef Möllerich had been hard at work and by the summer of 1940 believed he had made some progress toward a move to the United States for himself and Selma, as well as for his children in England. He had received an approved visa and affidavit at the end of 1938 arranged by his nephew, Otto Schwarz in New York, and was awaiting the conclusion of the extended financial audit and issuance of exit visas by the Nazi government, as well as clearance of the United States quota number. He had been writing to Otto and his brothers, Max and Eugen, as well as to his niece in Chicago (Hilde) to find a way to have his son and daughter come to the United States, either through the visa process or, in his son's case, as part of a children's transport he had learned about. In a letter to Hilde dated July 29, 1940,

Josef bemoaned the absence of any communication from Edith: "We simply cannot understand that Edith does not write at all." The letter continued: "We do not know whether Edith's papers are in order or whether she received your affidavit because it was originally planned that both children should travel together." Later, on February 6, 1941, Josef wrote to the family in Chicago indicating continued efforts to get the children to the United States. The letter also reflected significant confusion—that turned out to conflict with the facts—regarding the status of both Edith and Rolf: "We are amazed that Edith is not yet with you since her papers were already in order last year," he wrote to his niece in Chicago. "That Wolfgang is staying back is very regrettable." He again bemoaned the absence of a communication from Edith: "We have written several times via the Red Cross and have never had an answer. It appears that many letters to there are getting lost." Josef also renewed his request to find a way for both children to receive approval to immigrate to the United States. These efforts, however, came to no avail due in large measure to the difficulty in working out arrangements for his children in England solely via written communications with relatives in America that had to be circumspect due to Nazi censorship. As a result, despite Josef's written assumptions regarding his children, there was no record of any actual effort for their immigration to the United States during 1941 or throughout much of the remainder of the war. Rolf, of course, knew nothing about these letters at the time, nor did he learn much from a postcard he received from his parents, written in early 1941, expressing only the hope that they would be reunited soon. The next communication he received regarding his parents was a postcard from the International Red Cross in May 1942 informing him that his parents had died at the hands of the Nazis. The postcard indicated that Edith had been informed via a similar communication, and concluded, as he later recalled: "We regret that you will never see your parents again."

The stunning news of his parents' death could not have come at a worse moment for Rolf. Much of the progress he had made both in school and in adjustment to life in England, including the manner in which he had learned to interact with his peers, had begun to unravel with the onset of puberty. As Rolf approached his final year in primary school, he began to fall behind in some of his subjects, taking less interest especially in subjects other than math and science and remaining generally unaware of many of the events taking place around him besides the war. The more he fell behind, the more discouraged he became. "I felt that I was inferior to the English kids," he later recalled, "and that I wasn't worldly enough to know the names of important sports figures or even events in British history, like Guy Fawkes Day." Outside of school he made an effort to learn more by visiting the library and reading extensively. But he was easily distracted in some of his classes. During his first year in secondary school, at age 12, his teacher, Norman Kirk, discovered that Rolf had spit on the page of his book while he was reviewing that page with the class. Rolf could not later recall why he had done that other than he was bored with the discussion. As a consequence, Kirk had him hold both hands open and Rolf received three whacks on his hands with a thin cane, something that brought back unpleasant memories of his father in Wolfhagen; the pain in this case was enhanced by the relatively recent news of his parent's death at the hands of the Nazis.

Outside of school Rolf's behavior took a turn for the worse as well. Although he had been friendly with a few of the English boys who had been evacuated and were living in foster homes in Peterborough, as time went by and many of these boys moved back to their homes, Rolf took up with a group of local boys who spent much of their time engaged in mischievous behavior. "We would throw stones at a person's house," he later recalled, "and try to hit a window;" fortunately without success most of the time. They also would raid a shed that was used to collect metal for the war and throw cans into the street. There was an area in an open field that the gang called "The Spinny," where stood a solitary group of relatively small trees. The boys would climb the trees and cut down small branches to use as swords when they played. Rolf also recalled that Peterborough had an abundance of gooseberries and the boys would climb over the fences of private homes where there were gooseberries growing, steal them, and gorge themselves until they had their fill. "We—this bunch of guys—were out to do no good," he later recalled. "I guess we were typical teenagers."

When the boys were not engaged in mischief, they spent most of their free time playing sports such as football (soccer), cricket, and rugby. Rolf had never been coached in the fundamentals of these games, but because he was agile, fast, and very tough for his size, he was a natural athlete. The Jenkinsons had purchased a pair of football boots for him and he would take charge of the ball and race down the field easily with nobody able to catch him. But scoring was a different story; because he lacked the skills, and because the boys would line up in front of the goal, he found it difficult to score and this frustrated him. Sometimes he would take out his frustration by engaging in fights with other boys, and generally handled himself well. He developed a reputation as a tough kid on the field, and this may have compensated for his lack of training and relative newness to the sports. He also loved to play cricket and excelled at the game even though cricket was completely foreign to him, unlike football, which he had seen played in Germany. Despite the lack of training in cricket, Rolf specialized at throwing the ball past the batter and knocking down the wicket. He threw so hard, he recalled, that he developed a chronically sore shoulder which he aggravated later in life. The boys also played rugby, which was the roughest of the three sports, and Rolf did not enjoy this game nearly as much as the other two sports because he would get bloody noses during the scrums, and later in life he was diagnosed as having a deviated septum, possibly originating from playing rugby in Peterborough.

The sense that Rolf increasingly had through his primary school years of being different than, and inferior to, English children increased as he entered his teen years to a point where sometimes he was treated in an ugly manner. From his early days in Peterborough of being teased about his lack of English skills and general knowledge about England,

Rolf at times encountered outright hostility from his peers once he began secondary school. At first he believed it might have been because he was Jewish, as had been the case in Germany, but as time went on he came to understand that it was because he was German, and England was at war with Germany. This fact sometimes did not sit well with Britons, so much so that some of the oldest boys from the Kindertransport program—who were saved by the British from the hands of the Nazis because they were Jewish—ended up being interned and sent to Commonwealth countries such as Canada or as far away as Australia once the war started for fear they would engage in espionage against England. At Rolf's level, the xenophobia manifested itself among his peers by isolated incidents of bullying—often in the course of a sporting game—when many of the boys would gang up on him and he would have to fight off one or more at a time. "In my mind," he remembered, "I was a reject, being a refugee in England and having lived in Germany for eight years. This put me on the other side of kids accepting me." The ugliest of these incidents occurred during a rugby scrum. The boys were huddled up and "suddenly I felt something wet on my pants," Rolf later recalled; "Someone was urinating on me." He knew exactly who the perpetrator was, a chap named Perkins, and so "I broke out of the huddle and hit him hard in the face. They all turned on me and yelled, 'You Nazi bastard!'" This was not the only occasion he had been ostracized for being German during his time in Peterborough, but it was an incident he never forgot.

The other significant focus for Rolf during his early teenage years was his bar mitzvah. One evening in the autumn of 1942, well after Rolf turned 12 years of age, Rolf recalled that Mrs. Jenkinson asked him: "Don't you have to have a ceremony at the synagogue at age 13?" He responded: "Yes, my bar mitzvah." She told Rolf he needed to mention this to the rabbi so that he would be prepared. Rolf had a meeting with Rabbi Greenberg and Mr. Shaw at the synagogue. The rabbi told him that he had missed so much training in Hebrew that it was rather late to begin preparation for a bar mitzvah and he was not certain Rolf would learn enough to get through everything. "He was a nice man," Rolf recalled. The rabbi suggested that Rolf might consider doing less than most boys did for their bar mitzvah. But Mr. Shaw thought that was nonsense and offered to tutor Rolf in the Torah *trope* (chanted melody) and promised that Rolf would be prepared for both the reading of the scriptures and for participating in leading a portion of the service. Rolf was familiar with the melodies of the service, of course, having attended Shabbat services regularly ever since arriving in Peterborough over three years earlier. As he later recalled: "I knew the various parts of the service and was very involved and very comfortable with the service." But the Torah *trope* was a different story. Because there wasn't enough time for Rolf to learn these melodies from scratch, Mr. Shaw made a gramophone recording of his bar mitzvah *parshah*—the portion of the Torah from which he would read—with his beautiful singing voice, and Rolf practiced these melodies. Mr. Shaw drilled Rolf especially in his pronunciation of the Hebrew words, each week giving him a new sentence to learn. With the help of the recording and the hours Mr. Shaw devoted to Rolf in the months leading up to his bar mitzvah, the boy was able to learn and then put to memory his entire *parshah*, and in the week before the bar mitzvah service, Rolf recited it for Mr. Shaw, who literally beamed with approval. "I don't know what else I need to do for you," he told Rolf. "You know your *parshah*; you have memorized it and you are going to do just fine." Rolf's confidence surged, but Rabbi Greenberg was less optimistic and repeated to Rolf what he had told him months earlier, that he wasn't certain he would be able to get through everything because of his previous lack of training. This set Rolf back so that on the eve of his bar mitzvah his confidence ebbed and he became very nervous.

On Saturday morning, May 29, 1943, two days after Rolf's 13th birthday, a modest number of congregants gathered for Rolf's bar mitzvah service. For the first and only time while Rolf lived in Peterborough, Edith came to see him and share the day with him. She had spoken to him a month earlier and he had described his preparations for the

bar mitzvah. "I just hope you will accept that your parents won't be there," she had told him on the phone. Now, standing with Edith inside the synagogue just before the start of the service, Rolf expressed doubt about his ability to get through the service because the rabbi had no confidence in him even though he knew what to do. Edith put her hands on his shoulders and said: "You will do it—you will be just fine; I'm here." Strangely, the Jenkinson family was missing from the congregation that morning. Rolf understood their absence, however; they did not feel comfortable being inside a synagogue, but had been very supportive of his months-long preparation for his bar mitzvah. "They were there emotionally for me," Rolf later recalled, and they were joyful for me." And so as the service began, other than Rabbi Greenberg and Mr. Shaw, Edith was the only person present that Rolf knew well.

Just before it was Rolf's turn to come to the *bima* to recite his Torah *parshah*, Rabbi Greenberg gave an explanation to the congregation regarding what they were about to witness. He told the congregants that this was going to be a different kind of service than the typical bar mitzvah service because of Rolf's background. He described how Rolf had been rescued out of Germany by the Kindertransport and had been living in a foster home in Peterborough since the war began. He also explained that Rolf's parents had been murdered by the Nazis and that with the support of his sister and foster parents in Peterborough, Rolf had tried to put that behind him and continue his life. Listening to the rabbi's sermon, Rolf became increasingly nervous, so that "by the time I went up to the *bima*, my hand was shaking so badly that I knew the *yad* (the pointer used to follow the Hebrew words in the Torah scroll) was not going to work for me." Instead of following the words across the parchment, Rolf moved his finger down each line and as a result lost his place. "My mind was telling me that I was going to falter," he later recalled. "Then I saw my sister in the front row with tears in her eyes, so emotional, and I knew that I would be okay. I had memorized the entire *parshah* thanks to Mr. Shaw and everything went off like clockwork." Afterward, besides Edith, only one other person came up to congratulate Rolf; he was an American Jewish GI who just happened to come to the service that morning and shook Rolf's hand, telling him that he was "amazed" at how well Rolf had done considering his "background" that Rabbi Greenberg had described during the service. The GI handed Rolf a 10 shilling note, which was the only bar mitzvah gift he received that morning.

As it turned out, Rolf's bar mitzvah signaled the final stage of his time in Peterborough, as the seed of a plan for him to be moved elsewhere had already been planted. In January 1943, while Rolf was preparing for his bar mitzvah, Edith had registered a complaint with the Refugee Children's Movement about his overall situation, but particularly about his education. As a result of the increasingly poor behavior and lack of progress during Rolf's first year in secondary school, as well as telephone discussions that Edith had with her brother over the course of several months during the late summer and fall of 1942, Rolf had been transferred to a different secondary school in Peterborough during the middle of the school year. He later recalled: "I couldn't understand why I needed to change schools when I was just settling down and had friends" in the secondary school. The change contributed to his feeling that he was "going backward and not forward in life when it came to my education." Edith told him that he was "too critical" of himself and asked him to "go along with what I'm trying to do for you and trust me," Rolf later recalled. He had shown an interest in and aptitude for mechanics ever since his parents had given him the "mechano set" in Germany, and this interest continued to grow in England, where he spent many hours taking apart and repairing bicycle parts. Edith wanted him to go to a secondary school that focused on technical education, and Peterborough did not have what she felt was an acceptable option for that kind of education. But she did not want to disrupt Rolf's preparation for his bar mitzvah, and so it was arranged and recorded in his official file in February 1943 that Rolf would remain in Peterborough with the Jenkinson family until the school semester following his bar mitzvah, when he would be transferred to a technical secondary school "near his sister."

Things did not work out exactly according to the plan. It was not possible for Rolf to move back to London to be closer to his sister, and the Refugee Children's Movement had difficulty placing Rolf in a technical school in Peterborough or anywhere else for the beginning of the fall 1943 school year, and so he began the year attending the secondary school in Peterborough to which he had been moved the previous year. In December 1943, however, Rolf's situation in the Jenkinson household became strained. He refused to continue to go to the synagogue each Shabbat, which made Edith unhappy, especially because he continued to accompany the Jenkinson family to church every Sunday. According to Rolf's official file, the social worker recommended that he be moved from Peterborough to the city of Northampton, where there were several technical secondary schools to which Rolf could apply for entry, with the recommendation that he be permitted to spend holidays with the Jenkinson family in Peterborough. Although he was not happy about the move, he later recalled: "I understood my sister's point of view that I was stagnating in Peterborough and that is why she wanted me to get moving to an industrial area where I would have a better opportunity, and that was Northampton." On January 6, 1944, Rolf was moved from Peterborough to an orthodox boys' hostel in Northampton. Although he did not know it at the time, Rolf would never see the Jenkinson family again. Reflecting back on his more than four years living with them, Rolf later recognized the mixed emotions he had when he departed: "I didn't fall in love with them, but it felt like home living with them." He also acknowledged the immense positive influence that his experience with the Jenkinsons had on his life: "If I had the chance to see them again," he later recalled, "I would get on my knees and kiss them for saving my life and making me feel secure, and for making it possible for me to grow up."

The first thing that Rolf noticed upon his arrival at the Hollybank Boys' Hostel, located in the Cliftonville section of Northampton, was the size of the property, which was at least two acres with a large iron fence surrounding it. The building was set back from the road, where there was a gate at the entrance to the property and a long driveway with a large garage attached to the main building. Northampton was a modest-sized city located 35 miles to the west of Peterborough. Although its population was only a bit larger than Peterborough, Northampton was more industrial and, in particular, was known for its leather manufacturing industry. The inside of the hostel appeared to Rolf very similar to the London hostel, especially on the main level, with a very large living room area and dining room with tables arranged in a "U" shape, just like in London. The Hollybank Hostel was also similar to the London hostel in that there was space for 40 boys. Because the Hollybank Hostel had four levels compared to the two-level building in London, however, there were several more bedrooms and so the boys were not crowded into two large dormitory-style sleeping areas but spread out over the second and third levels of the house into bedrooms that mostly accommodated six to eight boys each. The top level of the building accommodated the few sleep-in staff. Behind the building there was a large vegetable garden, which was used during the growing season to feed the residents. The remainder of the property behind and to the side of the building had open space that was used by the boys to play sports and engage in other recreational activities.

The hostel director, Isadore Marx, was a bearded gentleman in his late 50s who, although not traditionally orthodox, often wore a black hat with a brim and insisted on holding three prayer services daily. Like Oscar Friedmann at the London hostel, Marx had the boys address him as "Rabbi" even though there was again some question whether he had ever received "*smicha*" (been ordained). Besides chores within the hostel, the boys were expected to study Hebrew, as well as Jewish history and ethics; they were given books to read and then were required to discuss what they had read with "Rabbi" Marx. Although the services were not a problem for Rolf, he often had difficulty with the books in Hebrew and with the readings in Jewish studies, for which he had sporadic training at best in the past. Marx took a liking to him, however, and went over the readings with him page by page, helping Rolf with the translation of the Hebrew when he faltered. Marx had a son with the same initials as Rolf—"RWM"—and Rolf believed this was partly why the director spent so much time helping him to overcome his education gap in Hebrew and Jewish studies. Rolf had received a billfold from Edith with his initials emblazoned at the bottom and asked Marx to store it in his office for safekeeping, which the director was happy to do.

Rolf's arrival at the Hollybank Hostel presented him with other challenges. For more than four years he had lived in a stable family setting, in a private home with a room of his own. Now he was expected to readjust to the hostel setting, where he had to share a room with five other boys on the third level of the building. Although Rolf was well past his 13th birthday when he arrived at the Hollybank Hostel, he was once again among the youngest of the boys, most of whom were teenagers and some, like in London, had reached age 20, including one of the boys with whom he shared a room. Most of the boys were refugees from Austria. There was Markus, who played the ukulele; Sigi, who was the oldest at age 20 and sometimes bullied the younger boys; Martin and Alan, who were twins; and then there was Josef Haberer who, like Rolf, was born in Germany, in a town called Villingen-Schwenningen in the southwestern part of the country and had come to England in early 1939 as part of the Kindertransport program. Joe was about two years older than Rolf and had thick, curly hair. The two of them hit it off immediately, establishing a close friendship that would transcend time and distance for several years.

Joe became the older brother that Rolf never had, taking him under his wing and helping to guide Rolf through probably his greatest and most consistent challenge throughout his youth, fulfilling his father's wish that he focus on obtaining a good education. In this respect, it proved fortuitous indeed that Rolf would encounter Joe Haberer at the Hollybank Hostel. Although outwardly friendly toward Rolf and adventurous by nature, which appealed to Rolf, when it came to formal education and learning in a broad sense, Joe was deadly serious and mature beyond his years (age 15 at the time Rolf arrived), and thus tended to set himself apart from many of the other boys in the hostel. He was also an excellent judge of character and correctly sensed almost immediately that Rolf was internally in turmoil and desperately needed to develop self-direction and the motivation necessary to achieve a solid education that would prepare him for adulthood and a career. Within a day or two of his arrival, Rolf got into a debate among his roommates, except Joe, over the location of his bed and the assignment of his daily chores. With respect to the latter, he was assigned to clean the bathroom. Rolf told the others that he didn't mind doing any number of chores but he refused to clean the bathroom, blurting out: "When you idiots come through there and pee on the floor, I will not clean that up." Markus told the others that they had to take better care of the room. Most of the boys wanted to rearrange the beds so that they were all perpendicular to the walls. Rolf didn't want to be in the midst of the other boys and argued for one of the beds near one of two windows at the end of the room, a bed that was currently occupied by a chap who had a propensity toward flatulence. It was agreed that Rolf could have that bed, but then, as he later recalled, he told the others that "I'm not sleeping in the same bed as the boy who farted," and he insisted on switching beds with the boy. Joe, who had observed this discussion silently, and who occupied the bed near the other window so that his bed was closest to Rolf's, took Rolf aside and said to him: "I have no axe to grind, but I heard how you interact with the other people here and it seems to me that you need to get yourself more educated so you can stand on your own feet and not be influenced so much by what others say." Thus began Joe Haberer's influence on Rolf Möllerich's education.

Rolf's educational future was very much in flux at the time he arrived at the Hollybank Hostel. Although Rolf's official file reflects that he had "settled down all right" with respect to life at the hostel within two weeks of his arrival, and his welfare report was considered "satisfactory," efforts made by the Refugee Children's Movement and Edith during the spring and summer of 1944 to have him placed in a secondary school specializing in technical education proved more difficult than they had anticipated. Rolf failed the entrance examination at the Paddington Technical College as well as for the Northampton Technical College, and he was deemed "too old" and "below standard" for entrance in the Northampton Junior Technical School. As a result, it was decided in August that Rolf should continue his general secondary education at the nearby Northampton School for Boys. Having experienced difficulty in two separate secondary schools while in Peterborough, Rolf had fallen so far behind in his general studies that it would require a true reversal in the way in which he applied himself to his education during the remainder of his time in secondary school if he would ever have an opportunity to obtain a technical education at the college level. Throughout 1944, neither Edith, nor the movement's social worker, nor especially Rolf himself had the confidence that the boy could change significantly with respect to his education. Rolf was particularly concerned because he felt he had taken steps backward in his education and that he was running out of time. Joe Haberer told Rolf that he had the time, that he needed to go to the library, read books, not only associated with school work but more generally in order to become more knowledgeable about his own environment as well as the world beyond his milieu. "He said that I was like him in that we were both torn away from our parents," he later recalled, "and that I had to be able to form my own opinions and get an education so that I would have the tools to succeed in life. That was the first time since leaving Germany that I felt like I had gotten my father's smack. It was a wake-up call that I had been wasting my time. That conversation was one of the most important ones I had the entire time I was in England."

Although in Peterborough the signs of war—namely bombing and strafing of the town by the Luftwaffe—had largely ended by the spring of 1941, in more industrial Northampton that was not the case. When Rolf arrived in Northampton in January 1944, the presence of war was more clearly visible. The city had a network of barrage balloons in place overhead, as well as anti-aircraft units and machine gun emplacements on rooftops all over the city and its environs. Bombings over Northampton by the Luftwaffe had virtually ceased by the spring of 1941, but periodically squadrons of German fighters would cross the North Sea and strafe the city, usually prompting dogfights with RAF Spitfires overhead. Rolf was fascinated by the aerial combat, which he witnessed from time to time, especially until early June 1944. After the D-day invasion there were few, if any incidents of attacks on Northampton by the Luftwaffe. "It was fun watching this in the air," he later recalled, "because the Spitfires would make loops and were able to outmaneuver the German fighters." Shortly after the D-day invasion, however, the Third Reich developed and deployed V-1 rocket attacks on England. Nicknamed "buzz bombs" by the British, the rockets were retrofitted pilot-less winged planes with a large bomb attached that would be fired from Germany and travel at around 350 miles per hour for a pre-set distance and heading, all the while announcing their presence with a loud buzzing sound that could be heard from the ground. Once a rocket reached its destination, the engine would shut off and the rocket would plummet to the ground and deliver nearly a 2,000 pound payload. It was estimated that Germany fired over 8,500 V-1 rockets on England—mostly on London but periodically on other industrial centers—and on the port city of Antwerp in Belgium once it had been liberated by the Allies. Fortunately, only slightly more than 50 percent of the rockets fired actually hit their targets; the remaining rockets were destroyed by a combination of barrage balloons, anti-aircraft fire, and RAF fighters. Sometimes the explosions from the shot down rockets, however, caused severe damage as they exploded on British soil. Unlike conventional German aircraft bombing raids, V-1 attacks occurred around the clock in all types of weather, striking indiscriminately, causing suspense and terror among the populations of British cities, especially London, which took a particularly heavy toll in lives lost and property damage, especially during the initial onslaught of launches beginning on June 13, 1944, one week after D-day.

For Rolf and his co-residents of the Hollybank Hostel, the incidence of V-1 rockets appearing over Northampton was fairly minimal, with the buzzing sound heard perhaps twice a week, and these occasions sparked considerably more interest than terror among the boys. Joe said to Rolf, "The next time we hear one of those V-1 rockets coming, let's go up on the roof to get a closer look." The window of the boys' third level bedroom overlooked a section of the roof of the hostel because that part of the building had only two levels at that point, so they could sit on the ledge of their windows with their feet firmly planted on the roof and watch the V-1s flying over the city. Most of these rockets were targeted for nearby and much larger and industrialized Birmingham rather than Northampton, and so the primary danger from these attacks would have been if the rockets had been incorrectly targeted or the engine failed, or if they were shot down by anti-aircraft or the RAF. Aside from watching the V-1 rockets during the summer of 1944, the boys who did not have jobs, and this included Rolf and Joe, spent most of their time riding bicycles around the town, participating in sports in the field behind the hostel or at a nearby sports complex, going to a local showing of a movie, or engaging in typical teenage horseplay.

In the fall of 1944, Rolf entered his final year of secondary school. He had turned 14 the previous May and had adjusted quite well to life in the Hollybank hostel since his arrival, even to the point of showing some improvement in his study habits regarding school. But with the summer break, Rolf began to fall back on his old study habits once the school year began. His preference after school was to ride his bike around the city, sometimes on his own and sometimes with other boys from the hostel who did not have jobs. But when he asked Joe to accompany him, Joe took that occasion to chastise him: "You see," he told Rolf, "this is what I'm trying to impress on you: riding is okay but you need to get to the library and use the books to help you decide what you want to do for your career. Look at education as the bridge that takes you on the path to your destination." Joe continued to remind Rolf about what his father had told him regarding the importance of education. "I told him," Rolf remembered, "that I was constantly aware of that but it was in the back of my mind." Rolf was, in fact, truly impressed with Joe's thirst for knowledge and focus on education. He later recalled that "it felt like a wakeup call each time Joe mentioned the word 'education.' He pounded me with it and never let up." The persistent encourage-ment from Joe eventually paid off. As the school year went on, Rolf not only applied himself in his classes but began to attend Shabbat services and programs held on weekends and during the evenings on week nights at B'nai Akivah, a local synagogue, where talks were held both on Jewish topics as well as on current events, especially on the war. Many of the boys at the hostel took great interest in Allied progress toward the defeat of Germany and listened to the radio reports on the BBC, which became considerably more positive once the Allies turned back the German counterattack in the Battle of the Bulge at the end of December 1944. Rolf began recording the increasingly favorable war news in a daily journal entry shortly thereafter.

The spring of 1945 brought several major events in Rolf's life. The week before Easter, which fell on April 1 in 1945, Rolf successfully passed his exams and completed secondary school. Then, on April 9, he began a full-time job as a maintenance engineer's assistant at Pettit and Sons Ltd. Trade Leather Dressers. The job had been arranged through the Refugee Children's Movement and had required substan-tial paperwork over the course of the previous several weeks to en-able Rolf to begin his first job. Rolf was assigned as a leather sorter in the inspection department, where he was responsible for grading the leather after the tanning process and then placing a rope around each bundle of inspected leather with the color corresponding to the quality of the product based on its assigned grade. As part of his training, the company also had Rolf attend basic engineering classes each Tuesday after work for the first few weeks of his employment. Another aspect of his indoctrination on the job was to locate a piece of equipment called a "long stand." For this Rolf had to go into the factory and ended up walking from one end of the building to the other, each time asking for a "long stand" and each time being told to wait while an employee presumably went off to fetch the equipment for him—except the employee never returned. After several futile attempts and considerable time walking around the factory and standing and waiting, Rolf noticed one veteran employee approaching him. "You're new here, aren't you?" he asked, as Rolf later recalled. Rolf nodded and said he needed the "long stand" because he was eager to get to work. The employee responded: "Haven't you had enough of a 'long stand' by now?" and broke out into laughter. "They were pulling my leg," he later noted, "and that was my introduction to the Pettit Company." Rolf did well enough at this job to earn several small increases in pay in fairly rapid succession.

The third major event in Rolf's life that occurred in the spring of 1945 was the end of the war in Europe. By that time, England had been at war for more than five years and victory had come gradually and at a high price. At the Hollybank Hostel the boys had been listening intently for weeks to the BBC reports on the war that became more optimistic virtually each day. Rolf recalled also hearing the sad news of President Roosevelt's death on April 12. He made cryptic notations in his daily journal (usually "good news") except every few days over the last few weeks of the war he would specify the news in brief detail if it was especially good. Even while he was in Peterborough, Rolf had listened with the Jenkinson family to Churchill's inspiring speeches broadcast on the radio. He found Churchill's voice "firm, but calming and assuring." The almost daily favorable war news in late April and early May 1945 met with cheers among the boys listening to the radio at the Hollybank Hostel. On May 7, at 9:00 p.m., the boys gathered around the radio in the hostel and listened to speeches by King George VI and by Churchill, who delivered the joyous announcement that Germany had surrendered unconditionally (signed on May 8). The next two days were national holidays featuring parades and celebrations throughout England.

Rolf continued working successfully at Pettit through the summer and into the fall of 1945, when he rather suddenly learned he would be moving again—this time to another hostel located in the city of Birmingham. The impetus for this move, once again, was Edith. Although she was satisfied that Rolf was successfully employed and earning a fair wage, she remained concerned about his education. At age 15 and having graduated from secondary school, Rolf was no longer required to attend school, but Edith remained keen on his pursuing his education in a technical field, as Rolf wished to do. The problem in Northampton had been that Rolf had not been able to qualify to attend the technical colleges there, due to his overall substandard general education performance and test scores on entrance examinations. After Edith consulted with the Refugee Children's Movement's social worker assigned to Rolf in Northampton, it was decided that Rolf should be moved to the much larger city of Birmingham where it might be possible for him to attend a technical college and continue working simultaneously. Rolf was informed of the move in mid-October but continued working until he received his release from Pettit on October 24.

That night Rolf packed his things and went to "Rabbi" Marx to say farewell. He also asked Marx to retrieve the billfold that he had left in the director's custody upon arriving at the Hollybank Hostel. As Rolf later recalled, Marx opened the safe and immediately became upset because there was a billfold in there with the initials RWM on it but he was certain that this billfold belonged to his son. He showed the billfold to Rolf, who said, "That's mine." Marx asked him how he knew it was Rolf's and not his son's billfold. "Mine has my initials at the bottom, just like this one," he responded. Marx then relaxed his expression, realizing that his son's billfold had the initials in the center, and acknowledged that the one he had taken from the safe belonged to Rolf and handed it to him. The two parted as friends, so much so that years later Rolf learned that Marx had moved to the state of New Jersey in the United States and he tried to locate him but was ultimately unsuccessful at reconnecting. After the encounter with Marx, Rolf spent the remainder of the evening saying his farewells to the boys at the Hollybank Hostel, especially the five boys with whom he had shared a room since arriving almost two years earlier. They spoke about remaining in contact and visiting each other, but Rolf was not certain at that moment whether he would see any of his friends again. Leaving Joe was particularly difficult, even though the two pledged to keep in touch, and did so over the course of several years. Reflecting on that relationship, Rolf later indicated: "I can honestly say that I thought that Joe Haberer was my big brother." The next day, October 25, 1945, Rolf moved to Birmingham.

The train ride between Northampton and Birmingham, located about 55 miles to the west, took only about an hour. The hostel was situated in the southwestern suburb of Edgbaston at 117 Gough Road, a heavily tree-lined street featuring large homes. The hostel itself was, in fact, a very large mansion-like building that accommodated 60 boys in 1945, along with a number of staff who lived there and several others who worked at the hostel but lived elsewhere. When Rolf arrived the hostel was nearly full. Like the Hollybank Hostel in Northampton, most of the boys living at the Birmingham hostel were at least teenagers if not older, and so Rolf again found himself to be among the youngest of the residents at age 15. Besides kitchen and maintenance staff, there was a small educational staff who were available for boys needing tutoring in Hebrew, since the hostel was traditional orthodox and daily services were conducted only in Hebrew, and also to assist those boys who needed tutoring in their secular school subjects. Rolf had by this time improved his Hebrew skills, and his secular subject knowledge as well, so that he did not require tutoring, especially since he expected to focus on technical education, which he presumed was the primary reason for his being moved to Birmingham. "I was doing better with learning," he later recalled, "but I needed help with social adjustment—how to deal better with people, how to interact better with my peers."

Fortunately for Rolf, there was a full-time counselor on site, whom he met almost immediately after his arrival. The counselor, it turned out, was a refugee from Vienna, and therefore was someone whom Rolf could easily relate to and so Rolf told him how he had come to England from Germany and quite a bit about his life in England, but he could not talk about the loss of his parents. "He told me he knew what I went through," Rolf later recalled about the counselor; "he understood the type of trauma that I had experienced." Rolf explained about his insecurities, and about some of his behavioral problems experienced in Peterborough with some of the other boys there. "He told me I needed to take charge of my own life," he later recalled, "that I should ask myself if something is appropriate behavior and if it is representative of how my parents would have wanted me to grow up." Rolf realized that he had heard similar words before with respect to education—from Joe Haberer—and that he needed to focus on his behavior as well as his education. "All of a sudden a light went on and I realized how bad my behavior had been for me. From then on, I became an introvert instead of an extrovert, and that carried me through for several years forward."

Rolf adjusted rather quickly to life at the Birmingham hostel and after two weeks he was ready to take on a new full-time job at the Sheridan Precision LTD Tool and Die Company, which was located just a short distance from the hostel on the south side of Birmingham at 5 Sherbourne Road. The company mostly produced ball bearings that served as fixtures to move both furniture and heavy equipment, similar to a very heavy version of ball casters. Because the manufactured products, which were called "jigs," could be used for military equipment, the British government was one of the company's best customers, as there was an urgent need to rebuild so much of what had been lost in the war. Rolf took a job as an apprentice general maintenance engineer, for which he received a very fair salary that dwarfed his wages in Northampton. He was placed under the tutelage of a gentleman whom he addressed as "Professor," and who was the master tool and die chief. Within a very short time he had learned about most of the hand tools required to produce the "jigs." He also learned to perform maintenance on the equipment and so, as he recalled, "I quickly had a pretty good introduction to tools, how to use them correctly, and how to care for them." He learned how the hand-operated punch presses were used to produce the "jigs," and observed the assembly line process, which required for the largest of the punch presses—a 10-ton press—a team of four women to produce a half-bucket of the finished products each day. The process was not only slow but required great physical stamina because of the repetitive arm motions needed to operate the press. It was also inherently dangerous operating the heavy equipment, even with built-in safety measures required to use it.

Rolf spent a few days observing how the assembly line process worked, especially for the largest punch press, and thought about a possible way to automate it in order to vastly increase the efficiency of the process and the volume of finished products. One day he waited until after 5:00 p.m. when everyone was gone and then set out on his task, beginning by making mental notes of every step necessary to automate the process. He conjured a way to make the press continuously feed, punch, and disgorge multiple finished units without stopping in between to reset itself and without overheating, allowing him to hold his foot down on the operating pedal so that the press worked without pause, punching out one unit after another with a rapid pop, pop, pop noise. After about two and a half hours, Rolf had filled six buckets of finished units. In doing so he had virtually solved the automation question but had taken risks by circumventing most of the built-in safety requirements in the process.

The next morning when Rolf arrived at work, the professor and several other workers were standing next to the filled buckets from the night before, deep in conversation. Some of the workers were scratching their heads. When Rolf walked in, the discussion ceased and the professor asked Rolf if he knew anything about the filled buckets. Rolf began to explain what he had done the previous day after work, that he had a passion for doing something creative to ease the physical burden on the women and at the same time make the production process far more efficient. As Rolf later recalled, the professor said that he must have worked straight through the night to have produced what he did. Rolf told him that it took less than three hours from start to finish. He said he stopped because he became hungry and so he cleaned up, turned off the lights, and left. The professor was far more angry than impressed. "What do you think you are doing here?" he began. "We don't allow this; it is dangerous for you to be alone, especially because you are an apprentice." He then told Rolf he would have to take him to see the company president because safety rules had been broken and what Rolf had done was "most unusual." Just at that moment the company president came out of his office and approached the group. The professor explained what he had discovered and what Rolf told him he had done after work the previous day. "Those buckets are filled to the top and are so heavy that it will take at least two men to carry them," he exclaimed. "I cannot condone what was done here." The president was far more impressed than angry. "I see a young man who is creative, who has ingenuity, and has taken initiative, and I applaud that." He told the professor and other employees to get back to work, and escorted Rolf into his office. He then said to him: "I know you did something that was close to your heart by finding a way to automate what we are doing here by hand, and I commend you for that. But you do not have to violate safety rules because I would never have forgiven myself if you had gotten hurt badly in this shop. I can see a young person with abilities and talent, someone who is a thinker, which is pretty rare around here. Automating this line would be heaven for me and for this company." He then asked Rolf to write down everything he thought about and then did—and the reasons for doing what he did, step by step. He asked him to diagram his ideas for automating the production process. He told Rolf he was going to enroll him immediately in courses at the Birmingham Polytechnic Institute. He would come to work during the day and take courses in basic mechanical engineering, along with mathematics and chemistry, every day after work. The president later handed him a certificate and a letter and said to him, "Whenever you want a job in an engineering firm, here's a letter of recommendation you can use."

And so it was that in the autumn of 1945, Rolf felt that he finally belonged somewhere. He had developed his English skills so quickly after arriving in England nearly seven years earlier that he spoke with virtually no German accent, although his was not a classic British accent either, and his writing skills were still improving. He was making a decent wage in a place where he felt useful and where he was able to contribute while embarking on an educational path that would lead to a career in engineering, thus honoring his father's wishes. His life for the first time seemed to have purpose and he had been true to his sister's instructions to put his life in Germany behind him. He had entered into a lively, ongoing correspondence with Joe Haberer and a few of the other boys from the Northampton hostel during the winter and early spring of 1946. Although they were not too far away from him in Northampton, Rolf found it difficult with his job and coursework to find the time to see them, but the exchange of letters cheered him and made it feel almost as if they were together. Joe, especially, filled many pages of correspondence with news about Rolf's former roommates at the Northampton hostel. Markus had gone off to Belgium and seemed to be happy there. Martin was working occasionally in London as an apprentice in an art studio and taking in a movie at least once a week. Joe had started writing short books and encouraged Rolf to describe what he was doing in great detail, which would help provide him with ideas for his writing projects. As always, Joe found a way to include advice for Rolf in some of his letters: "I am well and never worry," he wrote. "If there is anything to worry about I try to solve it to the best of my ability. That's the best policy." Between his job, his educational courses and his correspondence with friends, for the first time since he was a very young child, Rolf began to rediscover what it was like to be happy. Then, in April 1946, he received news that turned his world upside down.

# CHAPTER 6

—— ❧ ——

# Immigration to the United States (April–June 1946)

THE TELEPHONE RANG at the Gough Road Boy's Hostel in Birmingham the evening of April 11, 1946, with a call for Rolf from Edith. She told Rolf, in her flat, matter-of-fact tone that their United States visas and affidavits had been approved; they had cleared the United States immigration quotas and had been issued exit visas from the British government. Their cousins Gretl and Ruth in New York were arranging passage for them, and Edith told Rolf she would let him know their departure date as soon as she was informed, but that he should prepare himself for a one-way journey to the United States. Rolf was stunned, although the news could not have come as a complete surprise to him. He had been required to come to London to join his sister for a meeting with a representative from the American Consulate on February 26, 1945, in which they were both interviewed to begin the process of obtaining United States visas. The previous September Edith had told Rolf—who was at that time still in Northampton—she had engaged in an exchange of correspondence with their cousins Gretl and Joe Rosenthal and Ruth Schloss in which the cousins had expressed their intention of sponsoring the two of them so they could join the family in New York. The cousins pooled their limited resources and found the means to purchase visas for them and arrange passage once the complex immigration paperwork was fully approved. But the wheels of the immigration bureaucracies, both in the United States and in England, had moved at a predictably glacial pace and more than a year had passed since that time, in part because Edith had completed her final nursing requirements and had become a full-time nurse, and there were restrictions in England on active nurses emigrating from the country while England was still at war and even for several months after the war ended. It was not until January 1946 that new affidavits were signed and the paperwork process was completed with the issuance of exit visas at the end of March. Edith told Rolf he should inform the hostel director and his boss at Sheridan Precision that he would be leaving for the United States sometime after Easter—so that he could complete his coursework for the semester at the Birmingham Polytechnic Institute—and that he should pack so he could be prepared to leave on short notice, probably no later than the beginning of May.

There had been a time when news of a departure for America to join family would have been for Rolf a moment of great joy. He remembered the long discussions in Wolfhagen and again in Hamburg, all the planning his parents had done in hope of moving the family to the United States. He also remembered begging his cousin Gretl to take him with her to New York when she visited him in Peterborough in the summer of 1940. But he had been much younger then, before he had developed a vision of a future career and embarked on a path to get there. When Edith told him to prepare for the journey to the United States, Rolf later recalled, "I didn't want to go; I wanted to stay and continue what I was doing." He immediately wrote to his friends at the Northampton Hollybank Hostel, Joe and Martin, who were actually quite happy and excited for Rolf. "So you are going to dear old America," Joe wrote on April 29. "Congratulations—a good trip and all the best in America; I am sure you will do well there, at school and work." Joe asked Rolf to send along his address in America so they could continue their correspondence, and also indicated that he might be coming to America soon as well. The next day Edith called Rolf to let him know that their departure had been scheduled for May 2 and that he had to come to London to join her the day before that. Rolf took the train to London as he was told but continued to resist leaving England. "I kept telling my sister that I really wanted to stay in England," he later recalled. He was about to turn age 16 and believed he was prepared to be completely on his own. Edith would have none of that. She told him: "You have no choice—you are going;" and for Rolf that was that. Word then arrived that their departure had been delayed for two weeks and that they were now scheduled to sail to New York on May 17 on the Swedish American liner *Gripsholm*. Rolf did not enjoy having to share the flat in the Belsize Park section of London with his sister and three other women, but he could not go back to Birmingham, and so he sent one more letter to Joe Haberer, enclosing a photograph of himself, which his friend very much appreciated ("I carry it on me always," Joe wrote on May 15), and awaited his sailing to the United States.

Rolf and Edith arose early on the morning of Friday, May 17, 1946. They ate breakfast mostly in silence and then took a taxi loaded with their belongings (Edith's two suitcases and Rolf's one), to Euston Street Station, where they boarded a train bound for Liverpool, some four hours to the northwest. At exactly 9:45 a.m., the train left London carrying 600 passengers to Liverpool. As it turned out, the train was special in two respects: almost every passenger was immigrating to the United States, and each passenger on the train was sailing on the *Gripsholm*, and therefore the train took all the passengers directly to the dock area along the Mersey River instead of to one of Liverpool's railroad stations. Rolf recorded in his first journal entry of the journey: "As soon as we got near Liverpool, you could see water all around us." At approximately 2:00 p.m., everyone on the train was ushered into a building with a large hall divided into two sections, while scores of porters took away everyone's luggage for loading on the ship. Rolf and Edith had a seat and waited; it was not long before their names were called to join the queue to have their boarding passes checked and stamped. They then went to another table where a page was pulled from each of their travel documents. Once that was done, they passed into the second large hall, which served as a waiting area for everyone embarking on the ship. Here Rolf and Edith found seats and were served a light lunch of toast with jam, scones, tarts, and tea from the snack bar. It was close to 5:00 p.m. by the time passengers began boarding the ship. Boarding passes were checked twice more, once when Rolf and Edith departed the waiting area, and again at the gangway bridge upon which they boarded the ship. The line for this latter process moved slowly, so that by the time they had boarded the ship and were shown to their cabins, it was nearly 5:45 p.m. It had been an exhausting and anxious day for Rolf, but upon boarding the ship he could feel his excitement building.

When he stepped on board the *MS. Gripsholm*, Rolf had no idea that he was about to sail on a unique ship. The *Gripsholm* had been built in 1924 for the Swedish American Line by Armstrong Whitworth in Newcastle-upon-Tyne, and was the very first ocean liner propelled by diesel engines rather than steam power. A relatively modest-sized vessel even by early 20th century standards at just under 18,000 gross registered tons and under 600 feet in

length from bow to stern, the ship nevertheless provided comfortable to luxurious accommodations for the roughly 1,500 passengers on board depending, of course, on the class of cabin reserved. Originally built for transatlantic sailings between Gothenburg, Sweden, and New York, the United States had chartered the ship during the Second World War for the purpose of exchanges and repatriation. Beginning in 1946 the ship returned to its transatlantic sailings under a Swedish crew. The May 17 sailing from Liverpool was somewhat unusual in that the ship sailed from Liverpool under the auspices of the Cunard White Star Line, and in that more than one-third of the passengers were in immigrant status, most notably a significant number of unescorted young people who had been

brought to England in 1938 and 1939 as part of the Kindertransport program, among them Edith and Rolf Möllerich.

The cabins that Rolf and Edith occupied were located on E Deck,
the lowest passenger deck on the ship, situated about eight feet below the water line where all the cabins were assigned to "standard" or
third-class passengers. Rolf's cabin was 647, and he occupied the berth
labeled "B;" Edith's cabin was next door in 645, and she occupied the
berth labeled "A." Each shared their room with three other people so
that the room was cramped with double bunk beds, and was hot most
of the time. Later, once he had an opportunity to explore the ship, Rolf
would soon discover, much to his surprise, that "there was a vast difference between first-class and third-class" passenger status. At 6:00 p.m.
Edith and Rolf went to the third class dining room for supper, as they
were quite hungry by then. They were told that they had been assigned
to the second seating, which was not until 7:30 p.m., but the dining
room manager accommodated them for the 6:00 p.m. seating, which
they retained for the remainder of the voyage. This required them to
have breakfast at 8:00 a.m., dinner (lunch) at noon; tea at 3:00 p.m.;
and "supper" each evening at 6:00 p.m. Rolf enjoyed "a good meal"
that first evening and then went up to the top deck. He had met a man
on the train ride to Liverpool named Ray Kemp who had been a sailor.
The two had struck up a conversation and Rolf noticed him standing on
the deck and the two of them explored the ship. Given his interest in
machines, Rolf listened intently to Ray's explanation of the various parts
of the ship and how everything worked on board. They were eagerly
awaiting delivery of the luggage and interrupted the exploration of the
ship every 15 minutes to check for their bags. At around 9:00 p.m., while
searching for his luggage among a group of bags on E Deck, Rolf turned
to Ray and said, "It feels as if we are moving." Ray told Rolf that this was
not possible as the ship was scheduled to depart at 10:00 p.m. But they
rushed up to the top deck to have a look. "There you are," Rolf said to
Ray as they watched the ship slide away from the pier into the center
of the Mersey River and sail the short distance into the Irish Sea. Rolf

recorded in his journal: "I was so excited and I watched the coast until it was out of sight." When he returned to E Deck, he discovered that Edith already had both pieces of her luggage and Ray had one out of two of his. They searched again and Ray found his second bag, which he took to his cabin and he then returned to help Rolf look for his single bag. As he walked along the E Deck corridor, Rolf noticed a suitcase that looked quite similar to his, except that it was not in as good a condition as the one he had left with the porter at the terminal. He checked the label and, "to my astonishment," he wrote in his journal, "it was mine." It was after 11:00 p.m. Exhausted, Rolf said good night to Ray and took the bag to his cabin, where his three cabin mates were already in bed. He briefly introduced himself to the young man in the bunk below him whose name was George Wellworth, who was British and immigrating to the United States with his parents, who occupied their own cabin. Rolf's journal entry for that first day of the voyage concludes: "The small cabin was so hot and stuffy that it prevented me from going to sleep. The ship was swaying from side to side." The motion of the ship, however, eventually helped Rolf to fall asleep.

The next morning Rolf awoke feeling queasy. He had some breakfast and "felt a bit better." Rushing up to the top deck, he spent much of the day breathing in the sea air but feeling increasingly ill toward supper time. Not knowing what to do, he ate his meal and was just finishing his last potato when someone told him he looked "very pale." Rolf pushed himself from the table and made a dash for the lavatory, "and up it came," he wrote in his journal later in the voyage. So violently was he ill that his nose began to bleed, as it did from time to time because of the deviated septum that was diagnosed much later in his life. "I must have been two hours in that lav," he recorded, "because as soon as I tried to get up and go out, I felt all dizzy and sick." Finally he managed to drag himself down to his cabin, where he collapsed on his bed and fell asleep without getting out of his clothes. In the morning, he skipped breakfast, but asked George, who had the second seating, to bring back a couple of slices of bread. After wolfing down the bread to fill his empty stomach, Rolf got dressed and went topside, found a deck chair, and slept in the sun most of the day. When he awoke, it was evening and he recorded in his journal that he "felt a lot better." Before bedtime, he saw Ray and described his illness over the past 24 hours. Ray gave him some good advice, which he wrote in his journal and would remember thereafter: "When you feel seasick, always eat plenty of bread, plenty of solid food." Following that advice the next day, Rolf felt more like himself again; the beautiful, sunny weather contributed to his improved health. He spent much of the day on the deck, relaxing and listening to music played by the band. By the end of the day, Rolf felt completely well.

The next day, Tuesday, May 21, Rolf finally saw Edith again. It turned out that she had suffered seasickness from the moment the ship sailed, but finally felt much better. She had also made a couple of friends on board, and for the next three days she and Rolf, joined by their friends on the ship, spent most of their days on the outside deck, enjoying warm and sunny weather, calm seas, and relatively gentle breezes for the North Atlantic. Rolf discovered more about the world of first class on the ship, noting that every night there was dancing or films or concerts, the latter off limits to third-class passengers. He sometimes tried to get into the first-class shows and venues but mostly was sent away by staff stationed at the doorways. Once or twice he was "lucky" and "managed to get in some of these posh places." Sitting among the first class passengers and listening to a concert, he closed his eyes and visualized what it must be like sailing in first-class status. "When you are in first class," he recorded in his journal, "you can almost imagine you are in a palace, where only the lord and noblemen live." The idyll passed and Rolf spent the remainder of his evenings on board mostly watching films shown in the third-class dining room or listening to music and watching the dancing. During the days it became increasingly hot. Spending so much of their time on the deck, Rolf and Edith both became sunburned. On Friday, May 24, the weather began to moderate, much to Rolf's "relief." He heard rumors that the ship—although averaging a speed of only about 15 knots—would arrive in New York harbor at 9:00 p.m., more than two days ahead of schedule. "I was so excited that I tried to stay up until we were there, but I might have known it was only a rumor," he wrote in his journal.

Saturday the weather changed considerably, as the ship was shrouded in fog and when Rolf awoke he heard the ship's fog horn go off once every minute. After breakfast Rolf borrowed a pair of binoculars from one of Edith's friends and spent hours peering through the fog and haze. All he could see was an occasional group of what he thought at the time were sharks, but more likely were dolphins, as the ship sailed on. He noted in his journal that he had seen only six other vessels during the week the ship had been at sea. That afternoon the captain held his "farewell dinner." For the third-class passengers, this meal turned out to be the best of the voyage: chicken soup, chicken with roast potatoes and peas, spinach, and gravy, with assorted fresh fruit and ice cream for dessert. Rolf feasted on this meal and afterward was too full to walk the deck or stand at the railing. He sat down and peered out to sea with the borrowed binoculars. Out of the mist Rolf began to see the outline of "strange buildings" and other structures. By nightfall the ship approached Coney Island, all lit up, and Rolf could again see many "fantastic buildings" also outlined in light in the distance. As the ship approached New York harbor, it slowed considerably. Rolf went to bed around midnight, but recorded in his journal that "hundreds of passengers remained on deck" as he turned in.

On Sunday morning, May 26, passengers were notified that the ship would arrive in New York at noon, but due to having arrived a day early, the ship would remain anchored in the harbor until Monday morning. Rolf learned a little later in the day that the ship had to lie at anchor in the harbor to allow health officials to come aboard. Several passengers were in the sick bay with what the ship's doctor had diagnosed as possible infectious illnesses and so the health officials had to check on these passengers and record a list of their names before the ship could be allowed to dock. As recorded in Rolf's journal, the health officials took pains to assure the passengers that "there was nothing to fear; they were just checking the extent of those passengers who were ill." That process took but a few hours. Meanwhile the captain had advised the passengers to come to the top deck on the starboard side. Rolf rushed topside and managed to find a place along the starboard railing. There, just a few hundred yards away, stood the Statue of Liberty. The ship was anchored in such a way," he later recalled, "that there was a broadside view of the Statue of Liberty." He recorded in his journal: "The sky was blue, the breeze was invigorating, and the view of the 'Lady of the Harbor' prompted a flow of adrenalin within me."

After a while many of the passengers became impatient, anxious for the ship to dock, and made their way to their cabins to pack up their things, even though the ship would not reach the pier and disembark passengers until the next morning. Rolf remained topside at the starboard railing, taking in the view of New York City with great excitement. "The skyline was gorgeous," he later recalled, "and the Empire State Building was the tallest building at that time. I just marveled at the architecture that was very different from England, very different from what I remembered in Germany. The buildings did not have the ornamental designs like in Europe, but they looked as if they were piercing the clouds—at least it seemed that way to me." He also saw cars whizzing by in the distance along what he later learned was the West Side Highway. He was fascinated by the many yellow vehicles and didn't realize at the time that they were taxis. Gazing at the scene before him, Rolf suddenly became introspective. He thought about his life, how he had lived as a child for eight years in Germany; how he had spent his boyhood living eight years in England; and how now, as he approached adulthood, he was about to embark on a life in America. As had been the case all too many times in his still brief lifetime when he had been uprooted from what had been familiar and comfortable and compelled to face a new and unknown future, Rolf's rush of adrenalin faded and was overtaken by a sense of anxiety. "My thoughts there on the ship that morning were about what was going to happen to me when I set foot on US ground," he later recalled. "I was worried because there were no plans; we really didn't know where we were going to stay at the beginning." Edith had mentioned to him during the voyage that it was possible they would stay with one of the cousins who had sponsored them, but she left the impression that this would likely be temporary, at least for herself, in part because she had the feeling that the cousins in New York were not to be trusted. Although she did not elaborate at the time, in part because she had made plans to work as a nurse and at age 25 was very much inclined to be on her own, Rolf found his sister's self-absorption a bit unsettling. Of greater concern to him was his own immediate future. He had completed his required schooling in England and had begun a course of technical education toward a career as an engineer. He had spoken to some educators on the ship who had told him that he would probably have to repeat the senior year of high school in the United States because the education system in England proceeds at a more rapid pace. Insecurities about expanding his skills in English, especially his desire to read more and to learn more about history and geography, which had never been a priority during his early years of schooling in England, and which Joe Haberer had impressed upon him as essential to his preparation for adulthood, overcame him while he stared at the New York skyline. As he turned away from the ship's starboard railing and headed down to his cabin to pack, Rolf felt an all too familiar knot in his stomach as he contemplated an uncertain future in an unfamiliar land.

On Monday, May 27, 1946, which happened to be Rolf's 16th birthday, a fact he noted in the final entry of his journal maintained during the cruise, the *Gripsholm* docked at a pier located at West 46th Street along the Hudson River. Disembarkation was a long and exhausting process that began for Rolf and Edith at 10:00 a.m. and lasted most of the day, causing Rolf to conclude his final journal entry with the comment that "This was the worst day of the entire journey." The day remained etched in Rolf's memory because many years later when he was con-templating taking a cruise, he was reluctant because of the unpleasant disembarkation in 1946 and was very much relieved after having done so to discover that cruising was actually a wonderful experience. On the morning of disembarkation from the *Grispsholm*, third-class pas-sengers, who comprised a majority of the ship's complement of pas-sengers, were the last to disembark. It was well after 11:00 a.m. when Rolf and Edith were allowed to queue near the gangway and wait to exit the ship. Peering below at the dock, Rolf saw his Cousin Gretl among the rather large group assembled waiting to meet disembarking pas-sengers. He had last seen her in Peterborough almost six years earlier, but he recalled that she was easily recognizable and looked no different than at their last meeting, other than the fact that she had been almost nine months pregnant at the time he saw her in Peterborough. Just be-fore they walked down the gangway, Edith turned to Rolf and told him to stay very close to her "every inch of the way during the disembarka-tion process."

Once off the ship, Rolf and Edith had to find the proper line for the immigration and customs process, so that Rolf had no time to reflect that he had just set foot in America for the first time. It appeared to him that all 1,500 passengers had crowded into the terminal building at the same moment and were searching for their place to queue. Rolf had a serious concern about locating the luggage, and was "a little bit uneasy" about meeting his cousins; but there was nothing he could do about either issue at that time. Once they found the proper line, Edith and Rolf waited more than an hour for their turn with the immigration and customs official. When that moment came, Rolf was the first to be interviewed. He was asked whether he spoke English, to which he quickly responded, "Yes, of course." He gave his name and date of birth, and was a bit surprised that the official ignored the coincidence that it was his birthday. He then told the official that he was with his sister and pointed to her waiting about 10 feet away at the front of the line, but she was not asked to come forward yet. Rolf was then asked a series of questions about Edith, including the name of the school she attended in Frankfurt, which he had never known. He mentioned that Edith had trained to be a nurse and worked at the St. James Hospital in London, and was asked if she was an "RN." Rolf was not certain what that was, but of course knew that Edith had achieved a nursing certificate in England and later learned that she was certified as a Registered Nurse. At that point the official waved Rolf forward and interviewed Edith while Rolf was weighed and had his height measured, and was asked about his general health—whether he had contracted any illnesses recently, which he had not. Rolf believed that he was "a little on the heavy side because my height wasn't good," but he later acknowledged that he was in good health and "had a pretty good physique, even at age 16." He also later recalled: "I told them that I was a pretty healthy person, and that was the extent to which I was questioned. Nobody asked about my religion." Shortly after that, Edith completed her interviews, joined Rolf, and the two of them sought after their luggage, a process which took long enough that it was late in the afternoon by the time they had retrieved their luggage and passed through the gate to the place in the terminal building where people were waiting to meet disembarking passengers.

Gretl and Joe Rosenthal were standing near the exit gate and greeted Rolf and Edith almost at the moment they passed through the gate. Gretl presented Rolf with a birthday gift—a wide-style dress tie—and explained that they had made room in their apartment on Sherman Avenue in upper Manhattan, north of Washington Heights, for Rolf and Edith to stay with them. Rolf thanked them for the gift and for arranging for the visas and "for being caring enough to provide a place for us to sleep," as he later recalled. The luggage was loaded into the trunk of the sedan and off they went to the apartment. Rolf's first glance at the neighborhood on and around Sherman Avenue "left a terrible impression on me," he later recalled. It was very different from the places he had lived in England, which had fairly open spaces. Sherman Avenue was crowded with one apartment building after another. The building

Gretl and Joe lived in had five stories and no elevator. The Rosenthals lived on the fourth level, so the luggage had to be hauled up three flights of stairs. The apartment itself was quite small and the first thing Rolf noticed was that it was very hot and stuffy. There was not an open window anywhere, even though the weather in late May in New York was quite warm. Joe explained that they did not open the windows much because the people upstairs shook their mops out the window and the building was shaped so that the debris sometimes came into their apartment. The windows had small metal slats which could be opened a little without allowing debris or rain to enter, and that was the extent of the fresh air allowed in the apartment. Looking around, Rolf noticed that the furniture and the floor were heavily glazed with a coating of some kind so that "you could almost see your reflection in the floor, it was so shiny," he later recalled. Rolf and Edith were then introduced to Gretl and Joe's son, Harry, who in May 1946 was three months shy of his sixth birthday.

After the introductions it was time for the evening meal. Rolf and Edith had eaten nothing since breakfast on the ship early that morning and so they were both very hungry. Gretl served delicatessen—a variety of cold cuts known in the New York German-Jewish community as *aufschnitt*. This food was something which Rolf had never eaten in England. Because he was hungry, it looked very appetizing but afterwards it did not agree with him and so he did not feel well the rest of the evening. Joe explained that he built cabinets out of wood and worked in a shop on 27th Street, near Avenue of the Americas, farther downtown in Manhattan. The Rosenthals had purchased an extra bed for Harry's room and so Rolf was again sharing a room, which was a disappointment to him at first. "I thought I was finished sharing a room with somebody after all those hostels in England," he later recalled. But he found Harry to be smart and engaging, despite the 10-year age difference between them. Harry spoke to him at great length that first evening about New York and about school, since he was just about to complete kindergarten. Edith was going to be sleeping on the living room sofa, which converted to a bed, an arrangement that she found to be completely unsuitable. It did not help her disposition when Gretl and Joe made it clear that both Rolf and Edith were to abide by a 10:00 p.m. curfew. This was difficult enough for Rolf, who had been largely able to come and go as he pleased ever since he moved from Peterborough to Northampton, and especially while he was at the Gough Road hostel in Birmingham, when he was working all day and taking classes each night. He accepted the rule, nonetheless, recalling an early lesson upon arriving in England to be a good boy and "keep a stiff upper lip." But for Edith, who was an adult and who had been on her own since arriving in England at age 17, the imposition of a curfew was impossible to accept. She whispered to Rolf before going to bed that first night: "We are getting out of here at the first opportunity."

The next day Joe and Gretl began several days of taking Rolf and Edith around to meet with the relatives who were living in New York, almost all of whom resided in apartments in nearby Washington Heights. This neighborhood had a multiplicity of ethnic groups, but one of the largest was the community of immigrants from Germany, mostly Jewish refugees and their children. Many of the people Rolf met or passed on the street spoke German; "That didn't bother me one bit," he later recalled. "I might have understood some of what they were saying, but I preferred to shut them out—the ones speaking German." Rolf was more interested in meeting the relatives. He recalled his Aunt Sophie and Uncle Hermann and their large house in Volkmarsen, Germany. Rolf came to think of Sophie as the "Queen of the Möllerich family" in New York. He remembered his Uncle Hermann having the habit of whistling and saying "Wow!" every time a beautiful woman went by, and that he was something of "a comedian." He and Edith then visited three of their sons, each of whom was married and had their own apartments in Washington Heights. Rolf learned that his cousin Otto manufactured commercial diamonds and owned a large plant outside New York City. Eugen had completed medical school after arriving in New York in 1936 and was practicing medicine. The third Schwarz brother,

Max, manufactured ladies hats and other accessories and had a factory in downtown Manhattan. Rolf and Edith also visited their cousin Ruth Schoenthal (née Schloss) and her husband, Fred, who lived on West 181st Street in the heart of Washington Heights. Ruth had largely paid for Rolf and Edith's visas, for which Rolf thanked his cousin. Ruth could be abrasive, however, and so Edith wanted as little to do with her as possible. Unlike Rolf, Edith did not thank Ruth for sending the visas, which greatly angered Ruth, and so there was a strained relationship between the two women from the outset.

Edith was largely distracted during the days-long visits with family that first week in New York with other, higher priority concerns. She was anxious to find work and tried to locate a friend she knew from England who had come to New York and taken a job as a nurse and who might be able to help her get a job. There was also a man she had left behind in London—a young English Jewish physician named Michael Cronin—whom she had been dating and who was interested in pursuing a long-term relationship, possibly marriage, with her. Because Edith had gone to the United States, however, Michael did not believe it was possible to continue the relationship. Edith thought otherwise and had determined that she would find a way to return to England, marry Michael, and bring him back to the States with her. She believed this would take a little time to work out and so a more immediate priority was finding a job. But Edith's top priority was getting both herself and Rolf out of the Rosenthal apartment as soon as possible. Because it was necessary in getting from Gretl and Joe's bedroom to the kitchen to pass through the living room, potentially requiring both of them to walk past Edith sleeping on the sofa, in an act of defiance, she slept in the nude. Harry later recalled: "My mother was very upset over that; she told Edith that she couldn't do that with my father having to walk through the room." Edith also defied the curfew, staying out late several evenings, especially after she had connected with her friend from England. But one night she had gone out and then lost her apartment key and came home after 10:00 p.m., so she went up to the roof and climbed down the fire escape and tried to get in through the window. Some people saw her doing that and called the police. Joe and Gretl were furious about that incident and "bawled her out about that," Rolf later recalled.

After living with Gretl and Joe for about three weeks, Edith decided she had endured the situation quite enough and determined to find a new place to live. While it was clear that Edith had worn out her welcome with Gretl and Joe very quickly, so that they would have been perfectly happy to see her leave, Rolf was a more difficult matter. Although Gretl and Joe liked having Rolf living with them, they felt they did not have the financial means to feed and clothe him, nor look after his education, if Edith went off on her own. When Edith announced that she intended to leave, Gretl and Joe told her that she couldn't leave without taking Rolf with her. Edith was adamant about leaving; she explained to Rolf that she "needed to find her own path." Rolf was less interested in Edith's needs than his own at that moment and tried to talk her out of leaving: "How could you think of going somewhere else this soon?" he later recalled telling Edith; "it is so disrespectful to our cousins." She promised to find a place for Rolf where he would be well cared for but made it clear that he would not be living with her. Rolf was torn because while he could understand that Edith was old enough to be living on her own and he was not, he remembered his mother's last request before they boarded the train in Hamburg, that Edith should always take care of her little brother. The next day Edith made some phone calls, and on the morning of June 17, 1946, she and Rolf set out to meet with people who had prospective—and separate—living arrangements for both of them. Before he had hardly settled into a new home with his cousins in a new city and country, Rolf was about to be uprooted once again.

# CHAPTER 7

—— ⚹ ——

# Early Life in the United States (1946–1956)

Rolf gazed up at the woman standing with a stern expression in the doorway of the apartment on West 156th Street. She introduced herself as Miss Just, whom Rolf later described as "a spinster who kept her hair swept back in a bun like a *hausfrau*." It had been a relatively short subway ride from Sherman Avenue south to the 157th Street stop on the Broadway line and a very brief walk to the apartment building located one block south to West 156th Street and around the corner from Broadway on the block heading west toward Riverside Drive and the Hudson River. There had been very little conversation between Rolf and Edith on the way to the apartment, except that Edith had told Rolf to let her do the talking once they arrived. Rolf's mood during the trip was so dispirited that he found it difficult to speak in any case. Now, standing before Miss Just, who didn't speak to him even as he was introduced, Rolf half-listened to the conversation between Edith and the woman as they entered the apartment but remained standing in the foyer. It became clear almost immediately that this apartment was not going to be for Rolf and so he became a little more attentive to the conversation once Edith quickly came to an agreement with the woman on a room there for herself. She then asked Miss Just if she knew of anyone relatively close by who might be willing to take her brother in and care for him in a loving way, as he had been through a difficult time and needed someone to treat him more like family than a boarder. The woman immediately said that she knew of a couple—a Mr. and Mrs.

Simenauer—who lived within easy walking distance of her apartment and who she thought might be interested in taking Rolf in. She gave Edith the address and told her she would call them and let them know Edith and Rolf were on their way to see them.

The walk to the Simenauer apartment turned out to be quite brief indeed. Rolf and Edith only had to retrace their steps to West 157th Street and Broadway, cross to the other side of the street and turn east toward Amsterdam Avenue. The building in which Mr. and Mrs. Simenauer lived was the second in a series of six-story apartment buildings past the corner building on Broadway—at 547 West 157th Street. As they approached the entrance to the building, Rolf and Edith were greeted by an African-American gentleman who introduced himself as Mr. Harris, the maintenance man. He offered to show them to the Simenauer's apartment, which was number 2, located on the ground floor at the end of a long, very dark corridor. The few ceiling light bulbs in that corridor were 25 watts and so it was very difficult to read the numbers on the apartment doors. The maintenance man rapped on the door of apartment 2 and a man from behind the door responded in a gruff voice, "Yes? Who is it?" Mr. Harris said that there were some people there to see him. "I'm not expecting any people; go away!" the voice behind the door responded. Rolf then said that he was sent by Miss Just and asked the voice if he knew the name Möllerich. "No," the voice responded. "Miss Just called a few minutes ago and said somebody would be coming over but I don't know that name." Mr. Harris then said: "Mr. Simenauer, these are people who want to speak to you—open the door." Finally the door opened a crack and there was a chain across it. A pair of eyes squinted from behind the crack trying to see the faces outside the door because the light was so dim in the corridor. The door finally opened fully; Mr. Harris turned to Edith and Rolf and said: "You folks have a wonderful day here," and chuckled as he walked away.

Without saying much in the way of a greeting, Mr. Simenauer led his guests into the apartment, which was designed in a "railroad" style that was typical of apartments in that part of Manhattan, with one long corridor and all of the rooms directly off the main corridor. Ralph's first memory of the apartment was that it had a distinct and, for him, unpleasant odor which he could not identify but to which his sensitive nose reacted right away. Most of the rooms were on the right side of the apartment, starting with a bedroom that was occupied by a boarder named Mrs. Katzenstein, who had lost her husband and was living there by herself. The next room was a full bath and then a guest bedroom that Rolf soon learned was used by Mr. Simenauer. There was a dining room behind the guest room that was large enough to be used as a small restaurant, where several people came in and purchased dinner most nights. These were people who were very particular about their diet and who wanted someone to cook meals that would meet their dietary needs, mostly kosher meat and other products. The living room was behind the dining room and faced the street. The kitchen was located on the opposite side of the corridor from the living and dining rooms and was quite large for an apartment. There was a door that was closed off the corridor on the same side as the kitchen. Rolf at first thought it was a closet, but when he opened it he saw a very small room, with a single window overlooking a courtyard. Besides a small, single bed, the only other furniture was a small table, perhaps half the size of a bridge table, with a couple of drawers on the side, and a chair. The room was dimly lit by a light hanging on the wall with a small lampshade and a ceiling light, both of which had 25-watt bulbs. Rolf soon learned that this was to be his room. There was another bedroom next to the small room where Mrs. Simenauer slept, except when they had a third boarder, in which case that person used this bedroom and Mrs. Simenauer slept on the living room sofa.

Edith and Rolf sat down with the Simenauers in the living room and engaged in a pleasant conversation—except that Rolf said almost nothing, allowing his sister once again to do most of the talking while he sat quietly in an easy chair with his arms folded. Once again he resented that Edith was able to arrange his life according to her needs.

She wanted to be on her own, and so her first priority was to find a place she could live, which she had done earlier that day and now she was determined to get him settled in a place where he would be well cared for and not be a burden on her. The longer the conversation went on, the more Edith appeared comfortable having Rolf live in this apartment with this family. Although remaining silent, Rolf took a liking to the couple as well. He later recalled that Mrs. Simenauer reflected back on that day in their apartment: "Here was this young man—really a boy—sitting in the chair and not saying a word. I wanted to pinch his cheek so he would say 'ouch,' because he said absolutely nothing." The couple was "of course delighted" to have Rolf live with them. Edith agreed to pay a monthly sum to cover Rolf's room and board and it was all arranged. He and Edith immediately returned to the Rosenthal apartment on Sherman Avenue, grabbed their belongings, said farewell to their cousins, whom Rolf thanked but Edith did not, and moved into their respective new living quarters.

Rolf settled in very quickly with Mr. and Mrs. Simenauer and the more he learned about them the more comfortable he felt about being with them. Fritz and Henny Simenauer—Rolf soon learned their given names although he never addressed them as such—came to New York directly from Frankfurt-am-Main early in 1936, soon after passage of the Nuremburg Laws. They had the good fortune of being able to get visas and clear  the US quota right away. Rolf learned that the Simenauers did not have children; Henny had been pregnant in Frankfurt but the baby was still-born. The child would have been the same age as Rolf, and so Rolf had the impression, as he later recalled, that "they looked at me as a miracle child that came to them as a 16-year-old, and they treated me as if I was their son." Fritz had been an architect in Germany who specialized in castles. He also spoke often about Greek and Roman architectural designs, as well as sculpture and art, and had frequently testified in court as an expert witness, both in Germany and in the United States. Fritz invested heavily in the stock market and that, along with his court appearances and the restaurant in their apartment, provided sufficient income. Because they had lived close to a university in Frankfurt, Henny had developed a skill in embroidering emblems for students to wear on their blazers. She continued this work in New York and had a small shop not far from the apartment. The Simenauers had a cat named Mushie, who mostly lived outside, but came to the window when she was hungry and would enter the house to eat. It is possible the odor Rolf smelled when he first entered the apartment came from either the cat or the litter box. Most nights Rolf would wait until the guest diners had completed their meal and departed, and then he would join the Simenauers and Mrs. Katzenstein and "we all had a meal together," he later recalled, "and that was like a family dinner." He enjoyed talking to Fritz and helping Henny clean up with the dishes in the kitchen afterwards. Mrs. Katzenstein spoke very little English and so most of the time she conversed with the Simenauers in German. Rolf could understand a little of the German and from time to time spoke a few words in German with her so they could converse because whenever she tried to speak English she lapsed into German. But these conversations were very sporadic; "I was very surprised that I could understand when she spoke German," he later remembered, "because I had put the language behind me." As Rolf spent less time in the apartment, his conversations with Mrs. Katzenstein diminished. Nevertheless, he later recalled, "my life started to work favorably in that apartment right from the beginning."

The second day after Rolf and Edith moved into their separate apartments, Edith took Rolf to see about getting him enrolled in a school for the fall semester. She had spoken to some people and learned that there was a very good high school that provided both an academic and technical education, including a preparatory course of study that would facilitate Ralph's acceptance in a technical college and then a career in engineering. She told Rolf that although he had completed secondary school and begun technical college in England, nobody in the United States goes to college at age 16. Rolf had been prepared to repeat his final year of high school, having spoken to some educators on the ship. The school was known at that time as the Straubenmuller Textile High School (now part of the Bayard Rustin School for the Humanities), which was located in the Chelsea section of Manhattan between West 18th and 19th Streets. Rolf and Edith took the subway downtown and entered the massive, multi-story brick building. School was still in session, with most students taking final examinations during that third week of June, and as Rolf and Edith walked through the main corridor, some of the boys passing by stopped and stared, whistling and gawking at Edith who, at age 25, was what Rolf called "a knockout of a woman"—slim, with beautifully groomed wavy hair. The dean of the school, Norman Ford, came along and put a stop to the catcalls and ushered Edith and Rolf into his office. Edith explained that she and her brother had just arrived from England, where Rolf had completed secondary school, had always shown an interest in mechanical things—taking them apart, working on their components, building things with them—and that he wanted to pursue a career in engineering. Dean Ford said that children at age 16 were ill-prepared to know what they wanted to do in life and needed a better educational foundation in the humanities before pursuing a career goal at the college level. He asked about Rolf's school records from England. Rolf had lost the diploma he had received from the Northampton secondary school. Edith had written to the school, but had been told the school's records had been destroyed in a fire, and so it was impossible for Edith or Rolf to produce any written evidence of his having attended the school. Dean Ford suggested that Rolf take a battery of tests so that he could determine Rolf's placement at the high school. Edith suggested that Rolf take all the classes that a normal high school student would take during their four years at the school. Rolf was mortified; Edith wanted him to start high school from the beginning—ninth grade—without his having the opportunity to take the tests first. "It would have been nice to have known how much I knew, at the very least," Rolf later recalled. "I never found that out and with that Edith put me three years back right off the bat." Rolf was enrolled at the school for ninth grade beginning in September 1946, but Dean Ford suggested that Rolf get a head start by taking summer school classes at a school closer to where he lived. Edith said no, however, preferring that Rolf get a fresh start with ninth grade in the fall. "That was devastating for me," Rolf later recalled, "absolutely devastating. I felt deflated, as if I had been run over by a truck and flattened like a pancake." But reflecting back on that day many years later he acknowledged: "As it turned out, it was probably the best decision that Edith made about my life."

Rolf spent most of the summer adjusting to life in New York, learning a little about what the city had to offer, and getting further acquainted with the Simenauers and his immediate neighborhood. Soon after moving in he went up to the roof of his building and discovered that he could easily see the scoreboard of a large baseball stadium located just a couple of blocks to the east, which he later learned was called the Polo Grounds, home of the New York Giants. He walked to the Hudson River and enjoyed exploring park areas and sitting on the grass and sunbathing along the river. He also spent a little time with Edith when she was available, and called upon his cousin Otto and got to know his wife, Rose, a little better. Upon moving to the Simenauer's apartment and enrolling in school, Rolf had written a long letter to Joe Haberer, who was still living at the Northampton hostel, relating all that had happened to him in the month since leaving England and providing him with his new address. Rolf was thrilled to receive Joe's response, written on June 27, according to Joe's letter, just 10 minutes after he had completed reading Rolf's communication. Joe had the ability to assess Rolf's frame of mind very quickly, even in a written communication. He had learned very early on in their relationship, more from inference than from anything Rolf had specifically told him about his past, that Rolf had experienced a rough childhood—similar to his own but at a slightly younger age—and he came to understand that Rolf tended to focus more heavily on negative aspects of life, especially with respect to new experiences. Joe expressed interest and sympathy over Rolf's account of the sea voyage and all that had transpired since his arrival in New York, especially being forced by Edith to move so quickly out of his cousin's apartment, and was eager to point out the bright side. "But what is that compared with all that you have gained?" he wrote. "You're home, Rolf, home. No more hostels, no more being bullied by the Refugee Committee; you now have a place to enjoy life." Joe also wrote about how he had learned more about the world around him and to appreciate so many more things than he had before, especially the process of learning about new things. As always, Rolf was heartened by Joe's letter and his always sound advice, and about the prospect of continuing their correspondence from afar.

A few weeks after moving into the apartment with Fritz and Henny Simenauer, Rolf was riding on the subway, standing near one of the

doors, when he heard a voice calling his name. He quickly turned around and there standing before him was George Wellworth, the boy who had occupied the bunk below him on the *Gripsholm* on the transatlantic sailing to the United States. The two had become friends during the journey, but in the excitement and chaos of arriving in America, Rolf had not asked George for his address. As it turned out, George lived with his parents on Broadway and West 150th Street, not too far from the Simenauer's apartment. The unexpected reunion on the subway turned out to be fortuitous for Rolf, as it began a three-year friendship that exceeded any that he had known during his lifetime, including his early childhood friendship with Heinz Abel and even his friendship with Joe Haberer, because much of the time he and Joe were physically separated from each other. Unlike Joe, George served less as an older brother from whom Rolf sought advice and more as a day to day companion. Reflecting on their friendship, Rolf later acknowledged that George "had a profound impact on my life," exposing him to culture in general and classical music in particular. Rolf spent much of his time during the summer of 1946 with George going to movies and free concerts at Lewisohn Stadium on the campus of City College, exploring New York City, or just hanging out with George in his apartment, where he "witnessed beautiful parenting by George's parents," and where they would "experience family time listening to operas broadcast on the radio," he later recalled. "At times I wondered how a one-bedroom apartment could be so cozy." Although George was a year or so younger—but nevertheless considerably taller—than Rolf, they were both about to enter ninth grade, albeit in different schools.

Early in September, Rolf began the first of four years at the Straubenmuller Textile High School. His experience at the school was mixed in several ways, but overall he did very well in most of his subjects, even during his first year at the school. His early success was largely attributable to having taken some of the subjects previously in England. With each day during that first semester, Rolf's confidence grew; he actively participated in class discussions, which pleased his teachers. "I outsmarted the rest of the class," he later recalled. "I spoke with intelligence that amazed me." He even took up the French horn during his first year in school, and became proficient enough to play in the school orchestra before the end of his first year at the school, and with the school band as well later on in his high school career. He also learned to make repairs to the instrument, which impressed Fritz Simenauer enough for him to suggest that Rolf should pursue a career in mechanical engineering. But a couple of incidents in his classes during ninth grade set Rolf's confidence back. During a biology class, Rolf spoke correctly about the "cleavage of cells," which sent many of the male students into hysterics and caused the teacher to intervene on his side. "How dare you laugh," she told the class; "how rude that is!" In a second incident, the teacher of his social studies civics class had trouble pronouncing Rolf's last name, not because of the umlaut over the "o", which he had eliminated at the time he enrolled, but because of the "h" at the end. For some reason the teacher made a joke of his name by calling him "Molotov," which caused the rest of the class to laugh. In 1946, in the very early stages of the Cold War, the name of the Soviet foreign minister was fairly well known and highly unpopular among many Americans, so that the teacher's teasing "terribly embarrassed" Rolf. The result of these two incidents was for Rolf to resist speaking up in class, even to ask a question; it took a couple of years for him to regain his confidence with respect to participating in class discussion. He also changed the spelling of his last name to "Mollerick," replacing the "h" with a "k". During the course of his four years at the Straubenmuller Textile High School, nevertheless, Rolf did quite well, achieving good grades in most of his subjects, with the exception of ninth grade English and two years of Spanish, despite getting help after school from his teachers in these subjects. He excelled especially in mathematics and in the technical classes, and was able to fulfill the requirements for both academic and technical diplomas, although he took classes each of three summers in order to fulfill the requirements for both diplomas, and at the time he often felt that he struggled with many aspects of school.

Edith did what she could during the first several months to encourage Rolf. Through her friend, Francis, she had found a job in which she was assigned to care for individuals in their homes on a temporary basis. Most of these assignments were in New York City, which allowed her to see Rolf reasonably often. But in September 1946, she took a job caring for someone who lived in Greenwich, Connecticut, and so for several weeks she lived in that home. On Rosh Hashanah, which occurred on September 26, she sent a letter to Rolf wishing him a happy and healthy New Year and took the occasion to offer him a pep talk. "Please, darling," she wrote, "don't ever give up and have the ambition to get on in this world. . . . You are old enough now to realize that this life is not easy for anyone, but especially we, you and I, have to put all our strength and willpower into it to make ourselves independent from others. Learn as much as you can at school now—that is something nobody can take away from you." Edith also urged Rolf to try to find work in order to make some money, even if he could only work on Saturdays if he needed to spend weekdays after school doing his homework. She also urged him to continue to "go to places" and take advantage of all that the city had to offer, and to continue to see his cousin Otto.

Not long after Rolf received Edith's letter, a conflict arose with the Simenauers. The couple, especially Mr. Simenauer, wanted Rolf to know more about worldly things, not only about what was happening in his life, but about politics and history. Even though Rolf's friend Joe had emphasized the importance of this very point during their time together in Northampton, Rolf had little interest in discussing current events with Mr. Simenauer, who became very much annoyed by Rolf's indifference—so much so that he sometimes yelled at him and Rolf thus found him to be "dictatorial." Then, after about a month of school, Rolf discovered that his dimly lit room was straining his eyes, making it difficult to get his school work done. He asked Mr. Simenauer if he could get brighter bulbs for his room. "No," Fritz replied, "that would require more electricity." Rolf persisted, "But this is too dark for me to do my schoolwork." This further annoyed Fritz, who would not tolerate Rolf's "cheeky" mouth—deliberately using the British phrase. Rolf then went out and purchased two 40-watt bulbs, which at that time cost only a few pennies each, to increase the level of light in his room. This infuriated Fritz, who yelled at Rolf "with all his breath," Rolf later recalled. The sound reverberated in the enclosed courtyard outside Rolf's window to the extent that "I wondered what the tenants must have thought." Rolf immediately sent Edith a note complaining bitterly and comparing the living conditions in his little room, and his treatment by Mr. Simenauer to "a concentration camp." Apparently Edith spoke to Fritz and Henny about this and received an earful because when she responded to Rolf, as he later recalled: "Edith read me the riot act." She told Rolf that he was to remain with the Simenauers "whether I liked it or not and I was to be always respectful of them." She made it abundantly clear that they were in charge of his life: "I don't want to hear from them again that you were disobedient and mouthed back to them," Edith told him. He realized that he had gone too far and apologized to Mr. and Mrs. Simenauer, and from that time forward his life with them became "a loving and truly wonderful experience."

At the end of Rolf's first semester in high school—on January 27, 1947—he decided he should try to earn some money and was offered a job working for a florist in the neighborhood. The plan was for him to work a few hours in between school sessions and see how it worked out. His job was to deliver flowers and for this he would receive 10 cents for the few hours of work and he could keep any tips he received. When Fritz Simenauer heard about this he was outraged. He marched out of the apartment with Rolf at his heels and stormed into the flower shop, confronting the proprietor, as Rolf later recalled: "How could you pay this boy just a dime when he has worked almost half a day?" he bellowed. "You think he's worth only a dime? How cheap can you get? They ought to shut this business down if you cannot afford a decent salary for him." They took the argument into the street and there was some foul language exchanged. Rolf later recalled that "I never knew Mr. Simenauer had that capacity." A small crowd gathered to watch the shouting match, waiting for fisticuffs to break out. But Fritz discharged one last verbal salvo, took Rolf's hand like a parent would do, and said, "Let's get out of here." The incident ended Rolf's fledgling career in the floral industry. A few days later he received his end-of-semester grades, which were mostly good, and the result of a New York State Regents exam in English, which was not. After consulting with Edith and the Simenauers it was decided he should wait until toward the end of the school year to take on a job.

In late May, Fritz Simenauer introduced Rolf to Alfred Strauss, who sometimes ate dinner at the apartment and who owned a butcher shop. Strauss was in his 30s and single, and brought fresh meat to the Simenauer's apartment the first time he came for dinner, for which Mrs. Simenauer thanked him but asked him not to bring meat again because it was not kosher. It became Alfred's custom to come for dinner on Mondays when business was slow. He and Rolf hit it off immediately. Alfred offered him a job in his butcher shop, which was located on Broadway and West 148th Street. Rolf went there after school the next afternoon, which was a Friday, where he was told to observe how things worked in the front of the store. Alfred told Rolf to come the next morning at 7:00 a.m., before the shop opened, at which time he showed him what he wanted him to do. First Rolf learned to use the cleaver for cutting meat and small bones, but he was not to use the band saw for cutting larger bones. Rolf had to wear a coat every time he went into the refrigerator, which was the about 64 square feet in size. He had to learn all the cuts of delicatessen meat sold at the shop, as well as how to clean out and cut up chicken the way a customer wanted it. Besides the safety considerations, Rolf had to learn to cut chicken and meat in a manner to observe the required health standards for the products. Once Rolf learned his way around his responsibilities in the shop, Alfred had him come with him very early one morning to the wholesale meat market to purchase a quarter of a steer. Rolf helped carry the beef in one piece that weighed several hundred pounds to Alfred's car—a Hudson—which was stripped down in the back in order to haul the meat to the shop. Rolf started at a salary of 50 cents per hour and worked weekdays after school and on Saturdays (for Edith it had become more important that Rolf earn money than attend Shabbat services by this time) pretty much year round, even though he went to summer school much of the time that he had the job. Alfred was very pleased with Rolf's work; he wanted Rolf to become a licensed butcher and increased his salary a few times up to 75 cents per hour over the course of the two years Rolf worked for him. The two of them became good enough friends that Rolf was invited to Alfred's wedding and also came to dinner at Alfred's apartment several times over the course of the following year or so.

Besides his job, Rolf remained busy outside of school engaged in a budding social life. He joined a local chapter of the B'nai B'rith youth organization known as Aleph Zadik Aleph (AZA), which met mostly every Sunday during the school year for discussions, dances, and outings to museums and parks, and included day trips to Bear Mountain and to the Franklin D. Roosevelt Presidential Estate along the Hudson River at Hyde Park in upstate New York. Although still quite shy socially, Rolf quickly developed a comfort level in this group setting. He continued to spend extensive time with George. They would go to the movies often—sometimes every week—and also to concerts on occasion, or take strolls down to the Hudson River. He and George spent 10 days in Rochester, New York, between the end of summer school and Labor Day in 1948, much of it lounging on the beach along Lake Ontario. Although Rolf did not have many friends from school because it was located fairly distant from upper Manhattan, he befriended a classmate named Bert, who lived within walking distance of his apartment. From time to time they would study together or go to a movie or a walk along the river. Rolf also continued to spend time with several of his cousins who lived in Washington Heights, especially Otto, who took him on outings and also to his plant outside of the city where Rolf enjoyed learning about the production of commercial diamonds. Sometimes Rolf would have dinner with Otto and Rose and their children, Ronnie and Helen. He also visited Otto's brother Eugen, who was a physician, and who gave him an Omega watch as a gift. He visited Joe and Gretl Rosenthal perhaps only two or three times during his high school years, largely because he felt uncomfortable due to the way Edith had summarily taken him and moved out of their apartment, and he knew there was bad blood between Edith on the one hand and Gretl and his cousin Ruth on the other. Although Edith was often busy with her job or friends, she made time to see Rolf every couple of weeks. During the summer months they would go to Coney Island or to South Beach on Staten Island because they both came to love the seashore.

In April 1947, Rolf reconnected with Joe Haberer after a months-long hiatus. During that time, Joe had come to the United States, having moved in with an aunt and uncle in Oakland, California, where he managed to begin college without having to repeat any high school as Rolf had to do, something which he had complained about to Joe multiple times in their previous correspondence. Joe expressed understanding of Rolf's predicament and his somewhat negative outlook on life: "When I think it all over, Rolf," he wrote, "life could have treated you better." As always, however, Joe provided just the encouragement Rolf had been seeking: "If matters are not what they should be, 'grin and bear it' and try to improve them. You cannot afford to let them get you down. After all, we are lucky to be alive and in America." They enjoyed a series of exchanges over the course of the summer. Joe always described how he would read and then re-read Rolf's letters and ended his communications with expressions of friendship and love. He urged Rolf to do his best in school and encouraged him to think about what he truly wanted to do with his life and pursue education in college that would lead him to that goal. By summer's end, the written communications became inexplicably more sporadic and ended shortly thereafter, much to Rolf's disappointment. More than half a century would pass before Joe would enter Rolf's life again.

For the first time since he left Germany, Rolf celebrated his birthdays with friends and family, sometimes going out and sometimes having a party at the Simenauer's apartment. One of the diners at the apartment, who Rolf knew only as Mr. Wasserman, took an interest in him, engaging him in conversations and occasionally accompanying Rolf on walks. On Rolf's 18th birthday, May 27, 1948, Mr. Wasserman pointed out to Rolf that he needed to register with the Selective Service System, which he subsequently did, with Mr. Wasserman's assistance. Rolf also began to take an interest in politics, stopping to listen to a young Jacob Javits speak on the street corner while campaigning for his first re-election to Congress in 1948, and noting in his journal that President Harry Truman had surprisingly defeated Thomas Dewey in the 1948 presidential election.

Despite remaining busy and engaging in a reasonably active social life in New York, Rolf had virtually no experience with the opposite sex. This began to change, in a small and somewhat unique way, after his first year living in Manhattan. Henny Simenauer had a niece named Ilse Gimlicher living in England who planned to come to the United States in 1947 to meet her husband-to-be, who had found his way from Germany to Australia and had known Ilse in Germany ever since she was five years old. In an exchange of letters with Henny, Ilse had learned a little about Rolf and expressed an interest in meeting him. Ilse came to New York for two weeks on September 20, 1947, staying with the Simenauers and getting to know Rolf. The two of them took a liking to each other straight off even though at age 28, Ilse was two years older than Edith. Rolf showed her around, taking walks with her along the Hudson River, attending a party for her, taking her to Radio City Music Hall (his second visit there), and spending much of his limited spare time enjoying her company and learning how to converse with a woman. Just before Ilse departed for Australia on October 5, Rolf took her for a walk near the river and they kissed; it was the first time he had kissed someone "lips to lips," as he recorded in his journal. Over the course of the next two years, he began dancing with girls during socials as part of his affiliation with AZA, but never really dated anyone for the remainder of his time in high school.

Edith fared far better than Rolf in her pursuit of a social life. She enjoyed going out with friends and did so as much as possible. She had reconnected with Michael Cronin, her romantic companion in England, not long after her arrival in New York. The one and only instance in which she asked Rolf for advice, however, came unexpectedly late in 1946 in an impulsive decision she was about to make. She shared with Rolf that she was dating a man originally from Norway named Joey, who was not Jewish but she said to Rolf, "I love him but I also love Michael and don't know what to do." Rolf later recalled his response: "Our parents would have wanted you to marry a Jewish man and that should be your path," and—in what would soon prove to be an ironic twist—that is exactly what Edith decided to do. Michael was completing medical school in England during Edith's first year in New York; in the course of their correspondence, they agreed to get married. During a break in his studies in January 1947, Michael signed up for the merchant marine so he could travel at little cost to New York. Rolf had a chance to spend time getting to know Michael in the week following his arrival, and accompanied Edith and Michael when they were married at City Hall on February 3. The following week, Michael returned to England to complete his medical studies; Edith remained in New York. But in August 1947 she sailed to England so that she and Michael could have a private marriage ceremony with Michael's family and a few friends at the home of Michael's parents in London. They were wined and dined for three days and then had a few days' honeymoon at a "lovely country place in Essex." She described many of the local attractions in the area in a letter written to Rolf from Essex, which concluded: "Give my regards to Broadway."

Edith returned to New York alone in early October 1947, but Michael joined her shortly thereafter and shared the room in Miss Just's apartment in Washington Heights with her while she continued her nursing job and he took up a two-year medical internship. By the autumn of 1948, however, Michael arranged to open his own general practice in Rockville Centre on Long Island and Edith became his nurse. They rented an apartment not far away from Manhattan in Hempstead on Long Island, and Michael purchased a Humber Hawk automobile made in England by Austin Motors. Rolf occasionally visited them in their Hempstead apartment on Sundays or holidays. He was invited to spend Christmas with them in 1948, as both Edith and Michael not only had given up their observance of Judaism, but decided to hide their Jewish heritage once they moved to Long Island. In fact, Rolf learned that Michael had earlier changed his name from Cronick (which had been derived from a longer Russian name) to Cronin in England because it sounded Irish and not Jewish. He and Edith celebrated Christmas and had a decorated tree on their front yard. Edith went as far as to invent Christian parents from the Midwest and insisted that Rolf use the name Madison when he visited them in Hempstead. This did not sit well with Rolf and launched yet another long-term grievance with his sister that only worsened over time. He spurned their invitation, remaining in New York over the Christmas holiday, which annoyed both Edith and Michael so badly that Rolf felt compelled to send a letter of apology to them, conjuring a number of excuses, such as being worn out from school and work, when it was mostly because he felt uncomfortable celebrating Christmas with his Jewish sister and brother-in-law.

June 17, 1949, was the last day of classes for Rolf during his junior year at the Straubenmuller Textile High School. He performed with the school orchestra in a concert that evening with Edith and Michael sitting in the audience. Afterward, they drove Rolf to the Simenauer's apartment, had him pack up his things, and told him that he was going to move in with them in their apartment in Hempstead. Rolf was stunned. How could Edith tear him away from his home, especially on such short notice? He had a full year of high school remaining, not to mention his having to take his final examinations and New York Regent Examinations in a week requiring him to spend the next several days in intensive study. Edith said that she would explain in the car but that it was late and this wasn't the time or place to have that discussion. Fritz and Henny Simenauer were distraught over this unanticipated development. They had become quite attached to Rolf over the course of three years and his sudden departure was devastating for them. Rolf could barely bring himself to say goodbye, but promised he would visit them often. In short order, Rolf found himself on the way to yet another new home.

Things turned ugly the moment the car drove off from the Simenauer's apartment. Without giving Edith a moment to explain, Rolf launched his attack. Edith had no right, he told her, to uproot him again. For the first time in memory he had a tranquil life in a family atmosphere with a job that he enjoyed and friends and family close by. He had a routine that made sense to him living in Manhattan, and most of all, Fritz and Henny treated him like a son—something he had missed ever since leaving Germany. He reminded her that he was no longer a child, having recently turned 19 years old, and that it was high time that he had some say in major decisions affecting his life. Edith told Rolf that she and Michael had been paying for his room and board and that their move to Long Island and launching a medical practice was very costly and difficult for them to afford. Rolf should "have the common decency to listen to them and cooperate because of their financial limitations," as he later recalled. Rolf asked her if it was just about the money or if Edith wanted to take him away from the Simenauers for some other unknown reason. "She said that I was stupid," Rolf recalled, "and didn't understand that the Simenauer's apartment was not my home, that I was a boarder, and that I had no choice except to move in with her and Michael." Rolf could feel years-long pangs of resentment toward Edith welling up from inside him realizing that, like it or not, he was not capable of meeting expenses required to live on his own with his fairly meager salary from the part-time job at the butcher shop. He thought of Joe Haberer's advice to "grin and bear it" whenever life throws you a curveball, because you will come away from the experience all the stronger for having done so. He sat back in the rear seat and fell silent, realizing that "of course I had to leave, but it was a painful experience for me to have to move away from the Simenauers."

The tension never fully abated over the roughly two years Rolf lived with Edith and Michael in Hempstead. The apartment was relatively large, with four bedrooms, but the room he was assigned was small, although larger than the room he had in Manhattan. The primary problem with the room was that there was no desk on which he could do his work. He had to stack orange crates together and put a board with shelving paper on the top and that was where he worked. "I was uncomfortable working that way," he later recalled. He had become accustomed to eating quite well while living with the Simenauer's, "where the meals provided a balanced diet: protein, vegetables, fruit, bread, and a drink," he recalled. "At Edith's house, my need for food was not being satisfied. I didn't have a ravenous appetite, but a moderate appetite that required a balanced diet." Rolf also did not feel comfortable living in the house with a young, married couple, especially with his sister. He was particularly careful not to disturb them at night. But shortly after moving in, Rolf developed a problem with boils, which Michael lanced and treated. One night Rolf awoke in terrible pain from a boil that had become infected. The pain was so bad that he went to the bathroom and cried out, hoping that Michael would hear him and come to his aid, but was too shy to knock on the bedroom door. When there was no response, Rolf forced himself to bear the pain until the morning. Although his reticence to disturb Michael and Edith at night was largely an issue of his own making, that experience with the boils stuck in his memory and contributed to a growing discomfort with his living situation.

Edith made it abundantly clear from the outset that Rolf was going to have to work while living in her apartment, even though he had signed up for summer school to take chemistry. It was now going to be necessary for Rolf to commute between Hempstead and Manhattan on the Long Island Railroad, a much longer trip than the subway ride downtown from upper Manhattan. Because of the longer commute, Rolf had to give up his job at the butcher shop. He was eager to get a job, however, and so as soon as Rolf had completed his final exams the week after moving to Hempstead, Michael introduced him to the owner of a service station located on a street corner near his office in the town of Rockville Centre. The proprietor of the nearby service station, Harvey Hartung, was a young man in his late 30s. He and Rolf got along right away and when Harvey learned of Rolf's interest in taking apart and fixing bicycles, he offered him a job working as a mechanic at the garage. Harvey patiently instructed Rolf exactly how to perform the various tasks, such as setting the valves in the engine and the fuel aeration level so that he could perform oil changes and minor tune-ups. Harvey had a wife who was in her early 30s whom Rolf considered "very sexy." From time to time she would show up at the garage and engage Rolf in friendly conversation to the extent that he had the impression that she was flirting with him. Harvey would get annoyed and tell her to "stop distracting the workers" because Rolf needed to complete the job he was working on before the close of business. In early July, Harvey helped Rolf purchase a car—a used 1934 Plymouth. Rolf had saved perhaps half of his earnings at the butcher shop over the course of two years, enough to cover the cost of the 15-year-old car and several key replacement parts, which he installed after work during the rest of the month so that it was able to pass inspection and be registered on July 26. Meanwhile, Rolf practiced driving with Michael and Harvey and even with Edith on their many sojourns to the beach—Long Beach and Jones Beach in Long Island, Coney Island in Brooklyn, and South Beach in Staten Island—throughout the summer, so that he was able to pass his driver's test and obtain a license by the first week of September. Rolf worked at the garage on weekends and after school through the summer of 1949 and all of his senior year of high school.

Besides his frequent excursions to the beach, usually with Edith, most of the remainder of Rolf's leisure time during the summer of 1949 was taken up by joining the Malverne community band. The band performed a series of free summer concerts each year and needed a French horn player. Rolf spent an evening or two each week rehearsing with the band and then performed in concerts on three consecutive weeks in August. He considered participation in the band concerts good practice for his upcoming work in the school band and orchestra where, as a senior, he would be promoted to first chair of the French horn section. As a result of his full schedule, there was virtually no time during the summer of 1949 for him to visit the Simenauers, or George, or his relatives in Washington Heights. But he was invited to spend Rosh Hashanah and Yom Kippur with Fritz and Henny Simenauer, and this gave Rolf an opportunity not only to report on how things were going in his life since moving to Long Island, but to go to synagogue, something he had not done throughout the summer. He did not see Fritz and Henny again until the Christmas vacation when he drove to Manhattan for the first time and took them for a ride in his car. He also brought them each a Chanukah gift: a pen and pencil set for Henny and a pipe and tobacco for Fritz. Keeping up with George and some of his friends from the AZA club during his senior year of high school, however, was more difficult for Rolf. He only saw George a few times during the entire school year, and so their friendship, which had been so close for the three years in which Rolf lived in upper Manhattan, began to ebb once he moved to Long Island.

By his senior year at the Straubenmuller High School, Rolf had improved his overall grades and had amassed enough courses, thanks to three consecutive years attending summer school, to receive both an academic diploma and a diploma in technical studies. He had applied to eight colleges—mostly schools that focused solely on engineering and other technical degrees—and had been accepted by six of them. He had wanted to go to Massachusetts Institute of Technology, probably the finest technical school in the land, but did not make the cut. The same was true for Renssalaer Polytechnic Institute in upstate New York. Finances were an issue as well and so for Rolf the decision came down to two local schools, Pratt Institute or Brooklyn Polytechnic Institute. Pratt recruited him hard because he was older and had a more diverse life experience than typical students entering college. But in the end, Rolf selected Brooklyn Poly because it was ranked in the top 10 in the country in the field of engineering. Rolf took several advanced mathematics and technical classes during his senior year of high school to better prepare him for college.

When Rolf's graduation exercises were held at the end of June 1950, he had much to be proud of and to embrace the moment, but two circumstances put a damper on the event, one of which was of his own making. Rolf had received grades of "A" each semester in the orchestra class, as well as in the band class. The orchestra had been rehearsing to play "Pomp and Circumstance" at graduation, and Rolf practiced the first chair French horn part. He had expected to receive the orchestra award at graduation, as he had consistently worked hard over four years and had seniority, having played in the orchestra for three and a half years. But someone else received that honor, and the rest of the orchestra learned of that decision just before the graduation ceremony. Rolf was so disappointed by this that he chose to sit in the audience with other graduates rather than play the French horn with the orchestra. To make matters worse, the second seat French horn player could not be there to play. After the graduation ceremony, Mr. Klinger, who was the teacher and conductor of the orchestra, and who had a temper, confronted Rolf. "How dare you sit in the audience and leave me without a horn section?" he bellowed. Rolf expressed his disappointment at being passed over for the orchestra award. "Did you get a grade of 'A' from me each semester?" Klinger asked. "Yes I did," Rolf responded. "That was your reward," Klinger explained. "Had I known what you were going to do at graduation, you would not have gotten an 'A' this semester." This incident would have taken on even greater importance for Rolf, except he was already upset about something else: neither Edith nor Michael came to his graduation which, being held during the daytime on a weekday, conflicted with patient visits at Michael's office. The only person Rolf had attending his graduation was Fritz Simenauer. "He told me that it was such an honor for him to be at my graduation," Rolf later recalled, "seeing me graduate after all I went through." Fritz put his arm around Rolf and told him how proud he was that Rolf was able to push himself and achieve such a notable milestone in his life.

After his graduation, during the summer of 1950, Rolf continued to spend part of his days working at the service station but he also spent time at Jones Beach with Edith, who especially loved going to that beach. Despite the fact that Edith was pregnant and the baby was due in late July, she continued to visit the beach, and Rolf often accompanied her. Edith and Michael celebrated the birth of their first child, Johnnie, on July 24. Later during that summer, Edith encouraged Rolf to leave his job at the service station in Rockville Centre and find work at Jones Beach where he would be paid a bit more, since he would be starting college the following month. Rolf was reluctant to take on a new and more time-consuming job at the outset of his college career. He argued with his sister about this and, for once, a compromise was reached that he would attend Brooklyn Poly during the week and work at Jones Beach on the weekends. Rolf took a job working for the New York State authorities who managed Jones Beach State Park in a unit that was operated by State Troopers. Rolf's initial job was enforcing rules at the beach, such as removing clothing from the tops of beach umbrellas, and keeping the beach clean. Rolf enjoyed the work because he loved the outdoors, especially the seashore, and so he continued working at Jones Beach on weekends after the summer season was over.

Once autumn arrived, Rolf was placed on fire patrol, and part of his responsibilities included driving the ambulance to transport people, for whatever reason, from the park to a nearby hospital. Because there were fewer people at the beach during the off season than the summer, Rolf had little opportunity to drive the ambulance. Once, however, a pregnant woman went into labor and he had to transport her to the hospital. By coincidence, the senior staff was holding a meeting at that time and Rolf had been told not to use the siren if he had to transport someone in the ambulance. Because there was slow traffic on the road, Rolf had to weave around the cars, all the while the woman was moaning in the back of the ambulance. Rolf decided to use the siren in order to get around the slow traffic, and although he made it to the hospital in time for the woman to give birth there, he was chastised by the park staff when he returned because he had used the siren. That was the last time he drove the ambulance but he remained on fire patrol. One day he and his partner, a hulk of a man named Hank, who was the football coach at Hofstra College, came upon a small wildfire in the high reeds on the Jamaica Bay side of the park. They both had a backpack filled with water and also had walkie-talkies. As they approached the fire, the wind suddenly shifted and Hank told Rolf to drop the gear and jump into the water to escape the flames. Rolf waded out until he was up to his chin, realizing he did not know how to swim. Fortunately, the patrol squad sent out a boat because they had been gone 40 minutes without checking in on their walkie-talkies. Hank jumped into the boat while Rolf tried to tread water doing a sort of dog paddle, and then Hank reached out and "yanked me into the boat like I was a piece of paper," Rolf later recalled. The water was cold enough that Rolf was shivering by the time they got back to headquarters, but not Hank, who remained completely unfazed throughout the event. "That turned out to be one incident," Rolf later recalled, "that shaped me quite a bit because it indicated that I was overdoing it between college and my job." Rolf, nonetheless, was concerned that he needed money to pay for Brooklyn Poly. Michael had paid for his first semester of college, but Rolf paid for the second semester from his earnings at the service station and at Jones Beach during the fall. "Each summer I worked at Jones Beach," he later recalled, "and earned enough to pay my tuition each year and had some left over."

Rolf discovered during his first year of college that he had to work very hard in order to keep up with his courses. Unlike high school, where Rolf found himself spending fairly little time doing homework and tended to cram only before final exams, he spent long hours wading through a difficult and heavy set of reading assignments, mitigated in many cases by his keen interest in that material. He was expected to complete the readings outside of class and participate in discussions during class. Midway through his second year at Brooklyn Poly in early 1951, Rolf decided to move to Brooklyn and rented a room at a home owned by Mr. and Mrs. Zuckerman at 555 Rugby Road near Newkirk Avenue. Even though this required an additional outlay of funds, the amount turned out to be modest and Rolf had several reasons for making the move at that time. He found the commute between Long Island and Brooklyn twice daily five times a week to be both exhausting and time-consuming. The 15- to 20-minute subway ride to downtown Brooklyn where the college was located was quick, allowing him more time to work in peace in the privacy of his boarding house room. Rolf had never really felt comfortable living under the same roof as Edith and Michael; with the arrival of the baby, it became all the more difficult to concentrate on his schoolwork there. "I could see no future there with her for me," he later recalled. "I had to step out of that life and make my own life. That was a turning point; from then on I became in charge of my own destiny to the extent that I could." Nevertheless, Rolf spent considerable time at Edith and Michael's home during the summer months while working daily at Jones Beach. It was during the summer of 1951, while staying with Edith and Michael, that Rolf discovered something that proved to be ominous in his life.

During the summer of 1951, when he was not working, Rolf often accompanied Edith to Jones Beach. On one of these occasions she stepped on someone's blanket and fell. Rolf helped her up, checked to see if she was okay and asked what happened. She said she was looking away and tripped over the blanket and was fine. A few days later the same thing happened. Once might have been a coincidence, he thought, but twice in the same week was troubling. He mentioned this to Michael, who said it was probably nothing to worry about but he would look into it. When Edith fell twice more on the beach during the autumn when there were no crowds or blankets on the beach, Rolf went back to Michael to express his concern. Michael told him that there was, indeed, something wrong but he wasn't certain yet what it was. He also told Rolf that Edith was pregnant with their second child and she was due to deliver in early March 1952. He told Rolf not to worry about Edith falling on the beach because she had agreed not to go back there at last until after the baby was born. While visiting Edith and Michael over the Christmas school break, Rolf noticed that Edith was decorating the living room for Christmas. Because he had strong feelings against Edith and Michael celebrating Christmas, he went into another room when suddenly he heard a shout and a loud thud. He came running and saw that Edith had fallen off a chair and called for Michael. Fortunately Edith did not injure herself or the baby, but Rolf's concern for Edith's health continued to heighten.

There were other incidents during the next several months. On one or two occasions when Edith was driving with Rolf in the car, she stopped the car and slumped over the steering wheel. When Rolf asked what was wrong she said she was having trouble seeing. Once she was backing out of the driveway and went over a tricycle; fortunately nobody was hurt and not much damage was done to the bike. Then, about a month before she was scheduled to deliver her second child, she asked Rolf to take her to Jones Beach, which she missed very much, even though Michael had told her not to go and it was wintertime. This time Edith had a bad fall against a hard object, suffering a cut on her forehead and lacerations on her arm and leg. Edith for once was upset because she thought she might have sustained internal injuries or hurt the baby. Michael treated her cut and examined her thoroughly after that and found that everything was fine with the pregnancy. Rolf now demanded to know what was wrong with his sister. Michael told him that he believed that Edith would develop Multiple Sclerosis (MS) at some point in her life. He explained that MS is "a very insidious type of disease" that attacks the spinal cord and the body's muscles, so much so that in later stages it causes paralysis, loss of speech, and eventually death. But Rolf was told the disease itself often takes decades to run its course and Michael assured him he was confident that the episodes when Edith had fallen or had temporary vision issues were related to the disease but were preliminary signs and not symptoms of the disease itself, which he thought would take many years to set in. As if to punctuate this last point, on March 5, 1952, Edith gave birth to a second healthy son, Robbie. As Rolf later recalled, "It took 17 years for Edith to develop symptoms of MS that eventually became debilitating." But Michael's words explaining the nature of the illness in 1952 reverberated through Rolf's subconscious from that point on as a periodic reminder of yet another tragedy in the making in his life.

Although Rolf continued to find the work at Brooklyn Poly challenging, he made steady and impressive progress through his third year of full-time pursuit of his college degree. At the end of his junior year, he ran out of money and realized his summer earnings at Jones Beach would not be sufficient to pay tuition for his final year at school. In the fall of 1953, he determined that he would have to work full-time during the day and take courses at night. This would, of course, prevent him from completing the degree in one more year, but he felt that he had no other option. He took a job at Macy's Bureau of Standards, which he found interesting and very much enjoyed. He was responsible for testing consumer products for the department buyers, ranging from televisions and other appliances, to furniture, to shoes, before the products could be sold by Macy's. Rolf had joined the Reserve Officer Training Corps (ROTC) at Brooklyn Poly after his first year. Shortly after he took the day job at Macy's and began taking courses at night, he was dropped from the ROTC program at Brooklyn Poly because it was only available during the daytime. That eventually triggered a letter from the draft board in the spring of 1954 informing Rolf that he had been reclassified to 1A (eligible for military service) and he was ordered to report to Whitehall Chapel for a physical examination. On the morning Rolf came for his physical, the doctor who examined him turned out to be his brother-in-law, Michael Cronin. What a fortuitous coincidence! Rolf thought. "I said to him the least he could do for me was classify me 4F" (physically unable to serve in the armed forces), Rolf later recalled.

177

Michael examined Rolf thoroughly and pronounced him perfectly fit. "He said that if I had been nothing more than flatfooted he could have classified me 4F," Rolf recalled, "but there was nothing wrong with me." With that, Rolf had to place his job at Macy's Bureau of Standards and his college courses on hold after the spring 1954 semester.

Before entering into active military duty, Rolf became a naturalized American citizen on July 6, 1954. It was a fairly straightforward process and took place at the Kings County Courthouse in downtown Brooklyn. For the occasion of becoming an American citizen, he decided to officially Anglicize his first name, so that Rolf became Ralph. His naturalization paper thus identified him, for once and all time, as Ralph Wolfgang Mollerick. With that accomplished, Ralph went off to Fort Dix in New Jersey in August 1954 to undertake basic training. Once he had completed that, Ralph was sent to Fort Belvoir in northern Virginia not far from Washington, DC, in October 1954 for advanced training. Because he had been in a ROTC program at a technical college, Ralph was able to be assigned to the Army Corps of Engineers and was encouraged to take a commission even though he had not completed the ROTC program. This would have required a three-year commitment in the army. When Ralph explained his circumstances to his superiors, particularly his desire to complete his college degree in engineering, he was told that he could serve in a noncommissioned capacity for two years, and so he became an engineering specialist and, along with the rest of his advanced class of 30 men, was ordered to ship out to East Asia at the beginning of 1955. The war in Korea or, more accurately, "police action," had reached a point in which hostilities were over, with a "permanent truce" having been signed at Panmunjom in July 1953. Nevertheless, the thought of being sent into a post-combat zone in Korea appealed neither to Ralph nor to any of the 1,600 men sailing on his transport ship to Japan. As it turned out, Ralph was one of seven men from his advanced class at Ft. Belvoir—all of whom happened to be Jewish—who had been assigned to the largest engineering depot in Japan and so were considered "lucky" to have drawn an assignment in Japan rather than in Korea. As Ralph and that small group walked down the gangway of the transport ship in Yokohama, they were serenaded by a hearty "Bronx cheer" from the remaining GIs headed for Korea.

The large engineering depot to which Ralph was assigned was located in Sendai, one of two major cities in the northern half of Japan, which presently is perhaps best known as an academic center. It is also known for having suffered significant damage in 2011 as a result of a major earthquake that triggered a catastrophic tsunami. In 1955, however, it was the depot and not the surrounding area that was the focus of Ralph's life. He was assigned to help manage the flow of 17 million parts required to service military equipment shipped from Korea for repair. The work required not only a knowledge of the inventory of parts and their relationship to specific equipment, but also completing extensive paperwork to ensure that replacement parts were ordered, if necessary, so that equipment could be returned to Korea as quickly as possible. Sometimes it was necessary to improvise in repairing military equipment if parts were not available. The work turned out to be very much something for which Ralph felt prepared, and he caught himself more than once thinking back to how he took apart bicycles and reassembled them as a child growing up in England. He experienced several small earthquakes during his time stationed in Sendai, recalling that "the roof shook like a blanket but the building didn't collapse." After serving at the depot for a little over a year, Ralph inquired if there was any way he could shorten his tour of duty. His superior officer suggested that he apply for early discharge in order to complete his higher education, which could shorten his tour by three months. That is exactly what Ralph did, and in May 1956 he received his honorable discharge from the Army and returned to the States. He was eager to resume his full-time job at Macy's Bureau of Standards and complete his degree at Brooklyn Poly; but he was especially looking forward to returning home because of a major event that had taken place in his life just a few weeks before he had shipped out to Japan.

# CHAPTER 8

## Marriage, Family, and Career (1954–1988)

AT THE BEGINNING of July 1954, Ralph Mollerick was in need of a break. He had been working full time at Macy's Bureau of Standards while attending night classes at Brooklyn Poly since the past September; in a month's time he would be mustered into the United States Army. He had never been to Atlantic City—and, of course, loved the seashore—so Ralph decided to rent the basement of a summer house very close to the boardwalk for the Fourth of July weekend. Shortly after he arrived at the house he saw a young, pert woman doing laundry and thought she was the maid; when she greeted him he gave a quick nod and turned away. Going up to the front porch, Ralph was approached by a boy who was about 10 years old who introduced himself as Barry Laken, and who engaged him in conversation and explained that he was staying at the house for much of the summer with his family. Barry then asked Ralph if he had ever played miniature golf, which he had not, so he asked Ralph to take him to play miniature golf at a place located off the boardwalk a couple of blocks from the beach house. The two of them went off and returned perhaps a few hours later after playing "several rounds of miniature golf." During their time together, Barry told Ralph about his cousin, Marlene Penn, a young single woman who along with her parents and grandmother was staying with them at the beach house for the holiday weekend, and whom he thought Ralph would like very much. When Ralph and Barry returned to the house, Marlene's grandmother—they called her "*Baba*," which is Russian for grandmother—was furious that Barry had disappeared with a stranger without telling anyone and then scolded Ralph for taking Barry to miniature golf without asking permission. At first Ralph was somewhat perplexed that he had provoked this older woman's ire but then realized he should have mentioned to one of the adults present that he wanted to take Barry to miniature golf before going off with him. The incident demonstrated the level of Ralph's naiveté at the time when it came to human interaction.

Barry introduced Ralph to Marlene shortly after they returned from playing miniature golf. Ralph took one look at Marlene and said, "Oh, my God, I thought you were the maid here!" She laughed and said, "I know you did, but as you can see, I am not the maid." They both had a chuckle about that and then Ralph asked her if she wanted to play miniature golf with him that evening ("since I now knew how to play," he later recalled). As it turned out, Marlene had never played miniature golf before but beat Ralph anyway. "We had a good time," he recalled. They spent the evening getting to know each other a little and went out the next evening as well. Dating was virtually new for Ralph—he had been on exactly one real date, in 1950 at age 20 with a second cousin named Malka who was 16 years old at the time—so the prospect of going on a date made him a little nervous on the one hand. On the other hand he very much enjoyed spending time with Marlene over the holiday weekend. She gave him her address and they exchanged phone numbers before Ralph went back to New York and she returned to the family home in Springfield, Massachusetts, on the afternoon of July 5. Ralph had to work at Macy's the following day, which was also the day he became an American citizen. During the holiday weekend in Atlantic City he had learned that July 6 was Marlene's birthday—she had been born in 1931, which made her about a year younger than Ralph—and so he purchased a card, wrote a nice message, and mailed it to her. A few days later Marlene called him on the phone to thank him for the birthday wishes. "What a beautiful thing it is that you've done," she said to him; "nobody has ever done anything like that for me—remembering my birthday—other than my immediate family." Ralph told her that he just wanted to wish her a happy birthday and let her know how much he enjoyed meeting her in Atlantic City. Over the course of July, Ralph and Marlene spoke on the phone perhaps every other day. Around the middle of the month, at her invitation, he drove to Springfield to spend the weekend with her and the family.  She then invited him to accompany her to a cousin's wedding, which was to be held in Baltimore in mid-August. Ralph had explained to her in Atlantic City that he would be starting basic training at Fort Dix in August, but Marlene's invitation and the thought of seeing her again very much interested him, and so he told her that he would try to come to the wedding, if the army would allow him leave to do so.

Toward the end of July, shortly before the start of Ralph's basic training at Ft. Dix, Marlene visited Ralph in Brooklyn for the weekend. Ralph had to arrange with Mr. and Mrs. Zuckerman for a separate room for Marlene. Their relationship had progressed through the few days they had spent together over the course of the month and the regular phone calls, but neither of them had much prior experience with the opposite sex; nor had they learned much about each other. Despite the shortness of time since they first met, their lack of experience in developing relationships with the opposite sex, and utter inability—for a variety of reasons—to explore each other's background even superficially, Marlene told Ralph during her visit to Brooklyn that she wanted to become engaged and announce their engagement at the upcoming wedding of her cousin. Ralph was stunned at first, feeling a sense of excitement and reluctance all at once. He knew that he very much liked Marlene and sensed that he was developing deeper feelings for her. But even with his lack of experience—perhaps because of it—he sensed that he was hardly ready to make the kind of commitment that engagement signified. They both knew that Ralph was about to begin basic training that would launch probably a two-year commitment to the army. Although they had not discussed it, Ralph expected that after his basic and advanced training were completed, there was a distinct likelihood that he would be shipped overseas for a tour of duty in the Army Corps of Engineers. He was not certain that he was ready to become engaged to be married before undertaking his military service. Marlene was adamant and persuasive, however, and Ralph was not prepared to risk an abrupt termination of their relationship, and so he agreed. The engagement was duly announced with some fanfare at the wedding of Marlene's cousin in mid-August, barely six weeks after they had first met.

With Ralph at Fort Dix undergoing basic training and thinking about his two years of service in the army, he and Marlene spoke over the phone about setting a date for their marriage. Ralph saw little reason to get married until at least after completion of his overseas tour and suggested that they wait to set a wedding date until his return. As he later recalled, "I didn't think Marlene's parents would think it best for her to get married to me at that particular time." Marlene had spoken at some length about this topic with her parents, however, and she told Ralph that she and her family thought it would be best if they were married before Ralph was shipped overseas. "She begged me to get married before I went overseas," he later recalled. Although this notion went against Ralph's better judgment, to the extent he could trust his judgment in such a situation, he once again acceded to Marlene's pressure during a late September visit to Springfield in between his basic training and advanced technical training assignments, which commenced in October at Ft. Belvoir. It was midway through his advanced training course that Ralph learned he would be shipping out to Japan early in January. He and Marlene were married in a relatively small ceremony in a synagogue in Baltimore on December 19, 1954, before Ralph had completed his training at Ft. Belvoir. To Ralph's great disappointment, he learned in late November that Edith and Michael were going to be in

England through the holiday season and would not return until January, that none of his cousins in New York could be present, and that Fritz and Henny Simenauer were unable to attend as well, which meant that he would have no close family or friends at the wedding. Only Marlene's parents and relatives who lived in the Baltimore area were present for the ceremony. The couple had hoped to drive to Florida for a short honeymoon before Ralph went overseas, but there was insufficient time for that. Ralph then tried to convince Marlene to join him in Japan where it would have been possible to live in a billeting arrangement for married couples on the base, and where they could quickly learn more about each other and deepen their still growing relationship. Marlene was strongly against traveling to Japan, arguing that it would be best for both of them if she remained with her parents in Springfield until he returned. Besides her disinclination to live overseas, Marlene noted that the army would increase Ralph's overall pay if she remained in Springfield. The decision was made for Marlene to remain behind, which "was such a disappointment for me," Ralph later recalled.

The 15 months Ralph served in Japan could have proven disastrous to his new marriage, especially given the circumstances in the two weeks between the wedding and Ralph's departure, but perhaps somewhat to Ralph's surprise, time and distance had quite the opposite effect on their relationship. From the moment Ralph arrived in Japan, Marlene sent him daily letters, sometimes enclosing photographs of herself. "I must say she is looking better than ever," Ralph wrote to Fritz and Henny Simenauer in late December 1955. "I think she gets lovelier every day. She writes me such wonderful letters that she keeps me happy." In their exchange of letters, Ralph and Marlene discussed a variety of purchases he should consider while in Japan. Ralph would send her brochures and prices and she would list the items in which she was interested, including a set of china and cultured pearls. The two of them began counting the days until Ralph's discharge almost from the outset, and as time got closer they became all the more enthused about his return to the States to really begin married life. "Marlene is all excited about me coming home," Ralph wrote to Fritz and Henny the week before his return to the States. "She is such a wonderful wife and I don't think I could have found one better." Upon his return from Japan and honorable discharge from the army in May 1956, Ralph went straight to Springfield and he and Marlene stayed with her parents for a few weeks before moving back to the Zuckerman's boarding house in Brooklyn in time for Ralph to begin summer school at Brooklyn Poly and resume his day job at Macy's Bureau of Standards.

It did not take long for Ralph to discover that his marriage was going to be a complicating factor in an already stressed-filled life. Marlene made it clear from the outset that she wanted Ralph to finish school and get settled in a career. Her letters to him while he was overseas were filled with planning for their future. "She keeps saying that the sooner I am finished with school, the sooner I'll have a position in industry," Ralph wrote to Fritz and Henny shortly before the end of his overseas tour. Once they were settled into their room on the top floor of the boarding house on Rugby Road in Brooklyn, Ralph and Marlene found that the living conditions were unsuitable for a newly married couple. The room was brutally hot, as there was no air conditioning and they arrived there just at the beginning of summer. One of the other boarders on that floor was an alcoholic; the other boarder up there came from Switzerland and spoke hardly any English. It was impossible to move downstairs, as all the rooms on the second floor were rented, and the Zuckermans lived on the ground floor. Marlene found herself alone much of the time because Ralph worked during the day at Macy's Bureau of Standards and took classes every night at Brooklyn Poly, while she did not work. The managers at Ralph's job wanted him to take on the job of chief engineer, but that required certificates that would allow him to work on boilers and do electrical work, and he did not have those certificates, nor could he immerse himself in a job with such responsibility while trying to finish college. Instead he was involved in testing newly mar-keted merchandise, which he found both educational and interesting.

Ralph completed his undergraduate coursework and graduated from Brooklyn Poly with a bachelor's in mechanical engineering (BME) degree in May 1957.

No sooner had Ralph received his BME degree than Marlene decided she had more than enough of living in the boarding house and told Ralph they needed to move to a more private, spacious, and comfortable living arrangement. They found a one-bedroom duplex apartment in a relatively new section in the eastern part of Brooklyn known as Canarsie, located at 1099 East 99th Street near Avenue K. The neighborhood of mostly residences with businesses and schools scattered throughout had been built at least in part on landfill, and was about as far to the east as you could go in Brooklyn at that time before hitting swamp or Jamaica Bay. Eventually that swamp was filled and high-rise apartment buildings were erected on that site. But in the summer of 1957, Ralph saw this move as a major step up from the boarding house which, for a brief time, lifted Marlene's spirits because it gave them privacy in a place of their own. The move to Canarsie, however, significantly complicated Ralph's life because he had taken a new job in the summer of 1957 at the United States Testing Laboratory in Hoboken, New Jersey. The company tested and certified products used by the United States government to ensure the products met specifications for efficiency, safety, and the environment. The company was one of the largest independent facilities of its kind in the country, and so Ralph joined a large staff of mechanical engineers, with his work focusing largely on air conditioners. He landed this job as a result of a recommendation from one of his professors at Brooklyn Poly, who suggested that this sort of work would provide him with foundational experience for a career in mechanical engineering. The job, however, required Ralph to spend hours each day commuting by car from eastern Brooklyn to Hoboken. There was no Verrazano Bridge in those days and so Ralph had to drive around Brooklyn, through the Battery Tunnel to lower Manhattan, then through the Holland Tunnel to New Jersey in order to get to Hoboken. Ralph also entered into a graduate program at Brooklyn Poly under the GI Bill in the fall of 1957, leading to a PhD in engineering, but because of his full-time job and long commute, he could only handle one course during the evening each semester. All of these considerations made for very long days each week.

Shortly after their move to Canarsie, Ralph and Marlene learned that they were going to have a child. Marlene gave birth to their first son, Jeffrey, on July 10, 1958. Although Marlene stayed at home with the baby while Ralph was at work, the responsibilities of being a new father added considerably to his already stressful schedule. Marlene wanted her parents to spend time with their grandson. Because there was no room to accommodate them in their own apartment, Ralph and Marlene and Jeffrey drove the several hours from Brooklyn to Springfield for weekend visits at least once a month. During the ensuing year, at times Ralph felt as if he was living more in his car than at his apartment. Soon enough, Marlene told Ralph that the one-bedroom apartment was insufficient for a family of three and that she wanted a house of their own. The cost of a house anywhere in New York City or within the immediate environs of the New York metropolitan area was far beyond the capabilities of Ralph's salary, which meant they would have to move some distance away. This was fine with Marlene, who much preferred living far from the clutter and congestion of the city. It was less fine with Ralph, who had become accustomed to city life ever since arriving in the United States and who came to truly enjoy all the city had to offer. After considerable searching, the couple found a three-bedroom, new single family home in Old Bridge, New Jersey, which was located in Middlesex County, southeast of New Brunswick and southwest of Perth Amboy; they moved in at the beginning of July 1959.

It was shortly after the move to Old Bridge that Ralph made two decisions that would steer the course of his career and the lives of his family in a new and exciting direction. The first decision came about because Ralph was forced, as a result of family responsibilities, to reassess his priorities. He determined that it would no longer be possible for him to pursue the doctoral degree. At the current pace of one course a semester at night while working full time, even at a university closer to his home than Brooklyn Poly, such as Rutgers University, it would have taken Ralph many years and a commitment to a study discipline far beyond his capabilities to complete the degree. Ralph thus terminated his education, but he quickly found that his BME degree and growing experience in the field was sufficient to land a new and exciting job with the avionics division of ITT Corporation. The company had built an office complex with a 300-foot research tower during the 1940s in Nutley, New Jersey. Even though Nutley was located some distance from Old Bridge, it was a relatively easy and short commute for Ralph on the Garden State Parkway. ITT Corporation had developed into a major conglomerate since its inception that spread into a vast array of technological, aerospace, communications, transportation and hospitality industries on a global scale. The corporation also later included a shady history of involvement in international politics under its CEO, Harold Greene, who assumed that position in 1959, the same year Ralph joined the company. The avionics division at that time had several multi-million dollar projects under contract with the United States government's defense programs. Joining ITT was "when I began to blossom in my profession," Ralph later recalled. "I quickly demonstrated that I had good skills in management and in engineering." True enough, Ralph experienced a meteoric rise through the ranks of the company so that in less than three years he was selected to serve as project manager for one of the largest projects the avionics division had ever undertaken, through a multi-million dollar contract with the US Strategic Air Command (SAC). "I was chosen for this assignment, after a thorough interview process," Ralph later recalled, "because of my technical experience going as far back as my work in Birmingham, England." The promotion to project manager carried a hefty increase in Ralph's salary.

Ralph's new assignment meant that he would serve as field manager of project operations, which required him to be onsite first at Barksdale Air Force Base in Shreveport, Louisiana, and then at SAC headquarters in Omaha, Nebraska. In the spring of 1962, Ralph moved his family—which by that time included a daughter named Shari, born July 19, 1960—to Shreveport and closed the house in Old Bridge. The project turned out to be highly complex, involving computer technology when it was still in a relatively formative stage. But Ralph excelled at identifying what needed to be done and how to accomplish it. He was jokingly known as "Major Mollerick," because his military counterpart in SAC at Shreveport, a major in the United States Air Force, "didn't know shit," as Ralph later recalled, "but I needed to use his signature to proceed with the work." Ralph found it amusing that he did not have to salute the officers, even the generals at Barksdale, because he was a civilian contractor and no longer in the US Army. He was less amused by the way some of the senior officers spoke to him even though he was project director. "They treated me like a peon, but they needed my brain," he later recalled. Marlene, of course, was ecstatic about Ralph's promotion, so much so that she didn't mind moving the family to Shreveport, even though she was not fond of travel, and the logistics of moving two young children proved to be exhausting. It was during their time in Shreveport that Marlene gave birth to a third child and second son, Glen, on August 4, 1963. Only a month later, the family had to move on to Omaha, as the Shreveport phase of the project was completed and the remainder of the work had to be accomplished at SAC headquarters. The project ended in December 1963 and Ralph moved the family back to their home in Old Bridge and returned to work in Nutley. He was glad the project was finished because he found the responsibility "sometimes overwhelming" interfacing with the military and was "quite stressed out" by the time the work ended. He received highly favorable reviews for the successful completion of the project, however, and the company asked him to write proposals for a series of new contracts. But the market for engineers in the northeast was undergoing retraction in 1964. First RCA, a major electronics company, announced that 3,000 engineers would lose their jobs and then ITT went through a series of reductions in force, as well. Ralph made it through the first two cuts, but simultaneously with these cuts there was also a strike by the union that included the engineers. After seven weeks on the picket line, Ralph's funds were heavily depleted and so he crossed the line and returned to work, only to learn shortly thereafter that his job had been cut as part of a third wave of reductions at ITT that brought the total to 2,000 engineers having lost their jobs at the company. The termination of his job at Nutley was a monumental blow to Ralph, especially after accomplishing so much at ITT in such a short time. Just as his career seemed to be exactly where he had hoped it would be, he now had to face the prospect of rebuilding it from scratch with responsibility for a family of five, which would have been more than sufficient to send anyone into the depths of depression. For Ralph, however, the sudden collapse in his career came on top of an earlier, unexpected and highly disturbing disclosure involving his relatives in New York.

In the summer of 1956, Ralph received a phone call from his Aunt Sophie Schwarz who asked him to come by himself to Washington Heights to see her. It had been about a month since Ralph had seen his aunt Sophie, when he had taken Marlene to upper Manhattan shortly after his return from Japan so the relatives could meet her. During his last visit with Sophie, Ralph had noticed a marked change for the worse in her appearance. Her health had, in fact, been gradually deteriorating ever since shortly after the death of her husband, Hermann, in February 1951. Now, sitting with Sophie in her apartment, Ralph could see that she did not look well at all, but as was her practice when discussing her health, she waved off his expressions of concern and offered him a cup of tea. There was something important she had to say to him— something that he had a right to know, she told him—but first he had to promise her that he would not speak about it to anyone until after her death. These words elevated Ralph's curiosity, but there was something ominous in her tone that caused him to feel the beginnings of a knot forming in his stomach, now a characteristic warning sign to him that something momentous was about to occur.

Sophie began by explaining that what she was about to tell him had to do with her sons Otto, Eugen and Max and a shipment of crates that had been sent to them from Hamburg by Ralph's father 17 years earlier. From the dark recesses of his memory Ralph recalled that in the weeks and months prior to his departure on the Kindertransport, his father had been consumed with packing large crates known as lifts that he planned to ship to New York in advance of their much desired emigration to the United States. He specifically remembered helping his father organize a highly valued stamp collection to be included in one of the lifts. As Ralph learned many years later from documents found in a Hamburg archive and from letters obtained from cousins, his father had actually packed a total of four lifts and on March 20, 1939, had submitted an itemized list of the contents of the lifts to the Nazi Customs Investigations Office requesting authorization to ship the lifts to New York, one to each of Sophie's three sons living there at the time (Sophie and Hermann did not emigrate to the United States until 1941; Otto, Eugen and Max had been living in New York ever since 1936, and the fourth son, Ludwig, and his family arrived there from Israel around the time of Hermann's death in 1951). The fourth lift was to be shipped to Ralph's cousin Ruth, also living in Washington Heights. Josef had received approval to ship the four lifts on April 14, 1939, for which 2,500 RM was withdrawn from his frozen assets account on April 21. Five days later, Röhling & Co., Hamburg, a moving firm, collected and shipped the lifts to the four cousins in New York. There is no available record of the date of their arrival in New York, but each lift was received, probably during the late spring of 1939, with the instruction from Josef that they were to be stored unopened until he and his wife could obtain the necessary authorizations to emigrate and travel to New York. Storage of these very large crates was expensive; each cousin paid for the storage of the lifts under a promise that they would be reimbursed by Josef when he arrived in New York. Josef had made clear in at least one letter, sent on August 18, 1941, that the contents of the lifts were to be retained and given to "the children"—namely Edith and Ralph—"and not be used by them" (the relatives). "Let us hope," he had written to Ruth, "that it will be possible for the dear children to use the contents of the lifts themselves soon."

Sophie confirmed to Ralph during their conversation in 1956 that the lifts were received by the individuals to whom they were sent. She then indicated that her sons had agreed to store the lifts at their own expense because Otto had paid for and sent a visa affidavit for Josef and Selma at the end of 1938 and they all had expected Ralph's parents to emigrate shortly thereafter. With each passing month and year, however, it became less likely that the Nazi regime would issue exit visas. The storage payments for the lifts were mounting, and so Otto decided to open the lift sent to him, which he found mostly contained linens, china, and a variety of houseware items. He also found a cardboard box containing the stamp collection that Ralph had helped to pack in Hamburg as well as a sterling silver *Hanukiah* (menorah) that had been in Ralph's Wolfhagen home. Now Ralph's interest was piqued, and he asked about the other lifts. Sophie indicated that, one by one, each of the three brothers had opened their crates, finding similar items, except that one of the crates included only a sofa and a somewhat unique standing lamp, another included a table and some other furniture, and Sophie indicated that the lift sent to Ruth contained a settee along with a few smaller items. When Ralph then asked Sophie what had become of the contents of these lifts, she sighed deeply, paused, and then told him that Eugen had sold the items and used the money to help cover the cost of setting up his medical practice; Max had sold the materials in his lift and used the proceeds to start up his manufacturing business; and Otto sold the contents of his crate to help him establish his commercial diamond business. According to Sophie, the contents of Ruth's lift somehow also came into her sons' possession and were sold as well. Apparently Josef learned that at least one or more of the lifts had been opened because in his August 18, 1941, letter to Ruth he had indicated that he had instructed Sophie in Berlin, just before she came to America, to tell the children "not to sell any of Edith's things, not the sofa, quilts, beds, washables, even if not new, but to store everything," and was surprised "to hear" that the lift with the settee had been opened.

Trying to digest what his aunt had told him, Ralph fastened on the stamp collection and asked Sophie if she knew specifically what had happened to that. Sophie told Ralph that Otto had not sold that with the other contents of his lift but Edith had asked Otto for financial assistance so she could travel to England in the summer of 1947 to be married to Michael. According to Sophie, which Edith later confirmed to Ralph, Otto had not sold the stamps with the other contents of his lift and told Edith that although he could not give her the cash outright, he had her father's stamp collection that he was holding for her and if she allowed him to sell the stamps, he would give her the proceeds to help pay for her passage to England; and that is exactly what occurred with Edith's agreement. This story became somewhat more complicated when, in 2016, Ralph's cousin Harry Rosenthal recalled that his mother (Gretl) had told him that Otto had her father's (Moritz's) stamp collection and had promised to give it to her but later said, according to Harry, "the collection suddenly was stolen." The likely explanation for the confusion about the stamp collection is that it belonged to both of the brothers—Josef and Moritz—but because it was in Josef's custody when the lifts were packed, Otto probably assumed it belonged to Josef and had no problem selling it and giving the proceeds to Edith. Otto may have later told Gretl that it had been stolen as a means of protecting both Edith and himself from Gretl's ire. Learning about the stamps from his aunt, Ralph was furious; how could Edith have been so selfish? "She allowed Otto to sell the stamp collection which she knew I wanted," he later recalled. "That was one more reason for me to be pissed off at her." He then asked his aunt about the *Hanukiah*, which was the only other item he heard about that was of special interest to him because he remembered that his father had a silversmith design it especially for the family. Sophie told him that Otto sold it to the Jewish Museum in New York City.

Ralph was stunned by his aunt's unexpected revelation. He felt that his father had entrusted his cousins with the safe-keeping of his immediate family's possessions and they had betrayed that trust. He was especially upset about Otto. During the time he had lived in Washington Heights he had grown closer to Otto and spent more time with him than any of the other cousins. "Otto was my favorite because he would call up the Simenauers and invite me to come with him on trips," he later recalled. "I went with him a number of times to his plant and to other places. I just enjoyed his presence; he was a fun, outspoken guy with a big belly." Although he had seen less of Otto after moving out of Washington Heights, he always enjoyed the times they were together. He had spent less time with Eugen and Max, but they had been nice to him as well. He still wore the Omega watch presented to him by Eugen, whom he thought of as "a rich person—a doctor who had really made it," and Max had offered to give Marlene a "Lilly Daché" hat and some accessories when they had visited him. Ralph's cousin Harry, however, later remembered a very different side of the three cousins, especially Otto. "These cousins treated my mother horribly," he recalled. "They were vicious. . . . But Otto was the worst," because "Otto cheated her out of the stamps. What was in that crate certainly wasn't Otto's." He also recalled that when Sophie passed away, after the funeral "none of the cousins had room in their car to take my mother to the cemetery. They were so vicious towards her. She was standing on the street crying because they just left her."

Ralph was good to his word and said nothing to anyone about his aunt's disclosure at that time. He did, however, do some quiet checking on some of the information Sophie had provided. He visited the Jewish Museum to see if he could recognize a *Hanukiah* like the one from his home in Germany. Besides the custom design by the silversmith, it was also unique in that it was an oil burning lamp, which was fairly uncommon at that time. He examined the Judaica in the museum and before long his eyes came to rest on a unique and familiar *Hannkiah* with a price tag of $5,000 hanging from it in the case. Was this the family heirloom? He could never be certain, but later in life when he examined documents concerning his family in Hamburg, his broadening understanding of the circumstances convinced him that this was indeed the very menorah from the family home in Germany. Ralph was also curious about Sophie's mention of a unique floor lamp included in one of the lifts. He had a vague memory of a visit to Max's New York apartment years earlier in which he had noticed a very unusual lamp that reminded him of a floor lamp in his Wolfhagen home. "It had a very large, round leather shade that was open at the top and the bottom, like an open cylinder," he later recalled. He made a return visit to Max's apartment to confirm his initial impression. The lamp sat in the same location in the living room it had occupied during previous visits. "When I said that I seem to recognize that lamp," Ralph later recalled, "Max didn't say anything." Ralph left the apartment convinced that he had been looking at his family's lamp.

Sophie Schwarz passed away on November 8, 1956, just weeks after her disclosure to Ralph, who surmised years later that she knew she did not have long to live and needed to unburden herself of her secret. Ralph went to Edith and recounted everything Sophie had told him about the lifts and his follow-up discovery of the family's lamp and sterling silver *Hanukiah*. Just thinking about it agitated him and he grilled his sister on her allowing Otto to sell the stamp collection so that she could travel to England to marry Michael. He could not understand why she had not told him about that, since now it was obvious to him that she would have known that Otto had opened at least the one lift containing the stamps. Edith told Ralph that she thought he was too young at the time and still getting adjusted to life in the United States and didn't want to burden him with such a family issue. Ralph's explanation of the extent to which the cousins used the contents of the lifts infuriated her, however, as she realized that most of it was likely to have been designated for her by her parents, as later discovery of documents in the Hamburg archive would confirm. "I asked Edith about pursuing it with the cousins," Ralph later recalled, "but she told me to forget it."

She indicated to Ralph that there was nothing they could do to bring anything back since it had all been sold and that they should just move on. She found dealing with any of the family distasteful. She had recently accompanied Gretl Rosenthal to see a lawyer—Millard Ring, Esq.—to complete paperwork regarding a modest sum of money they were to receive in restitution from Germany based on a heavily deflated value of their fathers' business. In the end, the restitution awarded at the time was $40,000, half of which went to Gretl, and the other half was split between Edith and Ralph. Spending that time together with Gretl had been difficult for Edith and for her cousin, and Edith now wanted both she and her brother to put the family issues behind them. "Don't call them," she told Ralph. "It's not worth your aggravation. I want you to finish your schooling and get on with your career." Ralph peered at her closely as she concluded: "Listen to me—I'm older than you; just forget about this, just like everything else." Once again, even as a 26-year-old adult with a wife, Ralph felt compelled to follow his sister's instruction and so he never pursued the matter of the lifts with his cousins. "I just didn't see the point in bringing it up after that," he later recalled. "My parents were long dead; pursuing this with the cousins would not bring them back." While he considered his aunt's account about the lifts entirely credible at the time—after all, why would Sophie tell him what she did about her own sons if the story was made up? And documentation later discovered would corroborate much of it—without having confronted his cousins about the matter in retrospect he could never fully verify the accuracy of Sophie's disclosure. There were two significant consequences, nevertheless, of this disturbing episode concerning the lifts: it served to further alienate Ralph from most of his family, even from Edith; he also drew from this matter an unfortunate and likely inaccurate conclusion about the fate of his parents that he would carry with him into his senior years.

The layoff from ITT proved to be a turning point in Ralph's life. Weeks earlier, during the union strike, he had placed his resume with several headhunters specializing in employment opportunities for mechanical engineers. He also contacted his brother-in-law, Mitchell Penn, who worked for the Army Chemical Corps in Edgewood, Maryland, where there was an opening for a mechanical engineer at a GS-12 level, which turned out to be somewhat less salary than he had been making at ITT. Ralph later recalled telling his brother-in-law that "there was no way that I was going backward in life," and so he did not pursue that job opportunity. Ralph also received several referrals from the head-hunters and he had phone interviews with three or four firms in the area, none of which materialized into a job offer. One of the headhunt-ers reached out beyond the New York metropolitan area and found an employment opportunity for Ralph with the engineering and elec-tronics division of ACF Industries, Inc., located in Riverdale, Maryland, just outside of Washington, DC. The company made aircraft simulators, which was a growing field, designed to train pilots in the use of complex navigational equipment. His interview went well, as did a follow-up visit, and Ralph accepted an offer of employment. He purchased a house in nearby Lanham, Maryland, and the family moved in during the sum-mer of 1964, in time for Jeffrey, the oldest child, to begin first grade in the Prince Georges County Public Schools in the fall. The follow-ing spring, on the recommendation of a neighbor, the Mollerick family joined Mishkan Torah Congregation, a Conservative congregation of modest size located not far from their home in the heart of the original, New Deal era–built section of Greenbelt, Maryland.

About a year after Ralph joined ACF Electronics, the company was sold to Link Aviation, Inc., a component of General Precision Equipment Corporation. Most of Ralph's simulation work up until that point had been with military high performance jets; he had a keen interest in the space program, however, with which the company had no direct con-nection, but his supervisors asked him to be patient while they tried to find a job that more closely suited his interests. Meanwhile, Ralph had learned from Zev Hendel, a fellow congregant at Mishkan Torah who was employed at the National Aeronautics and Space Administration

(NASA) Goddard Space Flight Center in Greenbelt that the agency might have vacant positions for mechanical engineers opening in the next few months. Ralph submitted his resume to NASA in late 1965 and waited, all the while finding it increasingly difficult to continue with Link Aviation, Inc. Ralph told his superiors at Link that he was actively seeking a new job, but his immediate supervisor continued to work with him to find a project with which he would be happy. Ultimately that became a moot point. After weeks of negotiation, NASA offered Ralph a position at the Goddard Space Flight Center in April 1966 at a GS-13, step 5 salary that slightly increased his income from the Link job. Ralph embarked upon a 31-year career with NASA that would far exceed his loftiest expectations for a career in engineering.

Ralph's leadership experience in his early career meanwhile gave him the confidence to broaden his leadership outside of his profession. Mishkan Torah was a unique congregation among those affiliated with the Conservative Movement in that the founding members literally built the synagogue facility with their own hands and strongly encouraged all members, particularly those who had newly affiliated, to become actively involved. With Ralph and Marlene regularly attending services and their children attending junior congregation—and later participating in both the weekly Hebrew school classes and youth group activities—Ralph very quickly became immersed in the business of the congregation. Within weeks of becoming a member, Ralph was asked by the synagogue president to serve as chairman of the board of directors, which was different from the operational executive board in that he and one or two other members were responsible for making recommendations to the congregation about major policies. His first assignment was to look into options for expanding the number of classrooms available to the school, whose population was growing. There were three classrooms available but they were temporary rooms as part of the all-purpose area used as the sanctuary. The congregation owned a large space adjacent to the existing building. Ralph and his small group recommended hiring an architect to design a school building to occupy this space. It took only five weeks to get congregational approval to proceed with the design of a school building, but it took five years from then until the building was designed and constructed and then dedicated in 1970.

Zev Hendel became synagogue president in July 1969 and presided over the dedication of the Karp Family School Building, as it came to be known. He was impressed not only with the way Ralph had worked for the congregation throughout the decision-making process leading to construction of the school building, but also how he freely shared thoughtful ideas among the synagogue leadership and at congregational meetings. "They saw that I could get things done and had a vision for the future of the congregation," Ralph later recalled. At the end of his final one-year term as president, Zev asked Ralph—actually pleaded with him—to allow his name to be placed in nomination to succeed him as president. Although it was somewhat unusual for someone to assume the presidency without first having served on the executive board and as one of the vice presidents, Zev had every confidence that Ralph could do the job. Ralph assumed the presidency in July 1972. Unfortunately, the ensuing year would prove to be a tumultuous one for the congregation, and as president, Ralph of course was caught in the center of the maelstrom. Two serious issues arose simultaneously during that year: the first was a decision by the rabbi to terminate his relationship with the congregation at the end of the year because the congregation could not afford the financial package he sought, and he made the decision to leave too late for the congregation to have an opportunity to conduct a search, interview, and hire another rabbi for the next year. The congregation was also in negotiation with another nearby congregation seeking to merge with Mishkan Torah. Many of the Mishkan Torah members threatened to leave if such a merger took place, while others complained that negotiations were going too slow. When Ralph reported to the congregation on both these issues, "I was vilified and made the scapegoat," he later recalled. "I just didn't want to take another term as president."

Despite his rocky year as president, Ralph continued to contribute to Mishkan Torah business operations in significant ways over the next 25 years. He restructured the financial management of the congregation, digitized the treasurer's bookkeeping that facilitated both cash management and the budget process, and later served as the congregation's treasurer during the first half of the 1980s. He introduced a new category of membership known as "Associate Member" for those people who had retired or moved away from the area but wanted to retain their association with the congregation. He also organized a Men's Club for the congregation in 1967. In between his time as president and treasurer, Ralph continued in his original capacity as chairman of the policy board, at a time in which the congregation was considering dual membership in the Conservative and Reconstructionist movements, which it ultimately decided to do, Henceforth until this very day, all of the congregation's rabbis have been graduates of the Reconstructionist Rabbinical Seminary in Philadelphia.

Ralph's extraordinary service as a volunteer at Mishkan Torah took place concurrently with an exceptional career trajectory at NASA's Goddard Space Flight Center. Ralph impressed his supervisors from the very outset. He developed both his technical and managerial skills early in his career at NASA, working on such programs as the Advanced Earth Missions, the Earth Radiation Budget Experiment, and the Earth Observing System, as well as on several satellite programs. As a result he was told by a branch chief during that time: "The way you are going, you will be doing big things here at NASA." In 1977, he was reassigned to a branch that gave him the opportunity to design major technology for the space program. He designed robotics that allowed astronauts to work in space well before the space shuttle became operational. He also helped design a manipulating arm for the space shuttle that would actually allow the capture of another spacecraft while both were in space, "which happened several times," he later recalled. These projects took years—certainly a considerable portion of his career—to complete. During this time Ralph received a promotion to a relatively senior grade of GS-14. After the success of the robotics design program, Ralph was assigned responsibility for the Verification Program Definition for the Hubble Space Telescope and then was asked to design a shield for a space-launched telescope to protect it from the sun for the duration of an expected long-term, deep-space observation timeframe in a program then named Next Generation Space Telescope. Ralph designed an inflatable shield that deployed to the size of a tennis court. As he later recalled: "It was a major challenge, and I solved it; that was the capstone of my career." Ralph retired from his distinguished career as an engineer with the NASA Goddard Space Flight Center in 1997, but continued to work for NASA as a contractor on a part-time basis for another four years. At his formal retirement from NASA, Ralph received a plaque which read in part: "You have personally contributed to achieving and maintaining the nation's preeminence in the peaceful exploration, knowledge, and use of the earth, the solar system, and the universe. Through your efforts, 'the dream of yesterday' has become 'the hope of today' and will surely become 'the reality of tomorrow.'" Reflecting on his career at NASA, Ralph later recalled: "Never in my wildest imagination as a child playing with my 'mechano set' in Germany would I have anticipated that someday I would design major components for the United States space program."

With all the success he enjoyed in his professional career and as a volunteer leader at Mishkan Torah, during much of Ralph's adult life he faced multifaceted challenges that related in interconnected ways to his past. Most of these challenges involved relationships with Marlene and his marriage, with his children and the problems of parenting, and with his family, especially with Edith. The challenges also included financial concerns, and the memory of his parents and the traumas of his childhood. Each of these challenges manifested themselves over the course of decades, eroding his one-time, self-imposed invincible wall against the past and eventually causing him to question the very meaning of his life.

The center of Ralph's universe outside of his job was his home and immediate family. At the time of their move to Maryland in 1964, the Mollerick children were still young and very much under the influence of Marlene, who remained at home while Ralph worked. As the children got a bit older, Marlene wanted to move again, this time from Lanham to Silver Spring, in Montgomery County, where the public school system had one of the best reputations in the country. She was also interested in a larger house that would more easily accommodate the increased space needs of a growing family of five. In 1970, Ralph and Marlene purchased a home in the Kemp Mill section of Silver Spring that was large enough to comfortably accommodate the family, and included a circular driveway. The neighborhood at that time and for many years thereafter was heavily Jewish in population as well as one of the more affluent areas in Silver Spring. The move was a major upgrade in accommodations for the family but also carried with it a significantly higher cost of living. Nevertheless, everyone in the family felt very comfortable living in the Silver Spring community, including Ralph, whose commute to work and to Mishkan Torah now took twice as long as before, but he did not consider that drive too burdensome a sacrifice.

The move to Silver Spring, however, coincided with a difficult time in Ralph's relationship with his children as he struggled in his parenting role. He was very strict with his children, even when they were still quite young; it was what he had known based on the memory of his brief childhood in Germany. His father had been strict with him, using the cane to enforce discipline, and so that is how he treated his children, except he never used anything but the palm of his hand for corporal punishment. Ralph's experience with his father "had a profound effect on me," he later recalled, "because my kids told me that I had been too strict and I didn't know the limits of what a father can do, or should do, or must do." He became the enforcer in the family, and as a result the children tended to favor Marlene, who unwittingly exacerbated this situation by placing the responsibility for discipline solely on Ralph. "Whenever I came back from travel—and I traveled a lot for my job—the first thing Marlene would say is 'the kids were terrible,'" he recalled, "and she then proceeded to tell me all the things they did wrong and that I needed to punish them." At times punishment included spankings. Many years later Ralph recognized that these situations, in particular, only worsened the growing rift between the children and him, because he had not been there to see the poor behavior and his discipline often came long after the offense. He later believed it would have been better for Marlene to have handled the situation at the time, which she did not. The children, moreover, saw their father not only as strict but an angry man who made demands on them much of the time. Glen, who as the youngest probably had the best relationship with his father growing up, and who followed Ralph around just to be near him and learn from him as he did chores around the house, later recalled that "it took me a lot of years after my childhood to figure out why my father was the way he was. It all stemmed from the fact that he didn't have his dad, so he didn't really know how to raise children, and that all his anger was probably from his experience in the past, which we found out about many years later."

As bad as it was for Shari and Glen, Jeffrey as the oldest took the brunt of Ralph's struggle with parenting. Jeffrey had just turned 12 years old at the time the family moved to Silver Spring, and he tested his level of independence from his parents, as teenagers often do. He would disregard his father's requests for him to help out with chores around the house, or tell him he that he was too busy with schoolwork, or that he had to go out. Ralph recalled that this routine would occur so often that eventually he would demand that Jeffrey "do what I asked of him before he goes out." Even as a younger child, Jeffrey would walk on the side of his mother away from his father. "I was probably stricter with Jeffrey," Ralph later recalled, "and that's why he had a fear of me when walking and always moved over to his mother's side." Ralph recalled that "Jeffrey was often belligerent as a teenager; anything I asked of him he refused to do." Once Jeffrey asked his father for $35 to go to a Jewish youth function and when Ralph refused to give him the money there was a monumental scene in the house. He later told his father: "You were nasty to me." Ralph pointed out that Jeffrey's request had come immediately after he had refused to "participate in household chores." Jeffrey could not understand why he had no say in how he was being brought up, although he did not articulate his feelings about that until much later in life and then only briefly and in sporadic outburts.

Over the course of their childhood, each of Ralph's children reacted in different ways to his strict and often angry demeanor. Jeffrey confronted his father and their relationship deteriorated to such an extent that he carried his resentment of the manner in which Ralph treated him with him for the remainder of his life. Shari retreated into a world of her own, disdaining many of the standard conventions of teenage years, not to mention her Jewish heritage, leaving the house, and taking interest in such cults as Eckankar. Glen recalled that he "rebelled a lot as a child." He became a discipline problem in school that required intervention by his parents and consultation with a child psychologist. But he also internalized his issues with his father, getting along with him outwardly and suppressing his rage against the discipline. "I really didn't express anything at that age," he later recalled. "I held everything in." There was, in fact, little in the way of positive communication between the children and their father as they were growing up. "I did not have good communication skills in dealing with the children," Ralph later recalled; "they don't teach that at school." Reflecting on the manner in which he raised his children, Ralph later acknowledged: "It was a struggle for me that I really never knew how the kids felt until much later in life, and that I probably was not the best father. . . . I was emulating my father as the figure of authority, and I took on that role as a father recognizing that I hadn't liked that as a child, and yet I had done the same thing to my children. . . . I should never have accepted the role of sole disciplinarian as the father; I think that was one of the biggest regrets that I've had in my life that I allowed myself to do that."

A second challenge for Ralph throughout his life after leaving Germany was his preoccupation with the lack of sufficient financial means. It began when he arrived in England where, as he recalled," I had no money for most of the time I was there." He had been helpless and forced to depend on Edith for pocket change and on whatever the Refugee Children's Movement or the Jenkinson family could provide. "This bothered me for a long time in England until I started to work, and then I felt a bit more financially secure," he recalled. But the feelings of financial insecurity continued in America as well, and as time went on developed into anger and frustration. Ralph's struggle to make ends meet, especially paying his college tuition and for the necessities of life working in part-time jobs through high school and college caused him constant stress. He remembered that "my father acted as a wealthy man and as a family we lived quite well," but Ralph had no true understanding of the extent of his family's wealth in Germany until he learned something about that from his aunt Sophie and other relatives in New York. Then, when he was told about the lifts, he resented his cousins for taking away what little there was left of his family's possessions. "I didn't have money for tuition," he later recalled; "the lifts may have made a difference with regard to schooling. It could have made life a whole lot easier for me, because I had nothing from my parents." Despite being gainfully employed full-time and eventually experiencing a successful career and earning a very respectable salary, Ralph found himself pervasively worried about cash flow with respect to paying bills. "I was constantly at the table writing checks," he later recalled, "and figuring out which ones I had to pay now and which ones I could delay because I didn't have the money to pay them all at one time. For that reason I didn't have the money to do the things for the kids that I wanted to do." As time went on, Marlene developed a propensity to spend— sometimes indiscriminately. "She chased sales," Ralph later recalled. "She would purchase a dozen ketchup bottles because there was a special price for purchasing in bulk, or bring home dresses that were on sale, even if she didn't need them. An argument ensued because I would get bills I couldn't afford to pay." Even though Marlene worked for a considerable portion of her married life once all the children were in school—first as a part-time secretary at Mishkan Torah and later on in her own business in which she organized craft fairs—she "refused to share responsibility for household expenses," Ralph later recalled. "It was as much a psychological challenge as it was a financial challenge to understand and cope with Marlene's sickness to spend money," he later recalled. Although many people experience similar concerns about finances, Ralph believed that his particular circumstances dating back to his childhood exacerbated them and caused them to be a personal lifelong challenge that he largely suppressed.

One challenge that it took Ralph many years to recognize and that he suppressed throughout much of his adult life, related to his personal trauma from his early years in Germany through his experience growing up in England and continuing through adulthood. The most outward manifestations of the trauma were in nightmares and anger, the latter of which he failed to recognize and acknowledge until much later in life. But the nightmares were very real to him: "I used to dream about the struggles I had with my peers as a child," he later recalled, and often had visions or nightmares of Hitler Youth marching and of the Gestapo on street corners. When he left Germany to go to England, and especially after he learned that his parents had been murdered by the Nazis, he questioned how he would face the future and what it would hold for him. "I had to face new challenges and asked myself, 'Who am I and what am I doing here?'" He had trouble coping with his shortcomings in school, trying to keep up with his English peers. More often than not, he recalled, "I would cry myself to sleep and then experience nightmares." This pattern continued through his teenage years and into his early 20s, and then he realized that he could not change what had happened in his life, "so I trained myself to suppress it. . . . Edith helped me quite a bit in understanding that I needed to move on." For Ralph, the outward manifestation of suppressing the past and moving on turned out to be years of anger and frustration. Glen recalled that his father bore the scars of childhood most of his adult life: "I think that made him the man he was as an adult," he asserted. "He had to deal with never seeing his parents again, the anger against the German people, and having to live in hostels and being a foster child. He wouldn't let that go, he just held it and held it and held it."

For much of his life in New York and in Maryland with Marlene and the children, Ralph resisted speaking about his past. "I wasn't open to discussing my past, even with my wife," he later recalled. "Marlene never really asked about my time in Germany and England and perhaps may not have been interested." Glen recalled that his father "swore he would never discuss Germany." But the subject came up one time in what Ralph later described as "a very superficial discussion" during a Seder on the second night of Passover at a time when his children were probably beyond their high school years, possibly not until the late 1970s or the early 1980s. It occurred after Marlene's mother had completed her annual recounting of her exodus from Russia. Ralph decided he would speak up. "He didn't go into much detail," Glen later recalled, "because he had blocked so much out that he didn't say much." Ralph later had a somewhat different reaction regarding that night: "There was a lack of questioning and interest in knowing about my parents and my Kindertransport experiences. I was very disappointed by their lack of interest; this hurt me a lot." Thus, for the most part, Ralph continued to suppress the urge to speak about his past and confront his traumas for the remainder of the time the family lived together.

Still another challenge for Ralph during his adult years related to Edith. Theirs was a complicated relationship, especially for Ralph. It had evolved from chilly at best beginning when Ralph was a child in Germany, to one where Edith served as a surrogate maternal figure during their time in England and their early days in New York, to a somewhat less tumultuous but distant relationship during their adult years. From Ralph's perspective, although he loved his sister and appreciated what she did to enable him to survive in the absence of his parents, he resented her for the control she had exerted over him, for her self-serving manner particularly when it came to dealing with the family and the issue involving the stamps, and especially for willfully abandoning her Jewish heritage. These mixed emotions about his sister became heightened during the years after he was married and had children, at a time when Edith found herself losing her battle with multiple sclerosis.

It took many years for Edith's disease to develop to the extent that it was debilitating. Ralph had moved the family to Maryland, but every once in a while he received phone calls from Edith's neighbors with unsettling reports that his sister had been seen crawling on the floor of the basement of their home, or that there was a smell of marijuana coming from the house. He would call his friend Bob Kroll in Merrick, an attorney whom Ralph met while working at Jones Beach, and Bob would tell him to get up there and meet him at Edith's house. This came at a time when Edith's boys were already teenagers and out of the house and Michael was at his office seeing patients. When Ralph and Bob arrived, there was nothing wrong at all, but sometimes it was difficult for Edith to answer the phone and so Ralph made at least two trips from Maryland to his sister's house responding to a false alarm. Bob then told Ralph to call him first before making the trip from Maryland to New York and he would try to determine if there was a need for Ralph to travel there. Despite the cooling in his relationship with Edith as a result of the disclosure about the lifts, Ralph took his children to visit her several times over the years. "We did a lot of trips to New York," Glen later recalled. "My dad has friends who live in Long Island so when we went up there to see them we would also see his sister and her family on the same trip." Later on in the late 1970s and early 1980s when Glen was a teenager, he would accompany his father on trips to see Edith. Ralph had taken up flying lessons around that time and Glen recalled his dad learning to fly a single-engine Cessna while taking one of their trips from Maryland to New York. "I was the one who expected to get sick, but he was the one who got sick," Glen later recalled. By this time Edith was confined to a wheelchair, making it difficult for her to remain at home. Michael had placed her in a nursing home and subsequently divorced her; he married a woman who had served as his nurse in Long Island, leaving Edith very much on her own. Glen recalled visiting her at the nursing home without the past ever being mentioned. "Nothing was ever discussed when we saw her," he recalled. "Everything was so private."

Ralph nonetheless very much wanted to speak to Edith about his feelings toward her that had festered inside him since childhood. "I was at odds with what she had done," he later recalled, ranging from her forcing him to forget the past, to turning her back on the relatives, and especially her abandonment of Judaism. "Each of these actions had created friction between us," he recalled. He was finally able to have a conversation with Edith about these matters when he visited her at the nursing home without Glen. "I wanted to understand her way of life—what was inside her," he later recalled. She had never opened up to him in the past, deflecting any discussion by telling him: "Don't worry about what's inside of me; you worry about yourself." That had troubled Ralph most of his life, especially her abandonment of Judaism. He finally asked her, "After all you went through—after all our parents went through and the Jewish education you got in Germany—how can you turn your back on Judaism?" Ralph recalled Edith telling him that "persecution is very painful, that she had been much older than I was in Germany and so I had no idea how much pain and suffering she had." Ralph said that he certainly could imagine her pain and reminded her "that she well knew what my pain was, and my pain is exacerbated by her denying that she had Jewish parents." He asked her what she had against Judaism, which "is a beautiful religion, rich in history and culture," and said that Judaism did not need to excite anyone in order for people to embrace it. Ralph recalled Edith's response: "Just because Judaism was right for me didn't mean it was right for her. She had to live her life the way she saw fit to be best for her." That conversation was one of the last Ralph had with his sister. Her disease soon took away her ability to speak, and shortly after that—on April 25, 1987—Edith passed away without the friction in Ralph's relationship with her ever having been fully resolved and the scars from that relationship remained with him. "I had terrible regrets that I did not treat my sister fairly," he later recalled. "She saved my life, literally taking me by the hand as we walked on that train to freedom. We were separated for most of our lives and barely knew each other. I wanted time to know her better and show her my love and gratitude."

A final adult life challenge for Ralph concerned his marriage with Marlene. There had been a number of warning signs that the marriage was not doing well, but as happens in many of these cases, neither Ralph nor Marlene recognized them as such at the time they occurred. Ralph bore considerable resentment that Marlene had not accompanied him to Japan during his military service there when they were first married, even though it would have been quite possible for her to do so. Soon after Jeffrey was born and the couple moved to New Jersey, Marlene became homesick and made noises about moving the family closer to Springfield, Massachusetts, even though Ralph had just accepted a position at ITT that enabled him to launch his career. "This was a major issue between us," Ralph later recalled. "I knew at that time the road forward would be rocky," he noted in retrospect. Throughout the early years of their marriage, certainly up until the time Ralph had settled into his career at NASA and the family moved into their home in Silver Spring, Maryland, Marlene had put considerable pressure on him to be upwardly mobile, especially when it came to the size and comfort of their living accommodations. The most obvious warning sign, however, was the fact that they knew almost nothing about each other at the time they were married, that neither of them had experienced a real relationship with anyone else before they met, and they probably spent the equivalent of less than two weeks together from the time they first met in Atlantic City until they were married six months later, at which point Ralph went overseas almost immediately for 15 months. These circumstances prevented them from being able to build a foundation for a firm relationship in advance of marriage and parenthood. It was not until later in life that Ralph acknowledged: "I didn't know her very well; she didn't know me very well and yet, for some unknown reason, we were two needy people who were very lonely, very introverted, who found each other and started a life together."

Four factors contributed to great difficulties in the marriage. One involved Marlene's role in exacerbating the aforementioned friction that existed in Ralph's relationship with the children. He and Marlene would argue about disciplining the kids. Glen recalled: "They would start fighting and nobody said a word, because you didn't dare interrupt, and then if you did something wrong, it exploded back on you." Another factor had to do with the inability of both Ralph and Marlene to outwardly express affection. "Quite frankly," Ralph later acknowledged, "there wasn't much representation of love in our family, and that was a profound struggle for me." He wanted to say to Marlene, "I love you," but she was not able to reciprocate and so those words rarely were exchanged throughout their marriage. Although an introvert, Ralph considered himself "a warm and loving person, a hugging person." When the issue arose between them, Marlene would tell him that she was not a demonstrative person and that as much as she loved him, she said, "I'm not one that is going to shower love on you." Another factor occurred as a result of Marlene's personal business and her failure to keep accurate records that caused major problems when Ralph had to prepare his annual family tax return. He felt there was no accountability in her recordkeeping, and she felt that her business was none of his business and chastised him about this. They argued out loud on this issue in their house in the presence of the children, and each year at tax time the annual verbal fights became louder and more incensed to the point where Marlene told Ralph, as he later recalled, "that her first love was her business, her second love was her children, and I came somewhere after that." As if this was not sufficient, a fourth factor arose in the second half of 1975 when, with Jeffrey spending the year after his high school graduation in Israel, Ralph and Marlene learned that Jeffrey had to return home after being diagnosed with Hodgkin's disease. He went through a difficult time while receiving chemotherapy, but eventually the disease went into remission. Marlene had great difficulty coping with Jeffrey's illness, however, and distanced herself from most of her family responsibilities, concentrating on her concern for Jeffrey and on her business, leaving Ralph to take on a still greater burden which heightened the already significant dysfunction in their relationship.

Despite a growing realization that their marriage was deeply in trouble, Ralph and Marlene remained reluctant to sever the relationship. "They didn't want to jeopardize the family," Glen later recalled, "so they stuck it out as long as they could." In 1978 they tried marriage counseling at the Jewish Social Services Agency (JSSA) in Rockville, Maryland. "I told myself I could solve this," Ralph later recalled. "I thought I knew what my weaknesses were and felt that I could deal with them in a limited way." The counseling effort, however, came to naught. The first therapist they saw was new to her work and unable to stimulate meaningful discussion. A second therapist encouraged both of them to speak, but there were long periods of silence that made Ralph uncomfortable. The social worker said to him, "When you're ready, we'll talk about it." But Ralph was unable "to open up in that environment." The marriage counseling ended after just a few sessions. Life continued at home, but arguments became pervasive and the tension only increased. A short time later, in early 1981, Marlene became ill, for which she took an extended course of prednisone that caused her to gain significant weight and that had a severely negative impact on both her physical and emotional well-being. She was then diagnosed with lymphoma, for which she underwent a course of chemotherapy that put the disease into remission but again depleted her physical and emotional strength, contrib-

uting further to an untenable marriage. In June of 1984, with the children grown up and pretty much out of the house, Marlene told Ralph to leave. He said he would not get out of the house without a legal document of separation, which they both signed within a week, ending more

than 29 years of marriage. Ralph temporarily moved in with Jeffrey, who was living in a condominium in Bethesda Park in Rockville, Maryland. About a month later, Ralph purchased a townhome in Silver Spring and moved in. On February 10, 1988, Ralph and Marlene became formally divorced.

At age 54, Ralph found himself for the first time in his life completely alone in his own home. He had survived the horrors of the Holocaust, somehow managed to obtain a good education and had built a highly successful career in engineering; but in virtually every other respect he felt that his life had been a failure. Robbed of his childhood, his home, and his parents by the National Socialists, forced into an underdog role throughout his school years largely bereft of family support, he had struggled mightily just to get by. He had struggled and barely sustained a relationship with his sister, and now she was gone; he had struggled with and eventually abandoned any relationship with his cousins from Germany who had moved to New York, and now they were mostly gone; he had struggled through a disappointing and in many ways rocky marriage that may have been doomed from the start and was now over; and he had struggled with parenting that left his relationships with his children in varying states of disarray. He felt riddled with guilt over these failures, sensing that they were somehow connected to something greater, as he remained haunted by the traumas of his past in ways he could not quite understand and from which he had been unable to find relief. In the year 1988, as the book closed on a tumultuous phase of his life, Ralph Mollerick realized that he had survived but was unclear and deeply concerned about what the future would bring.

# PART II

## Redemption

# CHAPTER 9

— ❧ —

# New Beginnings (1988–1991)

THE PHONE RANG in Ralph's Silver Spring townhome one evening in May 1988. June Charney, a fellow congregant at Mishkan Torah whom Ralph had known for many years, had called with a request. June knew that Ralph had been actively involved in, and was the membership chairman of, an organization known as New Beginnings, which served as a unique support group for singles in the Washington, DC, metropolitan area whose marriages had broken up. June had a friend, also a fellow congregant, named Phyllis Jacobs who had recently experienced a messy separation. June encouraged Ralph to contact Phyllis and talk to her about New Beginnings as she believed Phyllis might find the organization helpful in dealing with her situation. Ralph was 15 years senior to Phyllis and really did not know her except that she was a fellow congregant and was active in the Mishkan Torah Sisterhood; nor did Phyllis know Ralph well either, more accurately knowing of him as a fellow congregant. Ralph nonetheless took June's request at face value: "I told June I would be delighted to do that," Ralph later recalled "and so I called Phyllis." They agreed to meet at the next Friday night service at Mishkan Torah, after which they spent considerable time talking. Ralph told Phyllis that June thought she might be interested in New Beginnings and that he very much liked his experience with the organization. Phyllis said that she wanted to hear more about it, and they made a dinner date for the following week at a Rockville, Maryland, restaurant.

The dinner turned out to be more than about introducing Phyllis to New Beginnings. Ralph and Phyllis hit it off almost immediately. The conversation was relaxed and very much devoid of the kind of pervasive tension and wariness that Ralph's interactions with Marlene or Edith had caused for him. Although they did not speak much about their personal lives at this dinner, Ralph and Phyllis immediately sensed ability in the other to listen and respond with interest to what each had to say, something that had been largely missing in conversations with their former spouses. Ralph spoke at some length about his very positive experience with New Beginnings. Phyllis listened intently and said that it sounded like an organization in which she might have interest. The dinner ended without their having discussed much about their failed marriages, their children, or other personal aspects of their past, but they both came away with enough interest in the other to keep talking. They agreed to have dinner the following weekend. "We went to a restaurant and we talked and talked," Ralph later recalled. Phyllis decided to join the organization and they continued to talk to each other outside the meetings, which resulted in a new beginning, indeed, for both of them.

It had taken Ralph close to four years to reach a place in his life where having dinner alone with a woman—for any reason—was possible. His separation from Marlene in June 1984, mounted upon years of frustration, anger, and pain regarding his childhood, had left him emotionally damaged. It was as if there was a profound weight on his shoulders from which his only relief was his career. Ironically it was during this time that he experienced some of his most productive work at Goddard Space Flight Center. When not at work, however, he was lonely and miserable, so much so that the extent of his volunteer work at Mishkan Torah lessened, although he sometimes frequented the Jewish Community Center (JCC) in Rockville. One day, shortly following his separation from Marlene, he encountered Shalom Fischer, a former congregant of Mishkan Torah whom he knew but hadn't seen in quite a while, at the JCC. "You look terrible," Shalom said to Ralph, "like you've lost your best friend." Ralph briefly told him about his separation. Shalom said that he was a member of a relatively new organization called New

Beginnings, a support group for people who are separated and divorced, and suggested that Ralph attend a session, which he did. He found the meetings very helpful; group discussions dealt with topics relevant to people hurting from bad marriages and helped them learn to cope with such post-marriage issues as anger management, relationships with children, improving communication, and dating again. "I took a liking to the group and attended for more than three years," Ralph later recalled. Primarily New Beginnings demonstrated to Ralph that he was not alone in having experienced a failed marriage, nor was the failure of his marriage his failure alone. Not only was this important for his self-esteem, but the discussions encouraged him to think deeper about his marriage and about other possible sources of his disquietude. As a result, not long after joining New Beginnings, Ralph sought personal counseling at the JSSA in Rockville.

The one-on-one counseling Ralph received at the JSSA, unlike the abortive attempts at marriage counseling in 1978, had a profoundly positive impact on Ralph's life. The therapist began by asking Ralph what he was feeling at the present time and that they would work back through his past from there. Ralph later recalled what he told the therapist: "I feel pent-up anger over my failed marriage, of having been overstressed about disciplining my children, and finding no path to reverse any of these failures." They had a long discussion about the roots of these problems deriving from Ralph's childhood. Over the course of months of sessions the therapist was able to help Ralph peel back the layers of his past that he had forcibly suppressed for half a century. Gradually Ralph found himself able to open up; he spoke about his father's manner of discipline, about his traumas from the way in which he had been persecuted by his teacher in first grade and his efforts, only sometimes successful, to escape being bullied by children after school and his need to protect himself both physically and emotionally from perceived and real threats from his peers throughout childhood in Germany and in England. He also spoke about suppressing his past—being told to "keep a stiff upper lip and act as an adult" by the social worker in England and about his sister's repeated admonitions to "forget the past and only look ahead." He spoke about pervasively experiencing nightmares throughout his life, reliving in his subconscious the traumas of his past. The therapist told him that he had been deprived of his childhood, that he had gone from being a little boy to an adult without the experience of enjoying his youth, and that this largely explained the source of his anger, which then manifested itself throughout his marriage and in his parenting in counterproductive ways. For the first time in his life, with the help of the counselor, Ralph was able to confront his past, to speak about it, and then analyze and eventually understand how so many of his perceived failures as an adult had been the result of his experiences surviving the Holocaust as a child. "The moment he said I was full of anger," Ralph later recalled, "I knew exactly what he meant; I understood better where certain stress points came from and began to see what my limitations had been and what caused them." Ralph thus achieved a level of self-awareness unlike anything he had experienced before in his life.

As a result of the months of therapy at the JSSA, Ralph made peace with himself with regard to his failed marriage. "I was happy—really happy—that I had finally changed my lifestyle, that I was now single again," he later recalled. "I felt that I was in a much better place being on my own again." He reached out to his children, especially to Jeffrey and Shari, with whom his relationship had been so poor for so many years. His children noticed an almost immediate change in Ralph's demeanor. They told him that he seemed like a new man, and he was not the father they knew. Jeffrey said to him that "had I been like this during his childhood, we would have had a whole different relationship," Ralph later recalled. He also recalled Shari telling him "that I even looked different, that I was now a person she wanted to love as opposed to being afraid of." Following this breakthrough, Shari was able to live in Ralph's townhome on and off over the course of seven years, despite her own issues that periodically estranged her from her family. Glen noticed a change as well, but his relationship with his dad had been considerably more positive, at least on the surface, than Ralph's relationship with Glen's older siblings. While the relationship between Ralph and Jeffrey warmed as a result of Ralph's counseling to the extent that they managed to get along fairly well outwardly, there remained a deeper level of resentment on Jeffrey's part that prevented a full reconciliation, and that situation would never be fully resolved.

In the broader scheme of things, Ralph's counseling sessions at the JSSA enabled him to face his past. He found himself, really for the first time, able to approach the topic, haltingly and with great difficulty at first, gradually achieving a very limited comfort level that allowed him to voluntarily enter his past in three very modest ways over the next few years. First, Ralph attended a few meetings of a child Holocaust survivor group, now known as the Association of Child Survivors in the Washington-Baltimore area (which is associated with the World Federation of Jewish Child Survivors of the Holocaust and Descendants, or WFJCSHD). Ralph found, however, that the few meetings of the regional group held during the mid to late 1980s that he attended were too difficult to tolerate. Some concentration camp survivors spoke about their experiences, and this led to open weeping at the meetings, which Ralph found depressing and too difficult to deal with at the time, and so he stopped going. Then, in 1989, Jeffrey learned about a planned 50th anniversary reunion conference of kinder being held in London in June of that year and encouraged his father to attend. But after his experience with the local child survivor meetings, Ralph was not ready to travel to England, even for a unique event dedicated to survivors of the Kindertransport.

A second example of Ralph taking small steps to confront his past involved his connecting with family. In this instance, Ralph continued to have difficulty reconnecting with his still-living older cousins he had known in New York. He did engage in a series of correspondence with more distant cousins, however, one of which was with a cousin, Walter Möllrich, who was most likely related to Ralph through his grandfather, Wolf Möllerich, and who emigrated from Germany well before the war and lived in San Francisco with his wife and sister. Ralph had visited them on a business trip in 1988 after Ralph's oldest children, Jeffrey and Shari, had met them in the early 1980s, and he had a brief correspondence with this cousin following his visit there. He also corresponded with two brothers named Walter and Ernst Möllrich. As best as Ralph was able to determine, the brothers were also related to him through his grandfather, Wolf Möllerich, and a likely first cousin of his grandfather, Samuel Möllrich, whose side of the family came from an area of north Hessen, not far from Wolfhagen. Today there are villages in the area bearing the name Möllrich. Both brothers had managed to escape the Holocaust. Walter lived with his wife Hansi in Flackwell Heath, Buckinghamshire, England, while Ernst and his wife Trude lived in Haifa, Israel. The original connection with the latter couple came as a result of the visits that Jeffrey and Shari made to Israel in the mid and late 1970s. Ralph had not personally made contact with either of the brothers until the late 1980s. The distant cousins were much older than Ralph, as had been the case with his first cousins who immigrated to the United States. The couple living in England, in particular, was quite a bit older. Ralph's correspondence with these cousins tended to be sporadic, sometimes occurring not more than once a year or even longer, and the topic of discussion focused mostly on current news about the family rather than on the past, which made it all the more tolerable for Ralph to communicate in this way. Unfortunately, the cousins in England passed away within a year or so of each other beginning in 1989. The cousin in San Francisco and the Israeli couple, however, remained part of Ralph's life well into the 1990s.

As for the third way in which Ralph began to reconnect with his past, much of that had to do with Phyllis Jacobs.

It did not take long once Ralph and Phyllis met each other for their acquaintanceship to develop into a deep friendship. After Phyllis joined New Beginnings, they saw each other at meetings, of course, but they began dating on a regular basis, often going to a movie, but especially going to restaurants where they would spend hours in conversation. It was not long before the talk turned personal, with each communicating about their past, not so much at first about the intimate details of their failed marriages but about their feelings, especially how their past had molded their frame of mind about relationships. Although Ralph and Phyllis were coming from very different places, there was an immediate chemistry between them, so much so that their conversations flowed freely over a wide range of topics. "I liked him right away," Phyllis later recalled. "I liked him because he was smart, and very gentle, and very kind." She also found him "settled," in that "he was older and had more life experience—he was just a good person." Ralph found Phyllis to be "a person who could easily listen; whatever I was talking about, she was totally involved in the conversation with me," he later recalled. This enabled Ralph to open up in ways that he had never attempted with anyone else, except during his recent therapy sessions. "Phyllis learned very quickly that I had some baggage, and she wanted to understand that baggage," he recalled. "Each time we went out on a date we talked a little more about our past, including our marriages and our children."

Phyllis had her own set of baggage. She had married Neal Jacobs at a young age and they had four children together: Rochelle, the eldest, was born in 1968; Philip was born in 1970; Jack in 1974; and Rebecca in 1979. They had lived in Laurel, Maryland, throughout their marriage and belonged to a synagogue in Laurel before joining Mishkan Torah in the early 1980s. Phyllis found Neal an increasingly difficult person to live with and, like the situation in the Mollerick home, the tension between the spouses predictably had an unfortunate impact on the children. When Phyllis left Neal in the fall of 1987, she moved into an apartment in Laurel with Rochelle and Rebecca, although Rochelle was old enough to be on her own and soon left to share an apartment with friends; Neal retained custody of the two boys. During their early conversations, Ralph recalled Phyllis telling him that she had been "denigrated by her husband, leading her to feel insecure and afraid." At one point Ralph asked what concerns she had in exploring a relationship with him. "She said she didn't like to be talked down to," he later recalled, "she didn't like being held accountable for what she was doing all the time, and she didn't like having to be forced into accepting someone else's opinion." It took very little time for Phyllis to realize that she would get none of that from Ralph. "I admired the fact that he has his head on straight," she later recalled, "that he's very ambitious about getting things done on the one hand, but not afraid to have a good time, on the other." Ralph later recalled Phyllis telling him at the time that "what she liked about me is that she could talk to me freely—that I listen and understand where she's coming from."

It did not take long for Ralph to open up to Phyllis not only about his marriage but also about his distant past for the first time outside of his counseling sessions at the JSSA. "She was immediately interested in the Kindertransport, in my life in Germany, in my life in England, and how I fared in the United States," Ralph later recalled. He told her about those components of his past and even about his long-standing dysfunctional relationship with Edith. "It was pretty early on that he told me he had been on the Kindertransport, and we talked quite a bit about it," Phyllis later recalled. "That happened pretty much in the beginning of our relationship." From the outset, Phyllis realized how difficult it was for Ralph to discuss his past. Through their conversations she encouraged him to speak because she wanted to understand about his past, not only because it would provide greater insight in what made him the person he was, but because she was a profoundly empathetic person who understood how important it was for Ralph to share his past as a means of exorcising the demons that had traumatized him for so long. She encouraged Ralph to talk about his past, however, without pushing him beyond where he was capable of going. "She was very understanding," Ralph later recalled, "and that was a completely different experience for me—the difference between Marlene's approach of demanding things to happen now and Phyllis' approach that we should talk about things together and see where it goes."

As quickly as the relationship progressed, there came a time fairly early on when Phyllis was prepared to advance to the next level but Ralph was not. "She told me that she thought this could work out for us," he later recalled, "but I told her that I was not there yet and couldn't make a commitment." He told her that his interest in her was as a person with whom he could engage in activities, such as movies and restaurants, and that perhaps after a while the romantic component could enter into it. "I wanted to take it slow," he later recalled, and felt badly because he sensed that Phyllis "was willing to advance the relationship more rapidly than I was." Ralph was not ready to have an exclusive relationship. "I told her I wanted to listen to other people, enjoy what they have to say, and I might date them," he later recalled, which he did for a brief time. At one point after Ralph and Phyllis had been dating for some time and even though Ralph and Marlene were legally divorced, Shari asked Ralph to consider reconciliation with Marlene. "Shari told me that I had to test my own needs and whether I'm willing to go in a different direction from Marlene," he later recalled. He and Marlene went on a date and Ralph attempted to discuss some of the problematic aspects of their relationship. "I didn't hear anything different from Marlene," he later recalled. But Marlene insisted that they try again and they went out twice more. "Each time I wanted her to say 'I love you' but I never heard those words," he later recalled. On the third date Ralph told her that he knew there was a part of him "that loved her very dearly from the very beginning when we met; however, as time went on, I did not feel loved—I felt like I was tolerated," he later recalled. They parted ways after that third date with the intention of remaining friends, which Marlene doubted would be possible. As it turned out, Marlene's prediction proved to be incorrect, although it took a couple of years and a major change in Ralph's life before the friendship materialized. Ultimately Marlene's health deteriorated and Ralph assisted with her medical expenses until they were formally divorced. She passed away on December 31, 1998.

Ralph may not have realized it at the time, but his abortive second effort with Marlene may have paved the way for him to accept a serious relationship with Phyllis. They became an exclusive couple and began to appear in public together with mutual friends. Ralph had met Phyllis' daughter Rebecca quite early on in their friendship and they each soon met the rest of each other's children. Phyllis got along with Ralph's children very well from the start, especially with Jeffrey and Glen. Ralph enjoyed spending time with Rebecca, who was seven years old when he first met Phyllis and she occasionally joined the couple on weekend outings once they began dating more seriously. Phyllis' divorce became finalized in 1990 and sometime around the beginning of 1991, Ralph and Phyllis became engaged. Although Phyllis recalled she never had a direct conversation with her children about marrying Ralph, she later declared that her daughters "took to him nicely" and "never raised objections to him." Ralph and Phyllis were married on May 12, 1991, before a gathering of family and friends. Phyllis and Rebecca moved into Ralph's Silver Spring townhome, and Ralph helped raise Rebecca in a loving atmosphere that had likely been missing in her life and had certainly been missing in Ralph and Phyllis' previous marriages. "I discovered that I still have the capacity to love and enjoy my own children and the children that I have affiliation with through Phyllis," Ralph later recalled. The marriage marked the onset of an extraordinary second phase in Ralph's lifelong journey and set the stage for an event that would change the trajectory of his life forever.

# CHAPTER 10

—— ❧ ——

# Return to Germany (1992–1993)

As HAD BEEN the case with most other turning points in his life, a new major milestone began for Ralph with a telephone call. Ralph answered the phone in his Silver Spring home one morning early in August 1992; his oldest son, Jeffrey, was on the line. "Dad," Ralph later recalled Jeffrey beginning the conversation, "I'm looking at your house from my hotel room in Wolfhagen." Ralph was stunned. He could hear Jeffrey's voice choking up as he delivered his message. Tears welled in his eyes as he tried to respond to his son: "I don't know what to say—I'm speechless to hear that you found the house that I had so much trouble describing to you from what I tried to remember of it." There was a period of silence as father and son attempted to gain control of their emotions.

The events immediately leading to Jeffrey's phone call were nothing short of remarkable. Ralph and Phyllis had celebrated the bat mitzvah of Phyllis' younger daughter Rebecca in June 1992. They had never taken a honeymoon trip and decided to travel with Rebecca to Israel at the beginning of July to mark both her bat mitzvah and their marriage. During the visit to Israel they had the opportunity to meet with Ralph's distant cousins Ernst and Trude Möllrich in Haifa. They also visited *Yad Vashem*, the extraordinary Holocaust Memorial museum and research center located on the outskirts of Jerusalem. There Ralph did some research and found information about his uncle Moritz, and about Julius Mansbach who, with his younger sister, Hilde had immigrated from Gudensberg to Chicago with their parents in the mid-1930s where Hilde had married Morris Hollander and they had two children, Kenneth and Sandra.

Seeing this limited information about his cousins in Chicago tweaked a distant childhood memory for Ralph that he had overheard discussions in the living room of his Wolfhagen home about family who had left Germany and moved to Chicago. Upon returning from Israel, Ralph told Jeffrey about the discovery of his relatives in Chicago. Jeffrey had taken a job with a wine distributor firm—Kronheim Wholesale Liquors of Baltimore, Maryland—some years earlier and frequently traveled on business. He had to make a trip to California and somehow found Hilde's phone number in a Chicago airport phone book while waiting for a connecting flight and called her from the airport. Upon his return to Maryland from this trip, Jeffrey convinced Ralph and Phyllis to join him on a trip to Chicago to visit the cousins, who very much wanted to see Ralph. The three of them—Ralph, Phyllis, and Jeffrey—went to Chicago almost immediately thereafter in July 1992 for a brief but very positive visit with Hilde and her family.

Jeffrey had been encouraged by his father's new and apparently growing interest in his past, especially following Ralph's trips to Israel and Chicago in short order. He had begun taking increasing interest in his father's roots, in fact, ever since meeting his distant cousins in Israel during the mid-1970s and more so in the wake of Ralph's breakthrough after undergoing counseling. Over the course of many months, he had sporadically been successful in getting his father to describe what he could remember about Germany, especially the house where he had lived in Wolfhagen. After the trip to Chicago, he had been assigned to travel to Germany in August of 1992 to visit vineyards along the Rhine and Mosel. Having completed his business task, Jeffrey drove his rental car to the north Hessen region and checked into the Alte Rathaus Hotel in the center of Wolfhagen (see photo on cover). He walked through some of the streets of the town searching for a large house opposite a bakery where his father had lived but could not find the house. That evening someone at the hotel told him of an English-speaking woman— a real estate agent—in nearby Zierenberg who knew something of the history of Wolfhagen, and so the next day Jeffrey drove to Zierenberg.

It turned out that the English-speaking real estate agent was also a historian who had done research about the towns in the area, and knew the name Möllerich. She invited Jeffrey to lunch at her home and made a couple of phone calls. She told him to go back to Wolfhagen and someone would be waiting at the site of the old family home, which she said was located just a short distance down Schützebergerstraße from his hotel. He was told to look for the large stone building with an unusual roof whose façade looked like steps. Returning to the Alte Rathaus, he walked along Schützebergerstrße about 100 yards and there, standing before him was the building with the unmistakable façade. The Steinkammer building had a restaurant on the ground floor and a cinema directly above. He found a door to the half-timber house directly to the left of the Steinkammer and knocked.

In fairly short order a woman opened the door, peered at Jeffrey, who smiled briefly at her, and she introduced herself in German as Frau Schiffmann. There were two immediate impediments to communicating at this point: first, Jeffrey spoke very little German and neither Frau nor Herr Schiffmann spoke much English. Jeffrey had also been cautioned by the real estate agent not to claim ownership of the house if he were to find it. Many of the townspeople who had lived in Wolfhagen for a long time knew which homes had been owned by Jewish families and could be quite sensitive if a stranger came to the town inquiring about one of these homes, concerned that they might claim ownership and want it returned to the family. In 1962 Ralph's cousin, Harry Rosenthal, had visited Wolfhagen in order to see the home of his grandfather, Moritz Möllerich. His parents, Gretl and Joe had never wanted any property back from the Germans, indeed really wanted nothing to do with Germany and refused to accompany him there. Harry nevertheless had written to the people who had purchased his grandfather's house and store, Herr and Frau Opfermann. When Harry arrived at the train station he was greeted not only by Herr Opfermann but also his attorney. "You knew immediately what they were thinking," Harry later recalled, "and they were never so happy in their lives when I left." Some years later, much closer to the time of Jeffrey's visit in 1992, Lutz Kann—who had been a classmate of Edith Möllerich in the elementary school in pre-Hitler times and who had escaped the Holocaust by going to Palestine, later returning to live in Berlin—had made his initial return to Wolfhagen and demanded to see his family home the first thing upon arrival. He had been a bit unpleasant during his visit and this had upset the current owner of the house and some of the other townspeople.

Jeffrey, of course, had no direct knowledge of these two previous incidents, but took heed of the real estate agent's admonition nonetheless when Frau Schiffmann opened the door. After Jeffrey had introduced himself, it is likely Frau Schiffmann recognized the name Möllerich, because she asked him in German, "Are you here to take this house away from me?" As best as Jeffrey could understand, Frau Schiffmann explained that she had paid a lot of money for the house, because she had purchased it under the Nazis and after the war when Germany became a republic she and her husband had to pay again for the house. Jeffrey, in his broken German, tried to explain that he was not there to take away the house, only to learn about his father's home and something about the family that he never got to know. He asked if he could see the inside of the house that his father had described to him. He was led inside and upstairs to the first floor where he met Herr Schiffmann, who told him they had made changes to the layout from the days his family had lived there. True enough, the rather uniquely situated half-bathroom that his father had mentioned he and Edith had used and that was located between the second and third upstairs levels, was gone. Herr Schiffmann said something about there being no good reason to have a bathroom at that landing. Otherwise, Jeffrey looked around the three-levels of living space in silence and reverence, as if visiting a museum or a cemetery, except for snapping some photos. He thanked Herr and Frau Schiffmann and went out to the street.

The real estate agent had earlier mentioned that there would be a performance in front of the regional museum later in the afternoon, and so Jeffrey made his way back to the end of Schützeburgerstraße and crossed the street to a complex of buildings that housed the museum. A small crowd had gathered in the area in front of the museum entrance and Jeffrey joined the group, listening intently to the speakers even though he understood little of what was being said. A woman who was a member of the museum staff at the time noticed this stranger and introduced herself as Frau Winter. Jeffrey introduced himself in English and told her he was the son of Rolf Wolfgang Möllerich and grandson of Josef Möllerich. "For a moment I was speechless," Frau Winter much later wrote in a letter written about this encounter. "This meeting touched me very much. I knew the sad and painful stories of both the Möllerich families—our guilt! What a coincidence, this meeting!" She told Jeffrey about the few items of Judaica on display inside the museum and offered to show them to him, and so they immediately left the event and went into the museum to see the very small, single display of Jewish culture. Before Jeffrey returned to his room at the Alte Rathaus Hotel, Frau Winter invited him to join her and her husband for the evening meal at their home and gave him their address. "What had inspired me?" she later wrote. "Jeffrey—alone in a strange town, where his father formerly lived and which he now wanted to get to know—these were my thoughts." Jeffrey readily agreed, but as he walked off Frau Winter recalled her doubts whether he would actually honor the invitation. "Would he come to a German house and have a meal with Germans?" she recalled questioning herself. But at 7:00 p.m. Jeffrey stood at their door. "It became a long, interesting, and exciting evening," Frau Winter later wrote, "without any resentments, no-ill-will." Jeffrey explained how he had come to Germany on business and his interest in visiting the town of his father's birth, even though his father had absolutely no interest in seeing Wolfhagen ever again. During the course of that evening, however, based on the conversation, Jeffrey became convinced that his father should make the effort to return, and determined to persuade him to do just that.

Jeffrey broke the silence created by the outpouring of emotion during his phone call to his father from his hotel room in Wolfhagen the next afternoon. He told his father: "Dad, I've spoken to some people here," Ralph later recalled. "They are all saying they would like to see you again." There were people whom he met in the town who remembered his parents and wanted to talk about that with him. Tears continued to run down Ralph's cheeks. Finally, he was able to compose himself enough to tell his son, "I'd like you to tell me all about your experiences when you get back, because I think it is fascinating that you were able to do what I was not able to do." With that, the phone conversation ended, leaving Ralph trying to visualize the scene Jeffrey had described, the sight of his home looking down Schützebergerstraße from the Alte Rathaus Hotel, the fields of bright yellow rapeseed encircling the town and glimmering in the afternoon sun. Instead, visions of Gestapo standing on street corners and Hitler Youth marching below the window of his house materialized in his mind's eye. He relayed the substance of this important phone call to Phyllis, who was immediately excited about the prospect of Ralph returning to his roots; but she could see that her husband was in turmoil and told him only that they should wait for Jeffrey to return from Germany to hear about his visit and see his photographs.

A few days after his return from Germany, Jeffrey came to his father's Silver Spring home. He told Ralph and Phyllis all that had transpired during his visit to Wolfhagen and they spent several hours discussing that and going through his photos from the visit. Ralph approached this initial conversation with understandably mixed emotions. On the one hand, he was highly interested in hearing about Jeffrey's experience in Wolfhagen, especially what the town was like and what the people said to him. On the other hand he had suppressed his memories for so long because of the trauma associated with them and because Edith had told him to, so that it was difficult for him to listen to what Jeffrey was saying let alone to contemplate actually returning to Wolfhagen. Jeffrey could see the anxiety on his father's face. "Please hear me out, Dad," he said, "because you need to hear through me what people in Wolfhagen are saying about your parents and grandparents." He mentioned people whom he met, including Frau and Herr Winter, Frau Thiele, and Herr Engelhardt, who still owned the bakery on Mittelstraße, where his grandparents had lived. "Hearing what Jeffrey was saying about the people there excited me somewhat," Ralph later recalled, "and yet, at the same time I said that I had forgotten all about this—you know, it is ancient history, it is over; I've made a new life." Phyllis was personally "thrilled" about a possible trip to Germany. "Jeffrey and I had become good friends, she later recalled, "and the prospect of traveling together was wonderful." She believed there was probably important information about Ralph's parents and other family members that he could learn from a visit to Wolfhagen and wanted him to go as soon as possible. After Jeffrey left, however, Ralph told her that "it's going to take me a while, because I am envisioning Hitler Youth marching in the streets of the town. I can't make myself go where I don't want to go and I don't want to go to Germany." Phyllis was supportive of Ralph and said to him, "I understand your concerns; let's just talk about it and we can go when you feel ready. You have to be okay with visiting Wolfhagen." Ralph appreciated Phyllis' patience and she and Jeffrey eased the pressure in order to allow Ralph time to reflect on a potential return to Germany, although they continued very gently to encourage Ralph to meet the people who knew his parents and to see what it would be like. Phyllis also told Ralph that she hadn't been anywhere in her life until 1992 and very much wanted to travel with him, and that a trip to Germany would be "a good opportunity" to travel with both Ralph and Jeffrey.

It took more than half a year of conversation and reflection—sometimes painful—before Ralph began to seriously consider a return to Germany. Beyond the constant but gentle urging of his wife and older son, Ralph mentioned a possible trip to Germany in a letter to his cousin Hilde in Chicago. On December 13, 1992, she wrote back to him: "What do you want to do in Wolfhagen? Of course now they are all good people but where have they been when we needed them?" She launched into a brief explanation of why she never considered going back to Gudensberg, but realized that "everyone is different," and so she wrote to him, "If Jeffrey wants you to go, so go with him." Early in 1993, Ralph finally acquiesced, telling Phyllis, "Okay, if this is meant to be, I'm ready," he later recalled. "But bear in mind that I am going to be very resistant to going where there is pain for me." Jeffrey then set about devising a plan for the trip. He had a number of ideas about how to proceed but one of the most important was that the three of them should not go directly to Wolfhagen but spend some time sightseeing in places in Germany distant from the town, even seeing portions of France and Switzerland. He developed a two-week itinerary for midsummer of 1993 in which they would fly to Frankfurt, rent a car, and spend a day in the Rhineland, two days in Alsace, two days in Switzerland, and then several days in Munich and other parts of Bavaria before heading north with stops along the way to Wolfhagen, where they would spend the final three days or so of the trip.

Jeffrey's strategic plan for his father's return to Germany worked to perfection, although it did not begin that way. During the overnight flight from Washington, DC, to Frankfurt, Ralph did not sleep much. The long hours on the plane allowed his mind to work overtime. He felt anxious about the prospect of visiting his town of birth. Thoughts of Edith indoctrinating him into forgetting the past and making a new life for himself, which he had done, re-emerged. He wondered if he could be "calm and accepting enough to go back and visit my home town," he later recalled. He questioned how he would react to people "who I'm likely to meet whom I have no love for and who destroyed our lives—not only for me but for other people and for my family." He also questioned how he would be able to communicate with people in the town, since he had long ago abandoned the German language. He even questioned how he would appear to Phyllis and Jeffrey in the setting of Wolfhagen. These concerns permeated Ralph's thinking during the long flight to Frankfurt. Once on the ground and in the car, however, Ralph joined his wife and son in the moment, experiencing the sights and sounds and aromas of the places they visited as would any other tourist. He was especially fascinated with the time spent in the Swiss Alps, where in midsummer they went to the summit of a mountain and threw snowballs. He had fun and particularly loved watching Phyllis experience Europe for the first time, He and Jeffrey and Phyllis truly enjoyed each other's company. For more than a week Ralph was distracted by the physical surroundings and his interest in the history of the places they visited, so that by the time they arrived at the Alte Rathaus Hotel at the foot of the main square in the historic center of Wolfhagen, Ralph was much more relaxed than he had been on the flight to Germany and felt as ready as he could possibly be to visit his past.

Ralph stood on the steps of the Alte Rathaus Hotel a little before 7:00 p.m. on Saturday, August 7, looking at the main square of central Wolfhagen and becoming a little lost in not-so-fond memories of his childhood, when a tap on his shoulder quickly brought him back to the present. A middle-aged, somewhat husky man stood beside him with his hand extended and introduced himself speaking flawless English with a British accent clearly recognizable to Ralph from living in England for almost eight years. "My name is Günter Glitsch," he said to Ralph; "I represent Bürgermeister [Mayor] Giselher Dietrich, who welcomes you to Wolfhagen. I will be at your disposal as your interpreter while you are here." During this greeting they were joined on the steps by Phyllis and Jeffrey, along with Lutz Kann, who had been in the hotel lobby when the Mollerick family had arrived less than a half hour earlier. Lutz immediately turned to Günter and spoke rapidly in German. Günter later recalled that "he said to me that he knows so much English that they don't need an interpreter. I thought, 'Oh, okay, then I need not stay tonight,' and asked about Sunday." Lutz then told Günter that he had a fairly full day planned with the Mollericks for Sunday as well, and so it was agreed that Günter would return on Monday morning, and then he departed; the others went inside and had dinner in the hotel's restaurant.

The presence of both Günter Glitsch and Lutz Kann at the Alte Rathaus that Saturday evening had been no accident. Jeffrey had made separate arrangements well in advance of the trip to Germany. He had written to Herr Winter to let him know that he would be coming to Germany in the summer of 1993, along with Ralph and Phyllis. Herr Winter gave the letter to the mayor's secretary, thinking that the mayor would be interested in meeting Ralph and perhaps might ask someone to serve as an interpreter. Herr Winter, who spoke regularly with Günter in order to catch up on town news, since Günter was a member of the council, mentioned to him the upcoming visit of the Mollerick family. Very shortly after that, the mayor called Günter and asked him to do some translating during their visit. Günter was an English teacher and the mayor was well aware of his English skills, and Günter was perfectly willing to be helpful, especially since it would be the summer when students were on holiday from school. He asked the proprietor of the Alte Rathaus Hotel to give him a call when the Mollerick family arrived, which she did on the evening of August 7, and Günter came right over to the hotel. As for Lutz Kann, Jeffrey had learned about the only other living Jewish former resident of Wolfhagen from Frau Winter during his dinner at her home in 1992. She had provided him with Lutz's address in Berlin. Jeffrey had contacted Lutz, who had been a former classmate of Edith Möllerich and who said that he would come to Wolfhagen to meet them at the Alte Rathaus over the weekend and bring with him "a suitcase full of photographs," as Ralph later recalled. Lutz had checked into the Alte Rathaus early enough to greet the Mollerick party when they arrived in Wolfhagen by car on August 7. So it was that Lutz Kann, a Jewish survivor of the Holocaust and former resident of Wolfhagen, determined to take charge of the Mollerick family without the presence of Günter Glitsch, a member of the town council and personal representative of the mayor, at least until Monday morning.

Ralph's first impression of Wolfhagen after almost 56 years had filled him with mixed emotions. "The center of the town looked pretty much the same as I had envisioned it back in the 1930s," he later recalled.

Some buildings were no longer there and had been replaced with newer ones, and the wall that had encircled the old center was gone, with only a stone gate remaining. Aside from the brief moment looking upon the main square and recalling unpleasant experiences from his childhood, he felt surprisingly calm as he and Jeffrey and Phyllis took a short walk along Mittelstraße after dinner. He became introspective during the stroll and was struck by a curious thought: "There was an eerie feeling that I was imagining that people were looking out the windows at me, but I couldn't see them," he later recalled. "My mind was saying, 'I wonder what they're thinking—here comes the Jew.'" He imagined how he was going to react when he visited the Jewish cemetery, and also when he was in one of the several places where there was an overview of the town. He had been told by Günter that the mayor had planned a "coffee reception" for Monday with several older members of the town who had known him, as well as his parents and grandparents, and he tried to anticipate how he would respond to meeting the mayor and listening to people speak about his family. He would have expected such thoughts to cause him anxiety, but that was not the case. He thought back to his brief meeting with Günter on the steps of the Alte Rathaus just two hours earlier: "I was immediately allayed of any fear the moment that hand touched my shoulder," he later recalled. "I figured that this visit was going to play out okay, that I just needed to be receptive to the people and what I was about to see and learn. It may not erase my memory, but it may act as an enhancement to the memories, so that I could better understand my feelings." Ralph went to bed eagerly anticipating the next three days.

On Sunday, August 8, after breakfast at the hotel, Ralph, Phyllis, and Jeffrey were joined by Lutz Kann shortly before 10:00 a.m. and they walked the short distance from the hotel to the top of the main square where the Lutheran church stood. They went to the opposite end of the church to the main entrance, where people were gathering and slowly proceeding inside the church for the Divine Service. Lutz left the

Mollericks outside and disappeared into the church, A few moments later he returned and said to Ralph that someone would be coming out of the church to see him. Before Ralph could respond, a gentleman of moderate build and with graying hair—about Ralph's height—came down the steps of the church. There was something vaguely familiar about this man, who approached him. Ralph turned to him and said, "*Möllerich.*" The man introduced himself as Heinrich Schwarz and asked, "*Bist du Wolfgang Möllerich?*" Ralph nodded, and before anything else could happen Heinrich noticed another man passing close by on his way into the church and called him over. This man turned out to be Kurt Giese, one of Ralph's childhood playmates. Heinrich asked Kurt in German, "Do you remember Wolfgang Möllerich?" "*Jah, Wolfgang, naturalich,*" he responded in a gruff voice that was characteristically the way he spoke. The three men stood together in silence for a moment looking at each other with tears welling in their eyes, and suddenly they embraced each other for an extended time, sobbing all the while as Phyllis and Jeffrey and Lutz looked on. It was a highly emotional moment that for Ralph involved more than feelings of joy. "We said nothing at first," he later recalled, "but it was a powerful message going around. I could see that there was great remorse on their part and I could also feel their warmth in their arms around me." But for Ralph, the pain of childhood memories of the way he was treated in the town intermingled with the pleasure of hugging boyhood friends, causing the reunion to be bittersweet. In that brief encounter the three men shared family photographs taken from their wallets, and Ralph and Kurt spoke quickly of their memories of riding tricycles as children. "That should have been a lot of fun talking about it," Ralph later recalled, "but it wasn't as enjoyable at that time as I had hoped." The brief reunion in front of the church, nevertheless, would later turn out to be a highlight moment in Ralph's life.

Once Heinrich and Kurt went into the church for the service, Lutz suggested they walk around the immediate area until the service ended, as Heinrich had requested they return after the service so they could speak some more. They walked down the hill on the north side of town to look for an area of land below the drop-off where Ralph's grandfather, Wolf Möllerich, had owned land, which had been leased to farmers. Ralph could see that the land was now partially developed and it made him sad to think about what might have been if he had inherited that property at some point in his life. On the way back to the church, Lutz stopped and pointed out the house in which he had lived. A woman came to an open window in the front of the house and Lutz spoke to her: "Are you taking good care of my house?" Ralph later recalled him saying. The woman scowled at Lutz and slammed the window shut. Ralph later learned from Günter that such an exchange had occurred on several occasions between Lutz and the current owner of the house, generally each time Lutz visited Wolfhagen, which had first occurred some years earlier, and each time he had been demanding and on the whole not particularly friendly toward people in the town. Recently he had spent more time in nearby Volkmarsen than in Wolfhagen when he traveled from Berlin to visit the north Hessen region. Observing the brief exchange between Lutz and the woman at the window, Ralph and Jeffrey better understood why Jeffrey had been told the previous year not to give the impression he was there to take back the family home, because of the sensitivity among current owners of former Jewish homes.

The group returned to the front of the church just as the Divine Service ended, and so it was but a few minutes before Heinrich and Kurt emerged from the church and joined the Mollerick party for a stroll around the main square. Heinrich was interested in having Ralph and Phyllis meet his wife, Gertrud. Phyllis mentioned that the mayor had planned a coffee at the Alte Rathaus Hotel for Monday afternoon and

invited Heinrich and Kurt to come with their spouses. During this exchange, Kurt—who spoke no English at all and said very little—blurted to Ralph in German in his typically gruff baritone voice, now again overcome with emotion, as Phyllis later recalled: "We never knew what happened to you but we are so glad to see you." He said that he would be pleased to attend the coffee the next day and hoped to bring his wife, Berta, as well. He and Heinrich then walked off in separate directions. Ralph told Lutz that he very much wanted to see the Jewish cemetery. The group walked toward the east end of central Wolfhagen. On the way to the cemetery they approached a shop and Lutz recognized a woman sitting in front of it who introduced herself to the Mollericks as Frau Thiele. Pointing to Ralph, Lutz said to her in German, "This is Wolfgang." Frau Thiele began speaking to Ralph in German, but Lutz interrupted and told her that Ralph doesn't speak German and that he would translate. "Wolfgang's dead," Frau Thiele then said. "No, this is Wolfgang," Lutz quickly replied. "I think I'm seeing a ghost," the woman said. The brief exchange highlighted one of Ralph's greatest concerns regarding his return to Germany—his inability to converse in German. "I was so ashamed of myself," Ralph later recalled; "the feelings were very real, very painful for me to accept that I could not remember the German language—I could not speak with the people in my native language." He could see the puzzled looks whenever he managed to say in German, "I have forgotten all my German," and they didn't believe that because the few words he spoke in German were in perfect Wolfhager dialect. Eventually Ralph would become a little more skilled at conversing in and comprehending the German language, but he never achieved any real comfort with doing so.

The Jewish cemetery of Wolfhagen was located on the eastern edge of the old town center just outside the former walls of the town, along a street named Wilhelmstraße. In his mind's eye, Ralph had visualized an open space about 150 feet wide and 100 feet deep, with a sign indicating *Jüdische Friedhof* (Jewish Cemetery). He vaguely recalled taking walks with his grandfather and passing the space as a child. What he saw bore scarce resemblance to that vision. The front of the space had a picket gate that was locked; on either side along the remainder of the front there were thick hedges standing at least 10 feet in height. Looking around, Ralph could see houses on one side of the space and a bank on the other side, and trees were located at the back of the space, with a multi-level parking garage directly across the street from the front of the cemetery. The greatest shock of all was that by peering through the gate, Ralph could see that the grass was at least two feet high and even higher than that in some places—so high, in fact, that it was impossible to see any headstones from the gate. All that could be seen from his vantage point was a single, large standing stone that later in the visit would be identified as a Holocaust Memorial. The sight of the cemetery in such condition left Ralph distraught and angry. He had hoped to visit the graves of his paternal grandparents and not only had this been impossible because the gate was locked, but clearly the town had allowed the cemetery to fall into disarray. He looked at Lutz for some explanation but he merely shrugged, as if to say, "What else would you expect from this town?" Ralph thus assumed the hedges and locked picket gate were there because the town wished the cemetery to be off limits to the public, including tourists. He walked back to the Alte Rathaus disappointed, upset, and disinclined to see more of Wolfhagen that day, including his family's homes. As a result, after lunch Lutz suggested that they drive towards Kassel to see the *Herkules* Monument—something that Jeffrey had planned on his itinerary for later in their visit.

The afternoon outing to the *Herkules* Monument proved to be a helpful but temporary distraction for Ralph. The 350-year-old monument was located outside of Kassel to the west of the city in the *Bergpark Wilhelmshöhe*. The monument of *Herkules* stands atop a large pyramid spire above a castle that overlooks a long row of cascades of water flowing down a gentle slope to a man-made lake. Ralph, with his engineering background, was always interested in man-made historical structures and found this site particularly interesting, becoming engrossed in learning about all aspects of its construction. By the time the group returned to Wolfhagen and had dinner, Ralph's frame of mind had improved considerably, although he was determined to get inside the cemetery sometime during his visit and have something done about its shabby condition. On that Sunday evening, however, his greatest interest was in the "suitcase full of photographs" that Lutz had supposedly brought along, especially because Lutz was scheduled to return to Berlin the next morning. After dinner he asked Lutz to show him the photos of Edith. He sat in the hotel lobby eagerly waiting to see what Lutz had brought in the suitcase because, although he had many photos of his sister from England and the United States, he did not have any from the time she was a child. Instead of a suitcase or even a folder, Lutz returned carrying a single photograph of his school class with Edith highlighted in yellow. Ralph and Jeffrey were stunned and disappointed. "What was supposed to be a suitcase full of pictures turned out to be one photo," Ralph later recalled, "and he wouldn't even part with it and that immediately framed him in my mind as a phony." The negative manner in which Lutz had spoken about the town during the day—no matter how much it may have been justified—had caught Ralph's attention, but he had been preoccupied with more important personal matters at the time. After the evening encounter over the photograph, Ralph was able to discern a more focused insight about Lutz: "There was a wedge that had begun forming between us that day," he later recalled, "and it continued to grow so that I felt that I could not be his friend." Ralph went to bed that night angry and concerned about a number of things. A day that had begun so hopefully had ended on a sour note.

The next morning, Monday, August 9, Ralph, Phyllis, and Jeffrey arose and ate breakfast early. Lutz joined them in the hotel lobby after breakfast, carrying his travel bag devoid of additional photographs. For a few minutes the group sat mostly in silence until Günter entered the lobby with gusto. Upon greeting Günter, Ralph's mood immediately perked up. He told Günter they wanted to see Nieder Möllrich and Ober Möllrich, the small villages south of Kassel bearing the name of Ralph's distant cousins from California, England, and Israel. Ralph's younger son, Glen, had a friend who had served in the army in Germany during the early 1980s who had told him upon returning to the States that he had been to these villages and wondered if there was any connection with Glen's family name. Ralph also mentioned to Günter that he wanted to visit Gudensberg, his cousin Hilde's birthplace, to see if there was any information about her family or about the synagogue that had been in the town when Hilde lived there. Günter was happy to show them these places, which were located quite close to each other, but Jeffrey said that first they had to drive Lutz to the train station in Kassel for his return to Berlin. The group of five piled into Jeffrey's rental car with Günter seated next to Jeffrey in the front and the others in the rear seat, and off they went to Kassel with hardly a word being spoken during the 20-minute drive to the train station. When the car arrived at the station, "Lutz just got out," Günter later recalled, "and the goodbye at the station was very cool, cold actually." Ralph and Jeffrey accompanied Lutz into the station and Ralph purchased the train ticket, as had been previously arranged between Jeffrey and Lutz. The moment Ralph and Jeffrey returned and the car drove off, the atmosphere immediately improved. This was really the first time Ralph, Phyllis, and Jeffrey had an opportunity to speak with Günter at length, and they all hit it off right away. "I turned around and talked to them in the back, and Jeff sat next to me, and we had quite a very good conversation then," Günter later recalled. "The funny thing was when I got to know them [the Mollerick family], it didn't feel like they were new people to me; it felt like I had known them for years. This is how I really felt about them very quickly, and Jeffrey made it very easy—he was very talkative."

The group arrived at the two villages bearing the names of Ralph's distant cousins. The twin villages were located very close to each other near the Eder River. Of the two, Nieder Möllrich was the larger, but both villages were quite small and so Ralph and the others spent only a short time there before driving on to the larger town of Gudensberg a short distance to the north in the general direction of Wolfhagen and Kassel. They all first inquired about the synagogue and were told it had been converted to a storage facility; they found the building and went inside. "Sure enough," Ralph later recalled, "there were buckets and bales of hay inside the facility; you would never have known it was once a synagogue." Ralph and Phyllis also inquired about information relating to Hilde and Julius and their parents. They went into the town hall but were unable to find any information about the cousins there. Meanwhile, Jeffrey and Günter sat at a table in the market square enjoying the midday sun and had something to eat and drink; Ralph and Phyllis joined them there once they were finished with the inquiries at the town hall. After the lunch break, the group drove back to Wolfhagen in order to arrive in time for the mayor's coffee reception. During the ride to Wolfhagen, Ralph mentioned to Günter his great interest in getting inside the Jewish cemetery and the poor condition of the cemetery he had noticed from outside the gate the day before. Günter said that he would get the key so they could visit the cemetery on Tuesday morning. He also mentioned that Ralph had an appointment with Mayor Dietrich on Tuesday afternoon.

The coffee and reception planned by the mayor was to be held in a large conference room at the Alte Rathaus Hotel at 4:00 p.m. When he learned that Ralph and his family would be visiting Wolfhagen from the letter that Jeffrey had written to Herr Winter, Mayor Dietrich realized that Ralph's visit could have significance for the town. "There had been an aversion against Germany at that time," he later recalled, "And I was pleased to learn that he planned to come to Wolfhagen." It is possible that the experience when Lutz Kann had first returned to Wolfhagen, where he basically just showed up and then made demands about his former house without anyone from the town knowing about it in advance so that townspeople could be prepared, had something to do with the mayor's decision to hold the coffee reception. It is also possible that, unlike the case with Lutz Kann's family, Ralph's father had been so well known and respected in the town that there that there were several people still living who remembered Ralph's family and wanted to see him. In any event, the mayor and his staff were able to locate several residents who remembered Ralph's parents, and even his grandparents, and invited them to the coffee and reception at the Alte Rathaus. Günter arrived with the Mollerick family on the early side, perhaps 3:30 p.m. The conference room had been nicely prepared with coffee and cakes laid out around a large oval table with many chairs

around it. Not long after their arrival, Mayor Dietrich came in and introduced himself to the family. He spoke no English and so Günter translated. For Günter this served as a warm-up for the meeting itself, in which the invitees from the town spoke virtu- ally only in German, while  Ralph, Phyllis, and Jeffrey spoke only in English. Almost immediately most of the invited people from the town arrived and everyone sat down around the conference table.

Mayor Dietrich said a few words of welcome and then everyone around the table introduced themselves in turn. Besides the mayor, the group included Herr Engelhardt (who owned the bakery across from Ralph's former house); Frau Schiffmann (current owner of Ralph's fam- ily home and the Steinkammer); Kurt Giese; Frau Thiele; Frau Vialon (Frau Thiele's daughter-in-law); Frau and Herr Wimmer (current owner of Moritz Möllerich's house and shop); Günter Glitsch; Frau Nagel (a neighbor whom Ralph vaguely remembered from childhood); Jeffrey Mollerick; Phyllis Mollerick; and Ralph Mollerick. Heinrich and Gertrud Schwarz arrived after the meeting started, as did a reporter from the local newspaper, whom the mayor had invited for the occasion. As each person from the town spoke, memories—sometimes vivid but mostly vague—of these people flashed in Ralph's mind. He could recall that most of them, with the exception of Frau Vialon and his boyhood friends present at the reception, had attended gatherings held by his father in his Wolfhagen home.

In turn, each of the invitees seated at the table spoke about what they remembered of Ralph's parents, and of himself as a child. Some of the stories were humorous; others were more serious. One of the people told the story of finding Ralph as a child hung up on a gate across from his home, which Ralph had forgotten until then but now remembered that boys had done this to him. He tried to remember if Kurt had been one of them, but Kurt said nothing when the story was told and at the time Ralph was "too afraid" to ask him directly and later concluded that it was more likely done by older boys in town who had bullied him. Several of the guests spoke about Ralph's father always wearing a suit and tie, and how his mother was "a fine woman, always well dressed," Ralph later recalled. He also learned at this meeting important information about the relationship between his mother and father and that his father had a sense of humor, something he had rarely observed as a child (with the exception of the exploding cigarette game, of course). This had to do with the reason why his mother spent so much time cleaning the floors. He was told that she wanted everything to be "spic and span," but his father would smoke cigars in the business and "deliberately flick the ashes on the floor," knowing that his wife "would come right after him and sweep up again."

The man who told the story about the cigar ashes—Herr Engelhardt—offered several other interesting comments at the meeting that sometimes baffled but also triggered Ralph's memory. "Do you know about my leg?" Engelhardt asked Ralph who, perplexed, responded that he did not and asked why he would have known about his leg. "I have a wooden leg," he said. "I lost my leg during World War I. Do you want to touch it?" Ralph said, "No, I don't want to touch your wooden leg; why would I want to do that?" Engelhardt then said, "Because you kicked me once on my wooden leg." Ralph then responded, "I have no memory of that, but I apologize for kicking you." During the translation of this exchange there were chuckles from around the table. Engelhardt then recalled that he once came into the store in the Steinkammer wearing his army coat and noticed Ralph staring at him, looking petrified. He asked Ralph if he remembered that occasion. "Indeed I do, but I was not petrified; I was angry because you had stolen something from me," Ralph replied. "Why would I ever steal something from you?" the baker asked. "I had a stubby pencil and you stole it from me," Ralph recalled. "Ah—do you know why I took it away from you?" asked the baker. "I did not want you to develop poor habits in penmanship from using a small pencil instead of a normal one." Ralph then responded, "Well, that incident ruined my image of you." Again there were chuckles around the table during the translation of this exchange. Engelhardt then became serious and said to Ralph, "Your father had a list of expenses that would have included loans, is that correct?" At that moment Ralph recalled little about the way his father had recorded business transactions and so he responded: "Now you are asking me something about which I have no idea, I really do not know if he had any debts to be collected or not, but I imagine he would have kept good records and would have resolved any outstanding business transactions before he left Wolfhagen." It occurred to Ralph at that moment that his father might have loaned money to Engelhardt and that perhaps the baker was concerned that he was there to collect any outstanding debts owed to his father. But Ralph had no knowledge of any specific outstanding debts and left the matter at that. "Actually, the baker and my father were pretty good friends," he later recalled. "They were also good business people." Ralph had earlier been told by Lutz Kann that he had heard stories about Ralph's father coming back to Wolfhagen after the move to Hamburg and that Herr Engelhardt had hidden him in the basement of the bakery so he would not be discovered by the Gestapo. But the baker denied that he had done this and nobody else around the table mentioned seeing Josef Möllerich in Wolfhagen after the move to Hamburg. It was years later that Ralph learned that his parents had returned at least once or twice to move the remainder of their things to Hamburg and presumably for his father to tie-up outstanding business in the town.

Once the invited townspeople each had an opportunity to speak, they said they wanted to know what had happened to Ralph, and to his sister, because they had heard nothing about his family from the night they disappeared until Jeffrey came to the town one year ago. Ralph then found himself telling his story—Hamburg, the Kindertransport, England, and America—before a group of people who were not immediate family for the first time in his life. He concluded by reporting on Edith's death less than a decade earlier. He spoke at some length, and was not accustomed to having his words translated, and so it was necessary for Günter to ask him to stop periodically so he could do the translation. By the time Ralph's comments concluded, nearly two hours had passed since the meeting began, and some of the people departed while others had more coffee and pastries and lingered to chat with Ralph and his family. Heinrich introduced the Mollericks to Gertrud and expressed the hope that they would be able to spend more time getting acquainted; they exchanged contact information. The newspaper reporter, who spoke some English, introduced herself to Ralph and asked him a few questions about his return to Wolfhagen before she left the room. Ralph then approached Frau Schiffmann and asked her if he could see the house his family had lived in. She became a bit unnerved and repeated to Ralph what she had told Jeffrey the year before—that she and her husband had paid twice for the purchase of the house. "I have not come here to take anything away," Ralph assured her, according to Günter's later recollection. With that she nodded and rushed out of the room. The Mollerick family then expressed their thanks to Mayor Dietrich for hosting the reception, and the mayor reminded Ralph that he would see him in his office the next day. They then joined Günter outside the hotel, as Ralph prepared himself to see his childhood home.

Once outside, Günter noticed the newspaper reporter standing near the hotel entrance with her husband, whom he knew well. The reporter asked where the Mollericks were going next and when Günter told them Ralph wanted to see his childhood house, the reporter asked if she could come along, to which everyone agreed. The walk down Schützebergerstraße to number 37 was no more than about 100 yards, but with a group of people talking to each other, the walk took several minutes. Ralph had carefully avoided the temptation to see the house when he first arrived in Wolfhagen nearly 48 hours earlier. At that moment he was not ready to deal with the emotions that he anticipated doing so would prompt. The issues surrounding his brief visit to the Jewish cemetery on Sunday and the subsequent problems that arose with Lutz Kann had distracted him from thinking about visiting the house, and he had been preoccupied outside of Wolfhagen earlier in the day and then with the reception during the afternoon. But after the unexpected and fascinating discussion at the mayor's reception that had just concluded, Ralph was now keenly looking forward to seeing his family's residence.

Just as the group approached the former Möllerich house and the adjacent Steinkammer, Ralph noticed a tall, slender man with his arms folded standing atop the steps of a shop in the building just adjacent to his house. Suddenly the man shouted into the street in German, "Wolfgang—is that you?" Günter later recalled that the man "jumped forward down the two steps and leaped at them like he was going to attack." The man stopped in front of Ralph, looked at him and said, "Heinz!" Ralph looked into the eyes of his best friend from childhood in the town. Without another word being said but with tears flowing down their cheeks, the two men grabbed each other and stood in the middle of the street embracing for what seemed to the others like an eternity. "We just watched," recalled Günter. "Even the lady from the newspaper said that she didn't want to take a picture of that because it was such a personal moment, so we stood there and waited and waited until they were finished." After that there was little time to speak; Heinz had to watch the shop, and Frau Schiffmann was waiting to allow Ralph to see his childhood home. Heinz quickly introduced his wife Gisela, and son, Uwe, who both spoke English; he then disappeared into the shop. Phyllis

chatted with Gisela and Jeffrey with Uwe, and the two ladies arranged for Heinz and Gisela to meet them at the Alte Rathaus later in the evening. Meanwhile, Ralph took his first glance at the half-timbered building that was once his home more than a half-century earlier, and then he looked up at the still familiar stone building with the unique façade that had housed his father's appliance store. For a brief moment Ralph was lost in his emotions and completely unaware of the others standing beside him. He then saw Frau Schiffmann peering from the window above and managed to bring himself back to the present by the time she came down the stairs and opened the door.

Ralph and Phyllis followed Frau Schiffmann into the half-timber house adjacent to the Steinkammer that was Ralph's home until July of 1937. As Jeffrey had reported nearly a year earlier, changes had been made inside the house, in particular the removal of the half-bath at the stairway landing between the second and third floors. "Oh, we took that out a long time ago," Frau Schiffmann told them. Instead of a single dwelling space, the upstairs portion of the building had been converted to six apartments. Ralph and Phyllis quickly went downstairs and then climbed to the top level of the Steinkammer above the cinema, which had been a massive storage area for grain when he lived there but now was empty. After taking more photos, they thanked Frau Schiffmann and went out to the street, having spent a very short time inside the two buildings. "There's really nothing left of what was there before," Ralph said to the group waiting for him. He later recalled, "This was a moment of joy and sadness—joy in that I had the privilege of living there and seeing it again; sadness in knowing that the house is no longer like it was." They proceeded past the alley that separated the Steinkammer from the half-timber building where his Uncle Moritz had his hardware store. The storefront now bore the name *Opfermann's*, which turned out to be the maiden name of Frau Wimmer who, with her husband, now owned the store and the home directly above it. This couple appeared to be more welcoming than had been the Schiffmanns. They readily offered to take Ralph and Jeffrey to the attic where Herr Wimmer showed them the desk upon which all the transactions of his father and uncle's business had been recorded. There were some books from the business reflecting the various columns of numbers and transactions for items such as bales of hay. Herr Wimmer said to Ralph: "Would you like this desk?" Ralph looked at Jeffrey and thought to himself that it was a nice gesture but "what am I going to do with this, it's a big old desk?" he later recalled. He and Jeffrey thanked Herr Wimmer for the offer but declined and then returned to the street where Phyllis and Günter were waiting for them with another of Ralph's childhood friends, Rolf Franke, who lived across Schützebergerstraße from Moritz's house. Ralph had a brief but emotional reunion with Rolf on the street, with the others looking on intensely.

The group returned to the Alte Rathaus Hotel, where Günter left them for the evening but told them he would return immediately after breakfast the next morning. Ralph, Phyllis, and Jeffrey had a light dinner and then waited in the hotel lobby for Heinz and Gisela. Both had been invited to the mayor's reception but could not come because their business was open that day and they could not get away. Heinz had hoped that Ralph would come to see the house after the reception and had come out of the shop at first glimpse of the group walking his way, leading to the emotional reunion in the street. He and Gisela arrived at the Alte Rathaus sometime after 8:30 p.m. and everyone went into the Ratskeller, the restaurant in the hotel, and sat down in the bar. They ordered drinks and began a discussion, but Ralph and Heinz felt that they needed some time alone and so they took their drinks to a different table, leaving Phyllis, Jeffrey, and Gisela to converse in English. Heinz knew hardly any English at all and Ralph, of course, had long ago forgotten most of his German and had struggled mightily, with great internal frustration, with his inability to communicate in German during the visit. But in this situation, Ralph discovered that he could understand German better than he originally thought, and so "we just made it work as best as we could," he later recalled. It helped immensely that Heinz spoke slowly and from time to time they would ask Gisela, who was across the room deep in conversation, to translate a phrase for them. Heinz said to Ralph at the outset: "One day you were here and the next day you were gone." He could not understand what had happened and had asked his parents and other people he knew in the town at the time if they knew "what happened to the Möllerich family," but nobody knew. Over the course of several hours and rounds of drinks, Ralph tried to explain, in his halting German, what had happened, recounting his life story that he had told earlier in the day at the mayor's reception. They also chatted about riding their tricycles as children and had several good laughs during that part of the conversation. Meanwhile, Phyllis and Gisela hit it off right away. Gisela talked about the business—they made curtains, which very much interested Phyllis—and the dual conversations in the bar continued late into the night. "We stayed there until midnight, maybe later, talking and drinking a lot," Heinz later recalled. Drinking was something that both Ralph and Phyllis did in great moderation, so the evening turned out to be quite extraordinary in that respect, as well. There were hugs all around when Heinz and Gisela went home. Heinz later recalled that in the middle of that night he and Gisela decided they would prepare a gift of curtains for Phyllis, which they wrapped up the next day and took to the Hotel Zum Schiffchen, located just outside the historic center of Wolfhagen, as the Mollericks had to move there because a radio station had booked the entire Alte Rathaus hotel for Tuesday night. As for Ralph, before falling asleep that night he reviewed the events of the day: spending the day with Günter, the reception hosted by the mayor, returning to his childhood home, and especially the wonderful evening reunion with Heinz, his closest childhood friend. The day had filled him with such warmth that he barely recalled the problems he had encountered the day before. What a difference a day had made! He smiled inwardly and then fell asleep.

The following morning, Tuesday, August 10, Günter appeared in the lobby of the Alte Rathaus shortly after breakfast, just as he had promised. Ralph, Phyllis, and Jeffrey were eager to return to the Jewish cemetery and actually go inside, but two things had to happen first: they had to check out of the Alte Rathaus and move their belongings to the Schiffchen hotel, and once that was done, Günter told them that he had to get the key to the cemetery gate, which he said was located at the mayor's office in the town hall and assured them it would not be a problem because he was on the mayor's council. The group walked up the steep hill on Burgstraße to the town hall and went to the second floor to the mayor's office. After speaking with the secretary, Günter explained to Ralph that the key was not there. It took a couple of phone calls before Günter learned that the key was currently in the possession of Dekan Eckhart Deutsch. They walked across the street to the parsonage of the Lutheran Church. Ralph remained silent during this very brief interval during which he recalled the scene outside the cemetery on Sunday morning—viewing the locked gate with the uncut grass visible in the cemetery and thinking that the town had intentionally restricted the cemetery from the public. This thought returned during the search for the key and Ralph could feel a knot growing in his stomach. At the parsonage, the Mollerick family briefly met Dekan Deutsch, who was quite friendly and handed a key to Günter and off they went to the Jewish cemetery.

The first thing Ralph noticed upon arriving at the gate to the Jewish cemetery—even before Günter unlocked the gate—was that the grass had been cut and the hedges on either side of the gate had been trimmed. There was an aroma of freshly cut grass in the air and the sight of this temporarily relieved Ralph's angst. How the cutting of the grass came about so quickly turned out to be an interesting story. At the end of the mayor's reception the previous day, Ralph had privately mentioned to Dietrich his displeasure with the condition of the cemetery. "It's a disgrace for a graveyard that was supposed to be supported by financial means from people who had paid for perpetual care," he later recalled telling the mayor. Dietrich had said little in response except to mention that the cemetery was under the jurisdiction of the Jewish Community Council in Frankfurt. "We couldn't do anything with the cemetery," Dietrich later recalled. "We couldn't trim the hedges or mow the grass" without authorization from Frankfurt. Such authorization apparently had nonetheless been quickly obtained by phone and someone in the mayor's office had undoubtedly arranged for the grass to be cut and the hedges trimmed very early that Tuesday morning.

Günter remained at the gate and allowed the Mollerick family to enter the cemetery. What they noticed as they walked from the entrance across the freshly mowed lawn toward the back of the site made their stomachs turn. All but one of the headstones—about 15 of them in total—had been knocked off their bases and in most cases lay either

next to or on top of a base. Behind this mess was a short stone wall about two feet in height that sat in front of several trees. The wall had been laid out in a pattern across most of the width of the cemetery near the rear of the space in a design where both ends of the wall turned toward the front of the area around which the headstones were located, while the center of the wall was set back near the trees in a semicircle. In front of this part of the wall stood the large stone monument—perhaps six feet high—that Ralph had first noticed on Sunday peering through the locked gate with the uncut grass behind it. At closer look the stones used for the monument and the wall had been pieces of gravestones, most of which contained fragments of engraving in Hebrew and German. The monument itself had a large plaque on the front with writing in Hebrew and in German that indicated that the monument is a memorial made out of the gravestones of some of the Jewish former citizens of the town, as a way of remembering them, as well as those killed in the Holocaust. It was later learned that this memorial had been erected by the US Army of occupation in 1946. The reason there were so few head-stones remaining in the cemetery was likely that the cemetery had been vandalized and most of the headstones broken apart during the Nazi era, probably on Kristallnacht or the following day (November 9–10, 1938), with the remainder having been knocked off the bases. By that time—or certainly shortly thereafter—most of the remaining small com-munity of Jews had left Wolfhagen.

The primary reason Ralph had wanted to visit the cemetery was to locate the gravestones of his paternal grandparents, Wolf and Richschen Möllerich. The sight of so few headstones and so many stone fragments used to erect the memorial monument and the surrounding wall caused his spirits to sink even further. He and Phyllis and Jeffrey got on their hands and knees searching among the fallen headstones

for his grandparents' names. It took some time to go from stone to stone because in sev-eral cases the engraved words were difficult to decipher. But after several minutes they were able to locate the headstone of Wolf Möllerich; it was face down on the base and located to the right of the Holocaust memorial monument. Ralph was heartened with this discovery and looked closely at the headstones nearby for his grandmother's stone, without success. "We had to go through the entire length of all these stones and finally found my grandmother's headstone on the opposite side to the left of the monument," he later recalled. Once again looking around at the condition of the cemetery, he said to the others, "This cannot be; this is not representative of Jewish tradition." On the one hand Ralph had been much "delighted" to discover the headstones of both his grandparents, overturned and knocked off their bases but still fairly intact. On the other hand he was "angry" that the cemetery, even after the grass had been cut, had been in such disrepair and no effort had been made to restore the headstones to their proper location— probably ever since the Second World War. Over lunch he shared his concerns with Günter and determined to speak to the mayor about this at their meeting that afternoon.

After lunch there was a bit of time available before the appointment with Mayor Dietrich, so Günter took the Mollerick family on a walking tour of the central part of the town to see a few places they had not previously visited. The first place they walked to was the site of a monument of a wolf at the east end of Mittelstraße, with a sign bearing the name of the town in front of it. According to legend, Günter explained, the town was named after a wolf because the original residents often saw a wolf standing on a little hill with a small wall surrounding it, howling, and this was at the site of the current monument and sign, near the edge of the historic center of the town. Günter then showed them the site of the former synagogue where Ralph had attended services with his father. The synagogue was gone, having been burned down on November 10, 1938, the day after Kristallnacht, and a Wolfhagen equivalent of a Woolworth's store that Günter referred to as "the Co-op" stood in its place. The only evidence that a synagogue once was located at the site was a small metal monument—perhaps three feet high and about six inches wide—standing on a patch of grass on the sidewalk in front of the building that said in German: "Here stood the Wolfhagen Synagogue, built 1859 and burned down November 10, 1938." There was a small menorah engraved above these words and a Star of David engraved at the lower end of the monument. Ralph was told that a historian had published a book about the town in 1980 and "thought it was important to have something there that represented where the synagogue was," he later recalled, but the monument actually was not erected until the spring of 1993—just a few months prior to Ralph's visit—and was paid for by private citizens rather than the town, something he would learn years later. So unobtrusive was this small monument that you would have to know it was there and specifically look for it to notice it. Viewing the site of the synagogue prompted Ralph to wonder about the *mikvah* (a small ritual bath used by observant Jews to purify themselves). Ralph later recalled that Günter had mentioned that this topic had come up before in the town and there had been a search for the mikvah. Members of the council thought it had been part of a tunnel, but they had found nothing. Typically the ritual bath would have been located in or near a synagogue or other Jewish structure, and there would have likely been some source of natural water nearby, but Ralph could see no evidence around the site where the synagogue had stood. They walked back toward the Jewish cemetery and came upon a small well with a couple of steps going down. Günter had no idea what this was, but Ralph thought it could have been the site of the mikvah, although after later research this could not be confirmed, nor was this well a likely location for a mikvah. Ralph much later learned that the mikvah had been located inside the old Jewish School building, which no longer existed.

It was then time to meet with the mayor and so everyone walked back to the town hall. The first and most important item of discussion that arose was Ralph's concern about the condition of the Jewish cemetery. Mayor Dietrich asked Ralph at the outset: "Is there anything we can do for you?" Ralph expressed his thanks for having the grass cut and hedges trimmed in the Jewish cemetery, but said that he was quite upset that the headstones had been knocked off their bases. "I want you to maintain that cemetery as you would any Christian cemetery," he later recalled telling the mayor. "I want those headstones to be stood up on their foundations so they reflect the people the stones represent." Dietrich indicated that this was something that would have to be authorized by the Jewish Community Council in Frankfurt and that somebody would have to contact these people to make the request. Ralph then raised a separate but related question: earlier that day while walking around the town Phyllis had suggested to him that perhaps they could put up a headstone for Ralph's parents in the Jewish cemetery; Ralph had immediately liked the idea and asked the mayor about that. The mayor thought that would be a good thing to do but again indicated that Ralph would have to get written authorization from the Jewish authorities in Frankfurt to mount a new headstone in the cemetery. Dietrich later recalled: "That was the wish that he expressed and I gave him the address of the place to make the request."

Ralph then mentioned that he would like to learn more about the history of the town. He had heard a rumor (from Lutz Kann and Frau Schiffmann) that there had been a tunnel from the Steinkammer that may have been used for hiding Jewish people during the time of the National Socialists. Dietrich nodded: "We thought there might be a tunnel somewhere in the alley next to the Steinkammer, but we have not found any evidence of this," he later recalled. Günter added that the town had dug up the street in that alley some years earlier but found nothing but a small cave. "There was nothing, not even a cellar," he later recalled. "Most of the houses had cellars in order to keep things cool because in older times they didn't have refrigerators." The mayor then indicated that if Ralph was interested in the history of the town, there were several books available, and there was a historian working in the building who might be helpful. He called the historian and a few minutes later, Horst Petrie entered the mayor's office. After introductions, Petrie said that he had written a book about the history of the old town of Wolfhagen that had been published the previous year and he would gladly give Ralph a copy. Ralph asked about records specifically relating to his family. The historian said that he had very little information on the history of specific Jewish families in the town but there was an old book in very poor condition—a log with handwritten entries that included occasions when Jews left or entered the town during the Nazi era. Ralph immediately asked to see that log, and Petrie said that it was very large but that he could show Ralph the pages covering the years 1934–1936 where he might find entries relating to members of his family. He went out and returned a few minutes later with a copy of his book, which he inscribed for Ralph, as well as the log he had discussed; it was indeed in very poor condition. Ralph identified a few pages with written entries relating to his family and copies were made of these for him to take away. The mayor then said that he and his colleagues would find more books concerning the history of the town, all written in German, of course, but he said that there were photos and charts that Ralph could easily understand. He then presented Ralph and Jeffrey with neckties and tie clips, and Phyllis received a scarf. He also gave Ralph a copy of the history of the town published in 1980. Ralph thanked both Dietrich and Petrie. "They were very kind," Phyllis remembered fondly. The mayor was also quite pleased that Ralph had returned to Wolfhagen. He later recalled: "I was very happy that we had the chance to get to know each other. We liked each other from the very first time we met."

After leaving the town hall, Günter suggested to Ralph that since he was interested in putting up a headstone for his parents in the Jewish cemetery, perhaps they should visit the local stonecutter and he could look at stones while he was still in Wolfhagen. Ralph agreed; Phyllis and Jeffrey stayed in town and went to visit Gisela while Günter drove with Ralph to see the stonecutter, whose workplace was located in a hamlet about 10 minutes from the town center. The stonecutter walked them through a part of the yard where there were many broken stones, which were of no interest to Ralph. He stopped at the back of the yard and showed Ralph a very large block of German black granite that he said would last for one thousand years. This stone already had writing engraved on it, but the stonecutter assured Ralph that he could remove that and engrave anything on the stone that Ralph wished to have placed on it. Ralph asked the stonecutter to keep that stone aside for him and he would let the stonecutter know once he received authorization from the Frankfurt Jewish Community Council to mount a headstone for his parents in the Jewish cemetery in Wolfhagen, and he would provide the stonecutter with the exact words both in Hebrew and German to engrave on the stone. Ralph also mentioned to the stonecutter that once the town received authorization from Frankfurt, he would like the fallen headstones in the Jewish cemetery replaced on their foundations. They shook hands on these arrangements and Günter then drove Ralph back into town where they met Phyllis and Jeffrey at the Schiffchen Hotel.

After the Mollericks had an opportunity to put their gifts—including the one left by Gisela and Heinz Abel and a ceramic plaque that said "auf Wiedersehen" presented to them by Günter—in their rooms, Günter noted that it was getting quite late in the afternoon and asked Ralph if there was anything else he would like to see before leaving Wolfhagen. Ralph told Günter he would like to go to a place where he could see a good overview of the town, maybe take some photographs from there.

Günter said he knew just the place and everyone piled into his car and they drove to the eastern outskirts of Wolfhagen, stopping in a slightly hilly and wooded area that at first glance appeared devoid of any opportunity to view the town. But then they saw a tall brick structure through the trees, about 100 yards away, which Günter identified as Offenberg Tower. The building was a plain brick cylinder with a diameter of perhaps 15 feet built in 1964 and had a 101-step spiral stairway leading to an outside platform around the small circumference of the structure, with a four-foot high red metal fence surrounding the platform. Only about 60 feet in height, the tower barely cleared neighboring trees, but it was possible nonetheless to get an outstanding view of the entire town of Wolfhagen from the viewing platform. Without hesitation, Ralph climbed the stairway, as did Jeffrey; after a few moments' pause, so did Phyllis and Günter. Once everyone reached the viewing platform, Günter went to the opposite side from the place where Ralph was standing in order to point something out to Phyllis and Jeffrey. They remained there several minutes in order to take photos, leaving Ralph on the other side, facing Wolfhagen.

It was at this moment that Ralph experienced a life-altering epiphany. Standing alone and lost in his thoughts, he gazed out at the town of Wolfhagen surrounded by farmland and meadows. He could see the bell tower of the Lutheran Church almost in the center of the town rising above the buildings and streets below. He looked skyward at "beautiful clouds" of various density pierced by the late afternoon sun. He imagined what it might have been like had he been able to grow up in the town. "I was thinking that I probably would have met a Jewish girl," he later recalled, "because there were more girls than boys so the pickings would probably have been pretty good." He thought about what it would have been like if he had been able to experience childhood in Wolfhagen under normal circumstances, with the freedoms and rights children had there today. He expected that as he had grown older his mother would have been more a part of his life, rather than his spending most of his time with his grandparents as he had as a young child, and that he would have had a closer relationship with his father. Then he realized that he might have inherited his father's and uncle's business, because his sister would have moved to a city to be a nurse in a larger hospital and would have married, and Moritz's daughter, Gretl had married Joe Rosenthal and moved to Wetzlar where Joe's family lived, thus leaving him as the sole heir to the business. His thoughts then returned to the beauty of the scene before him. "At that moment," he later recalled, "the clouds moved in such a way that a ray of sunlight burst through, shining like a spotlight on the town of Wolfhagen," while the surrounding countryside remained shrouded by overcast. "Suddenly I felt warm—something was happening to me on the inside," Ralph recalled years later. "Tears were running down my cheeks but I wasn't crying. I said to myself that I'm experiencing something that I've never experienced before, as if I'd been touched by a power that I had never felt before, and it changed my thinking. Suddenly I said to myself that I can forgive these people in this town and in this country, and when I was able to say those words internally, I felt calm—I felt at peace."

The afterglow from his extraordinary experience atop Offenberg Tower remained with Ralph long after he descended the tower. Sitting in the car during the return drive to Wolfhagen, Ralph said virtually nothing. Twice Phyllis asked him if he was okay, and twice he smiled at her and said, "I'm fine." The others conversed in the car but Ralph remained silent, apparently oblivious to what was being said or to the surrounding scenery. Over dinner at the Schiffchen Hotel's restaurant, once drinks were served and Günter had proposed a toast to a successful visit and to new friendships, however, Ralph described at length his experience at the tower. Listening intently, Jeffrey and Phyllis were filled with joy and gave each other a quick, knowing look; the trip had exceeded their highest expectations. Günter, being somewhat of a skeptic and not believing much in anything that sounded like divine intervention, nonetheless felt great pleasure in hearing about his new friend's revelation. After dinner, Ralph, Phyllis, and Jeffrey walked to the Alte Rathaus and met the Abels, Rolf Franke, and Heinz's older brother Albert for drinks in the Ratskeller. The evening was a fittingly joyous way to conclude the visit to Wolfhagen.

Although it was not difficult to discern a difference in Ralph's demeanor after the visit to Offenberg Tower, Phyllis and Jeffrey had been with him constantly for two weeks and so it was left for others in the family to quickly point out how Ralph had noticeably changed once they had returned from Germany. Glen Mollerick recalled that his father looked like a different person, that he seemed happy because that trip "changed his opinion of the German people. He was so adamant about never going back but the townspeople gave him the warmest welcome." Glen recalled listening with great interest to Ralph's description of his experience atop the tower: "He said it was like a huge release—like a great weight had been lifted off his shoulders. He felt like he could live as a different person than the one he was before because all the anger was gone." Phyllis later recalled that "when we came back to the States, my mother said to Ralph: 'You look like a changed person; you look calm and at peace.' She noticed. She noticed." In fact, Phyllis later recalled that "everyone noticed that Ralph seemed peaceful about Germany after we returned from the trip there." Although neither Ralph nor anyone in his family could have realized it at that moment, Ralph's return to Wolfhagen in the summer of 1993 and, in particular, his epiphany atop the Offenberg Tower, would transform his life.

# CHAPTER 11

—— ✿ ——

# Personal Redemption (1993–1995)

THE INITIAL WEEKS and months following Ralph's return from Germany left him and Phyllis virtually in a state of euphoria. Almost immediately upon arriving home, Phyllis had the hundreds of photographs taken on the journey developed and printed, and the couple spent the second half of August and much of September 1993 visiting relatives and friends, sharing their experience from the journey in great detail, and receiving highly positive feedback from nearly everyone in the process. Once things settled down after Ralph returned from a business trip to California, he and Phyllis began to communicate with several of the people in Wolfhagen with whom they had established a relationship or reconnected, beginning with Günter Glitsch. "Our thoughts and feelings of Germany, and especially of Wolfhagen, are still very vivid," Ralph wrote to Günter on September 3. "The scenery and the people left wonderful memories in our minds." Referencing the ceramic plaque Günter had presented them on their final day in Wolfhagen, Ralph indicated that he and Phyllis had hung it in a prominent place near their front door so that it would "remind us of an enjoyable time with you and a wonderful new friend we have made." He enclosed a note for Mayor Dietrich—an expression of thanks for the manner in which the town had welcomed them and especially for organizing the reception at the Alte Rathaus at which Ralph learned so much about his parents and their relationship with the people of Wolfhagen. He closed the letter to Günter with a hint of interest in returning to the town: "We are ready to go there again. . . . Who knows, maybe we will be returning to Wolfhagen soon."

The lasting impact the trip to Wolfhagen had on Ralph and Phyllis—as well as several of the people whom they met in Ralph's childhood town—cannot be overemphasized. In a follow-up letter sent to Günter on September 22, the day after they received a letter from Günter in which he enclosed several records from the town relating to Ralph's family, Phyllis described her feelings about experiencing the visit to Wolfhagen in gushing terms: "We are having a great time telling and re-telling of our fantastic trip to Germany and especially of Wolfhagen." She described how their friends have enjoyed looking at the photographs taken on the trip. "Everyone wants to hear about Ralph's memories of his childhood and his life in Germany. Many of our friends have actually gotten tears in their eyes when we tell of the older people who greeted us with their tales of Ralph's parents." She also provided some additional background information about her own and Ralph's extended families and enclosed several photographs for Günter to share with the many people of the town whom they had met. Ralph added to this communication his interest in knowing "what kind of reaction the people had to our short visit. I wish that I could have communicated better with them," he wrote. "Please give them our best regards." Two weeks later, Ralph and Phyllis sent Günter a pewter eagle as an expression of appreciation and friendship, knowing that Günter had mentioned that he was a collector of pewter. They wrote in the message accompanying the package: "We hope it will serve as our memento to you of our enjoyable time together and to a very excellent English teacher and a wonderful friend." Included in this message was yet another note of appreciation to the town: "What really is important to us are the people we met in Wolfhagen, and the friends we acquired."

On October 31, upon returning from a multi-day trip outside of Wolfhagen, Günter sent a long handwritten response to Ralph and Phyllis. "The pewter eagle is so marvelous and such a nice present that I had to show it to all my friends and acquaintances," he wrote. "You are very naughty doing such things but I appreciate it as a token of friendship very much." Several of the townspeople whom the Mollericks had met had expressed great interest in their visit and wanted to know more about Ralph's family and childhood in Germany, he reported. He also indicated that both Kurt Giese and Mayor Dietrich appreciated Ralph's messages. The mayor "was flattered" when he saw Ralph's message and told Günter that the afternoon reception in the Alte Rathaus "was the most moving moment for him in his job when everyone told stories about your parents and other relatives," Günter reported. "So I think your visit has stirred up quite a lot of Wolfhagen citizens and we all hope that you will be coming back soon and experiencing some more of our/your home country." Over the course of the ensuing weeks and months, the Mollericks established periodic but ongoing communications, especially with Heinz and Gisela Abel, and Heinrich and Gertrud Schwarz, along with the more constant exchanges with Günter. Shortly after Ralph left Germany, Heinrich wrote down his memories about his childhood in German and sent them to Ralph, but Ralph could not later find this letter. Subsequently Heinrich sent cards in English to Ralph and Phyllis. Each succeeding card from Heinrich displayed greater comfort with the language, so much so over the years that it is possible his written communications with Ralph were a major part of his improved skill in writing in English. Even Kurt and Berta Giese sent occasional cards in German, and Ralph sent Kurt a gift of a model of a NASA space shuttle. Because neither Kurt nor Berta spoke English, Günter was always the go-between, providing translations at both ends. The Mollericks also exchanged annual holiday cards with Herr and Frau Winter, along with their other Wolfhagen friends. Just before the onset of the holidays at the end of 1993, Günter sent Ralph and Phyllis a beautiful wooden nutcracker and *Lebkuchen*, a traditional German dessert that the Mollericks enjoyed with their family at Hanukkah. Thus began a series of friendships and communications between the Mollericks and several people in Wolfhagen that has grown and endured to this day.

Of course not every relationship Ralph and Phyllis established during their visit to Wolfhagen turned out to be quite so fulfilling. Despite the somewhat sour note upon which their time with Lutz Kann had ended the past summer, Ralph sent a long letter to Lutz at his home in Berlin describing his impressions of his visit to Wolfhagen and enclosing several photographs. On November 17, Lutz responded with a letter in German that Ralph had translated by a friend. In the letter Lutz expressed appreciation for the photographs and pleasure in meeting Ralph and Phyllis; but then he launched into a blunt reaction to Ralph's enthusiastic verbal description of his visit to Germany, and Wolfhagen in particular. "I do not want to trivialize your experiences; on the contrary I am pleased that you enjoyed your stay so much," Lutz wrote. "But I cannot avoid telling you my thoughts as a person and a Jew who lives in this country." He reminded Ralph "what the damned Nazis did to us, the Jews." He described how the Jews of Wolfhagen were so rooted in their town that "they thought about leaving their homes much too late, and their fate is known to us; may we never forget these people." With respect to the Jews of Wolfhagen, he also wrote: "They had a boundless confidence in their Christian fellow citizens, and this, dear Ralph, also applies to your murdered parents and other relatives of the Möllerich family, being one of the most well-known—and wealthy—families. They trusted their German fellow citizens; they stayed until the bitter ending." He explained that he had been older than Ralph during the time they had both lived in Wolfhagen and "can remember well the harassments I had to suffer as a Jewish boy." Revealing again his ongoing negative experience from his return visits to his childhood town, Lutz noted: "Unfortunately Wolfhagen did not do much to remember its Jewish citizens—victims of the Holocaust—with honor." He then cautioned Ralph: "Please take care that you are not being misused as 'advertisement' to show the bad or good conscience of the officials of the town of Wolfhagen. Nowadays there is a big need for a token Jew. . . . I really doubt the honesty of some officials when they show you so much sympathy."

The stark reminder of Ralph's past and the historical importance of the Holocaust transmitted in Lutz's letter caused Ralph to react in two separate but related ways. He believed first that Lutz's words—as historically accurate as they were—provided strong confirmation of the distinctly negative nature of his personality observed during their time together in Wolfhagen. Here was someone who had demonstrated animus, no matter how justifiable, toward some of the people in the town. Could his warning be true? Could the town be using Ralph as an example to satisfy their wish to let bygones be bygones? Or could it be that somehow the manner in which Lutz had interacted with the people of Wolfhagen, decades after the Holocaust, was symptomatic of Lutz's deep-seated personal issues he had with the town? Ralph instinctively surmised that the friendly welcome afforded to him and to Phyllis and Jeffrey by the people of Wolfhagen was genuine, and that the very different personalities and approaches to the town demonstrated by Ralph and his family in contrast to Lutz explained at least in part their different feelings about Wolfhagen. The letter from Lutz, nonetheless, left Ralph uneasy about sustaining a positive relationship with the only other living former Jewish resident of the town. It also reminded him that he had unfinished business he had begun to undertake just before leaving Wolfhagen, his personal commitment to placing a memorial headstone for his parents in the Jewish cemetery in the town as a permanent reminder to himself, his family, and to the residents of Wolfhagen of what had happened to one of the most important families in the town—a Jewish family—at the hands of the Nazis.

Although Ralph made his decision to place a headstone dedicated to his parents in the Jewish cemetery in Wolfhagen during his first visit to the town in 1993, it took him nearly two decades of research in the years thereafter to learn to the fullest extent possible of the fate of his parents and closest relatives who had remained in Germany. Prior to the 1993 visit to Wolfhagen, the only information Ralph had obtained regarding his parents came from two postcards received from them in 1940 and 1941 and the postcard he had received in May of 1942 from the International Red Cross informing him that his parents had perished. Over the course of the next half century, Ralph had been strongly disinclined to pursue a search for information relating to the fate of his parents, in large measure because of his sister's constant admonitions to forget the past and only look forward, and in part because of his bitter reaction to the disclosure by his Aunt Sophie about what had happened to the lifts his father had sent to his cousins in New York shortly after he and Edith had left Germany for England. As a result of his visit to Wolfhagen in the summer of 1993, and the fortuitous connection with his cousin Hilde in Chicago just prior to that trip and with his cousin Ruth Schoenfeld (née Schloss, who had moved from Washington Heights to Miami, Florida) shortly after his return from Germany, Ralph began to take an interest in seeking—and obtained—information relating to the fate of his parents, along with his maternal grandparents and his Uncle Moritz. Hilde and Ruth provided Ralph with a few contemporaneous letters received from his parents in Hamburg, as well as old photographs that began to fill in some of the gaps, and over the course of the next two decades he discovered small bits of additional information, usually from distant cousins. But it would not be until 2011 when Ralph conducted research in an archive in Hamburg before he was able to more fully learn what became of his family in Germany after he and Edith went to England on the Kindertransport.

The story, as it can best be reconstructed, began at the time Ralph and Edith departed Hamburg on December 14, 1938, with Selma's parents continuing to share the apartment on Beneckestraße with them and Josef's brother Moritz still living in his apartment on Isistraße. Josef and Selma had sent their children to England with reasonable optimism that they would, as promised, be able to join them there in about three months' time, based on having received affidavits from their nephew Otto in New York and hoping the prospect of the long-standing audit of the business was about to conclude, thus allowing the sale of the business, which had come under government control the previous year, to be completed. Many of their friends and most of their family members still remaining in Germany continued to have their papers processed and were issued exit visas by the German government mainly without complications. But such optimism became considerably tempered by the freezing of all Jewish financial accounts by the Nazi government in December 1938. Henceforth all transactions and, especially, requests for funds outside of an established monthly allowance, regardless how routine or minimal, required a formal, itemized submission and had to pass a strict and often arbitrary review by the government finance office before any funds could be approved. This process accounts for the protracted, month-long effort by Josef to itemize, request, receive approval, and have funds allocated for the shipment of the four lifts, consisting of personal belongings of the family as well as additional items meant to be used to start up a business in America, to Ralph's four cousins in New York in April 1939. The Hamburg archive also included records showing smaller requests for funds that were granted so that Josef and Selma could take English lessons during 1939 and 1940 at 1.50 RM per lesson, providing further evidence of their ongoing commitment to immigrate to the United States.

The sense of optimism held by Ralph's parents at the time their children were sent on the Kindertransport, however, continued to erode in 1940. The year began very badly, with a raid on their apartment conducted by the Gestapo on January 8, in which Selma's father, Jonas Meyer, was arrested. So distraught was Bertha (Jonas' wife) that she collapsed in the apartment with a stroke while on the phone describing the incident to a friend. She died the next day of heart failure at the age of 79. With Jonas being held by the Gestapo, Josef was permitted to withdraw funds from his own frozen account as an advance to the account of Jonas Meyer in an amount of nearly 500 RM to pay for funeral expenses and mourning clothing. Bertha Meyer was buried in the Jewish cemetery Ihlandkoppel in the Ohlsdorf neighborhood of Hamburg, where Jonas was able to purchase a plot large enough for both himself and his wife. Jonas was released by the Gestapo in time to attend the funeral, and there appears to be no further record of arrests during his time in Hamburg. For Josef and Selma the efforts to obtain entry visas from the United States and exit visas from the

German government remained stalled, causing increasing consternation. On July 29, 1940, Josef wrote dejectedly to Hilde and her parents in Chicago: "There is really nothing that you can do. The visa issuance is very slow and it is said at the moment that no visas are issued at all and by the time they will get to our number, nothing will be able to be done." He noted ironically that his sister Sophie and Hermann were able to get visas and an approved quota number because their son Max had become a citizen of the United States, but even their departure from Germany had been delayed because of limited availability of passage to America.

The efforts by Josef and Selma to emigrate yielded some hopeful developments early in 1941. Josef wrote to his sister Bertha and her family in Chicago on February 6: "Selma and I have been notified by the consulate [presumably of the United States] that we are to submit our papers because it will be our turn within the next few months. So it is possible that with normal conditions continuing we will be able to see each other again in 1941." He was also buoyed by news that Sophie and Hermann Schwarz had received notification in Hannover to come to Hamburg to pick up their exit visas so they could depart for the United States, having been able to obtain passage arranged by their son. "They are traveling on a preferred quota, "Josef wrote, "because Max has become a citizen. It does not apply to us because our old affidavits from late 1938 have to be renewed." He expressed some concern, however, whether Otto would still be "in a position today to issue such an affidavit" and noted that the total cost for the affidavits would be $2,000 USD plus the cost of approximately $600–$800 USD for the passage. He asked his sister Bertha whether she and her husband could serve as a backup in obtaining the visas in case Otto did not do so, reassuring her that it was unlikely they would need to call on her to provide the visas and in any event he would, of course, be in a position to refund the cost of the visas once they arrived in the United States. He added: "I plan to go to Wolfhagen one more time in the spring. It has been over two and a half years since I have been back." He did not mention the purpose of this visit and there is no record of whether or not he actually made this trip, which he clearly intended to be the final visit to the town before leaving Germany. Josef expressed his appreciation for the expected assistance with the affidavits and then it was Selma's turn to say a few words: "I think you should be so happy and content," she wrote, "that you can be together with your children. We pray daily to God that this might be granted to us sometime soon and to finally have our dear children with us again." She concluded with her own request for assistance: "I also ask you to help us with the affidavit. You would do us such a great favor." Having received no immediate answer from the family members in the United States regarding the visas, however, on April 12 Josef formally requested funds from his frozen account to purchase the visas directly. There is no record that he received a response to this request from the finance office controlling his funds.

The silence from the family in the United States and from the German finance office regarding Josef's efforts to emigrate during the winter and spring of 1941 proved to be an unfortunate omen of what was to come. In July, Josef received two letters from his niece Ruth in New York—one written on May 17 conveying birthday wishes (belated by more than six months), and the other written July 21 containing news about the family in New York. More importantly, Josef also received in mid-July the long-awaited affidavits from his nephew Eugen Schwarz required by the US consulate in Hamburg. Under normal circumstances this would have been cause for great optimism; but on July 8 the United States ordered all of its consulates in Germany closed, thus effectively removing any remaining possibility that Josef and Selma could immigrate to the United States. In a forlorn and desperate letter to Ruth written on August 18, 1941, Josef explained the circumstances in which he and his wife now found themselves: "When Eugen's affidavits finally arrived after about five months, the consulate was already busy with closing and we couldn't hand them in anymore. Only two weeks earlier would have been enough for them to process our papers." He asked Ruth to have Eugen undertake to learn from the US visa office in

Washington whatever alternative steps were available and to urge him to send that information to him as soon as possible. Realizing that with the closing of the consulate in Hamburg, any effort to move forward expeditiously with the requirements and approvals for immigration would likely be futile, Josef told Ruth that "we are not so full of hope and joy anymore to be united with all our loved ones; everything has gone down the drain!" In a note appended to Josef's letter, Selma reiterated her husband's lament: "It would have been so nice if we could have come to see you. However, unfortunately, it cannot be. When will we see our dear children again? The thought of it is terrible for me."

Less than two months later Josef learned that he and Selma, along with his brother Moritz, were scheduled for what would prove to be the first Nazi deportation of Jews from Hamburg on October 23, 1941. The three of them were designated to be sent to Lodz, Poland, where there existed a massive, overcrowded ghetto with such deplorable conditions that there was no proper water supply or sewage. In what would be the final communication sent by Josef found in his official file in the Hamburg archive, on October 7 he pleaded with the authorities to spare Selma—who had taken ill toward the end of the summer—from deportation to Lodz. There is no indication Josef received a response to this final request; he and Selma, along with Moritz Möllerich were deported by train that left Hamburg on the announced date. Selma's father, Jonas, did not receive deportation orders for October 23; he registered that same day with the German finance office that he had to move into a Jewish senior home at Jungfrauenthal 37 because he could not remain alone in the Beneckestraße apartment. He was later deported to what would become known as "the model ghetto" in Theresienstadt, located just to the north of Prague, Czechoslovakia, arriving there on July 16, 1942, and from there was sent to the extermination camp at Treblinka, Poland, shortly thereafter where he perished sometime in early 1943. The train transporting Joseph, Selma, and Moritz arrived at the Lodz ghetto on October 25, 1941. Records from Yad Vashem indicate that Selma died in Lodz, without reflecting a date of death. Almost certainly it would have been within less than two months of arrival, as most of the Jews deported to Lodz from Germany in the fall of 1941 were transported to the extermination facility at nearby Chelmno during the second half of January and early February 1942 and murdered forthwith in one of the first mass killings of Jews by the Nazis under the Final Solution, so the presumption is that if Selma died in Lodz it would have been before that timeframe. It is likely that Josef and Moritz Möllerich were among the group gassed at Chelmno, although there are conflicting written records indicating that Moritz was murdered either in May or July 1942, in which case he may have been among some of the Jews at Lodz transported to Auschwitz and killed there. No written record of Josef's death has been found, other than the postcards from the International Red Cross received by Ralph and Edith in England during May 1942 stating that their parents had died at the hands of the Nazis. Given the timeframe and the weeks it would have taken for the Red Cross to receive confirmation of his death and then locate and inform Ralph and Edith by postcard, it is likely that he was murdered at Chelmno early in 1942.

Could Joseph and Selma have avoided their ultimate fate? For many years, during his childhood and his youth, Ralph resented his parents first for not coming to England as they had promised and then for not getting out of Germany when most of his aunts and cousins did, despite the extensive planning to do so. As an adult, once his Aunt Sophie had disclosed what had happened with the lifts sent by his father to New York, Ralph's resentment of his parents turned to anger at his cousins. In the absence of additional evidence to the contrary at the time, he developed a theory that his cousins would not have sent visas for his parents because if his father had come to New York and claimed the contents of the four crates, he would have known that his nephews had sold them and used the proceeds for their personal purposes. Ralph reckoned that his cousins would have realized the consequences of being challenged by Josef for what they had done and determined not to send the visas. It would not be until much later in life, during the 1990s when Ralph was given the few precious letters by his cousins Hilde and Ruth that his father had written from Hamburg, that he would under-stand—from his father's own hand—that twice the cousins in New York purchased and sent visas and affidavits for Josef and Selma, despite their likely doubts that the Nazis would allow them to leave Germany. Even though Ralph no longer blames his cousins for his parents' de-mise, the anger about what they did with the contents of his father's lifts remains with him as a painful memory.

The fact is that Josef and Selma Möllerich's fate was likely sealed from the outset. Being a veteran of the First World War and a pillar of his community of Wolfhagen, Josef was among the many German Jews who were convinced their standing as German citizens would pro-tect them during the early years under Nazi rule. Beyond that he was, by nature, a meticulous man, especially when it came to his business, who dealt regularly with multiple and complex transactions, including a very substantial number of outstanding loans to people in and around Wolfhagen. These factors, more than anything else, determined the slow pace in which Josef's early efforts at emigration took shape. Even if Josef had acted promptly in 1936 to emigrate from Germany, howev-er, as most of his family did, it is highly unlikely that he would have been permitted to leave. The National Socialist government had established rules quite early after coming to power that placed the very substantial assets of the Wolf Möllerich Firm under careful scrutiny through an au-dit process that was slowed, first because Josef tried to hide his loans to Wolfhagen townspeople, and later because Jewish assets were fro-zen in December 1938. Beyond the complications with the business and personal assets, the very process of emigration to the United States was highly bureaucratic on both sides of the Atlantic, especially by late 1939, in which both Germany and the United States required multiple types of documentation, from properly submitted visa applications, to sponsors in the United States—preferably close relatives who had to sign affidavits—to certified tax information, to police dossiers, to au-thorization to leave Germany, to proof of booked and paid passage.

According to the United States Holocaust Memorial Museum's website, in fact, the latter two requirements often became something of a "Catch-22" scenario, as many shipping companies would not allow the purchase of passage without an exit visa and Germany would not issue an exit visa without proof of purchased passage to the Western hemisphere. In retrospect, therefore, Josef and Selma Möllerich, given their wealth, had virtually no chance to escape their fate while, ironically, those in Josef's family with far more meager assets were able to emigrate with relative ease.

Although Ralph would not come to fully understand the true nature of his parents' demise until years later, his experience in Wolfhagen in the summer of 1993, combined with considerable urging from Phyllis, compelled him to symbolically bring his parents back to his hometown—the place where many of the people there still remembered them—by placing a headstone in their memory inside the Jewish cemetery. "Suddenly I became overwhelmingly interested in Wolfhagen and the possibility of doing something like a gravestone in memory of my parents," Ralph later recalled. "That really reshaped my thoughts about Germany again; I wanted to go back, and that's counter to my original thinking before the 1993 trip that I would go once and that would be it." But in the excitement following the trip, Ralph and Phyllis were so engaged in telling friends and family about their experience, enjoying the photographs, and communicating with Günter and others whom they had met in Wolfhagen, that it took Lutz's letter to jar Ralph back to the task that he had set out for himself before leaving Wolfhagen. Nevertheless, because of multiple travel assignments regarding his NASA job and the crush of completing a major project, it was not until the beginning of summer 1994 that Ralph realized he had not yet begun the process of requesting the authorizations necessary from the Jewish Community Council in Frankfurt, as well as a similar organization in Kassel and a formal approval from the town of Wolfhagen that would permit the erection of the memorial headstone for his parents. He had also misplaced the contact information for the Frankfurt organization provided to him by Mayor Dietrich, and it had taken some time for him to track it down in his Silver Spring home. On July 18, 1994, he wrote to Günter: "I have still not written to the Jewish Community in Frankfurt regarding a tombstone for my parents." In this letter he also shared with Günter his misgivings about the tone of the letter he had received from Lutz Kann the previous November. "Unfortunately we do not have the same point of view on certain issues," he wrote. He explained that the friend who translated Lutz's letter into English was quite taken aback by what Lutz had to say. "I don't have the right to judge anyone," Ralph wrote, "but from his writings I cannot understand why he returned to Germany." Ralph also reported that he had received "a lovely card" from Heinrich Schwarz depicting the Alte Rathaus and Schützebergerstraße. "If I try real hard," he wrote, "I could just about see my parents' house." He indicated that he would have to reply to Heinrich in English. "If I could only write in German as well as he wrote in English, I would be very content." He also reported to Günter on his first visit to the United States Holocaust Memorial Museum, which opened its doors to the public on April 26, 1993, and which Ralph visited the following year, having become an associate charter member. The fact that Ralph would be able to visit such a place was likely made possible by his 1993 return to Germany and his visit to Yad Vashem in 1992, and he drew interesting comparisons in his letter to Günter: "I found this museum far better in its portrayal of the historical events of the Jews in Europe than that of the Israeli Yad Vashem museum. Having seen both museums, I can't help but feel a profound sadness when confronted by these exhibits, because they represent my people who, through no fault of their own, were denied the right of life, liberty, and the pursuit of happiness. It is something that we take for granted in this country."

It would not be until January 1995 before Ralph would have enough information, including the correct contacts in Germany to submit a request to the proper Jewish authorities to erect a memorial headstone for his parents in the Jewish cemetery in Wolfhagen, and the process turned out to be unexpectedly complicated and time consuming. On January 6, he sent identical letters in English to the *Jüdischen Gemeinden in Hessen*, located in Frankfurt, and to the *Jüdische Geimeinde* in Kassel, briefly explaining who he was and what he wanted to do, and requesting approval to erect the memorial stone and "the procedures to begin these dignified memorial plans." On January 24, the Frankfurt Jewish Community Council responded to Ralph's request with a brief letter in German, from which Ralph could barely get the gist. The letter included a few steps in the process summarized in handwritten annotation on the page, again in German. Phyllis wrote to Günter on January 30 asking him to read the enclosed letter from Frankfurt and let them know for certain what needed to be done. The Frankfurt letter indicated that they would first need written authorization from the town of Wolfhagen for the headstone to be placed in the town's Jewish cemetery. It also required information on Ralph's maternal grandparents and confirmation that the headstones for Ralph's paternal grandparents were standing upright in the Jewish cemetery in Wolfhagen. The letter also noted that it was necessary to provide specific information on the location of the placement of the headstone for Ralph's parents in the cemetery, and indicated that Ralph would need authorization from the Jewish Community Council in Kassel, to whom he had already written. On February 8, Kassel sent written approval to Ralph in a letter written in English, with a copy for Günter Glitsch, that contained an attached handwritten note in German as to whom to contact by phone. Günter also coordinated the request to the town of Wolfhagen, which sent a written approval dated February 2, 1995, through Günter to be sent to the Frankfurt and Kassel Jewish community councils. In her January 30 letter to Günter, Phyllis indicated that the rabbi at the synagogue where she worked in Potomac, Maryland, would prepare a template with the Hebrew letters and inscription to be placed on the headstone, and asked him to find out if the stonecutter he and Ralph had spoken to during their visit in 1993 had a fax machine to which she could directly send the materials to him from her office. She concluded her message: "Hopefully we can make this actually happen and we will see you soon."

Günter undertook the research necessary regarding Ralph's parents and maternal grandparents to send to the Frankfurt Jewish Community Council, but it took him nearly two months tracking down information from many towns and municipalities in central Germany before he found all the information he needed. This was a time when Ralph had virtually no information about his mother or maternal grandparents because they were not born in Wolfhagen. Twice during his search Günter thought he had reached a dead end, only to be rescued by a diligent clerk in one of the municipal offices. On April 11, he was able to write to Ralph and Phyllis that he had successfully completed the research and passed the information on to the authorities in Frankfurt. Meanwhile, Ralph had been working on the layout of the inscriptions on the gravestone, which Phyllis faxed to Günter on May 14. It included a template for the Hebrew and German words and letters, along with their size and the size of the overall stone to be used, instructions for the placement of the Hebrew words from right to left, that included an ancient Hebrew inscription that Ralph explained to Günter translated into English as, "May his (her) soul be bound up in the bond of life." Ralph had consulted a rabbi at the United States Holocaust Memorial Museum, who helped with the Hebrew letters of the inscription to be placed on the headstone. In his letter to Günter, Ralph also requested that the headstone be located close to his paternal grandmother's stone that was on the left side of the cemetery facing the large monument and wall, and he enclosed a photograph of this taken in 1993 for the stonecutter. For some reason, Mayor Dietrich wished this new stone to be placed in such a way that it would not be easily visible from the gate—probably because it was new and would stand out from the other headstones in the cemetery. "Your family, if they come to Wolfhagen, Ralph recalled Dietrich explaining, "will know why that is different from all the other stones." With the help of the rabbi at the synagogue where she worked, Phyllis had begun putting together an unveiling ceremony to be held during a planned visit to Wolfhagen at the end of July, in which they hoped their newly found friends would participate, including Mayor Dietrich and Dekan Deutsch. Phyllis began planning for a two-week stay in Europe and asked Günter for suggestions of places around Wolfhagen they could visit together during the first part of their trip, and Jeffrey and Phyllis also looked into more distant places in Belgium and the Netherlands the three of them could visit once they departed the Wolfhagen area.

It took three attempts for the stonecutter to get the inscription on the headstone correct, with Günter serving as the go-between with Ralph and Phyllis. On the first attempt, which the stonecutter sent as a template, the Hebrew letters appeared left to right; on the second, some of the letters appeared upside down. On July 8, with time growing short before their departure with Jeffrey for Germany, Phyllis and Ralph wrote to Günter inquiring if the stonecutter had completed the second round of corrections on the headstone. They also asked Günter to participate in the unveiling ceremony, and then asked him if he could locate a rabbi in Kassel that might be willing to officiate at the ceremony, but only under certain conditions. "We would be very interested in knowing the tone of his ceremony that he would be presenting," they wrote, "in order to better understand his outlook. I am sure you remember the offensive behavior of Lutz Kann when we were all together last time. We would be horrified if this rabbi behaved in this manner." So much had the relationship between the Mollericks and Lutz Kann soured over the course of their two days together in 1993 that he would not be invited to participate in the planned unveiling ceremony in Wolfhagen. As it turned out, the stonecutter was able to correctly inscribe the headstone on the third attempt. "The work was quite good, really," Günter later recalled. Phyllis sent to Günter the program for the unveiling ceremony, with a request to translate designated portions into German for Mayor Dietrich, Dekan Deutsch, and several of their friends in Wolfhagen to read and for Günter to distribute in advance of the Mollericks' arrival, and in the end Ralph and Phyllis decided there was no need for a rabbi to officiate at the ceremony. Günter arranged rooms for Ralph, Phyllis, and Jeffrey at the Alte Rathaus Hotel, as well as for a reception to be held in the Italian restaurant located in the Steinkammer following the unveiling scheduled for the afternoon of Saturday, July 29. The Mollericks departed Washington Dulles airport on July 27 for their flight to Frankfurt and return to Wolfhagen.

After checking into the Alte Rathaus hotel just before noon on July 28, where Günter was waiting for them, Ralph, Phyllis, Jeffrey, and Günter walked to the Jewish cemetery to make certain everything was in order for the next day's ceremony. The headstone for Ralph's parents was placed exactly as planned and looked both beautiful and dignified. The remaining headstones had been placed upright on bases since the 1993 visit. While Ralph and Phyllis admired the headstone for Josef and Selma Möllerich, Jeffrey knelt down at the base of Ralph's grandmother's headstone and stared at the engraved German letters on the base; they did not match the Hebrew name on the headstone. Jeffrey quickly looked at the other bases among the 16 headstones standing in the cemetery and found that most of them, when they had been set upright by the stonecutter sometime after the Mollericks had departed Wolfhagen in 1993, had been placed on the wrong base. When Jeffrey explained to the others what had happened to the bases, Ralph and Phyllis became very concerned because they wanted everything at the cemetery to be just right for the ceremony. While Günter contacted the stonecutter, Jeffrey created a chart that showed how the headstones and bases should match up with designated numbers and handed it to Günter and then placed masking tape labeled A and B with the proper numbers from the chart on the appropriate headstones and bases so they could more easily be matched up. They then went to the home of Heinz and Gisela Abel where they had lunch. As they finished their meal, Günter took a call and excused himself for a short time while the others lingered in order to catch up on what had transpired in their lives over the past two years and to talk a little about the next day's unveiling ceremony, in which Gisela would be participating with a reading. By the time Günter returned, everyone had been invited by Heinrich and Gertrud Schwarz to their home for coffee and homemade pastries for the first of many such occasions over the course of more than two decades. Ralph later recalled that although Gertrud spoke no English, "she can speak with passion with food and with baked goods she prepares, and you feel the warmth in the house of a family that had children who are now adults with children of their own. It is the family life that I always dreamed about but never really experienced. I always remember the tranquility of that house on each occasion we were in Germany, how

they took me in, and Phyllis, as if we were part of the family; that was the feeling—that was an amazing experience for me." It was also the beginning of a group friendship that included Heinrich and Gertrud Schwarz, Heinz and Gisela Abel, Günter Glitsch, and Ralph and Phyllis Mollerick that would be sustained over the course of two decades that neither distance, nor aging, nor illness, nor even death could dissolve.

Later in the day, on their way back to the Alte Rathaus, the Mollericks and Günter stopped at the parsonage of the Lutheran Church on the main square to see Dekan Deutsch. They spent some time going over the unveiling ceremony. Deutsch told them that he expected there to be a large number of congregants attending the ceremony because he had made an announcement about that during the previous Sunday church service and there was a considerable amount of interest expressed in attending the ceremony. He then invited everyone to join him at the bell tower at the top of the steeple to enjoy the view, and so they all climbed the steeple stairway to the bell tower. Because the time was approaching the top of the hour, Ralph became a bit nervous about being in such close proximity to the church bells when they would almost certainly be ringing while they were up there. Nonetheless, he and his family took in the extraordinary view of Wolfhagen and the surrounding fields laced with rapeseed from the tower, enhanced by the nearly cloudless sky as the late day sun created beautiful shadows in the village. Ralph was enjoying the moment, feeling very much at peace with himself when the silence was broken by the piercing sound of a trumpet. Everyone turned to see Dekan Deutsch playing the trumpet from the bell tower of the church. Instead of the church bells ringing at the top of the hour, the Mollericks and everyone else in Wolfhagen had been serenaded by a little trumpet concert. On the way down the steps, Deutsch explained that he did this from time to time because he loved playing and everyone had said they enjoyed hearing it so much that it became sort of a tradition in Wolfhagen. Although it was a small thing, the memory of Dekan Deutsch playing the trumpet from the bell tower of the Lutheran Church remained with Ralph over the years as a special moment among his visits to the town.

The next morning, Sunday, July 29, Günter came to the hotel just after breakfast. He and Ralph and Jeffrey walked to the Jewish cemetery so that Jeffrey could take another look at the headstones and the bases; he brought his chart with him. Jeffrey took his time going over each of the headstones and confirmed that they were all placed on the matching bases. Günter explained that the stonecutter and his assistant had worked the previous afternoon, matching everything up and affixing the proper headstones to their bases with epoxy so that all would be perfect in time for the unveiling ceremony. Before departing the cemetery, Ralph placed a cloth covering over the headstone for his parents. Returning to the hotel, Ralph felt very much at ease. Phyllis joined the group at the Alte Rathaus, having gone with Gisela to the Italian restaurant located in the Steinkammer to ensure that preparations for the reception following the unveiling service were in order, while the men were at the cemetery. They sat in the hotel lobby with Günter going through the materials they brought with them for the unveiling ceremony, double-checking that they had everything they needed. Although nobody was particularly hungry, they walked to the café on the square for coffee and a pastry, and relaxed while waiting until it was time to change clothes for the ceremony.

An impressive crowd had gathered inside the Jewish cemetery of Wolfhagen shortly before 3:00 p.m. on July 29, 1995, to witness something so unique that nobody there had ever contemplated such an event before. With the placing of a beautiful, German black granite headstone in the cemetery, in the presence of Mayor Dietrich (who had returned from a trip to Israel in time to be there and had purchased a hat while in Israel especially for the unveiling), Dekan Deutsch, other local clergy,  new friends and acquaintances in the town, total strangers, and the local and regional press, Ralph symbolically returned his parents to their home. Under a deep blue sky dotted with puffy white clouds, with just enough breeze to temper the afternoon midsummer heat, more than one hundred people stood, the men wearing black *kippot* (head coverings) brought from Maryland for the occasion throughout perhaps a 30-minute ceremony in which portions were conducted in English, Hebrew, and German that was at once solemn and moving—so much so that several in the crowd, including total strangers, openly wept. Jeffrey read the Hebrew prayers, including the mourner's prayers. Phyllis read an extract in English from the poem by Mary Elizabeth Frye, "Do Not Stand by my Grave and Weep" that ended: "Do not stand at our grave and cry; we are not there, we did not die." Dekan Deutsch recited the 23rd Psalm in German and other local clergy read prayers in German as well. Heinz Abel had written down some recollections of the Möllerich family from his childhood, which Gisela translated and read in English during the ceremony. She and Phyllis also each read prayers in English. Ralph then read a eulogy in English he had prepared entitled, "Home Again." He spoke about the conditions that his family—and all the Jewish families of Germany—had to endure under the National Socialists. He spoke of his parents being respected as "good people, hardworking, and pillars of the community," as people who "were giving to those in need and supportive in ways that promoted quality of life," and who were "people of strong faith and active in the synagogue." He spoke of the love they had for their children, so much so that they did something that many might have considered to be unspeakable but was, as Ralph believed, the ultimate act of love, by sending him with his sister out of Germany to "be safe from the perils that they themselves could not avoid." Ralph concluded: "It is with everlasting thought by their children

and grandchildren that we remember Selma and Josef Möllerich, and by this act return them to their hometown of Wolfhagen. *Olev v'shalom"* (rest in peace)." With these words, the headstone was uncovered revealing the engraved German and Hebrew words: "Children and grandchildren remember Josef Möllerich, 1885–1942; Selma Möllerich (neé Meyer), 1895–1942 who perished in the Nazi Holocaust; Josef ben Zvi; Selma bat Jonah." The inscription ends with the Hebrew phrase Ralph was given by the National Holocaust Memorial Museum abbreviated in Hebrew at the bottom of the stone.

At the end of the ceremony, Ralph invited all those who knew him or who knew his parents to join his family for a reception at the restaurant in the Steinkammer. But many people lingered at the cemetery, in some cases introducing themselves to Ralph and his family and for others—friends and acquaintances—stopping to say a few words of comfort and support or express their appreciation for being invited to the ceremony, or to pose with the family for photos. The reporters spoke to members of the family, clergy, and friends and took photos as well. Many of those who had attended the unveiling—perhaps 70–80 as later estimated by Phyllis and Günter—then joined Ralph and his family at the reception. Speaking of the preparations for the reception done by the proprietor of the restaurant, Günter later recalled, "He did that very well. . . .He laid out the tables and it was lovely." During the reception, many people came up to Ralph and Phyllis to thank them for what they had done at the cemetery.

As it turned out, the unveiling was not the only event for which the Mollericks came to Wolfhagen in the summer of 1995. They had brought with them several pieces of Judaica—a Kiddush cup, Seder plate, sho-far, 10 items in all—which they donated to the regional museum in Wolfhagen where Jeffrey had first met Frau Winter three years earlier. Jeffrey remembered how sparse the museum's collection of Judaica had been and so the family brought with them in 1995 a sufficient num-ber of items to fill much of the display case on the second floor of the museum. They had also prepared written captions explaining what each of the items represented. The presentation of the Judaica was accompanied by brief remarks by the curator of the museum and by

 the Mollerick family, as Jeffrey, Ralph, and Phyllis took turns ex-plaining the meaning of each item. The presentation conclud-ed with Ralph blowing the shofar as a demonstration. Years later Ralph reflected on this donation to the town, having learned a few years after the 1995 visit to Wolfhagen that there existed an exhibit in nearby Volkmarsen solely dedicated to restoring the history of the Jewish communities in the north Hessen region. "If I had to do

it over," he later recalled, "I probably would have preferred placing the Judaica in the Volkmarsen museum because it's more appropriate to the purpose of that project." Phyllis then reminded him: "But you lived in Wolfhagen and their Judaica exhibit was almost non-existent; it was better to place the items there."

With the "business" of the trip now concluded, it was possible for Ralph and his family to have some fun with their Wolfhagen friends and then move on for more than a week's worth of touring that included the Netherlands and Belgium. On the night of July 30, the Mollericks joined the Abels, the Schwarzes, and Günter to see an outdoor performance of *Anatevka*—a German language adaptation of the Broadway musical *Fiddler on the Roof*—being performed in a neighboring town. Ralph later recalled what he felt was a rather unusual reaction by an audience after a major theatrical production. "There was silence as people filed out; they were stunned and moved by the performance." At the end of the evening, Gisela handed Phyllis a handwritten note which she asked Phyllis to set aside until after they departed Wolfhagen. The next day the entire group piled into two cars and did some sightseeing outside of Wolfhagen before returning to the town for one final dinner before the Mollericks embarked on their tour of the Netherlands and Belgium the following morning.

Looking back on it in retrospect, placing a memorial headstone dedicated to his parents in the Jewish cemetery in Wolfhagen represented a personal redemption for Ralph. "I was delighted—absolutely delighted—about the attendance at the unveiling," he later recalled, and "that our presence there to perform something in the Jewish tradition would bring this gathering together to honor the memory of my parents." The cemetery, which had been moribund and vastly in disarray and largely hidden from public sight since the early years after World War II, in a town that once had included a thriving Jewish community but had been devoid of a single Jewish resident ever since before the start of the war, had been restored undoubtedly solely as the result of

Ralph's return to Wolfhagen in 1993 and had become part of the town consciousness with the unveiling of the headstone for Ralph's parents in 1995. This occasion would be the precursor to a series of events in Wolfhagen over the course of the next 15 years that would represent something of redemption for the town with respect to the Holocaust. More immediately and personally, as Ralph later recalled, "putting a new headstone in the cemetery represented the existence—and the memories—of my parents and brought tears to my eyes. I was so emotionally carried away in doing this that I felt I had finally reinstated them, at least their memories, in Wolfhagen." Thinking about his parents during the unveiling ceremony, Ralph found himself silently speaking to them: "You gave me life twice—once when I was born and the second time when you put me on the Kindertransport," he later recalled. He also felt that he had been able to do something that the town was not able to do by itself and in so doing, it changed the way he thought about Wolfhagen henceforth. "This unveiling ceremony was so unique for me that it categorically allowed me to say, 'Everything else now is okay,'" he later recalled. "That's the feeling I got in the joy of doing this, and yet I cried—I couldn't help it as I saw the ceremony transpire." The event thus allowed Ralph to achieve personal closure regarding Josef and Selma Möllerich, something he never expected would happen during his lifetime. "For the first time," he later recalled, "I had a feeling of satisfaction of purpose for being in Wolfhagen. I had symbolically brought my parents home." Thinking about the unveiling of the headstone more than 20 years later, Phyllis declared that "it was the best thing we ever did in Wolfhagen. Ralph always ends his talks with the phrase, 'I brought my parents home.'"

Sitting in the Frankfurt airport awaiting their flight back to the United States, Phyllis suddenly remembered that Gisela Abel had handed her a note, instructing her not to read it until the family had departed Wolfhagen. With all the traveling and sightseeing over the past week, she had completely forgotten about it. Now she found it in her bag, pulled it out, and read the note, dated July 30, 1995, out loud to Ralph and Jeffrey:

"Dear Ralph:

After 50 years you have found the way back to your childhood home. As you saw when you came back here two years ago, it is not too late; there are still your childhood friends and many people who remember your dear family. With your visit today you have deepened your ties to Wolfhagen, your childhood home. That is why I would like to say to you, Ralph, to your dear wife Phyllis and your son, Jeff—as often as is possible, find the way to Wolfhagen. You will always be welcome here with your whole family.

Yours, Gisela and Heinz"

# CHAPTER 12

— ❀ —

# Redemption for Wolfhagen (1995–2011 and Beyond)

RALPH MOLLERICK'S RETURN to Wolfhagen in 1993 and 1995—and especially the 1995 visit in which he was able to place a headstone for his parents in the Jewish cemetery in the town—had changed his life. It also set the stage for a remarkable series of events in Wolfhagen over the course of the next two decades. During this time, Wolfhagen experienced redemption of its own with respect to the Holocaust, and restored the memory and history of the Jewish community in the town to a considerable extent. This redemption occurred with the encouragement, support, and sometimes at the initiation and active participation of Ralph Mollerick, who returned to Wolfhagen seven more times between 1997 and 2011.

There was a double-pronged component that launched Ralph's involvement in Wolfhagen's efforts. First, the act of personal closure he experienced by placing a headstone for his parents in the town's Jewish cemetery—and the extraordinary level of support he and his family received from the town—served to reverse forever his lifelong commitment to forget his town of birth and everything else about Germany in his past. The July 29, 1995, unveiling ceremony in the Jewish cemetery in Wolfhagen proved to be not only a milestone for Ralph and his family, but also for the town. Two days after the ceremony, the north Hessen regional newspaper published an article entitled "Old Wounds Still Hurt" based on coverage of the unveiling ceremony. The article described at length the story of Jeffrey Mollerick's discovery of Ralph's hometown in 1992 and Ralph's initial visit to Wolfhagen the following summer when he was reunited with a few of his childhood playmates and learned more about his family from the townspeople. It described the moving unveiling ceremony at the cemetery and Ralph's remarks about his parents. The article also discussed Ralph's parents: "They [Josef and Selma Möllerich] became victims of the Holocaust, somewhere as nameless people. They died with the belief that their children would be safe from the Nazis." The article reported how Ralph's childhood friends had recalled that "in school he was especially harassed and tormented because of his faith." It ended by describing Ralph's emotions on that day: "His feelings are still mixed . . . when he is in his hometown. On the one hand there are still the old wounds of the past that hurt, but at the same time on the other hand there is the joy about the present which he can experience with his newly found friends from Wolfhagen." Accompanying the article was a captioned photograph showing the Mollerick family and town officials and friends surrounding the unveiled headstone for Ralph's parents. In September 1995, Dekan Deutsch wrote a piece in the newsletter of the Lutheran Church about the moving ceremony at the Jewish cemetery. "There was more to it than just remembrance and dignified commemoration," he wrote; "it was a matter of healing scars and wounds from the past." Deutsch briefly recounted Ralph's comments about how his parents saved his life—and his sister's—by sending them to England on the Kindertransport. The Dekan's article concluded: "The moving days of this visit have shown that reconciliation and peace can make infinitely free, can enrich and can lead to a new awareness. Who would have thought that this year 1995 which is full of recollections could lead to such human and cordial meetings? A stone of commemoration was the first occasion. We know now: the Möllerichs have come close to us and we to them. That makes us hope!"

The story of Ralph's return to Germany was considered newsworthy in the United States as well. Shortly after returning home, Ralph,

Phyllis, and Jeffrey were interviewed for an article that appeared in the September 7, 1995, edition of the *Washington Jewish Week*, entitled "Survivor Revisits German Roots: Local Family Erects Headstone in Wolfhagen." The article filled five page-length columns, beginning with Jeffrey's discovery during his 1992 trip to Germany that led to Ralph's two visits, which were described in some detail as well, including Ralph's epiphany atop Offenberg Tower during the 1993 visit. This article included the same photograph of the family and friends in Wolfhagen standing around the unveiled headstone for Ralph's parents that had appeared in the German newspaper. Ralph thought folks in Wolfhagen might find this article of interest and so he sent it to Günter, who translated it into German and showed it around to people in the town, including Ralph and Phyllis' friends there as well as Günter's journalist friend. The result of the latter encounter was a relatively short piece that appeared in *Hessiche Allgemeine*, the regional newspaper, on October 24, which Günter translated into English and sent to Ralph and Phyllis with the following handwritten annotation: "This is what the Wolfhagen newspaper made of the article you sent me on your visit. Note: She didn't use the words again that embarrassed you so much." Günter here referred to Ralph being identified in the two previous articles written about him as "The Jew." In this piece he was identified as "the former Jewish fellow-citizen." The piece focused on a few passages in the *Washington Jewish Week*, including: "The visit to Wolfhagen gave Möllerich a sense of closure and reconciliation that he had never thought possible." It also included a quote by Ralph from the original article: "I can't forget, but I am able to move on and forgive."

The translation of the *Washington Jewish Week* article and subsequent piece about the article in the *Hessiche Allgemeine* had a highly positive impact on the people in Germany who knew Ralph, with one notable exception: Lutz Kann. In early November, Ralph received what turned out to be a long, bitter, and personally offensive diatribe written by Lutz in German, which Ralph could barely comprehend, and so he sent it to Günter and phoned him with a request to translate the letter into English and send that back to him. Günter later recalled that after reading the letter, "I thought to myself, 'oh you can't translate that letter because it's really a very bad letter.' I thought it wasn't fair." Because he was torn, Günter showed the letter to Dekan Deutsch and they discussed what they should do. Günter later recalled that Deutsch told him "I think Ralph's strong enough; I think he can take that. If we talk to him beforehand and explain it to him, we should send back the translated letter." That is exactly how this played out, so that by the time Ralph received the English translation of the letter, he had been given a "heads up" with a phone call from Günter. The letter from Lutz went far beyond his communication two years earlier when he had warned Ralph about being used by the town of Wolfhagen for its own purposes. Referring to Ralph's 1993 and 1995 visits to Wolfhagen, Lutz wrote: "Fifty years after the end of the war they have finally found in you the American who hardly understands a word of German and who only lived in his hometown for 6 or 7 years; they have at last found their "Show Jew. . . . You have allowed them to misuse you in a hypocritical/deceitful way." Lutz then explained that instead of the town offering an official invitation to all Jewish survivors "as an act of forgiving and reconciliation" as had happened in "many towns and villages," he wrote, "You came and made them flatter you—and all that you claimed for you privately." He then launched into a complaint about not having been invited to participate in the unveiling ceremony for Ralph's parents: "It would have been a *mitzvah* [good deed] and an experience for me to participate in this ceremony if you had told me and had been interested in me. It would have been possible for me, too—because of my relationships— to organize a *minyan* of Jewish men [in this case at least ten adult males] together with a cantor from the Jewish community in Kassel for this ceremony. But you preferred the '*Goyim*' [non-Jews)] and they were closer to you."

Whatever prompted the second unpleasant communication from Lutz Kann—most likely his learning about Ralph's visit to Wolfhagen to unveil the headstone for his parents without being invited—it left

Ralph "horrified," as he later recalled. But having been forewarned by Günter and Dekan Deutsch about the letter's contents, Ralph took the verbal attack in stride. He viewed the letter as further confirmation of his initial impression from 1993 that he could not be friends with Lutz Kann, and this proved, in the larger scheme of things, to be a minor disappointment. Nevertheless, Ralph resented what he believed to be Lutz's misguided effort to "put me on a guilt trip for being a traitor to Judaism," as he later recalled. This particularly upset Ralph because with all that he went through and with all that his sister did to distance herself from her faith, Ralph had remained steadfast when it came to Judaism, even serving as president of his synagogue in Maryland. Lutz, of course, was not aware of that; he knew virtually nothing about Ralph at that time. Ralph believed that Lutz felt slighted both by the town of Wolfhagen and by him personally, especially for being left out of both the mayor's reception for Ralph held during his 1993 visit to Wolfhagen and the unveiling ceremony that Ralph sponsored in the Jewish cemetery during the 1995 visit. He also believed that Lutz was envious of the way Ralph had been welcomed by the town of Wolfhagen while Lutz had not. Beyond that, Ralph saw Lutz as a bitter man and suspected some of this may well have been as a result of the impact of the Holocaust on his life and therefore was justifiable to some extent. Ralph believed, nonetheless, that there was no excuse for bad behavior no matter how justifiable were the underlying causes. Speculation aside, the second Lutz Kann letter served to establish a chill in Ralph's relationship with Lutz that would largely remain in place for the better part of two decades during which their paths would cross several times, and this turned out to be the only negative aspect of Ralph's multiple visits to Wolfhagen and environs during those years. Nevertheless, and unbeknownst to Ralph or most of the people of Wolfhagen in the fall of 1995, Lutz Kann would soon play a key role in the redemption of the town with respect to the Holocaust.

The second factor influencing the onset of extraordinary developments in Wolfhagen in the late 1990s had very much to do with the fact that Ralph and Phyllis over the course of their two visits to Wolfhagen had established and solidified a number of friendships that grew closer not only with each subsequent visit, but with the ongoing communications by mail and phone that had closed the distance between south Florida and central Germany in the months and years between the visits. On September 19, 1995, a little more than a month after returning home from their trip to Germany, Belgium, and the Netherlands, Phyllis and Ralph sent a long letter to Gisela and Heinz Abel describing all they saw once they left Wolfhagen and expressing their joy and thanks for the extended time the Abels spent with them while they were in Germany. "When we were planning this trip, we said that this would probably be our last trip to Germany," they wrote, "because, after all, why would we want to keep returning? After two wonderful trips to Wolfhagen, we know now that we will return again and again. We want to keep in touch with our good friends and pay respect to Ralph's parents and grandparents." There had been some talk during the summer visit to Wolfhagen of Heinz and Gisela coming to visit the Mollericks in Silver Spring, as the topic also came up in the September 19 letter, with Phyllis asking when they would be coming. "I am already planning places that we can take you," she wrote.

True to their word, Heinz and Gisela arrived at Washington Dulles International Airport on May 8, 1996, just as Phyllis' oldest daughter, Rochelle, was about to go into labor with her daughter, Erin. Two days later Phyllis became a grandparent for the first time. Heinz and Gisela were more interested in meeting Rochelle and seeing the baby than in sightseeing; Gisela was shocked to learn that they could see the baby just hours after birth: "That's not possible," Ralph recalled Gisela saying to him. "In Germany we wait a minimum of a week to see the baby." In between the family excitement, Ralph and Phyllis were able to take Gisela and Heinz to Washington, DC, on sightseeing outings. One day they took the Metro into the city and visited the United States Holocaust Memorial Museum. They spent considerable time on the top floor of the museum where many of the videos and exhibits are in

German. Heinz was fascinated by the exhibits there and lingered while memories from his youth surfaced in a chilling way. It took hours to complete the visit at the museum and when the group finally sat down on a bench outside the museum to reflect on what they saw, Gisela unexpectedly said, "I am ashamed to speak in German here," as tears flowed down her cheeks. Over the course of the three-day visit, Ralph and Phyllis took their guests to the White House, the Old Post Office Pavilion where Gisela purchased souvenirs for their children and grand-children, and to the Kennedy Center to see *Joseph and the Amazing Technicolor Dream Coat*. After four days the Abels took the Amtrak train to New York and stayed at the Madison Hotel for a few days before returning to Germany. Over the course of the next several years, Heinz and Gisela returned a few more times to the United States but always stayed in New York, and Ralph and Phyllis would take the train and meet them there—including on one occasion when the two ladies celebrated their birthdays together.

In midsummer 1996, the Mollericks had another visitor from Wolfhagen. Günter Glitch flew to Boston, where he spent about a week touring the city and the New England countryside. He then took an Amtrak train to Washington, where Ralph and Phyllis met him at Union Station. Immediately upon arrival, Günter asked to see the United States Holocaust Memorial Museum, where he was particularly inter-ested in the exhibit entitled "Remember the Children: Daniel's Story." As was the case each day during midsummer, there were long lines almost all the way around the museum awaiting entry; but Ralph used his status as a charter member to avoid the long lines and gain virtually immediate entry into the museum. Having seen this exhibit, Ralph and Phyllis waited outside while Günter went through. About a half hour later, Günter came out visibly shaken. Ralph later recalled that "he was crying like a baby and could not stop." Over the course of the next several and far less emotional days, Ralph and Phyllis took Günter to the National Air and Space Museum where Ralph especially enjoyed explaining about the space program. They also took Günter on a tour of the White House and he visited several of the iconic monuments in the city. As with the Abels, Günter was treated to an evening at the Kennedy Center, this time to see *Beauty and the Beast*. On another day, Ralph and Phyllis took Günter to Baltimore's Inner Harbor, not far from where Jeffrey lived at the time, where he was treated to "a wonderful Italian meal" at one of the restaurants in Little Italy. He also had the pleasure of meeting Ralph's family, which gathered for a barbeque lunch at Glen's house, where he met Glen's young daughters, Hannah and Sara. Günter also met an older woman at Glen's house and later recalled asking Jeffrey to identify her. To Günter's surprise, Jeffrey responded: "That's my mother." Following a busy week visiting with Ralph and Phyllis, Günter completed his trip to the United States by flying to Tucson, Arizona, to visit a cousin of his mother. The combined effect of the dual visits to the United States by Günter and the Abels in 1996 was to enhance the deepening friendships of Ralph and Phyllis Mollerick with citizens of Wolfhagen, which encouraged them to return to the town of Ralph's early childhood multiple times over the ensuing years, and seal the growing bond between Ralph and the town of Wolfhagen.

The year 1996 was historically important for the town of Wolfhagen as it marked the outset of the town's public and official redemption with respect to the Holocaust. There were several factors that contributed to the timing of this important development for the town. One was simply the passage of time, with two generations of Germans beyond the generation of the National Socialists having grown up and lived during the postwar period. Many in the current generation of Germans thus were largely ready to confront the truth about their nation and their town's history during the Nazi era, something which began to unfold some years before 1996 in other parts of Germany but took time to begin in Wolfhagen, and this was due largely to other factors that fortuitously came together in the second half of 1996.

One of the most important influences on Wolfhagen's redemption, other than the visits by Ralph Mollerick, came not from Wolfhagen itself but from the nearby town of Volkmarsen where a man named Ernst Klein had for a number of years been conducting research in the history of the Jewish community in his town and in the surrounding towns in the area. "All my life I thought about the Jewish families who lived here in former times," he later recalled. "As a young man I could really do nothing; but I began to seek information about this." At first his research focused on the Jewish families of Volkmarsen and was sporadic because Klein owned a business. But as time went on, he found himself devoting more time to the research and less time to his business. He also found a number of people who shared his interest, especially his wife, Brigitte, and the group gradually grew over the course of a decade in the early 1990s. Klein sought to locate as many still-living Jewish former residents of the area as possible. He placed advertisements in German language newspapers in Israel, New York, and Buenos Aires based on information he had collected indicating some of the families were located in these places. The advertisements requested responses. "I used both German and English and I said that we must learn our history," he later recalled, "and we needed these people who have knowledge about our history." Slowly, Klein began to receive letters from people in Israel, the United States, Argentina, and even Australia. He sought funds to invite as many of the people with whom he had established contact as would come. The town mayor told him there was no money, and so Brigitte sent letters to 300 people whom the Kleins knew throughout Germany and they raised over 36,000 DM in donations, sufficient funds to cover the travel costs for 28 people, who gathered in Volkmarsen in mid-1996 for a meeting that lasted 10 days. A few of the participants had lived in neighboring towns outside of Volkmarsen, including Lutz Kann, originally from Wolfhagen but then living in Berlin. Interestingly, Ernst Klein did not know about Ralph Mollerick at that time even though Ralph had already returned to Wolfhagen twice, because Lutz apparently did not tell him about Ralph until after this very significant meeting (which will be further discussed in the Afterword section of this book, along with the remarkable development of Klein's small group into a major society and exhibit that has been recognized not only in the region but throughout Germany and the world).

The gathering in Volkmarsen attracted sufficient attention that the regional newspaper in Kassel sent staff to report on it, and this led to yet another important factor in the onset of Wolfhagen's redemption. Most likely during the course of the meeting, the outspoken Kann took the opportunity to speak to a reporter about his experience growing up in Wolfhagen and then probably had subsequent communications with one or more reporters and others associated with the newspaper, which undoubtedly led directly to the publication of several articles on the history of the Jewish community in Wolfhagen, dated November 9, 1996, the 58th anniversary of Kristallnacht, that filled most of both sides of a page. In a piece entitled, "Humiliated, Tortured, Expelled, and Murdered," Peter Soltau traced the history of the town's Jewish community—and mistreatment of members of this group—as far back as the year 1235, just 19 years after establishment of the town. The article described by name several of the Jewish shopkeepers and business owners in the town, how these families had thrived for a period of time, especially dating from the mid-19th century, and how everything had changed following the increasingly severe anti-Semitic policies under Hitler and the National Socialists culminating in the "pogrom" that occurred in Wolfhagen not on November 9, but the next day. The story of that event was outlined in a detailed chronology elsewhere on the same page of the newspaper, as well as in a separate article by Soltau on the next page entitled, "The People Disappear; Their Possessions Remain." The first article by Soltau began by noting the erection of a privately funded metal stand in the spring of 1993 in front of a discount store that was the site of the former synagogue on Mittelstraße as "a publicly documented confession of Wolfhagen citizens to the terrible end of the Jewish community of the town," an event that prompted Lutz Kann to write, presumably to Soltau later that year and quoted in the Soltau article: "I am particularly pleased that at last Wolfhagen is reminded of the former synagogue by setting up a memorial tablet by a citizen's initiative. . . . This act of redemption and remembrance by Wolfhagen took more than 40 years of great and abominable inaction . . . to acknowledge that Jewish citizens, like my parents, were deported and murdered, and Wolfhagen had every reason to confess to this unfortunate past." The second article turned out to be equally harsh on the officialdom of the town regarding land and property once owned by the Jewish community of Wolfhagen. The article noted: "A glance into the carefully recorded registry of Wolfhagen land records for former Jewish homes and landed property during late 1938 and 1939 shows that the silence about the fate of the Jewish community after 1945 might have been due to population groups being involved in the division of Jewish land ownership at inexpensive prices. . . . The largest beneficiary in the acquisition of Jewish land after the extermination of the Jewish community, according to the register, is the city of Wolfhagen itself."

The tableau of printed pieces in the November 9, 1996, edition of the regional newspaper focused public attention in Wolfhagen as never before on what had happened to its former Jewish community. What had taken place in the town during the pogrom 58 years earlier? One fact is certain: there were no demonstrations in Wolfhagen whatsoever on the night of November 9. Around 10:00 a.m. on November 10, an open truck arrived at the town square from nearby Arolsen carrying a group of men dressed in the uniforms of SS and SA stormtroopers. As reported in the chronology in the regional newspaper based on local records and eyewitness reports, a few local National Socialist Party activists joined them and they went to the Jewish school, which had been closed ever since 1933, and threw a large downed tree branch through the windows. The group then went into the synagogue where others joined the original group from outside of the town (perhaps 50 rioters in all, according to police records) and they threw the Torah scrolls into the street. The mob proceeded to the house of the Kron family, where a fire was set and then extinguished but the home was plundered, forcing Herr Kron into the street wearing slippers. At noon the crowd ransacked the Mittelstraße home of the Kann family. At 2:00 p.m. the mob went to Schützebergerstrße to the home of the Klebe family and looted the house, tossing furniture from the attic even though the family had already moved out of the town. The mob also looted the homes of the Winterberg and Block families, setting fires here and there near or at these Jewish homes and businesses as it continued its rampage through the center of the town. By nightfall, around 6:00 p.m., the growing crowd gathered at the synagogue where the uniformed SS and SA stormtroopers, accompanied by party activists, doused the building with gasoline and set the synagogue on fire, while a group of townspeople, including six-year old Heinrich Schwarz and his parents, stood watching in absolute silence. "My father, what can I say? He was not a Nazi—we stood there," Heinrich later recalled. "I cannot remember the size of the crowd of people who stood there, an audience, standing about 100 meters distance from the building. I don't remember any comments; no approbation, no regret." A fire brigade stood by to protect the neighboring houses. Afterward, according to the newspaper account, all the Jewish citizens who had been arrested were taken to the court building on Burgstraße, where many of the men were transported to the concentration camp at Buchenwald, as had happened on Kristallnacht to two of Ralph's cousins in other German towns and to so many young Jewish men throughout the country. "When this happened," Heinrich later recalled, "afterwards I never saw Jewish people in the town. They were not deported; they mostly moved to Kassel." A few of the families were eventually able to escape from Germany, as was the case with 17-year-old Lutz Kann, who made his way to Palestine. Young Wolfgang Möllerich and his family, of course, had moved to Hamburg in 1937. Most members of the Jewish community of Wolfhagen, virtually all of whom were gone from the town shortly after Kristallnacht, however, were murdered in the concentration camps, although the town's records have no details of their deaths, according to the newspaper account written by Soltau.

The two pages of articles marking the 58th anniversary of Kristallnacht that appeared in the Wolfhagen section of the regional newspaper included a remarkable editorial written by Tibor Pézsa entitled, "Why Remember?" The editorial drew upon the facts presented in the accompanying articles which, as strong as they were, suggested that more needed to be presented, and the editorial did just that. "What do we actually think of the outrages against people of the Jewish faith on 9 November (in Wolfhagen 10 November) in 1938?" Pézsa wrote. He questioned why only in 1996 and not in the previous decades has this question been raised publicly, noting that there had been in recent years private contacts between local citizens and survivors in Wolfhagen and elsewhere in the region. "Where was the official Wolfhagen in this reconciliation? Why did it require a private initiative to recall the destroyed Jewish house of God?" he wrote. Pésza quoted from Richard von Weizäkker, former president of the Federal Republic of Germany on the occasion of the 40th anniversary of the end of the war in Europe: "It is not a matter of pasting over the past, for you cannot change it or make it undetectable. Whoever closes his eyes before the past will be blind to the present. If you do not want to remember the inhumanity, you will again be startled with new incidents of inhumanity." In his editorial, Pésza put forward a call to action: "It cannot be a question of accusing each other, but only seeking and expressing the truth. Wolfhagen must put itself at the forefront." He called for an "official anniversary commemoration" of Kristallnacht "so that it cannot be forgotten."

The combined influence of the work being done by Ernst Klein in nearby Volkmarsen, the recent appearances in Wolfhagen of Lutz Kann and Ralph Mollerick, and especially the powerful call to action in the November 9, 1996, edition of the regional newspaper that reached so many citizens in Wolfhagen had an almost immediate impact on town officials. Sometime before 1996 the town parliament had established a working group to plan special official commemorations. After publication of the articles and editorial on the Jewish community of Wolfhagen in November 1996, the working group took up discussion of how the town should commemorate the date in the future as a way of raising the attention and consciousness of the town population. Membership on the working group included very key individuals, including Dekan Deutsch, Ernst Klein, Arne Pillardy (headmaster of the public school and a historian), Günter Glitch (who remained on the town council as well), Gabriela Oechsner, and a few others. The group determined as their primary mission to plan for an event commemorating the 60th anniversary of Kristallnacht, to be held November 9, 1998. Besides the expertise that Klein brought to this group, Pillardy had for many years been interested in the history of the area as well as in the events relating to the Holocaust. He later recalled that in school hardly any fellow students knew anything about the topic "because they couldn't talk about it and they wouldn't talk about it, so they just pushed it away." As a young teacher, he determined to speak to his students about it even though the parents "were afraid the children would blame them," he later recalled. "I had always wished that the students could learn about the history of this time, what happened and what was said, so that it wouldn't happen again." Although the working group reported to the town parliament, and thus Mayor Dietrich had little directly to do with its work, he strongly approved of its immediate mission to develop a program for November 9, 1998: "The program was prepared by the team; that was the official task of this group," he later recalled. It would be during the summer of 1997, while the working group was in the midst of its planning for the following year's commemoration that Ralph Mollerick would return to Wolfhagen.

By the summer of 1997, Ralph and Phyllis Mollerick were very excited about returning to Wolfhagen. During the visits to the Mollericks by Gisela and Heinz and by Günter the previous year, plans began to take shape and were firmed up during the course of the ensuing winter and spring for a very ambitious and exciting visit to Germany. This time, however, Jeffrey was unable to join Ralph and Phyllis on the trip and so Günter offered a spare bedroom in the basement of his home, which the couple gladly accepted. The visit included two major outings: Heinz and Gisela took the Mollericks to Berlin on a bus tour for a weekend, in part to reciprocate for the hospitality they received while in Maryland the previous year. The two couples had a glorious time in Berlin, where one of the stops was the Jewish Museum. Also during the Mollerick's 1997 visit, Günter and Heinrich accompanied Ralph and Phyllis on a day trip by fast train to Hamburg, where Ralph was most anxious to find the street where he had lived in 1937 and 1938. He had indeed remembered the name of the street—Beneckestraße—but oddly was unable to locate the street on any map of the city in advance of the visit. Upon arriving at the Central Station, a place Ralph had last seen on December 14, 1938, the day he and Edith departed on the Kindertransport, Ralph noted that the station appeared very much similar in many respects to the time almost 60 years earlier. The group went straight to the town hall to try to locate Beneckestraße. Several members of the staff tried to assist them but to no avail—the street apparently no longer existed. Curious and disappointed, the four friends spent the remainder of the day sightseeing around the city center, taking a harbor boat ride on the Elbe River, and enjoying lunch nearby. Ralph spent much of the time on the train ride back to Wolfhagen wondering what had happened to Beneckestraße. One of the people who tried to help in the town hall had speculated that the street may have been named after a prominent Nazi and therefore would have been changed after the war, but Ralph realized this was conjecture. He had wanted to see the neighborhood where he had lived but only remembered the name of the street and could not recall either the name of the neighborhood or where it was located relevant to the city center. Although they had spent a very pleasant day with Günter and Heinrich in Hamburg, Ralph was somewhat unsettled and disappointed that he could not see what he had gone there to see. It would not be until 14 years later that he would return to Hamburg and successfully see the neighborhood where he had lived.

Back in the now more familiar confines of Wolfhagen, Ralph and Phyllis had a leisurely visit with many of their friends and took the opportunity to renew acquaintances. They of course visited Mayor

Dietrich, who presented them with gifts once again. Lutz Kann was in town with his wife, Sonia, whom Ralph and Phyllis had not previously met. This encounter lacked the warmth that characterized virtually all their interactions with the townspeople, but remained civil nonetheless, despite the memory

of Lutz's November 1995 letter to Ralph continuing to grate on him. It also did not help that Sonia was offended when Ralph addressed her by her given name, as was typically the American custom, rather than using the more formal "*Frau* Kann," and so the chill between the two families continued.

Until the 1997 visit to Wolfhagen, Ralph had been largely unaware of the town's working group and its effort to plan a commemoration of the 60th anniversary of Kristallnacht. One day during the visit, Ralph and Phyllis were sitting in a café with Günter and Dekan Deutsch when Ralph said that he had been thinking it would be a good thing for the town, and something that he would very much like to see, for a memorial to be erected and dedicated to the Jewish families of Wolfhagen from the time of the Nazi era. The idea had actually come to him four years earlier, after his first visit to the town; but in the excitement and afterglow of that experience and then with the focus of the 1995 visit on the unveiling ceremony for the headstone for his parents in the Jewish cemetery, he had been too preoccupied to verbalize or even fully think through his idea for a memorial stone for the Jewish families of Wolfhagen. Now—at the café—he raised this question with Günter and Deutsch, who immediately liked the idea and told Ralph that there was a town working group currently planning an official commemoration for the 60th anniversary of November 9, 1938, and that both of them served on this working group. They told Ralph and Phyllis that they would share his idea with the other members of the working group at their next meeting and let the Mollericks know what develops. This proved perfectly acceptable to Ralph and Phyllis and after several more days of wining and dining and sightseeing with their friends in and around Wolfhagen, they returned home.

True to their word, Günter and Dekan Deutsch brought Ralph's proposal to the next meeting of the town's working group. "We talked about it," Günter later recalled, "and everyone said that it would be nice to do that." Because the working group had already begun planning for a commemoration of the 60th anniversary of Kristallnacht, and because that would be really the first major "official" town event relating to the Holocaust, members of the working group thought carefully about how to proceed with Ralph's idea for the town to erect a memorial stone dedicated to the Jewish families. "The working group had to be very cautious," Arne Pillardy later recalled, "because it had to be discussed what was good at that time—there was a time when it was probably not so good, but then it was decided that it was a good time to put up a stone, and that was decided by the group while planning for the November 9 commemoration." The group realized, however, that three aspects of this project had to be undertaken: identifying information about the former Jewish families of the town to ensure that the information to be engraved was accurate and complete; selecting a suitable location for placement of the memorial in the town; and selecting an appropriate stone on which to inscribe the information. The first step appeared to be the most difficult. "There were only a few people at that time who knew about the end of the Jewish history in Wolfhagen," Pillardy later recalled," so we thought it might be difficult to get the names of the people." But one of the members of the working group, Gabriela Oechsner, had a grandmother still living in the town that knew the Jewish families in the town from the Nazi era and also knew in which houses they had lived. She compiled a list of names and brought it to the other working group members. Ernst Klein had by this time begun to collect information about the Jewish families of Wolfhagen. "I worked together with this group on the dedication of the stone," he later recalled. Günter recalled that "Ernst was someone who had experienced that research all before we [the town of Wolfhagen] started, so we profited from his experience." Klein took the list prepared by Oechsner's grandmother and checked it against his own research. He had only recently learned from Lutz Kann about Ralph Mollerick existence after Ralph's 1997 visit and thus had not met him at that time, but he subsequently communicated with Ralph so that he could find out more about his family during the process of collecting information to be used for the memorial stone. "I did research on Wolfhagen," he later recalled, "and then I learned about all the Jewish people of Wolfhagen, the facts of their lives." It took considerable time to compile, double-check, and finally confirm all the information about the Jewish families needed for the memorial stone.

Meanwhile, plans moved forward for Wolfhagen's first official commemoration of Kristallnacht, which was held on the night of November 9, 1998. The program began in the town hall auditorium where somewhere between 200 and 300 people gathered, including children, which the Wolfhagen leadership and members of the working group found to be truly an impressive turnout for such a program. The keynote speaker was Herr Dr. Georg Maraun, a member of the town parliament. Speaking for more than a half hour, Maraun gave a detailed and sometimes graphic description of the wrongs done to the Jewish families of Germany under the National Socialists and, in particular, of Wolfhagen, focusing for extended time on the events of November 10, 1938, in the town. His was an impassioned plea for the citizens of Wolfhagen to face the past and dispense with suppression of the truth, to think about these events and take action to ensure such things will never happen again. He explained that the people of Wolfhagen had the opportunity to break down a barrier, such as occurred with the fall of the Berlin Wall nine years earlier, except this barrier is "an invisible monster" which "is locked in many heads." That is why the group is gathered "together here for the first time 60 years after the synagogue fire in Wolfhagen, in order to confess to the most gruesome event in

German history—everywhere in Germany and also here in Wolfhagen." Why now, after 60 years, was it time for the people of the town to face the truth? Maraun asked. It is only partly due to "the fact that a new generation is living, is responsible for the eradication of the events of 9–10 November 1938." Beyond that, it is for all Germans, including older generations, to recognize that "there is no excuse for the injustice that happened in Germany after January 30, 1933. Being silent and turning a blind eye are never the right way. . . . Fellow Germans—we have the chance to learn the power of these terrible, terrible events and contribute to overcoming them." Maraun then spoke at length about what happened in Wolfhagen, mostly on the day after Kristallnacht, and the consequences to the town's diminishing Jewish community—a community that had been important to daily life in the town—immediately thereafter. He concluded: "May our present remembrance . . . be an impulse to new thinking and action. . . . And to all of us I wish peace, peace in truth." Following Maraun's inspiring presentation, everyone took lanterns holding lighted candles and marched slowly in the November night's chill from the town hall to the Jewish cemetery, where prayers were recited. From there the group proceeded to the site of the synagogue that had been burned down 60 years earlier where members of the clergy, including Dekan Deutsch, spoke and more prayers were recited and a plaque that had just been mounted on the wall of the building at the site of the synagogue by direction of the town was then dedicated with the following inscription: "Here stood the synagogue of the Jewish community from 1859 to 1938. It was destroyed by fire in The Pogrom Night of 10.11.1938."

As far as it could be determined, not a single Jewish person was present for this program; nonetheless it had a lasting impact on the town. The working group in the months immediately thereafter made two key decisions: first, it determined that Wolfhagen would henceforth observe a commemoration on November 9 every year. Pillardy later recalled: "Since 1998 when we started the November 9 commemoration, it went around to all the other villagers around here so that many of the nearby villages wanted to know what happened here, and that interest was not there before, so this is the sort of reaction that happened then." Secondly, the working group recommended to the parliament and received approval to proceed with the creation of a stone memorial dedicated to the former Jewish families living in Wolfhagen at the time the National Socialists came to power in January 1933.

Ralph Mollerick answered the phone in Maryland one day early in the year 2000. Günter was calling from Wolfhagen, something that was a fairly routine occurrence as by this time he and the Mollericks spoke on the phone every few weeks. "There's some good news and there's some bad news," Ralph recalled Günter saying to him. "What would you like to hear first?" Ralph asked to hear the good news. "The good news," Günter replied, "is that Wolfhagen has given an official approval for the memorial stone for the Jewish families of the town." The bad news turned out to be that there was information for 29 families to be placed on the stone and the working group was certain there would not be a large enough stone to be found to hold all the information unless some of it was abbreviated or consolidated. Also, the working group was still trying to figure out the best location to place the stone in the town and whether there was sufficient funding to cover the cost of what would likely be a fairly large stone. Ralph immediately took the latter problem off the table by telling Günter that he and Phyllis and Jeffrey would pay for the cost of the engraved stone. This allowed for the working group to focus on finding the best location to place the stone. Several factors contributed to the decision. The first was that the group wanted the stone to be located in a place where everyone could see it, so this, plus the complicating factors of having to get approvals from the Jewish Community Councils in Frankfurt and Kassel, ruled out the Jewish cemetery. There was also some concern that placing it in the Jewish cemetery might invite acts of vandalism, which occurred sporadically at Jewish cemeteries still existing in some parts of Germany. "We thought that if it was in a place where everyone can see it, then nobody would do anything to it," Günter recalled in 2016, "and nobody has done anything to it so far." Finally, the working group wanted to establish a third and final location for the procession during the annual November 9 commemorations. Given that the procession began at one end of the town center at the Jewish cemetery and went next to the site of the former synagogue located near the center of the historic section, it made sense to find a location for the memorial stone for the families close to the other end of the historic center of town. "It took some time to figure out where to put it," Günter later recalled; "we walked around and thought about where to put it." Eventually the working group selected a spot at Freedom Plaza, a small park that slopes down a hill near the end of Schützebergerstrße, not far from the city's regional museum. It was ideally located to be in plain view but set into a serene spot off the street that would allow sufficient space for people to gather to conclude the town's annual commemoration of Kristallnacht. "We wanted the stone to be seen all over the town and that's why we selected Freedom Plaza," Pillardy later recalled.

With this decision made by the town, Ralph and Phyllis made plans to visit Wolfhagen in mid-July 2000 to help select a stone that would constitute the memorial and to visit with their friends who had been repeatedly urging them to return after a three-year hiatus. By the time the Mollericks arrived in Wolfhagen on July 17, some major changes had occurred since their previous visit. A new Bürgermeister, a young and energetic man named Reinhard Schaake, had been elected in 1999, as Mayor

 Dietrich stepped down after many years of service. Dekan Deutsch had also moved on, being replaced by Dr. Gernot Gerlach, a warm and thoughtful man who had become dekan of the town's main Lutheran Church on May 1, 2000, and who had

taken an interest in Jewish history even before arriving in Wolfhagen. He immediately joined in the meetings of the working group planning for the memorial stone. "I had heard about the new attitude to put up a stone sponsored by Ralph Mollerick," Gerlach later recalled. "I took part in the discus-  sions to find the right place and we discussed what should be written on the stone." Ralph and Phyllis immediately hit it off with both of these officials and their spouses, very quickly establishing a wonderful rapport with them that continues to the present day. The Mollericks again stayed at Günter's house and Ralph joined in the search for the best stone possible for the memorial to the Jewish families of Wolfhagen—a process which turned out to be a bit more complex than originally anticipated.

On July 18, Ralph accompanied Mayor Schaake and Günter to visit the stonecutter, the same one from whose yard Ralph had selected the headstone for his parents unveiled in 1995. There had earlier been some discussion among the working group about the shape of the stone and the mayor explained that it was thought that an irregular stone would make sense because the people had become scattered. Ralph disagreed; "Wolfhagen is a discreet location," he said. "It is not all of Germany." There were several pieces of German black granite but initially none of the ones they looked at were large enough to hold all the information about the families, and so they kept looking until they found one rectangular stone that was larger than the others. Ralph had it in his mind to have the stone cut into the shape of two tablets, "like in the movie *The Ten Commandments*," he later recalled. But that would have been too complicated and so he suggested that they use the large rectangular stone and set it with the longer side horizontally, which meant that the information about the families would have to be engraved in two columns. This required the information for families with children to be truncated, so instead of all family members having their given and last names engraved, it would have to be engraved only as "Family of Josef and Selma Möllerich," for example. The stonecutter was provided the information about the families and, as Günter later recalled, "He worked day and night to complete the engraving in time for the dedication ceremony," which the working group had decided to hold on November 9, 2000, as part of the town's annual commemoration of Kristallnacht.

With the selection of the stone completed, some of the members of the working group sat down with Ralph to discuss the details of the dedication ceremony. These members made it clear that they expected both Ralph and Lutz Kann to be present for the ceremony, which for Ralph would have meant a second visit to Wolfhagen within just a few months. Dekan Gerlach later recalled: "It was important for me that Ralph Mollerick and Lutz Kann should talk and pray and say what they want to say." On July 20, Mayor Schaake continued the practice of his predecessor by hosting Ralph and Phyllis and a few friends (in this instance Günter, Heinrich Schwarz, and Kurt Giese) in his office. As usual, there was a reporter from the local newspaper present, who was given an opportunity to speak to Ralph and Phyllis and take photographs. For the third time Ralph gave a summary of his sojourn from Wolfhagen to Hamburg to England and then to the United States and eventually his initial return to Wolfhagen in 1993 (including Ralph's epiphany atop Offenberg Tower) and the second visit in 1995 to place a headstone for his parents in the Jewish cemetery. For the first time, the article that appeared the next day in the newspaper presented virtually all of this information accurately and then went on to describe plans for the upcoming dedication of the stone for the Jewish families in Freedom Plaza. According to the article, Mayor Schaake said: "The town Council will support this project. . . . We regret the past," he said, and pointed out how important it is "to put up a sign of reconciliation." The article also reported that Ralph had responded to the mayor "that he had put his anger aside. The past could not be changed; one has to concentrate on the present and the future." At the end of the reception, as had become the town's custom with Ralph and Phyllis, Schaake presented them with a brooch and tie clasp with the insignia of Wolfhagen emblazoned on them. In response, Phyllis presented Schaake with a crystal vase as a "sign of friendship."

No sooner had Ralph and Phyllis returned home from Germany on July 28 than they began planning for a brief four-day return to participate in the dedication ceremony for the memorial stone for the Jewish families of Wolfhagen on November 9. Although they and the town were hoping that Jeffrey would accompany them to Germany for this ceremony, he had already committed to other travel plans for November so he could not join them for what would have been his fourth visit in less than a decade. Shortly before their departure for Germany, Ralph and Phyllis received an official invitation from Schaake with a copy of the program for the dedication of the stone in Freedom Plaza. An identical invitation also was sent to Lutz Kann, who came to Wolfhagen with his wife, Sonia. As it turned out, the program for the dedication itself followed the now becoming traditional November 9 commemoration of Kristallnacht format that began with some singing and readings by young people in the town hall. There followed the procession with people holding lanterns with lit candles to the Jewish cemetery, thence to the site of the synagogue, and this time ending at Freedom Plaza, where a crowd of more than 200 people stood in the chill of a clear and starry evening at 6:30 p.m. for a relatively brief but moving ceremony. Mayor Schaake gave introductory comments followed by a musical presentation. Then the school headmaster Pillardy gave a short but remarkable presentation that brought tears to the eyes of some of the onlookers as he discussed what had occurred in Wolfhagen 62 years earlier: "Most of our parents and grandparents looked aside. . . . People acted indifferently, everybody knew about the terror and expulsions of the Jews," he said. "Most would not allow themselves to feel that horror that was happening around them." With respect to the Holocaust in its broadest sense,

Pillardy told the assembled group that "We, as well as our parents and grandparents became guilty for the second time. We are guilty of allowing the memories of the horrors of the Holocaust to be repressed. We are guilty of not asking more insistently what happened to the surviving Jewish citizens of our hometown." He concluded, however, with a message of hope for the town: "Late, almost too late, the act of remembering has begun. We remembered the victims in a ceremony two years ago for the first time at the site where the synagogue once stood. . . . We do so now and we are grateful to you, Mr. Kann and you, Mr. Mollerick for being with us today on this day of Commemoration and Reflection." With that, the impressive black granite memorial stone was unveiled revealing the following heading: "We commemorate the former Jewish citizens of Wolfhagen." Directly below are the names of 16 families and 13 individuals in two columns with the following inscription at the bottom: "9 November 2000 – the City of Wolfhagen."

Fresh Flowers donated by the Mollerick family stood in large pots on either side of the memorial stone. Gabriele Oechsner then solemnly read the names inscribed on the stone, and Ralph and Lutz recited the mourner's *kaddish* (prayer) in Hebrew. Several prayers were recited by members of the clergy with Dekan Gerlach reading Psalm 130 in Hebrew and German: "Out of the depths I cry to you Lord; hear my voice. . . . Put your hope in the Lord, for the Lord is unveiling love, and with Him is full redemption."

In the immediate aftermath of the ceremony, Ralph and Lutz were the center of attention. They were interviewed together by local members of the press, who took a photograph of the only two remaining former Jewish citizens of Wolfhagen standing behind the newly unveiled memorial stone. Although Ralph and Lutz had their personal as well as personality differences, the subsequent article published in *Wolfhager Allgemeine* four days later reflects a common thread between the two men. Characterizing the moment when the memorial stone was unveiled as "a highlight of my life," Ralph indicated that he was "highly moved" not only by the manner in which the town had welcomed him back for a fifth time in seven years, but by the steps it had taken "to keep alive the memory of former Wolfhagen citizens who were murdered in the Nazi terror." As for Lutz Kann, the article reported that he "made it his business to remind people" about the town's history. "I must take care of the fact that the history of the German Jews will not be forgotten," he told the reporter. Speaking of the newly erected memorial stone, Ralph later told a reporter for the *Washington Jewish Week* for an article that appeared two weeks after the ceremony in Washington: "I believe the town put this up as a remembrance for this generation to look back with respect for the victims, and for the next generation to ask what happened here. Then the Jews won't be forgotten. They'll remember what Germany did." Once the interviews concluded following the ceremony in Wolfhagen, many of the participants adjourned for a celebratory dinner, and it was here that Ralph finally had the opportunity to meet and speak to Ernst Klein face to face, which turned out to be a singular moment for both of them and the beginning of an important relationship. There were additional discussions the following day involving Ralph and key members of the town's working group, and Ralph was especially pleased to have an opportunity to have an extended discussion with Ernst Klein about the history of the Jews of Wolfhagen.

Ralph's participation in the creation and unveiling of the memorial stone for the Jewish families of Wolfhagen had a lasting impact on him as well as the town. Like the placing of the headstone for his parents in the Jewish cemetery in 1995, he felt a very personal connection to the dedication of the memorial stone for the Jewish families in 2000, because, as he later recalled, "I saw my family's name on the stone." He also wondered, "Have we done enough? Is this sufficient, putting up the monument?" He may not have articulated it at the time, but he would have the opportunity to do more with respect to Wolfhagen's remembrance of its Jewish community in the coming years. Upon returning home, Ralph wrote to Mayor Schaake expressing his thanks for being included in the dedication ceremony: "The events of the evening and the day that followed will surely be recorded as an historical experience for the town," he wrote on November 29. "We can all feel proud that the Jewish families of Wolfhagen have been remembered. Let us hope and pray that this tribute . . . can ignite the minds and hearts of other leaders of townships and cities of Germany." The following year, in the wake of the September 11, 2001, attack on the United States, Mayor Schaake wrote to Ralph and Phyllis: "The events of September 11 have stunned us all—you, personally too as Frau Abel told me. To reach peace the knowledge about the past must be kept in mind. Thus, a memorial ceremony has taken place for the second time on November 9 at the 'Place of Freedom' where the monument now stands in Wolfhagen." In early January 2002, Günter sent Ralph a translation of an article about that 2001 commemoration of Kristallnacht referred to by the mayor that appeared in the *Wolfhager Stadtamzeiger*, describing the conclusion of the procession through the town at the site of the memorial stone unveiled the previous year with comments by Schaake: "The stone is a symbol of acknowledgement of the guilt for doing harm to the Jewish minority by citizens of our town. . . . At the same time it is also a symbol for the forgiveness and friendship by the relatives of the former Jewish inhabitants of Wolfhagen." Arne Pillardy gave brief comments similar to his presentation the previous year, as the article reported his comments: "The memory of torture and assassination of innumerable Europeans of Jewish belief by Germans forces us to admit that human beings could do horrible deeds to other humans and can still do so today. The terrorist attacks on the USA on September 11 show that this is still valid in present times. Our sympathy is with the relatives and friends of the victims."

For the Wolfhagen annual commemoration of Kristallnacht on November 9, 2002, the town asked Ralph to provide his written thoughts since he could not be there in person. These were translated into German and read by Günter Glitsch at the site of the memorial stone at Freedom Plaza during the conclusion of the solemn commemoration ceremony. The theme of the 2002 commemoration was "A Bridge Linking Generations." Earlier in the evening at the Culture Hall, students from the high school read poems and other writings created by children who were Holocaust victims. An article published in *Wolfhager Allgemeine* two days later recorded the scene: "It is dark in the Culture Hall and so quiet that one can hear a needle fall to the ground." The students read the names of the Jewish victims who formerly lived in Wolfhagen. Under the direction of headmaster Pillardy, the students from the ethics course gave their presentation. "Very impressive were the recitations of the students accompanied by the Wolfhagen youth symphonic orchestra." The group then faced "an icy wind" as the procession, as had become the custom, marched from the Jewish cemetery to the site of the former synagogue where Dekan Gerlach recited prayers and psalms, and then to the site of the memorial stone for the former Jewish families of Wolfhagen, where Günter read Ralph's prepared comments in the presence of Mayor Schaake, Ernst Klein, Lutz Kann, and some members of the working group who gathered around the memorial stone. "We are told that time has a way of healing, and remembering the past has a way of guiding us in making the right choices," Ralph wrote. "While we can forgive, we can never forget. . . . Let us not forget the families who were persecuted, humiliated, and murdered in streets and concentration camps. . . . The Spanish philosopher and writer George Santayana wrote: 'Those who do not remember the past are doomed to repeat it.'" The 2002 commemoration in Wolfhagen planted a seed of an idea both in Ralph's mind and among the members of the working group for the 2003 commemoration that would involve both Ralph and many of the young people of Wolfhagen. But before the planning for this event could fully take shape, Ralph and his family would be struck by tragedy.

Ralph and Phyllis sat with Jeffrey Mollerick in front row box seats at the minor league ball park in Richmond, Virginia, where Jeffrey had moved just three months earlier, having taken the position of president of Service Partners. The mid-July 2003 sun was warm; Jeffrey had invited his father and Phyllis to the ball game as a belated birthday and father's day gift for Ralph and the three had very much enjoyed the relaxed atmosphere. Ralph had for many years—perhaps since his counseling following his separation from Marlene but certainly more recently, after sharing the two trips to Germany—wanted to talk to Jeffrey about their relationship, which he felt had much improved in recent years. "I always felt that I wanted to share my joy over the trips to Germany," he later recalled, "and show my appreciation for his having directed me to those initial two trips that led to a journey and opportunity of my lifetime, and to thank him for his friendship." But he also had wanted to finally clear the air with his older son with regard to their earlier difficult relationship. Ralph turned to Jeffrey and apologized to him for having not lived up properly to his role as a father when Jeffrey was young. "I knew it had been difficult for both of us and that I had made his life miserable," Ralph recalled. He was then stunned by Jeffrey's response: "Your apology is NOT accepted!" Jeffrey blurted. "You were not a bad person; you were not a drunkard or a druggie. Had you been one, it would have been a hell of a lot easier for me because I would have left home. But you were not like that. . . . I don't know how I can convey to you how much living with you was painful," Ralph later recalled Jeffrey telling him, "and only now I understand what made you the way you were then." Jeffrey then told Ralph to drop the subject and just watch the game. Phyllis sat silently during this exchange holding back tears, but during the drive back to Maryland she angrily spoke out, telling Ralph that "she thought it was horrible the way Jeffrey spoke to me," Ralph later recalled, "and that I was not allowed to defend myself." She was angry at Ralph for not insisting on explaining his perspective. "She was annoyed that I didn't take control of that conversation and let him move me around like a rag." Ralph had been equally surprised that he was not given an opportunity to explain. He called Jeffrey twice during the next week in an effort to express his feelings about the issue. Each time Jeffrey told him, "Dad, I can't talk about this now—we'll talk about it another time," Ralph later recalled. That time never came.

Midmorning on July 23, Ralph received a phone call from his younger son, Glen. The voice on the line was choked so that Ralph immediately knew something was very wrong, which sent a chill down his spine. Jeffrey had been found dead in his apartment that morning; he had suffered an apparent fatal heart attack. He was 45 years old. Ralph knew that Jeffrey's health had been failing for a number of months, as Jeffrey had been diagnosed with congestive heart failure. When he had phoned Jeffrey during the previous week he had found his son sounding weak and unwell, and offered to come to Richmond. Jeffrey had told him that he just needed to rest and would feel better in the morning, as had been the case many times before. Jeffrey's best friend, Matt, from Baltimore had driven to Richmond the morning of his death to bring Jeffrey back to Baltimore for an appointment with a specialist at Johns Hopkins Medical Center, and it was Matt who found Jeffrey fully dressed on his bed. News of Jeffrey's passing, nonetheless left Ralph in shock. The next days and events passed for Ralph as if he were in a semi-conscious state, as he and Glen dealt with the apartment, arranging for transport of Jeffrey's body to Maryland, and for his funeral, which was held in Baltimore County, followed by interment at a cemetery just outside of Baltimore where Ralph's sister Edith was buried.

More than once in the days that followed the funeral and burial, Ralph thought about the way Jeffrey had confronted him at the baseball game. "I had thought that the two trips we had taken to Germany together were an indication and prelude to a better relationship," he later recalled, "and that things were on the mend and the friendship felt good." He regretted that he had not spoken out about his feelings the day of the ball game, to explain to Jeffrey that he now understood why he had acted the way he did and that it was important that Jeffrey try to lose the anger that he had inside of him the way Ralph was able to as a result of the changes that he had gone through during the early 1990s. "He could not let go of these feelings towards me from childhood times," Ralph recalled, "even to the time I asked for forgiveness one week or so before his death. Then it was too late." Because of the manner in which the argument at the baseball game played out, Phyllis had a theory that Jeffrey knew that he was ill and even perhaps that he did not have much time left, and chose to distance himself from Ralph—even after the years of getting along on the surface during the visits to Germany—in order that Ralph would not mourn as deeply after his death. Ralph thought there was merit to this, but it served to have the opposite effect on him: "The thing that was really the stab in the back," he later recalled, "was that he was willing to get me angry so I would not think favorably of him if he should pass away in the near future."

Ralph's grief over Jeffrey's sudden passing and the inability to experience closure with him, as he had with his parents and the Holocaust as a result of his return to Germany, sent Ralph almost immediately after the funeral into a grief-inspired depression. Phyllis' older daughter, Rochelle, noticed the change in Ralph right away; she took him aside and expressed her concern. "She said she loved me very much," Ralph later recalled, "and felt that I appeared extremely troubled. She suggested that 'grief therapy' would be very helpful and I agreed." Ralph remembered well the breakthrough he had experienced during the therapy he underwent following his separation—how it enabled him to face the demons from his past that had haunted him for half a lifetime. He found someone who turned out to be an excellent therapist, someone whom he continued to consult for more than two years. Over time Ralph achieved a greater understanding of himself and his relationship with Jeffrey and this allowed him to experience at least a partial personal sense of closure. This was due not only to the skill of the therapist, but in part to the positive effect Ralph's return to Germany had on his life: "The counseling alone may not have been as fulfilling," he later recalled," without the experiences in Germany which made me more receptive to understanding myself. I would not have been at peace in the same way or become the person I am today if I had not continued to go to Germany for many return trips." Less than four months after Jeffrey's death and even less time after starting "grief therapy," Ralph returned to Wolfhagen for what turned out to be a highlight of his life and one of the most extraordinary commemorations of Kristallnacht the town has ever experienced.

In early September 2003, Ralph received a phone call from Günter to explain what the working group had planned for that year's November 9 commemoration, and that it very much would center on Ralph and require his active participation. The theme of that year's commemoration was to be the Kindertransport, and Mayor Schaake wanted Ralph and Phyllis to come to Wolfhagen and for Ralph to be the keynote speaker for the occasion. Günter asked Ralph to prepare extended comments about his Kindertransport experience for a presentation before a large gathering to be held in the town's Culture Hall. He also asked Ralph if he would be willing to prepare a second presentation for a group of high school students at the school, which had been suggested by one of the new teachers there. "We try to do something different every year so that more people would be interested and come to see what's going on," Günter later recalled. "On this one year, that was when Ralph gave his speech on the Kindertransport." Dekan Gerlach also helped plan the 2003 program and was very much hoping for Ralph's personal participation: "Ralph always has a sense of peace and I got the impression that he can help people living in Wolfhagen to get to know and accept history and to learn from him."

Because it was anticipated that Ralph's speech would be substantial and he would be speaking in English, and because a large audience, many of whom may not understand English, would be in attendance, Ralph was asked to send along his speech in advance so that Günter could translate it into German. He had told Günter that he thought it was important to provide sufficient historical context to his explanation about the Kindertransport program: "Why am I here? Why did I do this with the memorial stone at Freedom Plaza? What is the meaning of that? What do we want to remember about that—and what does it tell us for future generations?" Ralph had the impression that the working group wanted to have the speech in advance to "make certain that I wasn't saying something that would create a disturbance in the community." He told Günter that if he were going to speak, he had to say "what I believe in and what I think is important to be heard. They may not like it all, but I don't think I will say anything outlandish that would disturb anybody," he later recalled. As it turned out, Ralph sent to Günter not only his speech but background information, all of which Günter translated into German. The only changes he could suggest to Ralph were grammatical: "He said, 'I like everything but I think you need to change the English grammar,'" Ralph later recalled and shared a chuckle with Günter that this critique had come from the now retired English teacher of Wolfhagen. When Ralph completed these minor edits, he sent the speech back to Günter, who then called to ask Ralph to mark a place every few sentences where he would stop for Günter to read the translation in German, and Ralph readily complied.

When Ralph and Phyllis arrived in Germany the morning of November 8, Günter was waiting at the Frankfurt airport and they drove the two-hour auto trip to Wolfhagen together. Once again the Mollericks stayed in the extra bedroom in the lower level of Günter's house and the first thing Ralph and Günter did upon arrival was rehearse the speech with the pauses for translation. Ralph already knew that Lutz Kann would not be present for the 2003 commemoration. He and Phyllis had an exchange of correspondence in late October—as they typically did around the time of the Jewish New Year—with Lutz and Sonia. Lutz was very kind, offering sincere condolences over Jeffrey's death: "From personal experience," he wrote on October 26, "I know how difficult it is when parents lose their children and grandchildren and mourn them." He then explained that he and Sonia had been invited by Mayor Schaake for the annual November 9 commemoration of Kristallnacht, but their children had surprised them with a trip to Portugal which would overlap with the Wolfhagen ceremony. For Ralph, news of Lutz's absence came as something of a relief, because he knew that he would be speaking to students and he planned on taking a different approach than Lutz did when he spoke to children about the monument for the Jewish families and about his experience. "He said we were ripped out of our homes, we were tortured, and we were taken to camps," Ralph later recalled. "It was true, of course, but I don't know why you would associate that with the monument, which is supposed to be something positive and educational for the kids to see." Phyllis agreed with Ralph's characterization: "Lutz would always rub their nose in the fact that it's the German people's fault that Jews no longer live there," she later recalled. "I felt that I had to say something," Ralph recalled, "that needed to be said in a way that future generations would listen and understand, and if I say it in front of hundreds of people, with newspapers and videographers and teachers and historians in that room, this would carry a better message than just knocking what Germany had done."

The program for the 2003 commemoration of Kristallnacht was unique in several respects. Because November 9 fell on a Sunday so people were not at work or school, and because the focus of the program was even more heavily on young people and education than it had been in the past, the working group had decided to hold the program during the day rather than at night. The first activity began at 11:00 a.m. at the site of the memorial monument for the former Jewish families of Wolfhagen in Freedom Plaza. Mayor Schaake offered some introductory comments, followed by a musical piece by a string quartet that set both a peaceful and somber tone. As had been the custom since 2000, the names of the families and individuals on the stone were read out loud, followed by prayers and psalms led by Dekan Gerlach and other members of the clergy. In silence, this assemblage adjourned to the Culture Hall for the main part of the program, where they were joined by other fellow citizens—many of them young people—as well as the print and television media, totaling perhaps 300 people and completely filling the hall. Ralph later recalled that one of the town officials spoke briefly about the importance of educating students about the Holocaust, explaining a little about what was being done in the school, and also mentioning the work that Ernst Klein was doing to preserve the history of Jewish culture and educating students. In September, Ralph had spoken to Deborah Oppenheimer, the producer of the documentary *Into the Arms of Strangers*, an Academy Award–winning documentary film with many personal reflections by kinder, and had learned that there was a version in German entitled, *In Eine Fremd Welt* (literally translated as "In a Foreign World"), and Günter had obtained a copy of this for the occasion. The film—which ran over 90 minutes—was shown in its entirety.

The large hall was hushed following the film, and many people were visibly shaken but came to life as Günter introduced Ralph as the keynote speaker. As Ralph climbed the steps to the stage and came to the lectern, the thought occurred to him that "A Jew had never been seen on this stage and that almost everyone in the room was not yet born when the Kindertransport made history." Although he had by 2003 begun speaking publicly about his personal experience and the Holocaust, he had never done so in Germany, nor to an audience anything close to the size of the one that he now faced standing at the lectern. Ralph began his comments with a brief history of the economic and political events in Germany that gave rise to Hitler and the National Socialists, and the systematic program of anti-Semitic policies that led so many German Jews to leave the country, as well as the consequences to those who remained, especially with the pogrom on the 9th and 10th of November 1938. Until this point in his talk, Ralph had been calm and his voice was steady. As he transitioned to the section of the speech that he called "My Kindertransport Saga," his voice suddenly shook with outrage and he momentarily deviated from the script as he spoke out about the atrocities inflicted on European Jewry. "I wanted people to know," he later recalled, "that while nearly 10,000 children were spared the horrors of the death camps through the Kindertransport, six million

Jews—including one-and-a-half million children—perished during the Holocaust." As Ralph paused for Günter to translate these ad-libbed comments, he could see that his words had a profound impact. Phyllis, who was sitting in the audience, later said that many of the people around her openly wept when Ralph mentioned the number of children murdered. Returning to his script, Ralph completed his description of his personal Kindertransport experience and a very brief explanation of his time in England. He then concluded by sharing a series of 10 lessons to be learned from the history of the Holocaust, ranging from prevention of discriminatory policies and activities to ensuring the preservation of personal liberties and rights to which all people are entitled. The talk—including the translations—had lasted more than 90 minutes, and yet the audience had hung on his every word and offered an extended standing ovation when it was over. Afterward, Ralph was surprised when audience members—many of whom spoke English—came to him to offer their warm appreciation.

Later in the day, Ralph participated in a roundtable discussion hosted by Mayor Schaake at the Alte Rathaus that included mostly educators and historians who took the opportunity to ask many questions about what at that time was the relatively obscure aspect of the Holocaust known as the Kindertransport, especially in Wolfhagen and its environs. Ralph answered the many questions posed but found it odd that among these approximately 40 highly intelligent individuals, not one thought to deviate from the details of the Kindertransport program to inquire about Ralph's feelings having to be separated from his parents forever and being forced to spend the greater part of his childhood alone, without family, in a strange country where he had to quickly learn a new language and customs. Although he recognized the utility of the roundtable discussion, the experience left him feeling a bit deflated, despite the success of his keynote address earlier in the day.

As it turned out, the next day—which Ralph later characterized as "my finest hour"—would prove to bring the satisfaction Ralph had sought at the roundtable discussion, and more. He had been invited to speak at the school to the older high school students and about 80 students filled every seat in the lecture hall. Ralph had planned to show perhaps 40 minutes of *Into the Arms of Strangers* and then lead a question and answer session so that his program could fit into the one hour that the schedule allowed. Unlike the previous day at the Culture Hall, however, everything went wrong with respect to the showing of the film. Despite the efforts of the teacher and many of the highly technologically savvy students, the film could not be made to work. Ralph had to scrap his planned program and speak to and with the students for an entire hour, virtually without a script—something he had never done in his life. After a momentary sense of panic passed, and he thought hard about how to capture the attention of young people whose knowledge of English was fairly good for a second language, but probably not colloquial, Ralph asked the group: "Suppose I told you that all girls in this room and throughout Germany are no longer allowed to play volleyball?" There was silence for a few seconds and a boy in the front then said, "That's not possible." Ralph explained that he was correct—that today something like that could not happen in Germany but that is exactly what happened in Germany to Jewish children like himself. Many of the students said that this was "a terrible outrage" and attentively listened as Ralph summarized his childhood in Germany and the Kindertransport experience. There were many questions asked and plenty of interaction following Ralph's presentation and before he knew it, the hour had passed. "These were kids who were 16, 17, 18 years old," Günter later recalled, "and they were not so shy; they asked good questions, and it turned out really well." Ralph later recalled that he concluded the session by telling the students: "Here is an opportunity for each of you to be ever watchful for maintaining your right to seek employment of your choice, to ensure freedom of expression, and the right to enjoy life." As far as Ralph could determine, not a single student spoke or demonstrated with body language any sign of disbelief during his presentation. Speaking to the teacher after the session, he learned that "of course" the students learn about the Holocaust as part of the school curriculum. He also learned that this is accomplished largely through the showing of videos and personal research, but with little or no discussion. "They don't want to talk about their grandparents," Ralph recalled the teacher telling him. Remembering the faces of the students as they left the lecture hall, Ralph could see there were no smiles and little conversation. "They are not proud of what some of their grandparents did," he later commented.

The other significant highlight of Ralph and Phyllis' 2003 visit to Wolfhagen—other than enjoying most evenings with their friends in the town—involved the opportunity to spend considerable time with

Ernst Klein and learn firsthand about his project in Volkmarsen and the remarkable work he was doing to preserve the Jewish heritage in the region. Observing the artifacts and documentation that Ernst and his wife, Brigitte, and their colleagues had collected and turned into an exhibit

and, more importantly, learning of the continuing and growing work of Ernst and his society to expand the collection, Ralph and Phyllis were thoroughly impressed. Ralph spoke at length about what he had learned about his family, which was at that time still quite limited. Ernst added to Ralph's knowledge by showing him documents he had found about Ralph's family as part of his ongoing research of Jewish life in Wolfhagen, which had begun around the time Ernst first met Lutz Kann more than a decade earlier. He also took Ralph and Phyllis to see the Jewish cemetery in Volkmarsen and to nearby Vöhl, where extensive work was being done to restore the synagogue there. Ernst was impressed by Ralph's description of his experience with the Wolfhagen school students the previous day. "I always say it's the best thing to go into the school," Klein later recalled, "so that our young people can hear directly from eyewitnesses about their lives." He also recalled the first time he met Ralph briefly in 2000 and the more extended conversations they had over the course of two days in 2003: "Sometimes we see people for the first time and know that it is good. There was a feeling of friendship the first time to see; there was an understanding between us without words." Before departing for home, Ralph and Phyllis left a donation for Ernst to further his work and promised to provide whatever documentation and artifacts they could find to bring to Ernst on their next visit to Germany when Ralph spoke to student groups both in Wolfhagen and in Volkmarsen and when he and Phyllis visited the Jewish cemetery in Volkmarsen. In fact, Ralph would also speak to student groups that Ernst would bring to his Volkmarsen project and contribute financially to the project during most future visits that he and Phyllis made to Germany after 2003.

Ralph's role in supporting and helping to guide the redemption of Wolfhagen with respect to the Holocaust had one more major component. Sometime after he and Phyllis visited the town in 2005 and before their next visit in 2008, the working group began considering the possibility of placing a *Stolperstein* in front of each home of a former Jewish resident of the town. "Stolperstein" (literally "stumbling stone") was the creation of artist Günter Demnig who, in December 1992, produced the first Stolperstein—a roughly four-inch square bronze plate set on a concrete stone into the ground, usually in front of the home of a former Jewish resident, with the phrase typically beginning "Here lived . . ." followed by the name of the individual being remembered, along with the place and date of deportation and date murdered (if known) engraved on the bronze plate. Today there are more than 65,000 Stolpersteine set in more than 600 towns and cities in Germany and in more than 20 other countries of Europe, generally countries which were occupied by the Nazis during the Second World War; additional Stolpersteine continue to be set each month. The purpose of the project is to perpetuate the memory of individual victims of the Holocaust and serve as a reminder so that what the Nazis perpetrated will never be forgotten.

Despite its popularity and continued use, the concept and implementation of the Stolpersteine became controversial almost from the outset and sparked heated discussion in many principalities and certainly among Holocaust survivors and their families. There were, to begin with, practical considerations. Bronze scratches and the coating on it tarnishes and must be regularly cleaned. Most municipalities where Stolpersteine have been set, in fact, have established regular schedules for cleaning and polishing the plates. The small size also limits the information that can be engraved. Perhaps more importantly, there was a strong theoretical argument to be made that the Stolpersteine were actually counterproductive to their purpose. Jews had been trodden upon throughout their history—they were slaves, they were expelled from places, they were subjected to anti-Semitism, murdered, and victimized in every conceivable way—and now the names of victims of the Holocaust would be placed in front of the designated Jewish homes on sidewalks where they would be trodden upon once again. To many Holocaust survivors and their families, the concept made no sense. In Münich, one of Germany's largest cities, the decision was made to reject the Stolpersteine project for that very reason, although most of the large cities in Germany, including Hamburg, participate in the project.

Ralph became aware of the controversy over the Stolpersteine project through his connections with the Kindertransport Association sometime before he and Phyllis arrived in Wolfhagen on July 2, 2008. For the first time, Ralph's younger son Glen accompanied them to Germany, and so the Mollericks did not stay at Günter's house but took rooms at the Hotel Zum Schiffchen, where they had stayed the final night during their 1993 visit. The primary purpose of this trip was to show Glen the town and region where his dad had lived, introduce him to their several friends in and around Wolfhagen, as well as spend a few days in Bavaria and in Iceland, and so the visit in Wolfhagen turned out to be a relatively brief three days. Glen, nonetheless, was suitably impressed. "I was so excited to see where he grew up," Glen recalled. "I had seen photos and heard stories from my brother about it but I never thought I would go with them, and when I did it was just amazing."

During the relatively brief visit, Ralph was drawn into a conversation involving the question before the working group on whether or not to place Stolpersteine in front of each of the homes of former Jewish residents of Wolfhagen. The working group had been debating the question for at least a year. Some members were in favor of setting the stones in the ground because the project had become so widespread and generally accepted in other locations in Germany. Günter, Ernst Klein, and Dekan Gerlach, among others, had done some research and understood the sensitivity and practical considerations weighing against the proposal. "I had read in an article that in Kassel that they were installing the Stolpersteine—quite a lot of them," Günter later recalled. "Well, some of us didn't want it here in Wolfhagen." When Ralph joined the conversation on July 3, 2008, he argued strongly against setting the stones: "I told them the Stolpersteine were not in good taste—they were not dignified enough," Ralph later recalled. "We said that if we have somebody here who is Jewish, we should ask him what he would prefer," Günter recalled, "and so Ralph said no Stolpersteine because in former times, under the Nazis, people tread on the Jews." Dekan Gerlach recalled the conversation as well: "Ernst Klein and I did not want this kind of remembering because of the same reasons which Ralph said." During the discussions the idea of putting up a plaque on the outside front wall of the homes rather than setting the Stolpersteine arose and quickly took hold. "We had this discussion and decided we wanted the plaques," Gerlach added. It took some time for the parliament to approve this recommendation and to obtain the permission of current owners of the buildings. The first plaque in memory of a former Jewish resident of Wolfhagen was dedicated on the home of Moses Bloch as part of the town's annual November 9 commemoration in 2009.

In an ironic twist, sometime during 2010 Ralph received a phone call from a woman named Christine Zinn, who was conducting research as part of a large project at the University of Hamburg about former Jewish residents in the city who were victims of the Holocaust, for the purpose of preparing published biographies and also for the city's growing Stolpersteine program. Christine had reached Ralph via a somewhat circuitous route. Her research involved a biography of families who lived on Isistraße, and so she had learned about Ralph's uncle Moritz. During her research in the archive at the university that commenced in 2010, she had discovered considerable information not only about Moritz, but about Josef and Selma Möllerich, perhaps even more information on them than on Moritz, and this piqued her interest in Ralph's family. From the archive files, she knew the family had moved to Hamburg from Wolfhagen, and so she visited the town to try to locate more information about the family. While there someone told her that Josef and Selma's son, Ralph, was living in America and had visited the town many times. She was directed to Günter Glitsch, whom she met and showed him the information she had collected on the Möllerich family in the Hamburg archive. Günter provided her with Ralph's telephone number and address in Florida. Now speaking to Ralph, she told him about plans to set Stolpersteine for his parents near the place where they lived in Hamburg and asked him if he would come to Hamburg to participate in the unveiling of the stones. Ralph later recalled: "I said that I would be delighted to be part of it but I could not come when the unveiling was scheduled in late 2010. I told her that I will eventually get there to see the Stolpersteine and would let her know when we were going to come." Christine also told Ralph about the documentation she found about his parents in the archive and offered to show him these records when he came to Hamburg, which very much interested Ralph. She then asked Ralph if he would be willing to pay for the cost of his parents' Stolpersteine, which amounted to about $150 for each one. Ralph politely declined. As he later recalled, Christine responded: "No problem—there are a number of people who are willing to put up money and so yours will be one of those paid by donation, but you will not know who the donor is." In retrospect, Ralph felt badly about not paying for the cost of his parents' Stolpersteine but realized it was caused by his strong objections to these stones, which he had articulated in Wolfhagen two years earlier. Christine was well familiar with these arguments and readily accepted Ralph's decision not to pay for the stones. "It's a special situation in Hamburg," she later recalled, "in that they don't have to get the permission of the Hamburg house owner to allow the Stolpersteine to be set, because the research has been done to be certain that it was a place where Jews once lived." As it turned out, in the case of the Stolpersteine for Ralph's parents, the location where they were to be set proved to be an interesting point all by itself, as Ralph would soon discover.

With the prospect of a visit to Hamburg in mind, Ralph and Phyllis decided to spend Ralph's 81st birthday in Germany. Once again Glen accompanied them and they arrived in Germany on May 24, 2011, for a stay of one week, dividing their time between Wolfhagen and Hamburg. Ralph was particularly interested in the visit to Hamburg and meet-

ing Christine Zinn and her husband, Thorsten Lührig. When the Mollericks arrived in Hamburg, Christine and Thorsten met them and first showed them Moritz's house at Isistraße 15, which was still standing, as well as the Stolperstein dedicated to Ralph's uncle. They then visited the archive at the University of Hamburg, and on their way to see the archive the visit to the campus solved the mystery dating back to Ralph's earlier visit to Hamburg when nobody could locate Beneckestraße. The street no longer existed because the campus had been built on and around it. Christine and Thorsten, however, showed the Mollericks the Stolpersteine for Ralph's parents that had been dedicated the previous fall. They were set among a series of Stolpersteine on the sidewalk near a large building on campus at the approximate place where the building Ralph and his parents and maternal grandparents had lived at Beneckestraße 26. The Stolpersteine for his parents had their names, dates of birth,

the house address, and indicated they had been deported to Lodz in 1941 and murdered. The Mollericks also visited the Jewish cemetery in Hamburg where Ralph's aunt Jette and maternal grandmother Bertha Meyer were buried and where they saw their headstones. The highlight of the visit to Hamburg, however, for Ralph in particular but also for Glen, was the visit to the archive where Christine showed them a stack of documents from two different files that was more than a foot tall. The documents were placed on a desk in a research room with a glass window so they could be watched to ensure the documents were not being abused or stolen. Most of the documents were from the Nazi's tax office and dealt with requests made by Ralph's father and others in his family for release of funds from their frozen accounts. "I was shocked to see a swastika stamp and a Third Reich seal," Glen later recalled, "on the bottom of these papers that said 'Heil Hitler' on each document." Glen also recalled that "we saw 'Denied' and 'Approved' stamps on many of these documents." For Ralph, seeing the place where he had lived in Hamburg was very different than his initial return to Wolfhagen had been 18 years earlier. On the one hand, the city had very much changed since 1938, whereas central Wolfhagen had not, so it was more difficult to experience the memories from childhood. On the other hand, the opportunity to see the documentation in the archive relating to his parents filled many of the gaps in his knowledge of his parents' past, and this further contributed to his sense of closure, as well as to his ability to speak more knowledgably about what had happened to them.

The few days that Ralph, Phyllis, and Glen spent in Wolfhagen during the May 2011 visit allowed time for several important items on their agenda. Glen wanted to see Buchenwald, and so he went there one day with his father and Günter. The Mollericks were, as always, invited by Mayor Schaake to visit his office, accompanied by Günter, Heinz and Gisela Abel, Heinrich Schwarz, and Ernst Klein, who then invited Ralph to speak to another group of school children at his project in Volkmarsen, which Ralph did the next day. It never occurred to Ralph at the time,

but by 2011 and beyond, it was no longer necessary for him to prepare in advance for a talk with students in Germany, so comfortable had he become with doing so. The group also celebrated Ralph's birthday at a dinner in the Greek restaurant in Wolfhagen. This occasion later turned out to be bittersweet because it was the last time Ralph and Phyllis saw their dear friend, Gisela Abel, who passed away in 2012.

Perhaps the most important moment for the Mollericks during their stay in Wolfhagen in May of 2011, however, was visiting the site of Ralph's former house, where a plaque had been mounted on the outside front wall of the Steinkammer and dedicated to his family the previous November as part of the annual commemoration of Kristallnacht. Günter had given a speech at the dedication of the plaque. As reported in the local newspaper at that time: "The memory must not fade. For this reason, the commemoration of the *Pogromnacht* in 1938 was again prepared with great commitment in Wolfhagen." Scholars presented in the town hall information about Judaism and the former Wolfhagen Jewish community, "especially about the family Möllerich, who lived here before the war, and about the son Wolfgang, who now lives in the USA." The plaque dedicated that night—which is about 8 by 15 inches in size and therefore is very much larger, clearer, and more informative than the Stolpersteine in Hamburg—was inscribed in German as follows:

"Here lived Josef Möllerich, 3 September 1885 and his wife, Selma, born Meyer, on 1 August 1895 and their children Edith and Wolfgang. The children were sent to England on the Kindertransport on 14 December 1938. The parents were deported to Lodz, Poland on 25 October 1941 and murdered."

The road to redemption taken by Wolfhagen as recorded herein is paved with the footprints of Ralph Mollerick. It is also paved with many other footprints from among the people of Wolfhagen and elsewhere. That Ralph had a profound impact on the town is undeniable, as is the fact that the town—perhaps more accurately the people of the town and the surrounding area—have had an equally profound effect on his life as well. Theirs was, and continues to be, a unique and mutually productive relationship. "If I had not gone back to Germany and continued to go back for many return trips," Ralph later recalled, "I would not have been at peace in the same way, nor would I be the person that I am today. It has been a very rewarding part of my life experience to see the positive influence I have had on the town, experiencing personal redemption and helping Wolfhagen to experience its own redemption."

One is tempted, nonetheless, to consider the question of whether Wolfhagen would have undergone the kind of transformative growth with respect to preserving the history of its Jewish community and the education of present and future generations, especially its youth regarding the Holocaust, had Ralph never returned to the town of his childhood. The views of key participants in this regard are both essential and insightful. Günter—who probably knows Ralph better than anyone else from Wolfhagen—is convinced that his return to Germany served as a catalyst for the town coming to grips with its past as a form of its redemption with respect to the Holocaust. "To have him as an eyewitness—this is the most important thing and that is why he went to so many school classes and why so many children come to hear him speak," Günter later recalled. "I think it's very important that the young generation now knows what happened in those years so that it will never happen again." Arne Pillardy, the school headmaster and historian who spoke so eloquently at the dedication of the memorial stone for the Jewish families of Wolfhagen—and on other occasions—concurs with Günter's sentiment: "It is really important to have someone here who has been through it and to whom you can ask questions and get eyewitness answers," he later recalled. That is why he believes that "his visits go hand in hand with the concept of redemption and reconciliation." Ernst Klein, whose project in Volkmarsen has done so much to restore the history of the Jewish communities in the area, and whom Günter and Pillardy characterized as "the spine of the working group in Wolfhagen from the very beginning," also recognizes the importance of education and Ralph's role in that regard. "For all these young people in Germany, we say that they are not guilty for what came before but they have the responsibility that this never happens again," Ernst later said. "Every month, perhaps three, four, five times, I tell about Ralph Mollerick, always when I have school classes come here. It is a very special thing for me to explain about Ralph's life and tell the stories about his life that he has brought to us." Dekan Gerlach echoed these sentiments: "It's terrible that the guilt is passed from one generation to another generation. Our people must learn to get in contact with their past and accept the consequences. I am very thankful to Ralph, who meets with our people and speaks to them in a way they can better understand what happened in the past. Therefore, his visits are so important for us."

Ralph's importance to Wolfhagen's redemption has extended beyond his many visits, as his presence has regularly been felt by the town even when he could not be there. For one thing, the people of Wolfhagen are constantly reminded of him each year during the November 9 commemoration event that concludes at the site of the memorial stone at Freedom Plaza that he and his family sponsored. Then there are the periodic but ongoing reminders of him—and of his family—that appear in the local newspaper. For the 70th anniversary commemoration of Kristallnacht, the November 8, 2008 issue of *Wolfhager Allgemeine* contained several articles about the history of the Jewish community and, in particular, about Ralph's escape from Nazi Germany via the Kindertransport. It also included an interview Ralph had given by telephone with reporter Hannah Cosse in which he summarized what had occurred during his childhood in Germany along with his personal recollections of his parents and the Kindertransport experience. He discussed the importance of his initial return to Wolfhagen in 1993, reconnecting with childhood friends and establishing new and lasting friendships in the town, and sharing some of his visits with his sons. In response to a question of why it is so important to remember such days as November 9, 1938, Ralph explained in this way: "It is most important to continue to tell the stories of the awful persecutions of the Jewish people during the Holocaust era. Every child must know that intolerance and hatred must be recognized and acted upon at all levels of our society so that it never will happen again. I am so proud of the wonderful people of Wolfhagen who stood together and erected a monument in the center of town in memory of the Jewish families who once lived in Wolfhagen prior to the Holocaust era. My thoughts and spirit will be with the people of the town in the 70th commemoration day coming up on November 9, 2008."

Ralph's contributions to the redemption of Wolfhagen have continued unabated to this very day. As recently as 2016 during a visit to Wolfhagen, he spoke to a group of students at the invitation of Ernst Klein with only one day's notice and without notes. In a unique event held in Wolfhagen, the Lutheran Church and a committee that included Mayor Schaake, Ernst Klein, and multi-denominational clerical and public leaders (including the chairperson of the Jewish community in Kassel) had planned a special service to be held on May 8, 2015, on the 70th anniversary of the end of the Second World War in Europe and official end of the Nazi regime. At the request of Dekan Gerlach, Ralph sent a personal message and prayer that was read during the service. In that message he reflected on the horrors and atrocities of the Nazi era, but, more importantly, focused on the future: "As we progress in life we must not hold our memories anchored to the evils that were committed in the past. The present is now, and life is for us to live and enjoy. The future is yet ahead and only God knows of its outcome. As we pray, may we find relief in our hearts and minds that forgiveness can be found and that peace can be achieved." With respect to the question posed whether Wolfhagen would have undergone the redemption that it did—at the time that it did and to the extent that it did—without the support and participation of Ralph Mollerick, there can be no definitive answer. Arne Pillardy put it in perspective, however: "It would not have been the same without him."

Had Ralph's story concluded with his role in the redemption of Wolfhagen, it would have made for a sufficiently compelling narrative. But there were two other major developments in Ralph's life over the course of more than two decades that ran parallel to, and were largely made possible by, his return to Germany. These developments, when combined with his experience in Germany, ultimately make his life story truly extraordinary.

# CHAPTER 13

— ❦ —

# The KTA—Filling the Historical Gap (1989–Present)

As a result of his renewed interest in his past and in the historical events surrounding the Holocaust and the fate of the Jewish communities of Europe sparked by his return to Germany, Ralph Mollerick immersed himself deeply in the work of the Kindertransport Association of North America (KTA). The organization had formed in 1989 as the direct result of an international 50th anniversary reunion of children who had participated in the Kindertransport program. The reunion was held in London in June 1989 and attracted over 1,200 people including kinder, along with their spouses and children. The event was the brainchild of Bertha Leverton, a kind living in London, and drew kinder from the United States (where roughly 2,500 from among the nearly 10,000 children saved by the program had been living), as well as from Israel, Canada, Australia, the United Kingdom, of course, and several other countries throughout the world. Many attendees from North America returned from the London reunion excited and eager to maintain contact with each other. Eddy Behrendt and a few others seized upon that enthusiasm, as well as the sense that somehow in the already vast and still growing historical interest in the Holocaust the Kindertransport had been largely omitted and quickly organized and launched the KTA. Hundreds of their fellow kinder and family members joined this new organization. In 1989, Ralph Mollerick had learned about the upcoming London reunion when Jeffrey had urged him to go. But Ralph had not been ready to face his past at that time and declined ("Oh, how I regret

that now," he recalled in retrospect). It was not until 1998 when the KTA
held a national meeting in Crystal City, Virginia, located directly across
the Potomac River from Washington, DC, and therefore in close proximity to Ralph's home in Silver Spring, Maryland, that Ralph was ready
to engage with the KTA. By that time Ralph had returned to Germany
three times and achieved closure with his past by placing a headstone
for his parents in the Jewish cemetery in Wolfhagen and so he decided
he was ready to find out what the KTA was all about. "I think he was
ready to do it by then," Phyllis later recalled; "it was so close to home
and so we went." He and Phyllis registered for the Crystal City meeting,
and that turned out to be a momentous occasion for both Ralph and
the KTA.

The 1998 meeting of the KTA in Crystal City was an eye-opening
event for Ralph. "I had returned to Germany and there were some
memories that were lingering in my mind," Ralph later recalled. "The
Kindertransport was part of my life that held meaning and a connection
to my childhood and I wanted to better understand the essence of its
rescue mission." During the early part of the conference, he and Phyllis
enjoyed meeting people—many people who shared a similar historic
experience with Ralph—and learning about the organization, its history,
purposes, and how it functioned. "Every other year," he later recalled,
"the meetings are held in a different location, and the biggest turnouts
are at the meetings held on either the east coast or the west coast." He
learned that one of the organization's purposes, especially in the early
years, was to find and unite kinder and their families with each other,
including fellow kinder who had known each other in the past, something that Ralph would experience firsthand just a few years later while
attending a KTA national meeting. Another function of the organization
is to increase public awareness of the Kindertransport as an important
part of Holocaust history. Melissa Hacker, current president of the KTA
whose mother was on the Kindertransport and who, as a filmmaker produced the documentary *My Knees were Jumping: Remembering the
Kindertransport* in 1996 that was nominated for a Sundance Film Festival

award, later recalled that "When the Kindertransport Association was first formed, really the awareness of the Kindertransport was very, very low." The third aspect of the organization's mission is to raise money and public awareness to help children—particularly refugee children—in need today. In recent years the organization has contributed to efforts to assist children after a terrible earthquake in Nepal, those who are among Syrian refugees uprooted by the civil war in their country, and those who came alone to the United States from Central America and are held essentially in captivity. "It's about advocating for children in need," according to Hacker, "who have had a similar experience as the Kindertransport children."

During the course of the 1998 meeting, Ralph participated in sessions where kinder spoke about their personal experiences and where expert speakers discussed aspects of the history of the Kindertransport program and related topics. Ralph was immediately drawn in, particularly during side conversations about how best to engender interest among kinder and their families living in the Washington, DC, metropolitan area, in which he actively participated. Phyllis recalled Ralph's reaction to attending the conference: "It was such a positive experience; we had a good time and I think he felt comfortable being there." Ralph had learned that there were local chapters of the organization in the New York area and covering places in and around Philadelphia but not in the Washington or Baltimore region. Laura Gabriel, who was the KTA officer-at-large on the national board and had observed Ralph's enthusiastic engagement during these discussions over the three-day conference, approached him on the final day and asked him if he would form a chapter of the KTA for the Washington, DC metropolitan area. In the past—throughout much of his adult life—Ralph would never have been able to attend such a conference, let alone immerse himself in the discussions as he had, and certainly not consider such a request. But at that moment, without hesitation, Ralph agreed. Undertaking a leadership role in an organization was something he had done before over the course of many years at Mishkan Torah Congregation, as well as experiencing years of organizational and magerial work for projects at NASA. He had also reached a comfort level with confronting his past and the Holocaust as a result of his visits to Germany. Shortly after the Virginia conference he sent a proposal to Kurt Goldberger, then president of the KTA national board, to establish a Washington, DC, chapter of the KTA, and he received approval and a list of the participants at the 1998 meeting who lived in the Washington, Baltimore, and northern Virginia areas and some general information about the KTA and the existing national bylaws. With Phyllis' help, he went to work organizing the new chapter.

The plan initially involved bringing together as many kinder from the area as possible for an organizational meeting that was held on Sunday, September 13, 1998, at the home of Bertl and Morris Essenstad. Bertl was one of the kinder who lived in Maryland not far from Ralph's house. Ralph contacted each of the names that had been provided by the New York office of the KTA, and then advertised at the Washington and Baltimore area Jewish Community Centers. Everyone was asked to bring along desserts, and this was an astute decision, because a few of the kinder who attended that first meeting turned out to be outstanding bakers. In all, about 40 kinder attended; with some spouses also attending there were perhaps 60 people in all—a very impressive turnout for an initial effort. The host had placed an easel with a map of Europe in the room and each of the kinder placed a color-tipped pin at the place on the map from which they came. Somewhat to Ralph's surprise, the greatest concentration of pins covered Vienna, Austria, and not one of the larger cities in Germany, where the pins were more spread out over many parts of the country. Ralph and the small group of organizers of this meeting took great pains to balance the time spent at the meeting between socializing and discussing how to organize and launch the chapter. The group decided to meet quarterly and that there would be three basic purposes to the chapter: service—primarily donating to needy groups in the area; social—providing an opportunity through meetings and special events just to enjoy each other's company; and educational—at most meetings people spoke about their personal Kindertransport experiences or expert speakers were brought in to discuss a particular theme. At the initial meeting the attendees also established a dues structure and decided to elect officers and establish bylaws. One of the founding members was a KT2, (an immediate descendant of a kinder)—Diane Harab, the daughter of a kind. Her husband, Jeffrey, was an attorney who specialized in organizational law and helped draft the chapter's bylaws. These were approved at the next meeting, the first "official" meeting of the chapter, in May 1999, when Ralph was elected the chair of the chapter, a position in which he would remain until he and Phyllis moved to Florida in June of 2006. "I was the motivator," he later recalled with pride. "Those early meetings were important because we were able to characterize what the organization was all about. When we met we had discussions about how we can give back to society—that was a big thing."

Within the first two or three years, the number of kinder in the group grew to 68, and in those days it was a very active organization. "People were a lot younger and healthier than now and they were willing to help," Phyllis later recalled. "They wanted the group to be social and they always talked about their personal stories, but they also wanted to be philanthropic. They would donate to children's organizations, and during Hanukkah and the High Holidays we always donated food to needy Jewish families." Some members of the chapter also volunteered to read in nursing homes. But the topic of discussion at each of the quarterly meetings proved to be a central aspect of the Washington, DC, chapter of the KTA. Sometimes Ralph brought in a speaker, but most of the time the kinder spoke about their personal stories. This did not come easily; like Ralph in years past, many kinder had to overcome their reluctance to speak about their past—at least partially. "Overwhelmingly the people wanted to talk about their experiences in England and not in Germany or Austria," Ralph later recalled. This raised an interesting point: why prefer to speak of their time in England rather than their country of birth in a setting that was so supportive? Reflecting on this question later, Ralph recalled: "I believe it was because England was the only country at that time, really, that opened its doors to us; England was our ticket to freedom. People gave thanks to England for taking them in and for giving them another chance at life." Some of the stories told during the chapter meetings reflected this perspective in graphic ways, situations where parents who had survived the concentration camps came for their children who they sent to England on the Kindertransport only to find that these children were now grown and had started a life of their own; or if they were younger many of them had settled down with an English family and did not want to leave. Ralph recalled a story about a boy from the Kindertransport who had been taken in by an English family. "He came there as an eight-year-old, just as I did, and was treated by the family like their own child. His parents came back when he was 16 years old—no longer a child—and he didn't recognize them and didn't want to go with them." Of course most of the kinder never saw their parents again and of the nearly 10,000 saved by the Kindertransport, the vast majority remained in England. Only those few whose parents returned or who had relatives in the United States or other countries, such as Ralph and Edith, moved on and that is why only about 25 percent of the total kinder eventually came to the United States. "Although we all went to England, the stories were very different," Ralph recalled. "Each of the kinder had an experience that was dramatically different from another." Ralph and Phyllis recalled that many of these stories told at the chapter meetings were difficult for the kinder to tell and difficult for them to hear, eliciting significant tears, despite countries of birth hardly being discussed because there were so many traumas attached to these childhood experiences. This was certainly once true for Ralph, as well, until he managed to return to Germany and face his past and make peace with it. The Washington, DC, KTA chapter remained active until at least 2006 but over the course of some years, especially after its first three years, some of the kinder—especially those who were among the oldest on the Kindertransport—gradually became ill or passed on.

Some of their children (KT2) and even grandchildren (KT3) joined the chapter, but with a smaller number of kinder, perhaps 20–30 attending the chapter meetings on a regular basis after the first few years, and with time not on their side, the very important personal storytelling at the meetings ebbed.

Besides the quarterly meetings of the Washington, DC, KTA chapter each year over which Ralph presided, he and Phyllis attended each of the biennial meetings of the national organization. Attendance at these meetings had two significant results: it was not long before Ralph was asked to become involved in the work of the national organization; it was also at his third national meeting in June of 2002 that Ralph experienced a singular moment in his life. Conference attendees convened that year in Philadelphia. Shortly after the opening session, Ralph noticed a vaguely familiar face across the room and immediately approached this bald-headed gentleman. "I know you from England," Ralph later recalled saying. "I think you're Joe Haberer. You had a lot more hair at that time." The man nodded and said, "Indeed I did." But even after Ralph introduced himself, Joe had only a vague recollection of him until Ralph reminded him that they had been roommates at the Northampton hostel during the war and that they had sustained a correspondence that had continued until after they had both come to the United States. Ralph learned that Joe and his wife Rose lived in West Lafayette, Indiana, where Joe was professor emeritus of political science and Jewish studies—was founding editor of the latter program's newsletter (now a peer-reviewed journal), *Shofar*—at Purdue University, and was currently doing research for a new book. Joe had been one of 12 members of the Purdue University faculty profiled in *Bitter Prerequisites: A Faculty for Survival from Nazi Terror*, by Purdue history Professor William Laird Kleine-Ahlbrandt that was published by Purdue University Press in March 2001, and in which it was revealed that Haberer's personal history as a survivor of the Kindertransport closely paralleled Ralph's. Joe was also chair of the Midwest chapter of the

KTA, so Ralph and he had that common thread in their lives more than half a century after their childhood friendship and correspondence had ended. "When I saw Joe at the KTA conference," Ralph later recalled, "it was like the sky had opened up and gold was raining down." After the conference, they struck up a limited correspondence that focused both on personal and KTA topics, beginning with an exchange of New Year's greetings in late December 2002. "This has been an especially good year," Joe wrote to Ralph. "One of the highlights was our fortuitous reunion—which gave me much pleasure and the remembrance of it always provides a lift in spirits." As opinionated as ever, Joe launched into *ad hominem* commentary on the state of the KTA: "My Kindertransport connection remains somewhat tenuous," he wrote. "The national leadership seems moribund. . . . I am pressing for change but will not over commit until I see some change."

Not long after their unexpected reunion, nonetheless, in 2004 Ralph and Joe were both asked to serve on a committee to revise the KTA national organization bylaws. Ralph was appointed chair of the four-person committee, which included, besides Joe Haberer, Anita Grosz (a KT2 attorney), and Robert Sugar (historian). The bylaws revision took two years and four drafts before it was approved. As chair, Ralph had to spend long hours on the phone or communicating via email both with his fellow committee members and with the organization's board leadership. Melissa Hacker, who joined the board in 2004, later discussed some of her impressions of Ralph and the way he undertook the responsibility of chairing the bylaws revision committee: "Ralph is engaging, alert, lively; he is really dedicated to the KTA and takes his work quite seriously. When he makes a commitment to do something, he really does it, he does it thoroughly, he does it well, he persists—when he takes things on he sees them through." During the course of the protracted work on the bylaws, Ralph and Joe found themselves in disagreement with respect to the basis of the organization. "He wanted to make the organization more inclusive of other survivors," Ralph later recalled, "and I felt that the Kindertransport was a unique aspect of the broader history of the Holocaust." Joe wanted to write the by-laws "in a way that included all orphaned children of the Holocaust, including camp survivors." Ralph believed that would have "significantly changed" the focus of the organization had the KTA taken that route. While the "purpose" statement of the revised bylaws ultimately approved reflects the continued focus of the organization on survivors of the Kindertransport, it also includes a broader provision to "engage in activities to aid, support, and assist in efforts to locate and bring together those individuals who fled the Holocaust as minor children."

As for Ralph's relationship with Joe Haberer, they continued to communicate, but far more sporadically than in the past and usually to discuss KTA business. Joe and Rose had extended a number of invitations for Ralph and Phyllis to visit them in West Lafayette over the course of a decade: "He told me he had a big house with plenty of room for Phyllis and me," Ralph later recalled; "he kept telling us to just come." But for a variety of reasons—most notably their move from Maryland to a new home in Lake Worth, Florida, in 2006, which required them to travel multiple times each year thereafter to visit children and grandchildren in Maryland, and the ongoing trips to Wolfhagen and to national meetings of the KTA—Ralph and Phyllis put off the visit to the Haberers and this was something that in retrospect Ralph very much regretted. Joe passed away in June 2013 after suffering for some time with pulmonary health issues. His passing caused great sadness for Ralph, as he later reflected on the relationship he had with Joe in England and during his first year or two in the United States: "Joe was perhaps the person who influenced me the most and steered my life in the best possible direction at a time when I needed it most." In an obituary for Joe Haberer published in the KTA newsletter, Ralph wrote: "Joe was a very special person. . . . He stressed the importance of an education and often it felt like he was the brother I never had."

In 2010 Ralph was appointed to the KTA national board as officer-at-large. By that time he and Phyllis were firmly ensconced in their Florida home, where they had joined the local chapter of the KTA. Under the revised KTA bylaws for which Ralph chaired the preparation, the officer-at-large had a broad portfolio of duties that focused primarily on serving as board liaison with each KTA chapter chair—a rather extensive undertaking by itself that involved reporting to the board on chapter activities, monitoring chapter financial matters, representing board initiatives to chapters and motivating chapters on their growth as well as national KTA matters. The position also called for carrying out special projects as assigned by the KTA board. It also turned out, as Ralph later recalled, "that I kept the Florida KTA organizational documents and made certain they were up to date." One of the areas of his duties to which Ralph has devoted extensive time and effort is outreach, in particular finding ways to connect with kinder who have disengaged with the organization. "There's an issue now of people being older and on the one hand are sort of isolated and want contact," Melissa Hacker described; "but on the other hand they are set in their ways and don't reach out—and one of the things we're trying to do is reach out to isolated KTA members." As the kinder have aged, Ralph has sought to address the issues for kinder KTA members related to aging. "Some of them don't drive anymore," Ralph later recalled. "Some of them are ill and some of them have caregivers so it is difficult for them to go to meetings. We are trying to get them to form smaller local groups and meet as often as they want." Hacker has been particularly impressed with Ralph's efforts in this regard because the KTA leadership realizes that time is not on their side with respect to the aging kinder membership. "He has been a great, persistent ally in that effort," she recalled. "He really reaches out and I'm sure suffers with frustration and disappointment because often he's reaching out to chapters that are dormant, that haven't kept active."

The latter point is especially true with respect to the fate of the Washington, DC, chapter that Ralph had established and chaired until he and Phyllis moved to Florida in 2006. The chapter had remained active during Ralph's chairmanship, holding quarterly meetings, often with guest speakers, but essentially became moribund over time without Ralph's vibrant and full-time presence. "That was the reason the chapter fell apart," Phyllis recalled, "because we moved away and Ralph wasn't there to keep it together. He was the spark that got the group going and the glue that kept it together." An effort has been made in recent years—mainly by KT2 members of the Washington, DC, chapter—to meet regularly and to encourage kinder to participate. Ralph's sense of this, from the perspective of his position as officer-at large on the national board, is that the second generation effort to revive the Washington, DC, chapter has not been successful from the point of view of some of the kinder members. "People I've spoken to tell me that it's a mess," he recalled. "It's unorganized, meetings don't happen very often, and when they do the discussion is carried mainly by KT2 members, who often focus on the question of how to deal with their aging parents—the survivors."

Changes have also been made and continue in the way the national organization functions as a result of the aging and now more rapidly diminishing population of kinder and the availability of technology. Ralph later recalled that "at its height the organization had I think 678 kinder as dues paying members; now [2016] the number is down to about 300 members who are actual kinder." National KTA board meetings are now held by conference calls, so that members like Ralph and others who are geographically located far from the New York City metropolitan area need not travel to participate in the meetings. This is especially important because the board has continued to be largely populated by kinder, although an increasing part of the organization's support functions, such as producing the newsletter and maintaining the website, are now being performed mainly by second generation members. As for the biennial conferences, the 2012 meeting held in Irvine, California, was the first one to be organized largely by second-generation members. "That was the first time that the first generation said that it was too much work for them to do it," Melissa Hacker recalled. The board had been thinking that the 2012 meeting might be the final national conference that the organization sponsored. But the Irvine conference turned out to be the most well-attended conference and there was such a positive reaction by attendees that there was interest in having another national conference. Hacker recalled: "I and a few other people who organized the conference felt that it didn't feel right to make that one the last conference. We wanted to have one that we were acknowledging would be our last national conference." This turned out to be held not two years, but three years later (October 9–11, 2015) in Farmington Hills, Michigan, located just outside of Detroit, and site of the Holocaust Memorial Center Zekelman Family Campus. Ralph later recalled: "They had railway tracks and cobblestones already in place, and it was similar to what I saw at Auschwitz." The center also houses the "KTA Quilt" and the organization's archives, as well as the archives of the World Federation of Jewish Child Survivors of the Holocaust and Descendants (WFJCSHD). At the Michigan national meeting of the KTA it was announced that henceforth the national KTA meetings would be part of the annual meetings of this latter organization, but the KTA would otherwise continue as a unique organization.

Ralph continues to serve on the KTA board as officer-at-large. Besides his liaison work with the chapters, he has confronted a question that is of both personal and organizational importance especially in recent years as a result of the KTA's closer association with the WFJCSHD, namely, what constitutes a Holocaust survivor? This is a question that has been debated both within the KTA and other Holocaust-related organizations as well as among historians and commentators. According to the Holocaust Memorial Center, Holocaust survivors are "any persons, Jewish or non-Jewish, who were displaced, persecuted, or discriminated against due to the racial, religious, ethnic, social, and political policies of the Nazis and their collaborators between 1933 and 1945. In addition to former inmates of concentration camps, ghettos, and prisons, this definition includes, among others, people who were refugees or were in hiding." The KTA website's definition matches the above almost verbatim, but adds, specifically: "The Kindertransport children are child Holocaust Survivors." Ralph, nonetheless, recalled that "I struggled with the idea of whether I really was a Holocaust survivor, because there are people in the KTA who feel that they didn't suffer the horrors of the camps." Ralph also experienced similar arguments while attending meetings of the WFJCSHD. "I don't agree with that premise," he later recalled. "There's trauma for kinder from being denied the love of their parents, having to go without them on a train to another country where another language is spoken, and where there are different customs." Perhaps more than any other issue regarding the Holocaust, this question continues to resonate with Ralph today and his views on it are best left for him to express personally (see the *Epilogue* of this book).

Ralph has, nonetheless, persisted as part of his KTA board duties, albeit from a distance, in efforts to revive interest in meeting together among kinder members of the Washington, DC, chapter that he founded in 1999. As recently as 2016, while engrossed in the extensive recording of oral history interviews for this book, Ralph organized a reunion of the Washington, DC, KTA chapter. "We're trying to reactivate that chapter," Melissa Hacker recalled, "which hadn't had a meeting in some years. Ralph's effort was fantastic." Indeed, Ralph spent hours on the phone and communicating in emails to firm up plans for the reunion, which he and Phyllis sponsored, which was held in April 2016 at Leisure World in Silver Spring, Maryland, and which attracted over 40 members, including kinder and children of kinder. The purpose of the reunion, according to Ralph, "was to have people meet one another and reignite enthusiasm for the chapter, and to select several volunteers to serve in a leadership role." While the event proved successful with respect to attendance, and while several KT2 members stepped forward initially, providing Ralph with enough encouragement to create a 2016 directory of key local and national names from the KTA register for these individuals to get the group started, there has as yet been insufficient follow-up from the volunteer KT2 members to indicate sustained enthusiasm for the chapter.

Despite lingering personal questions posed during his experience in a leadership role both at the local and national level of the KTA, as well as frustration in his ability to revive the Washington, DC, chapter, two facts regarding Ralph's role in the KTA remain clear: his energy, commitment, skill, and focus on the task at hand have made a difference in the organization; and his immersion in the activities of the KTA—where the demons of his past were so ever-present—would not have been possible had he never returned to Germany and experienced closure there with his past. "The return to Germany motivated me in ways that I wouldn't have considered before that," he later recalled, "including going to my first KTA meeting in Virginia in 1998. The Germany visit was the spark that ignited my interest in the KTA and other aspects of the history of the Kindertransport." Ralph's accomplishments for the KTA have ultimately been uniquely significant. Melissa Hacker summed it up succinctly and effectively: "Ralph has been a great asset to the organization—he really has."

# CHAPTER 14

— ✂ —

# Telling the Story (1994–Present)

As in the case of his involvement in the Kindertransport Association, Ralph Mollerick's return to Germany in 1993 led directly to a second significant development in his life with respect to speaking publicly, not only about his personal history but about the historic importance of the Kindertransport within the broader context of the Holocaust. Unlike his KTA experience, however, where Ralph largely dove into leadership responsibilities from the outset, he developed and engaged in public speaking presentations incrementally over the course of more than two decades. The result has been an extraordinary legacy of accomplishment that one can argue has been considerably more impactful than his work with the KTA, especially with respect to educating generations of young people both in the United States and in Germany.

Ralph and Phyllis walked silently out of a movie theater near their Maryland home one night in 1994, having just seen *Schindler's List*. The movie would win seven Academy Awards, including best picture and best director and add considerably to Steven Spielberg's legacy in the process. But the film would have far-reaching consequences on a global scale beyond its artistic and box office successes. Spielberg told a reporter for an article that appeared in the November 10, 1994 issue of the *New York Times*, that during the making of the film in Poland, "at least a dozen survivors journeyed there using the film as a cushion to find closure with their nightmares. They showed up, and often through tears began telling us their stories." Spielberg asked if they would be willing to do that in front of cameras, and they agreed. This was the

353

impetus for what would become a massive project for Spielberg under the Shoah Visual History Foundation. Over the course of five years beginning in late 1994, the project would conduct interviews and preserve on film the personal two-hour testimonies of more than 50,000 Holocaust survivors mostly living in the United States, but also located in more than 50 other countries; and the interviews would be conducted in more than 30 languages. Today the Shoah project film archive is available at sites in the United States, Europe, Australia, New Zealand, and Israel, including the United States Holocaust Memorial Museum and Yad Vashem. When the Mollericks viewed *Schindler's List*, at the end of the film there was a screened notice for Holocaust survivors interested in telling their story that included a contact phone number. Phyllis quickly wrote down the phone number of the Washington, DC, office for the project before she and Ralph left the movie theater.

There would have been a time when Ralph would never have watched a movie such as *Schindler's List*, let alone consider telling his story in front of a camera, but the timing of this opportunity was right. Ralph had recently returned from his first visit to Germany. He had faced his past and in doing so had undergone a life-altering experience. During that visit he had also been able to speak at some length about his past before a group of strangers at the reception held by Mayor Dietrich at the Alte Rathaus Hotel. Like many others, Ralph and Phyllis had been moved beyond words while viewing *Schindler's List*; but over the next several days they discussed the opportunity for participating in the Shoah project. "It didn't quite register for me because at first I didn't think of myself as a Holocaust survivor," Ralph later recalled. "I felt that I was fortunate enough to have parents who were willing to get me out of harm's way. But because of my return to Germany, 1993 was a year of awakening; prior to that I had nothing formulated about my past." Phyllis called the phone number she had written down in the movie theater and Ralph soon received a long questionnaire in the mail, which he completed and submitted. Some weeks later, during the first half of 1995, as Phyllis later recalled, "we had an interview with a very nice woman, who later returned to conduct the formal interview in front of the camera." There was an interval of a few months between the initial interview and the filming. During that time, Ralph became a bit nervous and began to have second thoughts. "Seeing that movie really stirred me up," he later recalled, "because it was telling a story about the Holocaust and I hadn't done that yet. I hadn't even thought about it until then and I was actually a little bit concerned that I would never succeed in talking about that before an audience." But in this instance, he would be speaking before an audience of two: the interviewer and the camera operator. Members of the family could be included in the interview but they would not be permitted in the room while Ralph was being filmed. This would make the process "easier" for Ralph, as he later acknowledged.

By the time the day arrived for filming the interview, the summer of 1995 was approaching and Ralph and Phyllis were busy planning their second visit to Wolfhagen and the unveiling of a headstone for Ralph's parents in the Jewish cemetery. Ralph was now ready to be interviewed, and the camera operator set up the lights in the living room of the Mollerick's Silver Spring town home. "They needed absolute silence," Ralph recalled. "I had to turn off the air conditioner and the living room became much hotter because of the bright bank of flood lights." Phyllis, Jeffrey, and Glen went into the basement to be out of the way and to stay cool, and waited for their turn to be interviewed. Because the interviewer had already reviewed the questionnaire and had the notes she had taken in the preliminary interview, the filming went quite smoothly. "The woman asked a question and I gave an answer," Ralph later recalled. "I was nervous about what questions I would be asked on the one hand, but very calm about my having answers to the questions, because I knew what I was going to say and felt surprisingly confident that I could tell the story as it unraveled in my mind." At only two points during the interview did Ralph pause. At one point he was surprised by the number of questions he was asked relating to his bar mitzvah, which took place in Peterborough, England—how well can you read Hebrew? Can you *daven*? Do you know *trope*? Do you remember your *parsha*?" He responded that he could do all of that but would have to review his bar mitzvah *parsha* first, "because I'm not that fluent in Hebrew," he recalled. At another point he described the scene at the railroad station in Hamburg the morning he and Edith boarded the train as part of the Kindertransport. He explained that "there was a part of me that was scared because I was told that my sister was going to take care of me, and that was such a red flag for me. Then I clammed up, and the interviewer said she detected a behavior adjustment in my tone of voice." Ralph explained a bit about his complicated relationship with Edith that had persisted throughout their lives and remained difficult for him nearly 60 years later and almost a decade after Edith's death. "I described my mixed feelings, being excited about taking a journey, but being scared about what the future would hold and especially about being with my sister," he later recalled. Ralph later acknowledged that while he calmly could respond to questions about the historical facts of his experience, "I did have difficulty expressing my feelings to the interviewer." Toward the end of the filming session, Phyllis and Glen each had a few minutes to be interviewed separately. When it was Jeffrey's turn, ironically, he was unable to speak in front of the camera. "My brother was so happy to get my dad to return to Germany," Glen later recalled, "but he couldn't even talk on that interview. He just totally broke down."

The interview for the Shoah project, nonetheless, proved to be a singular moment for Ralph. He later acknowledged that the experience brought him "great satisfaction" because "in my mind I kept telling myself that I didn't want to talk about this, yet the prompting kept coming and I kept responding, and I kept surprising myself that I was able to open up, and I felt pleased that someone was recording it because I was uncertain I would remember what I had said and be able later to recount my responses." Not surprisingly, the interview brought considerable satisfaction to Ralph's family: "I was proud to be there," Glen later recalled. "I was nervous for him, but we were proud and excited," Phyllis remembered. "I thought it was important for everybody to know his story and his interview would now be part of the Holocaust Museum; it was something very, very special." Ralph's one regret, he later recalled, was that "my daughter Shari was not up to being interviewed and was not present that day." Later in 1995, Ralph received CD recordings of the interview but it was not until mid-1997 that he received the DVD video that would become a permanent part of the historical project, along with a brief letter from Steven Spielberg. "In sharing your personal testimony as a survivor of the Holocaust," he wrote to Ralph on July 17, 1997, "you have granted future generations the opportunity to experience a personal connection with history. . . . Far into the future, people will be able to see a face, hear a voice, and observe a life, so that they may listen and learn, and always remember. Thank you for your invaluable contribution, your strength, and your generosity of spirit."

It turned out that the Shoah Project had a profound impact beyond the intrinsic value of the video recordings. Ralph later learned that most of the kinder who would soon become members of the Washington, DC, chapter of the KTA also participated in the project. He also learned that other kinder from far and wide not only were interviewed for the Shoah project but kinder participated in other documentary film projects and written accounts that began to appear in greater numbers in the years following the Spielberg project interviews. "There was a dramatic change from before 1995," Ralph later recalled. This proved to be particularly true for Ralph: "I felt that the Shoah interview prepared me for speaking publically about the connection between the Kindertransport and my life's story," he recalled. This set the stage for remarkable achievements a bit later in Ralph's life as they unfolded over the course of the next two decades.

The phone rang in Ralph's Silver Spring home one day during the first half of 1998. A teacher named Cynthia Peterman at the Charles E. Smith Jewish Day School in Rockville, Maryland, wanted Ralph to speak to her high school level class about his experience as a Kindertransport survivor. She knew of Ralph's background because she had worked with Phyllis at one of the local synagogues. Having never spoken to young people before about this topic—really having never spoken about his life before any public audience, save for the small group in Wolfhagen during his first visit there in 1993, Ralph had nothing prepared in writing to guide him through his talk. Previously the thought of speaking about his life history had filled Ralph with dread. But he had now returned to Germany three times, having both re-engaged and experienced closure with his past there, and he had been interviewed for the Shoah project. Rather than back away from the teacher's request—which he could easily have done because although he had retired from his NASA job the previous year he almost immediately had gone to work on a contract basis with Swales Aerospace in Beltsville, Maryland—Ralph embraced the opportunity to speak to young people about his life experience. "I was excited," he later recalled, "because now I had to put something on paper and organize my thoughts. For the Shoah interview I was just answering questions off the top of my head, and telling my story that way didn't make sense to me; it was insufficient because it lacked historical context." He focused on aspects of his life that he thought would resonate with the children. He spoke about his childhood, about Hitler's rise to power and how he had been harassed by his peers. He described the Kindertransport experience. "I tried to explain how difficult it was to talk about this because of memories and mixed emotions at the time, and about how my poor relationship with my sister created ongoing problems for me and how I felt about my family," he later recalled. "But I also told them how Edith pushed me to not look back but keep looking forward." One of the students asked him how he was able to turn his back on his family and his past and move on. "I told them that it was simply a matter of putting the persecution by my peers out of my head," he recalled. "I also said to them that my grandmother had always told me I was a good Jewish boy and not to worry about these things." Ralph felt that the students responded well to his presentation and to the answers he gave to their numerous questions, and that although it was difficult for him both organizing his presentation and speaking about lingering trauma from his past, the positive interaction he experienced with the children left him feeling satisfied with having taken the opportunity to speak to them about his life. He began to realize that doing so was not only useful for him but could contribute to greater understanding for future generations. This level of self-awareness and recognition of his educational value, especially for young people, nonetheless, came gradually over the next several years during which he only spoke one or two more times to school groups in Maryland. He made a video recording of a presentation for another school group because he could not be there for a live presentation, and this limited speaking was due in part to his contract work with Swales Aerospace and also because he became deeply engrossed in his ever-growing responsibilities with the KTA.

The one major exception to Ralph's years-long hiatus in speaking about his childhood and the Kindertransport experience came in 2003, of course, with his three major presentations in Wolfhagen in conjunction with the town's annual commemoration of Kristallnacht. The speaking engagements, especially his largely impromptu session with the students at the high school, left Ralph feeling so encouraged by the response to his presentations that upon returning to Maryland he organized the next quarterly meeting of the Washington, DC, KTA chapter and its annual Hanukkah celebration to focus on his recently completed visit to Wolfhagen. Meeting at Leisure World in Silver Spring on December 21, the chapter completed the business part of the meeting, lit the menorah, and settled down to hear Ralph's description of his experience in Wolfhagen the previous month in a presentation he called, "Going Back—Speaking Out." The presentation was quite comprehensive in describing his central role in the formal activities during the town's commemoration, and also his first opportunity to see the work of Ernst Klein during the same visit, who had not only showed him around Volkmarsen but had taken him to nearby Vöhl. Ralph's speech to his chapter was unique in that the focus of his comments was on his experience in Germany, with respect both to the previous month's visit and to the topic of his presentations that discussed his time as a child in Germany as well as the Kindertransport experience. Most of the chapter's discussion topics—especially those involving kinder member presentations—tended to focus on life in England rather than in Germany or Austria. Ralph's comments to the chapter that day concluded: "By returning many times to Wolfhagen, the town where my family once lived, and speaking to friends I have made, I have found the strength to speak out about my past and tell the Kindertransport story of my life." The other significant aspect of that 2003 visit to Wolfhagen was that Ralph had prepared several written documents that had been translated into German for the program, and the English-language originals became the basic written materials that Ralph would use for his future public presentations.

It would not be until after Ralph and Phyllis moved to Lake Worth, Florida, in June 2006, however, that the number and range of Ralph's speaking presentations relating to his personal Kindertransport experience would mushroom. Ralph had joined the Jewish Culture Club at his Florida community. As soon as the group discovered a little about Ralph's past they asked him to speak at one of their meetings. This 2007 presentation went so well that it was not long before the word spread throughout the many active adult communities heavily populating South Florida between Ft. Lauderdale and West Palm Beach. Ralph was asked to speak at many culture clubs and Yiddish clubs in these communities. He had also joined the Florida chapter of the KTA and established an excellent relationship with its chair, Anita Hoffer, who often used him as a resource for speaking engagements. As a result of that, as well as the word being spread by many who had attended his talks, Ralph spoke not only to senior adult groups but soon began speaking at schools. "Somebody might have heard him at a talk at one of the neighboring communities," Phyllis later recalled, "and then somebody called and asked if he would speak at a high school down in Hollywood.

The school was located on an Indian reservation but the students were not all Native Americans." Ralph developed one basic presentation for adults and another for students, and he would tweak each presentation based on the specific audience. For example, when he spoke to a Yiddish club, he recalled, "I asked them if everybody there speaks Yiddish—maybe I would have to give the talk in Yiddish, and they said to me, 'Oh no, we're just learning Yiddish!' and that broke the ice."

Over the course of the last 10 years, Ralph has spoken not only at schools and adult communities and organizations, but at synagogues, a church, and even at a theater in the South Florida region. "I always said 'yes,'" Ralph later recalled. "I don't think I ever turned anybody away." Of the dozens of public speaking engagements he has had in Florida, two in particular stand out. He was invited to speak at local chapters of Hadassah, and it was at his first Hadassah presentation, which was held at his own community on February 22, 2011, that Ralph received his first standing ovation for a talk in Florida. A large crowd had gathered in the community clubhouse ballroom to hear Ralph's presentation. The massive turnout was certainly due in part to the fact that Ralph had been speaking to clubs around the area, including in his own community, for four years, but also to the fact that a long article about his life had appeared in the January–February issue of the community newsletter, *The Villagio Voice*. The article covered the main threads of Ralph's life, not only his Kindertransport experience but his education and career in the United States, his founding of the Washington, DC, chapter of the KTA and his continuing involvement in the national KTA organization, as well as his return to Germany and making peace with his past. It also noted: "Ralph mentions that it often takes considerable concentration to overcome his emotions when he talks about his one-way trip on the Kindertransport. As he matured, Ralph realized that he lost his childhood because the circumstances required him to behave as an adult." The article summed up the author's assessment of Ralph in the following way: "Ralph is an exceptional individual. His sensitivity toward others, his warmth and willingness to share the trauma he endured have enabled him to rise above the nightmares. Ralph really savors the joy each day brings."

A second personal highlight with respect to Ralph's speaking engagements in Florida turned out to be truly unique. One day in 2011 Ralph received a phone call from Anita Hoffer of the Florida chapter of the KTA. A documentary on the role of Sir Nicholas Winton in the Kindertransport in Czechoslovakia had just been released, and Sir Nicholas' son, Nick would be speaking about the film and his father's life in several locations in the United States, including at schools in Lake Worth and Boca Raton. Ralph was asked to join Winton on the program at these two venues, one of which was a high school and the other an elementary school. "We spent a whole day with Nicky," Phyllis later recalled. "He and Ralph shared the podium." Winton spoke about his father's role in rescuing 669 Czech children through the Kindertransport and Ralph spoke about his personal Kindertransport experience leaving Germany. "The interesting thing that came out of those sessions with Nicky," Ralph recalled, "was that the questions were mostly directed to me, about how I fared as a child going through the Kindertransport experience. Nicky was speaking about his father but I was speaking about myself, giving an eyewitness account." As Ralph had earlier discovered from his talks in Germany, what he had to say carried great weight with audiences because he had been present during the events he was describing. During that same day, Ralph also joined Nick Winton on a program about the Kindertransport sponsored by the speaker's bureau of Florida Atlantic University in Delray Beach in the university's theater. Phyllis, in particular, found the day spent with Nick Winton to be "one of the most exciting days" she and Ralph had experienced among his many speaking engagements.

By the end of 2011 Ralph had achieved a high level of comfort in public speaking and took great joy in his presentations, especially those with an educational purpose for young people. Until that time, however, he had only engaged in writing about his life to the extent it was used for oral presentations. He had, of course been quoted in many newspaper and newsletter articles, in Maryland, Florida, and Germany. He had also written newsletter articles distributed to members of the Washington, DC, chapter of the KTA but these had been about chapter business and were not in any way related to telling his story. In early 2012, Anita Hoffer sent around a notice to the Florida KTA chapter members about a call for papers for a special issue of *Prism*, the journal of Yeshiva University that would be devoted to the Kindertransport. "I said to Phyllis that this was something that I would want to do but there was a lot of work involved," Ralph later recalled, and he felt ill-equipped to technically produce this kind of written product. But Phyllis reminded him that he had a thick binder of various iterations of materials he had written and used for his speaking engagements that could form the basis of his article, and so Ralph set about drafting the story of his Kindertransport experience. "I put together all that information and then I wanted to personalize the story," he recalled. There were formatting and length requirements he had to meet, and he worked very hard over the course of months writing his story "without going back and forth," as he was prone to digressions when he spoke informally or when he wrote. The article summarized his childhood under the Nazis in Wolfhagen and Hamburg and described his experience on the Kindertransport journey to England, and then summarized what his life was like growing up and attending school in England and learning of the death of his parents at the hands of the Nazis. It concluded with his arrival in America and a reflection on the meaning of what his parents did—sending him along with his sister to the relative safety of England. He found a few photographs to insert and submitted the article manuscript to the journal editor, who forwarded it to a panel of three judges for review, along with more than a dozen other submissions. After several weeks had passed, Ralph received a note from the editor of the journal congratulating him on his manuscript having been accepted for publication. He then worked closely with the editor of the journal through several draft revisions before the article was ready to be published. Entitled "No Place to Hide," Ralph's article appeared in the March 2013 issue of *Prism*. "You left me teary eyed," the editor wrote in a note that accompanied Ralph's copy of the published journal. Publication of his article stands as a singular moment in the long list of accomplishments in Ralph's life.

Despite the extensive work on his article, Ralph continued his speaking engagements in Florida. On several occasions the documentary *Into the Arms of Strangers* was shown to school groups and Ralph was asked to provide his personal perspective. "They would introduce me," Ralph later recalled," by saying that although I wasn't in the movie, I had similar experiences to the people shown in the movie, and because I was present, I could answer the students' questions." Over the course of time, especially once Ralph had the chance to review and digest all the information he had learned from his visit to the Hamburg archive in 2011, he began to include in his presentations an ever-increasing amount of information about the broader historical context of the Kindertransport and the Holocaust, as well as more extensive details about his past and especially his family. Speaking before two separate groups of students in Florida on the occasion of the 75th anniversary of the Kindertransport program in 2013, Ralph drew extended and stark comparisons between the conditions in which people live in the United States and those in which he was forced to live as a child under Nazi rule in Germany. "The lesson I want to leave with you," he told the students, "is that there were many people who worked tirelessly planning the Kindertransport rescue mission that made a difference in my life and the lives of so many innocent children, saving us from being murdered by the Nazis. . . . I hope that you will take it upon yourselves to make a difference by ensuring that freedom of speech and religion, and the right to pursue happiness will always keep us free." Ralph also began to incorporate into his talks many of the details about his life-altering return to Germany in 1993 and more recent visits to Wolfhagen, and the impact these visits have had on his life and on the town of his birth. He concluded a very comprehensive talk presented to one of the local community Yiddish clubs on January 14, 2015 with the following: "I now feel that I fulfilled my father's wish for me to get an education, and per-haps more importantly—with love in my heart and a sense of closure—I symbolically brought my parents back home."

After 2013, however, Ralph's very busy speaking schedule began to taper off. At first blush one might draw the conclusion that he had spoken to so many organizations in the area around his Lake Worth home for several years so that new audiences were hard to come by. This might have been true for his adult audiences, but was certainly not the case with respect to student audiences, as each year one grade of students was replaced with a new one. The number of Ralph's talks to students, nonetheless, also tapered off after 2013. There were two rea-sons for this: Ralph joined the board of his community's home owner's association (HOA), which required an extensive amount of time and ef-fort during his two-year tenure because his term of service coincided with a major refurbishment of the community clubhouse. There were at least two occasions during this time when Ralph was not in Florida but had to fly home to attend emergency meetings of the HOA board, such was the level of his commitment to this responsibility. Secondly, and from his perspective more importantly, Ralph believes "the drop-off in speaking engagements was primarily due to the increase in work as officer-at-large on the KTA board." As he later recalled, "This responsi-bility became time consuming." The decrease in his speaking engage-ments in Florida notwithstanding, Ralph would make the time for one very unique opportunity to tell his story.

One day during the second half of 2013 Ralph received a call from a man who introduced himself as Pastor Chris Anderson from Muskegon, Michigan. He had read Ralph's article in *Prism* the previous spring and wanted Ralph to serve as keynote speaker in an upcoming symposium sponsored by a program in which he was involved called The Center for Holocaust and Genocide Studies. Pastor Anderson explained that each year in April the center held a two-day symposium on some aspect of the Holocaust and that as a result of reading Ralph's article and learning about his Kindertransport experience, he was planning the 2014 symposium to focus on the Kindertransport. Ralph was, of course quite interested in this proposal, but his calendar for 2014 was solidly booked up with KTA board and community HOA board responsibilities. Pastor Anderson was understanding but persistent and immediately proposed to hold the program on the Kindertransport the following year instead, and Ralph readily accepted. The pastor, who was also an educator, told Ralph that "he felt that he wasn't teaching about the Holocaust as effectively as he could," Ralph later recalled. "He said that adults are tired of hearing about it but the kids are studying the Holocaust." The sense Ralph had was that having someone who was an eyewitness to the events being discussed would draw the audience in more effectively than would scholars or the showing of films—something Ralph had heard before from his friends in Germany and had experienced through his many speaking engagements—and so Ralph was to be the keynote speaker and a local kind named Edith Maniker was invited to speak at the 2015 symposium as well.

The symposium was divided up into two major events. On the first day—Sunday—the program would take place in the pastor's church, followed by a dinner. On the second day Ralph was invited to speak to a group of 80 high school students representing eight schools in the area. As the late April 2015 date for the symposium approached, Ralph for the first time in many years—after so many speaking engagements—experienced a sense of uneasiness. "This was a big deal," he later recalled, "because for the first time I would be speaking in a church and also I didn't know how much the audiences knew about the Holocaust." He was also nervous because Phyllis could not accompany him to the symposium due to a bout with the flu, and Ralph had become accustomed to Phyllis' presence at his speaking presentations. The church was filled with about 200 people for the first day of the symposium on Sunday afternoon. The audience consisted not only of adults in the community—including the local rabbi and several of his congregants—but many of the high school students who were studying the

Holocaust. Edith Maniker spoke first and focused largely on the historical chronology, but also discussed her Kindertransport experience and life in England. Ralph was told that as keynote speaker he could take as long as he wanted because everyone at the session was invited to the dinner that followed. He spoke at some length about life as a Jew in Wolfhagen before Hitler came to power and how everything changed under National Socialism. He spoke from personal experience based not only on his memory of the events but what he had learned about his family and himself as a result of his recent years of research. After speaking for an hour there was another half hour devoted to questions and answers. "There were questions about how I felt leaving my parents the way I had to," he later recalled. After the formal session several people congratulated Ralph on his presentation and asked follow-up questions. "There was one woman who came up to me and said something to the effect that Hitler was trying to do a good thing to get the country back on its feet economically and politically and that the Jews had it coming," Ralph later recalled. "She told me not to take it personally and I asked her how I—or any other Holocaust survivor—could take her comment any other way but personally. I told her that in all the years in which I had been in the United States I had never had anyone say something like that to me. It reminded me that even in America in current times anti-Semitism existed." Ralph's memories of that day had been largely positive, but this one comment remained with him, and had the conference ended then it would have left him with a sour taste in his mouth.

Fortunately for Ralph, the second day of the conference in which he spent the day with the 80 high school students turned out to be a highlight among his speaking experiences. Ralph spent much of the day listening to the teacher speak about perception and reality with respect to history or current events, and also with respect to the Holocaust. When it was Ralph's turn to speak, he looked from the podium at the students and said to them, "I am the reality." Using a single slide projected on the overhead screen—a photo of Hitler Youth marching through the streets of Wolfhagen that showed Ralph and his father watching from the window of his house (included in Chapter 1 of this book)—Ralph spoke about his childhood experiences in the town, of being harassed and not fully understanding why. "The circumstances I described from the photo intrigued the students and I think the teachers in the room as well," he later recalled. Ralph's presentation went over quite well with the students. "When I spoke," he later recalled, "you could hear a pin drop." During the question and answer session that followed his presentation, one student asked him if there were any good Nazis, a question he had been asked before during presentations to students. "I said there were no good Nazis," he recalled. "However, there were people who went along with the Nazi Party line because they had to or else something bad could have happened to them." In the case of the symposium, however, as well as in his other presentations to students, Ralph quickly learned to focus the discussions "not so much about Nazism but more about my personal experience dealing with what happened to me as a result of Nazism—how I was treated by my parents and at various schools and by my peers," Ralph recalled. "The students seemed to relate to that because they were kids themselves."

The Muskegon symposium might well be considered the capstone of Ralph's experience speaking to students about his past and about the history of the Holocaust except for the fact that he continues—albeit more sporadically—to speak to students today. Like his involvement in the KTA, his extensive experience in telling his story, especially speaking to students, is a direct result of his having returned to Germany in 1993. "I would never have done that before I went back to Germany," he later recalled. "I was at the opposite end of the spectrum; I didn't want to talk about my past." Over the years, speaking about his life has evolved, having conducted research about his family and having formulated opinions about what others were saying. Speaking publicly for Ralph "has very much been a growing experience," he later recalled. "I learned a lot about how I survived as an individual having gone through what I did in life without parents to guide me and serve as role models. I think the Kindertransport experience opened me up for that; I wanted to be able to speak more. I've asked myself these questions several times: Have I done justice to the Kindertransport program? Have I done justice to my parents for what they did to get me out of harm's way? How did I survive and grow? All of that went into my thought processes and into my speeches." What began for him as a tiny opening with respect to speaking about his past through the Shoah project interview, and what took root and inspired Ralph during his presentations in Wolfhagen in 2003, has blossomed into polished, highly effective educational speaking engagements over the course of years that not only has brought a higher purpose to his life but has strengthened the world around him. Today he concludes many of his talks to students by encouraging them "to make a difference in life" and closes with the Hebrew phrase, *Tikhun Olam*, which has taken on the meaning of repairing the world from a social, economic, and political perspective. For Ralph, it is meant as a motivational message of hope in the future, something for which he has indeed served as a role model.

# CHAPTER 15

———— ⚭ ————

# *"Ich Bin Ein Wolfhager"*
# (February 2013)

THE TOWN HALL in Wolfhagen was completely filled shortly before 7:00 p.m. on February 13, 2013. The atmosphere was electric with greater anticipation than Ralph had ever seen during his several visits to the town to participate in large programs, even his 2003 presentation on the Kindertransport held in the slightly larger Culture Hall. He presumed the town hall had been selected for this ceremony because of its superior acoustics to the Culture Hall and because the lighting was a bit better suited for the several television video cameras positioned on tripods at the front of the hall. Gazing around the room, Ralph also noticed members of the print press with cameras near the front of the hall—more of them than usual compared with the other events he had attended in Wolfhagen. Members of the town council and parliament, as well as its working group devoted to event planning, stood chatting in front of the stage, which was completely bare. A podium with a microphone had been placed on the floor at the center of the hall directly in front of the stage; this had been done specifically so that Arne Pillardy could present his speech, which was a central feature of the program, without having to ascend the steps to the stage. Several hundred seats were arranged on either side of a center aisle all the way to the rear of the hall, and musicians stood along a side wall awaiting the start of the program. Ralph and Phyllis were assigned seats in the front row near the center aisle, with Lutz Kann and his family and the American family seated along the same side of the front row. Mayor Schaake and other dignitaries from Wolfhagen and Kassel were assigned seats in the front row on the opposite side of the center aisle. Günter selected a seat just behind Ralph so that he would be available to assist if there were any questions during the ceremony, which was to be conducted entirely in German. Ralph could see Heinz Abel sitting with his daughter Britta, and Heinrich and Gertrud Schwarz seated together a few rows back. He then noticed members of the press approaching him and he looked at his watch, hoping that the program would begin soon, as the knot he had felt upon awakening that morning began to form again in the pit of his stomach.

Ralph and Phyllis had spent a quiet afternoon at Günter's house earlier that day following lunch with their other Wolfhagen friends. It was here, sitting in Günter's living room, that Ralph learned the precise nature of the honor he would receive that evening. The town had officially voted to bestow honorary citizenship upon Ralph and Lutz Kann. This came as a bit of a shock to Ralph, who had been thinking that perhaps he would receive something symbolic like the "keys to the town." The decision by Wolfhagen had come relatively easily but was taken with supreme seriousness, as it was considered a particularly important honor by the council and the parliament. How this decision came about, however, was something that Günter kept to himself at that moment sitting in his living room, but which Ralph later learned was a story filled with considerable irony. The initial proposal came from the same parliamentary working group that had planned the annual commemoration of Kristallnacht and recommended the stone dedicated to the memory of the Jewish families of Wolfhagen, and also the plaques on their homes. After some discussion in the working group, Dekan Gerlach recalled: "I spoke to the mayor, Herr Schaake and asked what we can do so that we can honor Ralph Mollerick and Lutz Kann." The idea of honorary citizenship arose and everyone involved in the decision thought it would be a good thing for the town to do. "They thought the time was right," Günter later recalled. It was then discovered, however, that the town had taken such action only once before, as many towns in Germany had done, and this was for Adolf Hitler. "And so of course they had to undo that declaration first," Günter recalled. "It was very important to me that before we honored Ralph Mollerick and Lutz Kann," recalled Gerlach, "we must deal with the proclamation about Adolf Hitler. We discussed this and said it cannot be that one honorary citizen was Adolf Hitler and then the next were Ralph Mollerick and Lutz Kann," the only surviving former Jewish residents of Wolfhagen. "I was on the council at the time," recalled Pillardy, "and we had to figure out how to throw Hitler out of that citizenship—it was tricky, not because people didn't want to do it, but because we didn't know how to do it, never having done something like that before." The town officials located the decision to bestow honorary citizenship on Hitler, "and the next decision of the town parliament was to take it away from Hitler," Gerlach recalled. "That was done and then the town parliament voted to make our special friends honorary citizens." As soon as Ralph had digested the news about his honorary citizenship, he told Günter he needed to make a minor change in his speech to reflect this specific honor, and so Günter translated the additional language, and a final version of the speech—transliterated for Ralph—was prepared in Günter's house.

While sitting with Günter, Ralph and Phyllis also learned a little more about two other events that the town would be hosting while they were in Wolfhagen. The first was to be a large reception in their honor, as well as for Lutz, immediately following the ceremony that evening. It was to be held in a restaurant and would include the mayor and several of the officials from the working group and the town parliament and council, some of whom Ralph and Phyllis had never met before. "I don't remember the name of the restaurant we went to," Phyllis would later recall, "but it was late—it was already probably 8:30 or 9 o'clock and it was in this huge place; there were a lot of people at a long, long table." Ralph and Phyllis also learned that the Americans they saw during breakfast at the Schiffchen that morning, whose family name Phyllis later recalled was Stuhlman, were direct descendants of one of the former Jewish residents of the town—Salomon Kron—and that there would be a ceremony the next night for the dedication of a plaque at the site of the Kron home. Typically the town held these plaque dedications as part of the annual commemoration of Kristallnacht, but it turned out that February was a more convenient time for the family members to come from the United States. Günter recalled that Mayor Schaake "had the idea that he could invite the Stuhlman family" to come and the town would have the citizenship ceremony one night and the dedication of the plaque on the Kron house the next night. "It all came together, you see," Günter recalled. "It was quite good, really, because we had two American families—Mollerick and Stuhlman—and the Kann family, and together this included second and third generations." The thought of standing outside in the bitter cold February night, even wearing Günter's warm coat, did not appeal much to Ralph and gave him a momentary chill, but his hesitation passed quickly. He had missed the dedication of the plaque on his family's home in November 2010 and felt a strong sense of obligation to attend the dedication at the Kron home, especially because he had such an instrumental role in the town's decision to put up the wall plaques instead of Stolpersteine. At the plaque dedication ceremony the next evening, representatives of the Stuhlman family publicly said "how terribly proud they were that the town was recognizing their parents and grandparents in that way," Ralph later recalled. By the time the discussion ended in Günter's living room, it was getting late, and so Günter drove the Mollericks back to the Schiffchen so they could get ready for the upcoming citizenship ceremony at the town hall.

With several minutes still remaining before the start of the ceremony, there was no way Ralph could avoid the members of the local press bearing down on him from the side of the room. Why did Ralph feel uncomfortable speaking to the press at that moment, when he had routinely been interviewed during all nine previous visits to Wolfhagen, and they had always spoken to Ralph in English? Given the circumstances,

Ralph likely feared a reporter would ask a question in German, and "a question in German would have definitely embarrassed me," he later recalled. Ralph's nervousness regarding having to offer his remarks in German had been pervasive virtually all day long, and this probably contributed to his angst at the approach of the reporters. It turned out, however, that while most of the reporters were new to him, much to his relief the questions were casual and posed only in English. As usual, he was asked many of the same questions that had been covered in years past. A couple of the reporters "wanted to know about my previous visits and how this one was different from the others," he later recalled. "I told them this moment was special to me and that I was excited about being honored in the way I was about to be honored." He then posed for photographs during which he glanced over to see Lutz Kann standing nearby also answering questions from the reporters.

Once the press contingent concluded their questions and photographs and just before the ceremony was scheduled to begin, Lutz approached Ralph and indicated he wanted a word with him and so the two men stood together for a private moment amidst the din in the hall. Other than their curt greeting during breakfast, Ralph and Phyllis had not seen Lutz and his family throughout the day. When Lutz approached him before the ceremony, "I had a feeling that there were going to be some words spoken that might set me off," Ralph later recalled. To his great surprise and relief, "that never happened." Instead, Ralph later recalled that Lutz said quietly to him: "I owe you an apology; I came on too strong with you years ago and I did not mean to belittle you or defame you in any way. I just felt that you were too receptive of these people who did such harm to your family. I would like to be forgiven." Stunned for a moment, Ralph looked into Lutz's eyes and said, "I accept your apology," and the two men shook hands. He later recalled: "I don't think anyone from the press picked up on that conversation even though they were very close by."

In the immediate aftermath of the visit to Germany for the citizenship ceremony and their private conversation in the town hall, Ralph and Lutz would have one exchange of correspondence in which they each would express their views about the honor bestowed upon them. On February 25, Ralph sent a brief but cordial note to Lutz: "Over the 20 years we have returned to Wolfhagen," he wrote, "this visit will be the most memorable. It felt like the people of the town were trying to show that there were terrible times for the Jewish families during the Third Reich and that it was time to acknowledge that it was wrong and that it must never happen again." Lutz responded on March 8 with an uncharacteristically gracious message of his own that he had trans-lated into English by his friend Peter Soltau: "The last visit to my former hometown and town of birth has been a big surprise and a great ex-perience," he wrote. "Not only the presentation of the honorary citi-zenship, but also the big interest of Wolfhagen's citizens during the several events, impressed me deeply." The letter went on—much to Ralph's surprise—in which Lutz ascribed to himself personal credit for the changes that had taken place in the town over the past two de-cades: "If you walk today in the streets of this little town of Wolfhagen," he wrote, "you will see many places of an honorable memory of the Jewish citizens and that is in fact in my view a result of my activities in my hometown in the past." Lutz concluded his letter with a cordial salu-tation ("your friend, Lutz"). Reading Lutz's words, it seemed to Ralph at once typical of this man and completely incongruous with the facts that he should take sole credit for the redemption of the town without a single mention of Ralph's role. True, Lutz had exerted influence that contributed materially to the town's establishing the annual commemo-rations of Kristallnacht. But it had been Ralph who had insisted that the Jewish cemetery be restored and properly maintained; it had been Ralph who had inspired and later funded the stone monument placed in Freedom Plaza in memory of the former Jewish families of the town; it had been Ralph who had influenced the town to place wall plaques on the homes of the former Jewish residents; and it had been Ralph who had spoken so eloquently about the Kindertransport and his life expe-riences so many times to students in the area. Ralph could feel a wave of resentment toward Lutz rising up after reading this communication, but he managed to suppress it quickly, preferring to remember Lutz's apology at the town hall: "That's how I wanted to end it—with that apology," he later recalled. The unexpected rapprochement with Lutz just before the citizenship ceremony in Wolfhagen in 2013 turned out to be fortuitous, as that was the last time Ralph would see Lutz, whose health deteriorated shortly thereafter to the extent that he would be unable to come to Wolfhagen during Ralph's next visit to the town in May 2016, and Lutz passed away in Berlin later that year, leaving Ralph as the sole surviving former Jewish resident of the town. The difficult personal relationship between the two gentlemen notwithstanding, the town of Wolfhagen undoubtedly had gotten it right by honoring both Ralph and Lutz.

It was finally time for the ceremony and there was a hush that came over the audience as everyone took their seats. The program began with musical presentations by a children's chorus from the synagogue in Kassel and a brass band. "There was a lot of music at first," Günter later recalled. "It was quite good music." The musical presentations set the tone for the evening. Thinking about how the program unfolded, Günter later recalled: "I liked the ceremony; it turned out really very nicely. The people were very solemn—it was a situation that you don't get every day." After some housekeeping announcements by one of the mayor's assistants, Bürgermeister Reinhard Schaake offered a few words of welcome to the honorees and the descendants of the Kron family, noting the presence of the officials from the town council and parliament and the parliamentary working group, as well as dignitaries from the regional government in Kassel. The featured speaker for the evening, former headmaster of the school, Arne Pillardy, came to the podium, which had been lowered so that he could sit in a chair while delivering his address. Günter had spent long hours translating Pillardy's speech into English so that the Americans in the room could hold the translation in their lap and follow along as Pillardy spoke in German.

For many in the hall, especially those who had missed Pillardy's remarkable but far more abbreviated comments during the dedication of the stone for the former Jewish families of Wolfhagen in November 2000, his extensive and comprehensive presentation was at once powerful, informative, thought-provoking, and moving. "Bestowing honorary citizenship was very important," Pillardy later recalled. "Because it was such an important event for the town, I felt there had to be an important speech made." Referring to the occasion at the outset of his presentation as "a special day in the history of our town," Pillardy noted that the two recipients of honorary citizenship, Ralph Mollerick and Lutz Kann, "had to leave Wolfhagen" and both "only survived because they had left Wolfhagen" and that they "remember Wolfhagen not only as a place of warm childhood but also of coldness, rejection, and brutality." Pillardy then traced the history of the Jewish community of Wolfhagen in considerable detail, noting both the town's congruence but also its differences with the historical treatment of Jews in Germany as a whole. He described the discrimination and persecution the Jewish citizens of the town had to endure during the Middle Ages and beyond and how, during the late 18th and especially the 19th centuries "there were some new improvements for the Jewish communities" as "the demand for tolerance, equal status, and peaceful cooperation became stronger," especially in professional and cultural fields. "This revolutionary process changed Jewish communities, particularly in large cities," where for many Jewish citizens, "this development led to complete assimilation." Even in Wolfhagen, the Jewish community experienced significant growth, from 127 citizens in 1827, to 300 citizens in 1874—roughly 10 percent of the town's population. But, Pillardy noted that by 1912 the Jewish population of Wolfhagen shrank by more than 75 percent, to "only 81 persons." He explained that this marked decrease in the number of Jewish citizens of Wolfhagen, which continued for more than another quarter-century, was due not only to a flight to urban centers where there were greater opportunities for economic promotion and assimilation, but also to a high rate of acceptance by Wolfhagen citizens of the nationalistic and anti-Semitic precepts espoused by the National Socialists. The numbers, he indicated, were dramatic: in 1932 the National Socialists received around one-third of the national vote but received more than two-thirds of the vote in Wolfhagen. "It is shocking to recognize . . . that in this town," he asserted, "prejudices and resentments were so strongly embodied." He commented: "We have often described the events of the Nazi regime. . . . We do not doubt any more what happened in those days and we are shocked." Moreover, he continued, long after World War II, even beyond the 1980s, "the aversion to coming to terms with this problem was very persistent, more so than in most towns." When, in 1985, he noted, some members of the town parliament proposed to invite still-living former Jewish citizens to Wolfhagen, that proposal was turned down. It was only with the establishment of the parliamentary working group that planned and coordinated the annual commemorations of November 9 beginning in 1998 and the unveiling of the memorial stone for the former Jewish citizens in 2000 that Wolfhagen began the long-delayed healing process. In closing, Pillardy recognized the important role played by Ralph Mollerick and Lutz Kann: "We are grateful, Herr Kann and Herr Mollerick, that you have stretched out your hands for a new beginning and reconciliation . . . We are grateful that you support our work of remembrance. We are grateful that you have come to us—in spite of the injustice you had to suffer in Wolfhagen." Pillardy then concluded his remarks with an expression of hope: "The memory of the Jewish history of our town has to make us think . . . about ourselves as human beings. . . . It has to make us sensitive towards others. . . . We have a constitutional right which we ought to take seriously. It is the most important demand in our constitution: 'Human dignity shall be inviolable.'"

During the opening section of Pillardy's speech, Ralph had been attentive as he followed along in the translation, but as Pillardy recounted the lengthy history of Wolfhagen's Jewish community, Ralph found his mind wandering and his thoughts becoming introspective. He reflected on the wonder of his lifelong journey of survival and redemption—and of the people who made a difference in his life so that he was able to make a difference in the lives of so many others. As he did earlier that morning, Ralph thought first about his parents, who gave him the gift of life a second time by sending him with Edith on the Kindertransport safely beyond the reach of the ultimate horrors of the Holocaust that befell his parents and millions of other Jews. He imagined they would have been proud of how he had persevered and had overcome the challenges in his life, the traumas of his past, and of all that he had accomplished, especially returning to Wolfhagen so many times, returning them to their hometown, and in doing so achieving redemption and playing such an instrumental role in the redemption of the town—an achievement for which he was being recognized that day. He thought about his sister, Edith, how she had saved his life and ultimately enabled his survival, despite their difficult personal relationship and strong differences. He thought of his son, Jeffrey, who despite lingering resentment of the way in which his father had treated him when he was young, had been the catalyst for Ralph's initial return to Wolfhagen and had stood by his side in support of Ralph's efforts to restore the memory of his parents in the town as well as the memory of the other former Jewish residents of Wolfhagen. How Ralph wished Jeffrey could be there to share this moment with him! He also thought about how his father had impressed upon him the importance of education, and this brought to mind the memory of Joe Haberer, who had been there for Ralph at a crucial turning point in his life to remind him of his father's charge; and how Ralph successfully had applied these lessons in his life not only through his own education and professional training but through teaching the lessons he had learned throughout his journey from survival to redemption to future generations. Ralph thought about his many friends in Wolfhagen—how they, as well as the town had embraced him upon his initial return and made it possible, in fact imperative, for him to return again and again. He remembered those who were gone and whom he missed, his childhood friend Kurt Giese and dear Gisela Abel, who provided so much enjoyment for them whenever he and Phyllis traveled to Wolfhagen. Finally he thought of Phyllis sitting next to him intently following Pillardy's comments from the translated pages on her lap. He thought of the joy she brought to his life at a time when he wondered if he would ever truly experience happiness, and how she had gently but persistently stood by his side, encouraging him every step of the way along his journey of redemption.

Sitting there so fully immersed in his thoughts that he was completely oblivious to the words Pillardy was speaking, Ralph was overcome by emotions he had rarely experienced. He felt profound gratitude to all the people he had been thinking about who had such an extraordinary influence on his life. He felt a supreme sense of satisfaction for having persevered and overcome so many challenges, and for all that he had accomplished in his life professionally, of course, but especially in the two decades since experiencing personal redemption with his return visits to Germany. Suddenly Ralph felt an overwhelming sense of calm. Gone were the nerves about having to deliver a speech in German, replaced by a rush of adrenalin and boundless anticipation for what was about to occur. The mention of his name toward the end of Pillardy's remarks abruptly returned Ralph from his inner musings to the present. As Lutz Kann came forward to receive his honor and spoke briefly to the audience in German, Ralph knew that he was ready, and that his moment was at hand.

Upon hearing his name called, Ralph took the very short walk forward to the podium accompanied by a thunderous round of applause the likes of which he had never experienced before in his life—but which would be eclipsed by the standing ovation he would receive following his comments just a few moments later that would conclude with an iconic and highly popular phrase. With Mayor Schaake standing by his side, a senior regional government official from Kassel presented Ralph with a certificate of honorary citizenship and then read the citation: "The City of Wolfhagen awards Mr. Ralph W. Mollerick the Right of Citizenship in recognition of, and with great respect for, his presence as a living witness of the former Jewish community and his tireless, years-long efforts in restoring its past while maintaining loyal allegiance to his hometown Wolfhagen and to the mutual desire for a peaceful future."

Waiting for a second round of applause to subside and holding the certificate in his hand while gazing out upon the audience, Ralph's eyes fell on his friends, Heinz Abel and Heinrich and Gertrud Schwarz, and then on Günter eagerly awaiting his comments, and finally on Phyllis sitting before him in the front row smiling up at him, eyes brimming with tears of joy and pride. Ralph felt completely at peace as he looked at the page of text in German and began to speak:

"When I left Germany I lost everything. I lost my parents, my home, my childhood, my country. But through it all, I chose LIFE. I chose to survive, to get an education, to make a successful life for myself, and to make my parents proud. I survived the most unspeakable adversities, but I made it and I am happy and healthy today. In Hebrew we say *Yasher Koach*, which means congratulations for a worthy accomplishment.

I thank you for this honor today, for granting an honorary citizenship of Wolfhagen, the town where I was born and where I spent the first eight years of my life. I thank the people of Wolfhagen and Bürgermeister Schaake.

*Ich bin ein Wolfhager!*"

# AFTERWORD

—— ❧ ——

# An Interesting Parallel— Germany's Redemption

DURING THE COURSE of conducting research for this book—and based on my personal observations over three visits to Germany in the past five years and on information collected subsequent to the book research— it occurred to me that there may well be an interesting parallel between the personal redemption experienced by Ralph Mollerick through his return to Germany, the redemption of the town of Wolfhagen largely experienced during the two decades following Ralph's initial return to Germany and directly related to his subsequent visits to Wolfhagen, and a broader redemption with respect to the Holocaust that Germany as a nation has experienced during that timeframe and continues to experience today. Like what has transpired in Wolfhagen, the nature of Germany's redemption with respect to the Holocaust can be divided into two separate but related major areas: projects to restore and remember the history of Germany's Jewish communities and the consequences of the Holocaust—including the Kindertransport—and programs to educate the population, but especially Germany's youth, about what occurred during the National Socialist era. What follows is by no means a comprehensive discussion of everything Germany has done or is doing with respect to the restoration of the history of Jewish communities in Germany and, in particular, the Holocaust—nor is it meant to serve that purpose. Rather, herein are anecdotal observations and general conclusions that suggest, rather than prove, that such a parallel does exist at the three levels mentioned above, and that this parallel is by no means merely coincidental.

One aspect of Germany's redemption with respect to the Holocaust relates specifically to timing. The nation was not ready to face its past prior to the mid-1980s at the earliest. Efforts to restore the history of Germany's Jewish communities and deal with the Holocaust developed gradually at that time and gained momentum over the ensuing three decades. Prior to that time the German population mainly consisted of people who reached adulthood at the time of the National Socialist Era and their children, who reached adulthood during the 1960s and early 1970s. Some second generation—or postwar—Germans, such as Arne Pillardy and Ernst Klein, took an interest in the fate of the Jewish communities of Germany even at a young age, but they represented but a small portion of the overall population. The Holocaust was not taught in the schools at that time. "My generation learned nothing about the Nazi era in school," Ernst Klein later recalled. "I never heard anything about this time when I was going to school," Günter Glitsch noted, "and that was in the 1950s. . . . The parents were afraid that the teachers might blame them and then their children would blame them." Pillardy had a similar experience: "It was a difficult topic to discuss in the homes and in the schools. . . . So many students at school who were as old as I had never heard anything about this topic—nothing! This was because the teachers had already taught during the Third Reich." It would take yet another generation of Germans before a critical component of the population was ready to face and accept the most horrific chapter of its nation's past and the consequences for its former Jewish population. This was especially true in smaller towns such as Wolfhagen. "I think it was good that Ralph Mollerick came to Wolfhagen in 1993," Pillardy later recalled, "whereas it would not have been quite so good if he had come in 1983 because the time was not right. In 1983 there were still people who probably would think that Ralph would recognize them and then they would have feared that perhaps he would remember that they had thrown a stone."

A second factor in the timing of Germany's redemption was the return to Germany of a small but significant number of former Jewish residents and their descendants, including Ralph Mollerick. It was important for Germany to have people like Ralph, who had undergone the traumas of the Holocaust in his life, and other Holocaust survivors, to provide a firsthand account of their experiences, especially to young people so that second and third generations of German citizens could better understand about the Holocaust. "We must learn our history," Ernst Klein noted, "and we need these people who have personal knowledge about this history. . . . Younger people in Germany would like to know that in this country today there are other people from the Nazi time." Referring back to the question of timing, but in this instance with respect to the Jewish survivors returning to visit Germany, Günter asserted: "I think the time was right for that because there were still eyewitnesses who could tell something about that time." To facilitate the return to Germany of Holocaust survivors, many municipalities or private organizations have sponsored visits for former Jewish citizens since the mid-1980s, but especially over the past two decades. It has been a crucial window of opportunity which is now rapidly closing as the generation of eyewitnesses passes from the scene. These visits, nonetheless, have fortuitously coincided with the nation's awakening awareness of and interest in that aspect of its past.

There are hundreds and probably thousands of projects to restore and memorialize the Jewish communities of Germany, and this has been largely a grassroots movement that began in individual communities but over the years has expanded to national proportions. Some are, of course, concentrated in major cities, such as Berlin, Münich, and Hamburg. Berlin and Hamburg, in fact, display monuments dedicated to the Kindertransport that were created by artist and Kindertransport survivor Frank Meisler. The majority of these Holocaust era–related projects, however, are located across all of Germany, many in small towns or at the site of former concentration camps. A vast number of these projects constitute memorials. Virtually every city and many of the towns of Germany in which a Jewish community once existed have erected a monument in memory of the people of these communities or placed a plaque or some other marker identifying the site of a former synagogue, some of which existed in medieval times but virtually all of which were destroyed during the pogrom of November 9 and 10, 1938. Many of these towns have restored—or plan to restore—these synagogues even though there are no longer Jewish residents. A significant number of Jewish cemeteries desecrated during the Nazi era have been restored as well, and in many of these one is likely to find a memorial to the Holocaust victims. Many of the former concentration camps are now both memorial sites and historical information centers. In virtually every state of Germany, organizations have formed dedicated to restoring the history of Jewish communities at the regional level. Most of these organizations are populated with highly motivated volunteers and have established networks with each other in order to share information, coordinate programs, and further their mission in as many ways as possible. One such truly remarkable organization was founded by Ernst and Brigitte Klein in Volkmarsen in north Hessen.

As a result of their interest and success in locating many of the still-living members of the former Jewish community of Volkmarsen and the surrounding area, Ernst and Brigitte Klein formed a group of around 20 colleagues in the spring of 1994 and officially established their working group, *Rückblende Gegen das Vergessen* ("Flashback Against Oblivion") in June 1995. Like so many similar projects throughout Germany, it was the return of former Jewish residents themselves that made possible the early work of this group. It was not easy convincing the survivors to return. "Some of the people said they would never come to Germany," Klein later recalled, "but I always tried to persuade them." This effort eventually led to the group's very first reunion in 1996 consisting of 28 invited guests that included former residents from Volkmarsen and a few surrounding towns. During the 10-day reunion that year, there was initial resistance by the visitors to speak. "The first two days," Klein recalled, "there was distance between us; but after that—with each day—there grew friendship." How did Ernst and Brigitte bring about this transformation? "I knew they had a bad life and bad memories of Germany," Klein later related. "I said to them: 'There were terrible crimes, and therefore there is a deep gap and we cannot close this gap between Jews and others in Germany, but we can build a bridge; let us build a bridge.' And the visitors said, 'Okay, we will build a bridge together.'" That experience, said Klein, "was the beginning of really deep, deep friendships." In the case of one such person who eventually escaped to the United States but lost the rest of her family to the Nazis, Klein later described, "I had to work very hard to get her to agree to come. When the 10 days were over she took me in her arms, and with tears said: 'Thank you so much; you have taken away my hate. I had 50 years of hate and you have taken me away from that.' This was something I can never forget; if it was possible for me to change her feelings that way then it is a very good thing." The woman returned to Volkmarsen two more times. In this way Ernst and Brigitte Klein have enabled people such as this woman to experience a personal redemption very much like the redemption Ralph Mollerick experienced by returning to Wolfhagen and placing a memorial headstone for his parents in the Jewish cemetery there.

Although most of the survivors who returned to Volkmarsen in 1996 are now gone, the friendships have extended to their descendants and those of a broadening number of survivors and their families from the region such as Ralph Mollerick and his family—second and third generations who continue to provide documentation, photographs, artifacts, and personal testimonies. These materials, along with Ernst's extensive research in the towns of the area and at the centralized archive on former Jewish residents in Germany at nearby Bad Arolsen, have formed the basis of one of the society's most important components: a permanent exhibit. Both the society and the exhibit began slowly. There was an initial two-week exhibit in Volkmarsen's town hall soon after the 1996 meeting of former Jewish residents that featured the artifacts and photographs they had brought with them. Over the course of the next five years, after Klein had conducted extensive research and collected documents and photographs and received additional artifacts from a still-growing number of donors, the society opened its first permanent exhibit in a local school room in 2001. This space soon proved inadequate for the type of permanent exhibit envisioned by the Kleins and their colleagues, but good work often begets good fortune. One resident of the town had passed away without leaving behind any heirs and so he donated a sizable building—really an old house—to the town of Volkmarsen and the town then offered the building for use by Klein's

society without requiring rent so the group is responsible only for paying utilities and the cost of maintenance. That building currently houses the society's now extensive and impressive permanent exhibit that fills seven rooms, each devoted to a separate sub-theme. It is in Room 1, for example, where information based on artifacts, photographs, and documents relating to the town of Wolfhagen and specifically to its former Jewish families such as Lutz Kann and Ralph Mollerick are displayed.

Over the years *Rückblende Gegen das Vergessen* has grown as a society from 20 to approximately 150 members, although it is still very much driven by the continued leadership and dedication of Ernst and Brigitte Klein. Growth in the organization has allowed the society to expand beyond its exhibit headquarters to restore the Jewish cemetery in Volkmarsen, identify and develop a restoration program for the former mikvah located just off the town square, participate in the restoration of the synagogue in nearby Vöhl and, of course, through the personal participation of Ernst Klein, play a leading role in the parliamentary working group in Wolfhagen that has overseen that town's redemption with respect to the Holocaust. Hundreds of visitors view the society's exhibits annually, usually leaving behind both moving testimonials in the guest book and donations to the society, with guests coming mostly from Germany but also from the United States, Israel, United Kingdom, Canada, and Australia, as well as from other countries of Europe. The purpose of the exhibit, according to the organization's website, is education: "Our exhibition is not a museum in the usual sense; rather it is a place of learning for everybody, young and old. Our aim is to make knowledge available and to make people think." Likewise, the goal of the organization as a whole, according to the website, "is to plug the gaps of our regional history and to make it impossible to suppress, falsify or deny the substantive events from the past. It is our intention that this view of the past will generate a greater awareness of current problems and will lead us to a future where mutual respect is natural for every one of us." Ernst Klein also published in 2012 a comprehensive guide to the exhibit, in German, that includes information on Ralph Mollerick and the Kindertransport, as well as the Möllerich family. It is the educational component of *Rückblende Gegen das Vergessen* and organizations like it throughout Germany where the two major aspects of the nation's redemption with respect to the Holocaust coincide.

Education—both anecdotal and formal—has been a major aspect of Germany's redemption. Today throughout Germany the topic of the Holocaust is taught as part of the standard curriculum. "The topic is intensively taught and discussed in all schools," Arne Pillardy recalled, "at all levels—primary, middle, and high school." Ernst Klein recalled hearing a rabbi say that "we must remember not only that six million people were murdered, but also that so many of those people lived here." For that reason, his approach in the project often focuses on individual lives rather than on the staggering numbers. Pillardy recalled that in Wolfhagen primary school students read a book about an individual child who lived during the period of the Third Reich and what he had to experience. "I do think these books about individuals are more important than pure historical data because they leave an impression on the children so that they will never forget them," he asserted. High school students are required to undertake a research project on some aspect of the Holocaust. Students comprise a significant component of the visitors to Klein's project in Volkmarsen. "The schools in the region all come here," he noted. Based on personal observation, these students are eager to learn and are willing to ask questions, especially when Klein is able to have a guest speaker who is an eyewitness to history, such as Ralph Mollerick. "There are many aspects to the way students learn about this topic," Pillardy later explained. The role, therefore, of organizations such as *Rückblende Gegen das Vergessen* and others like it throughout Germany in educating the country's youth about the Holocaust cannot be over-emphasized; it is a key component of Germany's redemption.

Likewise, in perhaps a smaller but still significant way, have projects dedicated to the restoration of synagogues and other aspects of Jewish life all over Germany contributed to the nation's redemption. Hundreds of such projects can be found dotted across the landscape of the country. The stories behind each project, however, are crucial to understanding their importance. One such story is based on personal observation with respect to the town of Niederzissen, located in the district of Arhweiler in the state of Rhineland-Palatinate, roughly midway between Bonn and Koblenz. The Jewish community of Niederzissen dates back at least to the year 1250. The most recent synagogue was dedicated September 3, 1844 and was destroyed November 10, 1938 as part of the Kristallnacht pogrom. The property later became a metalwork shop. On November 9, 2009—the 71st anniversary of Kristallnacht—the town council approved the purchase of the property on which the synagogue had been located. The following year the council approved an expense of 370,000 euro for reconstruction of the synagogue. The impetus for this project began with Brunhilde Stürmer, whose commitment to restoring the memory of Jewish life in the town and surrounding region also led her to produce a history of the Jewish cemetery as well as a book on the history of the Jewish families of the area. As a result largely of her efforts, and those of friends and colleagues in the community and especially of then-Mayor Richard Keuler, it was possible to see the synagogue restoration project through to completion. The dedication of the restored synagogue in Niederzissen took place March 18, 2012, with descendants of two families of the town's former Jewish community in attendance. "Some just hoped, only a few believed," Mayor Keuler said during the dedication ceremony. "A large number of people thought the hopers and believers were crazy.

But the village council trusted the idea and the result proves them correct and is a pleasure to all of us." A Holocaust sculpture donated by one of the family descendants from the town, entitled "Never Again" was placed inside the synagogue and unveiled at the dedication. A side room of the building displays documentation, photographs, and artifacts collected by Brunhilde and others. "We owe

it to our own history and to our children to let them know what happened," Keuler said at the larger ceremony inside the town hall immediately following the synagogue dedication, "that it not only happened in foreign countries but it happened also here in Niederzissen, and it must never happen again."

So immersed in his work on restoring the legacy of the Jewish communities of Germany has Ernst Klein become that he has visited the restored synagogue in Niederzissen and met Brunhilde Stürmer. More to the point, his work is now recognized and acknowledged nationally and internationally, due to two key developments. First, *Rückblende Gegen das Vergessen* has grown far beyond the confines of the building which houses its exhibits. There is a fairly constant demand for Ernst to speak both to adults and students outside of his own sponsored programs. "Because many people have heard of me, I am now asked to come to schools and to speak in evenings to report on what I've learned," Klein noted. The society, moreover, is linked with dozens of other programs through a network within the state of Hessen; Klein represents the north Hessen region at the meetings of this network. "We have a really good network," he said with considerable enthusiasm. Klein has also been involved "for some years" in the activities of a network of programs that has 35 regional components throughout Germany, yet another indicator of the depth and breadth of programs within Germany focused on the Holocaust.

The second factor that has elevated knowledge about *Rückblende Gegen das Vergessen* and, in particular, its founders, is that Ernst and Brigitte Klein are recipients of the highly prestigious Obermayer German Jewish History Award. Established in 2000 by American philanthropist and activist Arthur S. Obermayer, the son of a German immigrant, and in conjunction with the Leo Baeck Institute, the Obermayer Awards recognize and encourage those non-Jewish mostly, but not exclusively, German citizens who have distinguished themselves for raising awareness of Jewish history and culture through projects and programs such as the restoration of synagogues, Jewish cemeteries, and other Jewish landmarks; establishing monuments and memorials in remembrance of victims of the Holocaust; publishing books and articles and preserving historical documents and artifacts relating to former Jewish communities in Germany; and undertaking educational programs and exhibits. Each year the Obermayer Foundation selects five deserving programs to receive an award that is presented at a formal ceremony on or around International Holocaust Remembrance Day (January 27, in commemoration of the liberation of the Auschwitz concentration camp in 1945, and now a national day of remembrance in Germany). The ceremony is held at the *Abgeordnetenhaus* (which houses the Berlin Parliament) and the awards are usually presented by the president of the Berlin Parliament. In one of several letters of nomination in support of Ernst and Brigitte Klein, Ralph Mollerick wrote to the award jurors in the summer of 2008, speaking of their role in his reconnection with the communities and people where he and his parents once lived: "I cannot adequately put into words all the feelings of gratitude that I have for these two wonderful people, Brigitte and Ernst, who have dedicated their lives to creating and restoring places and culture that were so brutally torn apart. I salute both these individuals for their dedication and realization that this piece of history must not be forgotten." Ernst and Brigitte Klein received their Obermayer Award in Berlin on January 27, 2009, and are now among nearly 100 recipients honored by the award.

The recipients of the Obermayer Award are but the most distinguished among the hundreds of projects and programs located across Germany that are at the heart of the nation's redemption with respect to the Holocaust. Such programs, nonetheless, involve a relatively small percentage of the total population of Germany and this certainly raises a question about the validity of Germany's redemption. Ernst Klein's perspective is noteworthy: "My town is not unlike most towns in Germany. For a long time the older people tried to forget but we younger people said we can never forget—we must learn from our history. I think this is the same in most areas in Germany. There are many who say this is not my thing, learning about those former times. In the last 20 years, however, we have made very good progress to move forward and make it better, and now I think we have a good basis to fight against this question of not speaking about the Nazi time." The fact is that it would be impossible for all Germans to understand and accept the importance of what has taken place all over the country over the past two decades. Because of the work being done by such projects as *Rückblende Gegen das Vergessen*, however, and through formal education curricula in the public schools that has reached nearly a full generation of younger German citizens over the course of this time-frame and, in fact, the very existence of the Obermayer Awards, it can be reasonably argued—albeit in this instance somewhat impressionis-tically—that Germany is undergoing redemption at a national level in much the same way, and parallel to, the redemption experienced by the town of Wolfhagen and the personal redemption experienced by Ralph Mollerick.

> *"It is not incumbent upon you to complete the work, but neither are you at liberty to desist from it." (Pirke Avot 2:21) [Ethics of the Fathers]*

# EPILOGUE

꼭

# *A Personal Reflection by Ralph W. Mollerick*

REFLECTING UPON MY life, from my struggle to survive through the Kindertransport experience and the challenges of growing up without parental guidance, to my redemption achieved more recently as it unfolded and as described in the pages of this book, there are several thoughts that occur to me. I had feelings of helplessness and confusion as a young child living in the small town of Wolfhagen, Germany. Elementary school, during the time when the National Socialists were in power, instilled feelings of being unwanted and I experienced aggressive hatred. Because I was too young to comprehend the reasons why my life had suddenly changed for the worse, the memories of those childhood feelings of sadness and anxiety remain vivid today, and for a long time caused me nightmares. Phyllis told me that I made noises in my sleep and tried to wake me. But now I am able to shrug these off because I have become a person who realized that I had a second opportunity in life. I believe that my parents knew the dangers that lay ahead and desperately attempted to find safe passage out of Germany for my sister Edith and me. Thanks to the creation of the humanitarian Kindertransport program, my parents had the wisdom and lovingkindness to place us on a life journey that distanced us from certain danger and probable death at the hands of the Nazis, and set us on a course of hope for a new beginning in England.

As an adult I have often thought about what it must have been like for my parents to send Edith and me out of harm's way on the

Kindertransport. Having to make that decision so quickly, without ample time to fully weigh the potential consequences, they must have felt that it was something of a gamble with our lives. Knowing that things worked out for us in the long run perhaps would have given them solace had they survived long enough to be certain that we were okay. But that was not the case and I have always wondered if just knowing we were safely in England was sufficient consolation for them in the days before their ultimate demise. I found it interesting that most of the kinder survivors who spoke about their personal experiences at Kindertransport Association (KTA) meetings shied away from discussing their feelings about this question. Was it only because they could not face their childhood before they were sent to England or was it also because they experienced a sense of abandonment by their parents and were unable to shed that as their lives progressed as adults living in the United States? I know that I was only able to achieve clarity on this question once I had experienced closure with my parents by returning to Germany and placing a headstone for them in the Jewish cemetery in Wolfhagen many years later. This symbolic act was something very few of the kinder I have known were able to do and I believe that is why so few of them have been willing and able to talk about their experiences as an educational tool for future generations, as I have done.

Looking back, my hopes and dreams for survival served as the fiber for my life and sustained me through my traumas and challenges, especially as a child and throughout early adulthood. My father's last words to me at the train station in Hamburg, to get a good education stayed with me, with the timely assistance of Joe Haberer, who pounded into me all the time the need for me to look at myself, get a good education, and figure out what I wanted to do with my life. This part of my youth and early adulthood was a struggle, but through it all I have a great sense of satisfaction that I achieved my goals through education and training and had a successful and fulfilling professional career in engineering that helped provide me with the maturity to live my life as best as I could under sometimes very difficult circumstances.

I learned to understand that life is the most important thing; I survived and Hitler did not win. We, the children of the Holocaust, grew up and had families who now know what happened during those horrible years that witnessed the most inhumane behavior the world has ever known. I survived and, therefore, my children and grandchildren were able to experience life.

Although most Holocaust scholars and organizations today readily accept the concept that children of the Kindertransport are considered Holocaust survivors, there has been some controversy on this question among survivors that was brought home to me so graphically in a personal incident that it has remained etched in my memory. Phyllis and I attended one of the annual meetings of Holocaust survivors—not a KTA meeting—but a conference sponsored by an organization with a broader focus. Many of the people at this conference had experienced the horrors of the concentration camps. One such woman sitting next to me at a discussion group spoke about her experience in the camp. Turning to me, she asked, "What camp did you survive?" When I explained that I had been on the Kindertransport and was sent out of Germany as a child without my parents, she told me that I was not really a Holocaust survivor and asked what traumas I had experienced compared with hers. I told her that I could not begin to imagine the horrors of the camps but that I was eight years old when my parents sent me to England after I had been thrown out of school and denied a proper education in Germany, and never saw my parents again. She apologized profusely and acknowledged that I indeed had suffered trauma. She then turned to Phyllis sitting on the other side of me and asked her if she had also been on the Kindertransport. When Phyllis responded that she was born in America but that she was my wife and fully supported and participated in my involvement with the KTA, the woman told Phyllis that she did not belong in that meeting room, that she could not speak freely with Phyllis present, and then asked her to leave the room. I was horrified and asked the woman why she couldn't speak freely in front of Phyllis. She responded that Phyllis had not experienced what she had as a Holocaust survivor. I realized that while I had not experienced the horrors of the camps, I certainly experienced trauma at the hands of the Nazis, and my parents experienced exactly what the woman had, except they had not survived. When I told that to the woman, she fell silent. The incident caused me to reflect further about my life and the importance of speaking out to make possible a true understanding of the Kindertransport within the broader history of the Holocaust.

My current forward-looking understanding of life's personal meaning, moreover, would never have been possible for me if I had not had the courage to reconnect with my past—after so many years of intense effort to put that part of my life behind me—by returning to Germany, finding healing, and ultimately experiencing redemption. This emotional journey not only allowed me to seize an opportunity for a second chance at life, but in so doing, serve as the catalyst for the redemption of Wolfhagen, my childhood home. For this opportunity I will forever be indebted to my oldest son, Jeffrey, who opened the door for me by discovering the village of Wolfhagen and, with gentle persistence, persuaded me to overcome a lifetime of resistance and make the journey that changed my life forever. Standing in silence at his gravesite during his interment, overcome with grief, alone in my thoughts, I recalled the opportunities for reconciliation that had escaped us—heartbreaking chances passing like the wind, forever. It was a terrible moment for me, as I realized that I wanted to thank him for that journey of my life back to the past, but knowing that it was now too late. I will always remember that we had a deep love for each other and never once took the opportunity to express those words, and now it is but a memory.

Despite this deep regret, I feel that the result of that first return visit to Wolfhagen led me down a path of redemption and allowed me to pursue and experience considerable accomplishments and, more importantly, find an inner peace and the ability to share my story with the world, something that I could never have imagined possible before. If I had not returned to Wolfhagen I would never have met the people who knew my parents, nor learned what kind of person I was in the eyes of my childhood friends. Knowing this enabled me to have a better understanding of the circumstances that made my life what it was and had a therapeutic influence on my future. Equally important for me has been reconnecting with childhood friends and meeting new and caring and wonderful people—cherished friends—who have inspired me, and of course Phyllis as well, to return to Germany over and over again for more than 20 years. These visits have enabled me first to experience a personal redemption I would have never believed possible and then to find myself centrally involved in the redemption of Wolfhagen with respect to the Holocaust that included restoring the Jewish cemetery; placing a headstone for my parents inside that cemetery in a ceremony that connected so many of the people of the town to my life in new and hopeful ways; sponsoring the monument dedicated to the Jewish families of Wolfhagen that is now part of annual observances of Kristallnacht; encouraging the town to place commemorative plaques to these families on the houses in which they lived; and perhaps most importantly, speaking to the community and especially to the students during so many of my visits and providing an eyewitness account that furthered the understanding and education of future generations of Wolfhagers. Each time I recall these accomplishments, I feel reinforced that I have taken the path my father would have had me embark upon, and I am filled with satisfaction that I have made the most of my second chance.

There was a direct and absolute connection between my return to Germany and my accomplishments there with two other separate but related aspects of my life: my involvement in the leadership of the KTA and telling my story. With respect to the KTA, I saw an opportunity to step up and organize a Washington, DC, chapter. Instead of letting that opportunity pass, as I likely would have done 10 years earlier, I seized upon it, and I believe this was a major turning point for me because an important aspect of the work of the chapter was to allow members to tell their stories, and this was at a time when the Kindertransport experience had been largely missing in the history books. The opportunity for kinder to express themselves at KTA meetings encouraged some of them to speak publicly and in other ways make possible the recording of the history of the Kindertransport as an important aspect of the study of the Holocaust. I became one of these people and take pride that I was part of the Shoah Foundation's video history that tells these stories, which led to my personal commitment to speak publicly so many times over the course of two decades both in the United States and in Germany. It is we, as survivors, who must speak to audiences, whether they are adults or children, and put forth the message that life is precious and it must go on, and that we have to face up to persecution wherever it occurs, along with so many other problems in the world today. We must be ever watchful because there will be leaders who try to have it their way and not the people's way. That is the lesson that I have learned from my life's experience and that is the lesson that I try to convey whenever I get the opportunity to do so. It is through educating our young people and imparting our knowledge that allows vigilance and the preservation of our freedoms and democratic way of life. I therefore can say with great pride that this broadening of my experiences into something productive through my involvement with the people of Germany and my leadership of the KTA, that I have "walked the walk," and through my educational presentations I have "talked the talk," and I can hold my head up high with the knowledge that I have accomplished so much in spite of virtually lifelong challenges that I faced and ultimately overcame.

There have been amazing rewards along the path I have chosen, especially over the past two decades and more—not monetary rewards but personal satisfaction and knowledge of achievement as I reflect upon what I've done with my life. It is important for me to say in closing, however, that none of these experiences and accomplishments would have been possible without Phyllis. Her persistent encouragement, support, and love have sustained me through my journey of redemption. Of all the crossroads I have encountered and all the paths I have chosen, sharing my life with Phyllis was the best decision I have made.

*Ralph W. Mollerick*

CPSIA information can be obtained
at www.ICGtesting.com
Printed in the USA
BVOW09s1709090917

494451BV00024B/576/P

9 781548 067458